Wittgenstein's Secret Diaries

Also available from Bloomsbury

Introduction to Peircean Visual Semiotics, by Tony Jappy
Peirce's Twenty-Eight Classes of Signs and the Philosophy of Representation, by Tony Jappy
Portraits of Wittgenstein, edited by F. A. Flowers III and Ian Ground
The Bloomsbury Companion to Contemporary Peircean Semiotics, edited by Tony Jappy
Wittgenstein's Family Letters, edited by Brian McGuinness

Wittgenstein's Secret Diaries

Semiotic Writing in Cryptography

Dinda L. Gorlée

BLOOMSBURY ACADEMIC
LONDON • NEW YORK • OXFORD • NEW DELHI • SYDNEY

BLOOMSBURY ACADEMIC
Bloomsbury Publishing Plc
50 Bedford Square, London, WC1B 3DP, UK
1385 Broadway, New York, NY 10018, USA
29 Earlsfort Terrace, Dublin 2, Ireland

BLOOMSBURY, BLOOMSBURY ACADEMIC and the Diana logo
are trademarks of Bloomsbury Publishing Plc

First published in Great Britain, 2020
Paperback edition published 2021

A catalogue record for this book is available from the British Library.

A catalog record for this book is available from the Library of Congress.

ISBN: HB: 978-1-3500-1187-8
PB: 978-1-3502-7755-7
ePDF: 978-1-3500-1189-2
eBook: 978-1-3500-1188-5

Typeset by Integra Software Services Pvt. Ltd.

To find out more about our authors and books visit www.bloomsbury.com
and sign up for our newsletters.

Contents

Dzh hrxs nrxsg hxsivryvn pzhhg, pzhhg hrxs nrxsg hxsivryvn
(Whereof one cannot write, one must not write)
(MS 107: 75, 1929, my translation).[1]

Foreword vi
Acknowledgements ix

1 Introduction: Silence and secrecy 1
2 Symptoms 17
3 Cryptography 53
4 Cryptomnesia 95
5 Fact or fiction 127
6 Cryptosemiotician 163
7 Tentative conclusion 203

Appendix: List of coded passages from Wittgenstein's *Nachlass* 213
Notes 231
Bibliography 249
Index 266

1 Was sich nicht schreiben lässt, lässt sich nicht schreiben.

Foreword

Cryptography and semiotics: Dinda Gorlée's in-depth analysis of Wittgenstein's secret diaries

Marcel Danesi
University of Toronto

As a science of signs and how they are used in representational ways, semiotics has never ventured, as far as I can tell, into the domain of cryptography—an area that would actually lend itself concretely to exploring sign theories and methods. Aware of the significance of cryptography as a mirror of human thinking, Edgar Allan Poe used it as a central element in one of his best-known mystery stories, "The Gold Bug" (1843), which literary critics aptly emphasize was the main reason for the huge success of the story. Ciphers and codes are now found throughout the crime fiction literature greatly enhancing its appeal. Aware of its importance to the study of the "semiotic brain," Dinda Gorlée is the first semiotician to look at cryptography from the lens of semiotic theory, focusing on the secret diaries of Ludwig Wittgenstein, and in the process establishing him as a semiotic epistemologist, whether this is acknowledged or not within the field. If there is one phrase that encapsulates the main insight of Gorlée's book, it is that the human mind reveals its features best when it is engaged in "the mysterious." As the American writer Henry David Thoreau once remarked, for some truly enigmatic reason, "we require that all things be mysterious and unexplorable" (1854: 485).

As is well known, the philosophical-mathematical theory of reference, formulated by Gottlob Frege in 1879 as a distinction between reference and sense, was taken up by Ludwig Wittgenstein in his 1921 *Tractatus*. For example, Wittgenstein saw sentences as Fregean propositions about world facts; that is, he viewed them as representing features of the world in the same way that pictures did. However, in his posthumously published *Philosophical Investigations* (1953), he became perplexed by the fact that language could do much more than just construct propositions about the world. So he introduced the idea of "language games," by which he claimed that there existed a variety of communicative games (describing, reporting, guessing riddles, making jokes, and so on) that went beyond simple Fregean semantics. Wittgenstein became convinced that everyday language had a substantive impact on the language faculty itself. Reading Gorlée's book, I have finally understood why Wittgenstein felt this way. He wanted to literally "play" with language forms in order to experience what this would yield psychologically. One of his games was cryptic or secret writing. Gorlée focuses on the latter, showing us two important things: (1) how cryptography mirrors the semiotic process of a form *X* standing for a meaning *Y*, and (2) how cryptographic writing can help shed light on this process.

Gorlée's book is rich with details about the reasons why Wittgenstein wrote his private thoughts in code—he was a very secretive and private person, turning to cryptography to encode his private thoughts in his diaries, so as to keep them "silent." The reasons for his use of secret writing provides significant light on the inner workings of his mind, which was enwrapped in turmoil, in part because of the troubled times (politically and socially) in which he lived. Calling him a "cryptosemiotician," the central value of Gorlée's treatment is that it focuses on how Wittgenstein used cryptography to reveal his inner Angst—which he could hide on the surface through a cryptic code and thus be able express himself below it freely.

Secret writing has ancient origins. The sacred Jewish writers, for instance, concealed their messages by reversing the alphabet, that is, by using the last letter of the alphabet in place of the first, the next last for the second, and so on. This code, called Atbash, is exemplified in Jeremiah 25:26, where "Sheshach" is the encrypted word for "Babel" (Babylon). Gorlée suggests that Wittgenstein unconsciously understood the emotional power of such writing. To understand himself, and for others to understand him, a first-order decoding of his messages was needed (the actual form-based unraveling of the code) and then, a second-order decoding would allow for their psychological interpretation. The semiotician Roland Barthes (1957) maintained that this kind of two-level process is what generates meaning. Like riddles, cryptograms are puzzles that cry out for a meaning; and like any riddle, if a cryptogram remains unsolved it seems to leave us in a quandary. The "key" to solving them is the *code*—the system understanding the message. As is well known, this term was introduced into semiotics by Ferdinand de Saussure, as a system of signs structured in a specific way (1916: 31). Essentially, the code is the method of determining how we extract meaning from signs, and the end result is what Saussure called *valeur* (value), a form of conceptualization that crystallizes through an unconscious set of relations among the signs within the same code. In a phrase, to understand anything it must be decoded semiotically.

In a fundamental sense, the methods of all the sciences are akin to this cryptographic method, which Gorlée calls appropriately, "cryptosemiotics." Leibniz characterized scientists as cryptographers, suggesting that their primary objective was to crack the infinite array of ciphers that nature presented to them. Because we have to decode and interpret Wittgenstein's secret messages as analogous kinds of ciphers, we become involved directly into what Gorlée calls his "vision of multiple realities." Using the sign theories of Charles Peirce, a cryptogram is at a prima facie level an iconic form which allows the writer to model his thoughts through a code; at a different level it is an indexical form, pointing to something that the reader must discover through the decipherment key; and at a psychological level, it is a symbolic form that reveals the cryptographer's mind in its cultural context.

Gorlée maps Wittgenstein's mode of secret writing against the study of symptoms as signs that are produced by nature, but which require human intervention to be understood—that is, they must be decoded not only biologically but also historically and culturally. When we ignore the relation between the two domains—the biosphere and the semiosphere, as the Estonian semiotician Yuri Lotman (1991) pointed out—then we end up with "cryptomnesia," a kind of memory loss that must be recovered through the writing process itself—hence a "cryptobiography." The latter, as can be seen in Wittgenstein's diaries, obliterates the boundary line between fact and fiction. So they can be read as fiction and as therapeutic self-analysis at once. However, there is a price to pay for all this—the codes we acquire in cultural contexts constitute mental and emotional filters for interpreting the world, guiding us constantly in our attempts to grasp the meaning of that very world. If no meaning can be found, then we end up, as did Wittgenstein, in an emotional quandary. For this reason, the idealistically minded Wittgenstein resorted to secret writing as a way to attenuate his psychological distress over the state of a troubled world and his relation to it. It allowed him, as Gorlée writes, "to rid himself of the madness of the psychic alienation he deeply suffered."

Oscar Wilde stated that "Life imitates Art far more than Art imitates Life," because, as he put it, "the self-conscious aim of Life is to find expression" (2007: 94). Wilde used the example of the London fog to make his case. Although fog is part of London, it goes unnoticed because people have become habituated to it, and may thus miss its metaphorical implications. So, it is the "poets and painters [who] have taught the loveliness of such effects. They did not exist till Art had invented them" (95). Wittgenstein was seemingly immersed in the fog that enwrapped the world in which he lived. As Gorlée so brilliantly shows, when the meanings of that world are encoded in a cryptic form that requires clarity of mind to resolve, the fog dissipates and brightness returns.

Acknowledgements

My warm thanks go to those who have generously given me access to Wittgenstein's Nachlass deposited in a total of approximately 5,000 pages, existing in notes, typescripts, and dictations. The manuscripts have been transposed into electronic form (the project of HyperWittgenstein) at the Wittgenstein Archives, associated with the Institute of Philosophy at the University of Bergen (Norway). My friend and colleague Professor Alois Pichler, director of Wittgenstein Archives, has welcomed me as a research fellow, enabling me to study and write about the extensive linguistic and cultural material of Wittgenstein's published and unpublished heritage. The extensive legacy of the unpublished parts of Wittgenstein's writings supplies the unfamiliar diaries in uncoded plaintext but equally those in coded script (*Geheimschrift*) (Pichler 2006: 143–146). This combination of coded with uncoded will be investigated in this book to analyze Wittgenstein's cryptography to illustrate the supposed secrecy of the secret diary. The machine-readable transmission of Wittgenstein's total heritage, including the transcription of his diaries (see the list in the Appendix), provides both the construction and perhaps the deconstruction of the technical side of the logical notations to all his writings. Alois Pichler's helpful comments and generous encouragement have supported me during my visits to write this monograph.

I am grateful to German–English translator Liesbeth Wallien for revising the translations of Wittgenstein's diary paragraphs. In particular, my thanks go to my son Jorrit van Hertum and my friend and colleague Professor Myrdene Anderson for reading and commenting on sections of the manuscript in its early stages and revising with expert advice my errors. Editor Andrew Wardell has welcomed my book into Bloomsbury Publishing; his interest in my work and his generous assistance have supported and encouraged me. The editorial support of my co-workers has been for me the act of love, showing me the right way to decode Wittgenstein as I have called him as a cryptosemiotician.

1

Introduction: Silence and secrecy

Whereof one cannot speak, thereof one must be silent.

(*Tractatus Logico-Philosophicus*: 7)[1]

Diary as secret message

As an introductory note to the topic of this book, a picaresque anecdote. During a conversation I had some years back with an eccentric colleague from Belgium, he gave me his visiting card. The card was printed with three addresses: first his "public" domicile, officially shared with his wife, then his "private" home, where he went for holidays, and subsequently his "very private" residence, destined for rendezvous with his *maîtresse*. The printed information was used jokingly on the card. He demonstrated in strictest privacy the few words to be remembered by the receivers for some minutes or perhaps treasured for generations. The card tells the unique "story" of the life of this colleague; his intimate "things are stories" cannot be the "whole" or "finished" stories but are the complex signs as an apocryphal "story of stories" (Bär 1979: 193). The Belgian's self-described history was fragmented into the cryptograms (or visual pictograms). The outside story was the invisible autobiography of the pleasure and pain of his life—as narrated in Roland Barthes's ([1977] 2010) autobiographical scenes—but he was caught red-handed in the visible story of the visiting card.

After these humorous opening words, I move on to the real subject: the cryptic labyrinth of the codification of Ludwig Wittgenstein's (1889–1951) diary, which he wrote from 1914 up until close to his death. The metafictional diversity of Wittgenstein's literary and scientific works inspired and influenced the secrecy of his life, in which the philosopher formed and shaped the "private" identity of his "public" works written in a strange code. Wittgenstein as literary narrator, or even conversational *raconteur*, used different styles of writing to relate the events of his private thoughts to the outside world. In philosophy, Wittgenstein was "naturally" self-taught. He wrote approximately 20,000 pages of his philosophy of language but did not seek public recognition as a scholar. Wittgenstein was a modest man. His published writings consisted of a single book, the *Tractatus Logico-Philosophicus* (TLP) of 1922, announcing to the world the rule-guided foundations of the logical status of language. But in the *Tractatus*' last words, Wittgenstein argued the fate of undecipherable and unmentioned words, for which he summoned the non-argument of "silence" (TLP: 7; Gorlée 2012: 42, 73–78). Silence—which is not the same as secrecy—was supposed to be the fame, or infamy, of Wittgenstein's philosophical discourse, as argued in the fragments of his diary and discussed in this book, *Wittgenstein's Secret Diaries*.

To break the instantaneous silence and secrecy of Wittgenstein's *Tractatus*, he shifted from the overall aim of using the rules of language to learning the game/puzzle of the linguistic word-tool of human language. On every page, Wittgenstein "confused" the linguistic rules with the adjustments required to ensure consistency in our language. As a habitual fault-finder, Wittgenstein slandered the "confusions" made in the "ordinary" use of language. He analyzed the many competing paths of making and unmaking the creative and innovative "grammar" of language and put it into "good" philosophical use. Wittgenstein focused on practical examples, but avoided theories of interpretation and doctrines about how speakers should teach the use of language. Wittgenstein's writings set the example of his experience: during his life, he wrote a large number of "public" manuscripts in the form of unpublished notebooks, lectures, articles, conversations, letters, and reviews, which included the "private" diaries written in the coded script. Wittgenstein's public and private works were written together in his notebooks, some of which were penned for intimates but still kept private. After Wittgenstein's death, the trustees had the diaries removed from the philosophical text when posthumously published. Under the trustees' aegis, the secret diaries were thought of as belonging to Wittgenstein's "private" life kept secret but bordering on the conspiratorial, since he had disguised his life with a professional code. The trustees decided that readers did not need to read Wittgenstein's diary, since it was not meant to be made "public" property.

The inaccessible print of Wittgenstein's secret diary had to render the personal news from "hidden places, disguises, locked doors" (Kahn [1968] 1974: 452). The "meaningless" messages of Wittgenstein's "hidden" diary in coded script were regarded as different news from the "open" story of contemporary postcards arranged as a series of uncoded messages sent openly in a semi-transparent envelope (Derrida 1987). The secretive matter of the autobiographical diaries are "open" signs, but the "hidden" content had to be deciphered through the fantasy and imagination of the possible future readers of the diary. Composed as creative reflections by Wittgenstein, the real content must be imagined as not interpreted by diarist Wittgenstein but through the fantasy and imagination of the possible future readers of the diary. Wittgenstein enjoyed the modern practice of sending postcards to family members and friends, going against the traditional principles of letter writing (Net 2009: 62–63). Away from the family circle at Vienna, he sent cheery postcards home, obviously taking delight in the cunning deception of crazy messages sent in "open" messages.

In the European fin-de-siècle after the First World War, Wittgenstein was searching for a new outlet for his artistic energies. The postcard symbolized the psychological escapism of the "lost generation" avoiding in short messages the private "closed" memories to be interpreted by the flux of creative messages. Wittgenstein's diary entries were psychologically "open" signs to be observed and analyzed through the painstaking work of learning the "hidden" words, syllables, and letters to gather the close ties with his own soul-searching identity and the threatening environment around him. Indeed,

Wittgenstein spoke in a relaxed and less formal tone about his "open" diary, while asking, encouraging, and even stimulating his possible readers to welcome the habits of the *stream of consciousness*. He captured the sense of selfhood, but he opened up to the flow of human experience in the thoughts and responses of other readers.

Some of Wittgenstein's obligatory messages were more conventional communications, as in the correspondence from holiday places, work trips, and even military posts. He wanted these letters to be remembered as formal tokens of his life addressed to family members and friends (McGuinness, Ascher, and Pfersmann 1996).[2] But other messages were more creative signs, providing his epistles with pictorial images and references to the sense of biblical proverbs, lyrical poems, and other quotations. Some of Wittgenstein's private messages were written in a collection of postcards to illustrate the brief story of the anecdote in question. He scorned these emotional notes as the art of sending "nonsense" (*Unsinn*) (TLP: 5.5303, 5.5321) sent to his *intimi*. Wittgenstein's self remained open to facing the ambiguous and contradictory habits he had as a private person from a wealthy home in Vienna, but he needed to face, as a private teacher and scientific scholar, the task of somehow psychologically assimilating the political horrors of his time in his writings.

Wittgenstein himself spread his philosophy in the new style of journalistic culture. The satirical journals *Simplicissimus, Der Brenner,* and *Die Fackel*, as well as other journals, told of the politically turbulent times of Austria and Germany. These journals provided the readers with contemporary text, illustrated by caricatural pictures and cartoons (*Culture and Value* [CV]: 22), that made no logical sense and after the First World War moved into the fragmented style of Dada and surrealism. The "degenerate" forms of nonsensical art made politically brutalized art, since it is "harder for defeated soldiers to adapt to civilian life than victorious ones" (Buruma 2018). After the humiliation of losing the war, the old culture of the Habsburg Empire was reformed into the political and cultural style of the "degenerate" forms of nonsensical art, sympathetic to the political Left.

Wittgenstein even dispatched crazy greetings and funny jokes to his closest friends, sometimes written in dialect or scrawled out in intimate codes (Schulte 2001; Monk 1990: 265–267). The jokes would perhaps amuse, delight, and puzzle the receivers. However, Wittgenstein's levity of the new style of writing seems to be more aggressive than simple humor sent to his closest friends. He even frustrated the jokes by adding the pseudo-notation (*Begriffsschrift, Begriffsätze)* (TLP: 5.333 and following) by adding phrases or epigraphs to point a moral to the readers' social taboos. Such "riddles of technology" (CV: 22) maximized the personal curiosity of Wittgenstein's self-conscious mood of the old soldier in the First World War. His temperament was one of a creative thinker ready to strip the sign-receivers down from the attitude of blasphemy to the taste of kitsch. He communicated the political belief in the "ordinary" jokes of fellow citizens who served as soldiers. Acting as fool or trickster, he lifted up the word taboos to parody the sociocultural habits of the old Hamburg Empire to embrace the new style of communication (Waugh 1984; Perloff 2016). The jokes made the history more approachable. Wittgenstein provoked his correspondents with a shock of aphoristic wit to share the use of popular forms in ideological (that is, political and religious) use to abuse the speech of language (Tilghman 1984: 88).

Wittgenstein introduced the art of writing in brief fragments (epigrams), which often turned quite ordinary statements into ponderous news about his situation and environment. His experiments in caricature were a means to criticize the anxious tidings of the time, particularly the tragic *Anschluss* of his Austrian homeland by Nazi Germany in 1938. Wittgenstein deeply resented the heroic (and unheroic) dangers to life of the fate awaiting him and his family members and other Jewish citizens of Austria. The private monologue of Wittgenstein's diaries was garbled with the fictional dialogue to visualize his political troubles to survive difficult times. The mixture of "political" realism with quasi-"romantic" supplements was probably not meant at that point to be given wider circulation. Yet the restriction of Wittgenstein's style has completely changed in today's digital age, when "open" and "closed" messages are no longer opposite terms excluding themselves but can be almost considered as near synonyms.

"Ordinary" readers can first read the bitter style and sentiments of Wittgenstein's "unknown" journals in print (*Geheime Tagebücher* [GT]; *Denkbewegungen* [DB]). Beyond the early diaries made during the First World War, the real *Tagebücher* of 1930–1932, 1936–1937, and further years invite the ideal readers to decode and disclose the profoundly personal thoughts of Wittgenstein's youth in the new style of writing. Wittgenstein kept the critical intimacy to himself: he felt like a displaced person surviving in a time of war and therefore had to write in a secret code. By incarnating his unvoiced interior monologues into dialogues, he used no public statements. Wittgenstein's style of writing has a special significance: the specialist-expert reader needs to rearrange their understanding of the secrecy of the secret code to identify the possible answers to Wittgenstein's cultural and political questions. Finally, the readers have to reply to Wittgenstein's passionate attitude with some objectivity and a certain dispassion. Scholarship needs to frame a hypothesis to reflect on what Wittgenstein as a philosopher probably meant with the hidden significance of the diary-like entries coded in "quasi-language"[3] and mixed with the pages of philosophy. The short micro-episodes, taken from Wittgenstein's own life and integrated in the philosophical notebooks, reflect the tension he felt between the objective shape and subjective content, going back and forth, to give the fragments not *the* meaning itself but *any* meaning to puzzle the readers.

The pseudo-autobiography of Wittgenstein's diary entries is bound up with the linguistic ego and non-ego of his identity, secretly including the cultural self and selfish emotions, discussed in this book. The emotions are translated (self-translated and retranslated) in the postmodern fashion of acknowledging self-identity, self-knowledge, and self-criticism of his self (Colapietro 1989). The selfish symptoms of Wittgenstein's diaries are the immune reaction to the tolerance and intolerance of his anxieties and fears in his environment (Sebeok 1979: 263–267). In the diary entries, he spontaneously reflected the desire to self-analyze the complex and inconceivable circumstances of his life in the "adventures" of his writing. In the philosophical discourse and the diaries, he provided the double anxiety of positive and negative feedback. The emotions of rephrasing the ego-symptoms alternates with the pseudo-ego, which self-controlled the mixed style of both genres into the speech of his life.

Meanwhile, among philosophers, social scientists, psychologists, and literary thinkers a strong opinion has developed to imagine the rhetoric of Wittgenstein's modalities of writing the diary in a different way. The diary seemed to be derived not merely from the mind but also from the heart. The experts are expected to divide and subdivide the occasions of the auto-messages into the analysis of the episodes and then into the whole structure of his life (Gorlée 2016a). This structure forms Wittgenstein's paradox, since the first-person diaries are intertextualized into the scholarly work and cannot be studied alone. Some scholars have even approached the secret diaries with a certain ironical tone, providing allegorical fragments about the choice of the literary genres. Wittgenstein's style of writing, indeed, did not present the finished book but rather the unfinished thoughts of fragmentary writings. Today, the game or joke of Wittgenstein's coded and uncoded diaries is the unclear transaction, which must be solved.

Wittgenstein's works were not presented alone as solid diaries in splendid isolation from his scholarship. Instead, he described the self-emotions within his life episodes; strangely assembled and mixed together within the pages of his philosophy. Also, he did not keep his journal separate from his philosophy. Instead, each entry is a kind of epigram or inscription, knitted together with other pages in "private" and "public" notebooks. The diaries were even transposed into "very private" aphorisms and anecdotal material made of intimate paragraphs, allowing the reader to see the entire narrative spectrum of his natural and secret self in the infinite range of values and possibilities. Wittgenstein's diary opens the reader's eye to the truth of the mixture of his "forms of life" (*Lebensformen*) (Glock 1996: 124–128).

Wittgenstein's style of writing was not fluid narration; his diaries were sporadic episodes coming from deep emotions, whisked off by the real logic of his mental scholarship, and back again to affect his heart. Wittgenstein seemed to make the tone of his words a secret mystery, primarily because he transliterated his vitriolic tone into the diary's secret code (*Geheimschrift*). The "naïve" or unknowing readers were unable to decipher the paragraphs, while scholars felt the private secrecy needed further attention and reflection to become a symbolic form, drawing from mythical code to reach human understanding to comprehend the contents. The secret script was a method of security, guaranteeing secrecy and confidentiality in the encryption of the text. Wittgenstein seemed to keep his self-evident thoughts to himself, but until when?

The "classic" interpretation of Wittgenstein's broken and unbroken series of diary entries would be that they reflect the private language as a mirror image of the public, but most of the philosophical work and writings was unpublished during his life. This approach has over time turned into a technical argument about what can be noted and noticed as *standing for* the truth (or untruth) to judge Wittgenstein's sense of privacy of speech as the mirror image of his life (Eco 1984: 213–219). Meanwhile, the debate about Wittgenstein's own private language has become increasingly problematic. The notion of private language has provoked the intellectual or even dogmatic controversy now that Wittgenstein's coded biography and uncoded autobiography have become available for reading and studying. The Wittgenstein Archives at the University of Bergen provide readers open access to Wittgenstein's works (see Appendix; Wittgenstein Online 2018; Wittgenstein Source n.d.).

Wittgenstein's modalities in different genres and styles raised scientific questions for cognitive scholarship (Gray 1969: 7–19). Wittgenstein wanted to invent a "new" approach for the more socializing style applied to his writings and sayings. The journalistic style he used was close to simple speech, written in short paragraphs with hardly any extraneous terminology. At the same time, his self-knowledge encouraged him to keep the diary fragments not broken but intact. In the exclamatory fragments of Wittgenstein's diary, the fragments lift some of the curtain to reveal the cultural identity. Both the philosophical text and the diaries were written simultaneously and side by side on the right and left pages of his notebooks. Under the cover of the carefully coded and uncoded art of style mediating between science and humanities, Wittgenstein's secret code remains for uninitiated readers far removed from ordinary realistic journalism, but (as shall be argued) there is no secret mystery involved.

Wittgenstein's occasional papers, conveyed in "strange" messages through the pages of "serious" works, create a garbled collection of paragraphs with popular sayings, proverbs, and allegories. They episodically follow each other on alternating pages of the single scripts of Wittgenstein's manuscripts. Interrupting each other, the cultural genres are reciprocally exchanged or abandoned in the edited works, leaving an unread vacuum. However, when studied, the clarity of Wittgenstein's alternative ideas and thought created a tangle of interpretation, underinterpretation, and overinterpretation to disentangle the real "facts of life," thus problematizing any conclusion that one of Wittgenstein's selves was a "serious" writer. Thereby, the stylistic turn of personal diaries must be more than the dramatic cry of the heart to express the sense of mental misery he suffered in his life.

The subject of this book is the problem Wittgensteinian thinkers face in their social duty to offer, when possible, the most appropriate philosophical, linguistic, theological, and other orientations of Wittgenstein's diary as desired, hoped, or intended by Wittgenstein himself. As argued in this book, the fragmentary concept of Wittgenstein is based on unwritten material, it requires one to study the hidden subjectivity between the objective manuscripts of philosophy of language and the subjective emotion or desire of the diary. Steering between the dispute of art and the cultural event of artifact, the evidence of the *ménage à trois* was probably revealed by the visiting card of my Belgian colleague. It demonstrated, by analogy, that Wittgenstein's diaries clearly and unclearly display the necessary self-statements of his tragic life experiences. Wittgenstein seemed to mirror the internal sensations into his outer thought. But the question remains—were his diary entries directed to insiders or outsiders?

Semiotics

While Wittgenstein's early diaries, written during the First World War, were almost "real" diaries, in the later ones he acted as the "cryptosemiotician," that is, a "late modern thinker involved with but not thematically aware of the doctrine of signs, still a prisoner theoretically of the solipsist epistemology of modern philosophy" (Sebeok 1979: 259, quoted in Deely 2015: 1:98). The close association of Wittgenstein with semiotics draws on Ferruccio Rossi-Landi's (1921–1985) lecture "Wittgenstein, Old and New" (1992: 87–108), which emphasized Wittgenstein's interests in the enculturation and multicultural nature of analyzing speech events (Chatterjee 1991).[4] Rossi-Landi emphasized in a lecture at the 2nd World Congress of the International Association of Semiotic Studies (IASS) in Vienna (1979) that "Wittgenstein was not a semiotician, yet he made a great though indirect contribution to the foundation of twentieth-century semiotics and to the development of some of its branches" (1992: 87). Importantly, Rossi-Landi added that "Wittgenstein is an iceberg, by which I mean that there is an emergent portion of his work which is known already, but also a submerged and bigger portion which—whether recently published or still unpublished – has begun to be explored only in the last decade or so," so that finally,

> There is what Wittgenstein *says* in either the emergent or the submerged portion, and then there is what he *shows*, and what he *points to*, and what he *stands for* or (some times very symbolically) *represents* as against the background *finis Austriae*, the background of the Viennese heritage but also of the great changes which have intervened in our way of life and out cultures during the span of Wittgenstein's life and since his death. (1992: 87)

Following Rossi-Landi's premature death in Trieste in 1985, I have taken up the duty of prolonging his work about Wittgenstein's logico-formal philosophy of language, now approached from the general perspective of semiotics. The work of Wittgenstein is, in Charles S. Peirce's (1839–1914) words, "perfused with signs, if it is not composed exclusively of signs" (*Collected Papers of Charles Sanders Peirce* [CP]: 5.448 fn.). My "perfusion" to Wittgenstein in my profound attachment to the heritage of his *Nachlass* in the Wittgenstein Archives has revealed the secret script as the secret code of his diary entries—unfortunately omitted from the published works. This codification has thrown a new light on the lantern of Wittgenstein's semiotic writings. The effect of my investigation is presented in this book, published with the expectation that the interpretation of Wittgenstein's work and writings fully deserves a legitimate renewal from the reading of analytic philosophy to adopting the methodological scholarship of semiotics.

Wittgenstein's language used encrypted script for the open and closed, thought and unthought, entries of his diary. Can we conclude that the self-thought from language to quasi-language did not generate a rough-and-ready habit of codified entrances for possible readers? Instead, most of the time Wittgenstein was a teacher accustomed to developing different thoughts into transitions and to generating a variety of movements of thought (*Denkbewegungen*).[5] Wittgenstein's thought-movements gave direction to the course of his life by writing autobiographical lines, essentially written in a journalistic and poetic tone. He seemed, during the storms of his life, to weigh on different scales the literary genre of his diary—in the transcription of the text into secret code, Wittgenstein drew the readers' attention to the coded and uncoded scripts. He also refined the text in a postmodern style rather than affecting the personal observation in the pseudo-literature of his early works. The lines in Wittgenstein's diary open up complex areas of linguistic inquiry to comprehend the cultural understandings of the possible readers.

To judge the zero point of writing his philosophy of language, Wittgenstein's diary pages suggest an open and closed code of silence and secrecy. The diaries build a point of freedom from the alternative philosophy, but stay fitted by diarist Wittgenstein into unfitting pieces of fragmentary self-examination. Although the "metaphor" of the diaries introduced the emotional and energetic paragraphs strangely intertwined into the logical textbook, the fear of accepting the epistemological uncertainty of the secret script led to the open-ended relativism of obeying or not Wittgenstein's use of language. The cryptography reflected the complex and continually shifting glance at the alien language to make strange literature for readers. Today, the scholar needs an empathetic and interdisciplinary understanding to appreciate Wittgenstein's fictional and metafictional manuscripts in order to comprehend the autobiographical significance of his diary. True scientific inquiry must involve reasoned debate, ensuring a level of legitimacy about Wittgenstein's vision of multiple realities, including the cultural reality and psychological irreality of Wittgenstein's life and works (Schutz [1962] 1967: 207–286).

The study of "making meaning" of language is often in the hands of linguists, who "by their study of language are also semioticians; they are scholars of signs their nature and variety," but,

> Their claims to being scholars of semiotics go deeper. They have helped the unifying concepts embodied in the term *semiotics* to emerge. Typically linguistics does not focus on the relationship among alternative forms, as does the broader discipline, semiotics. However, precisely this focus provides value to scholarship and research. (Sebeok, Lamb, and Regan 1988: 1)

The vulnerable point of Wittgenstein's secret code is concerned with the method of pursuing interdisciplinary semiotic models to analyze sign systems. Rather than following the prerogative of Ferdinand de Saussure's (1857–1913) outlook of analyzing word-signs in rational language governed by structural rules, the pervasive power of Peirce's logical system can explore the irrational and flexible sign models of semiotics through the form of the individual sign and provide a linguistic-cultural meaning. Peirce's method is reflected in the judgment of Wittgenstein's "quasi-mind" by the codification of his diary. Peirce's triadic doctrine of semiotics can provide a strong, sound methodology to look afresh at the ideogrammatic and pictographic reasoning of the linguistic "sign" coded to the "object" to focus on the network of human interactions with other readers in Peirce's variety of "interpretants."

The semiotic signs are not simple things but multidimensional expressions interconnecting with the didactic experience "at the basis of education, namely, mind, meaning, learning, and information" (Sebeok, Lamb, and Regan 1988: 1; Gorlée 2012, 2017). In Wittgenstein's language philosophy, we think with language about language including, when possible, the estrangement of quasi-language. Language works with a sign-system with logical rules but with non-logical exceptions. The duality of subject language and object language turns into a circularity of linguistic systems explaining nothing. However,

> While it may at first glance seem reasonable to say we think only with language, that we communicate only with language, that we learn only with language, it is

> not. Such an incorrect assumption lies at the basis of many decisions in education. Unless by a circular logic everything with which we learn, think, and communicate is called language, then the narrowness of this view is seen as soon as we encounter an Einstein, a Picasso, a Moore, or a Mozart ... The variety of modes or ways of human thinking, creating, communication can be appreciated by implementing a semiotic perspective in education. Therefore, semiotic inquiry has a fundamental importance for education. Semiotics has a broad perspective. (Sebeok, Lamb, and Regan 1988: 1–2)

If humans think by language and learn by language, semiotics includes "the study of language and all the ways that human beings remember, think, learn, make meaning. [We] call what we can do with these verbal and non-verbal modes the four C's: *categorization, conceptualisation, creation, communication*" (Sebeok, Lamb, and Regan 1988: 1–2).

As early as 1923, early Wittgenstein and late Peirce had been brought together in the influential book *The Meaning of Meaning* (Ogden and Richards [1923] 1969). This book upgraded the old term "symbolism" to have the definition of 1920s modern linguistics, based on the semiotic findings of human psychology, social psychology, psychiatry, psycholinguistics, and aesthetics. The common reason for all the interdisciplinary disciplines was that linguistic words and sentences do not exist as real things in reality provided with a static meaning, as in Saussure's "simple" analysis, but need, in the diversity of meanings of Peirce's semiotic doctrine, to be interpreted as an intellectual challenge, both humanistic and scientific. The different events can have the meanings of an enigmatic puzzle as the analog of modernized symbolism. This break-up of disciplines brought bodily emotionalism back to the emerging linguistics to treat afresh the rationale of Wittgenstein's language philosophy and the diaries.

In 1923, *The Meaning of Meaning* greatly helped the reputation of the still unknown logico-semiotic works of Peirce, who had died tragically in 1914 while his papers and correspondence were unpublished and practically unknown (Brent 1993: 320–321). His "successor"—Wittgenstein—brought the inquirers nearer to the personal avowals of his individual acts to prove the truth of who he really was (Foucault 2014), but his works were also basically unknown manuscripts (beyond the published *Tractatus*). The emotional tone of Wittgenstein's language announced the upcoming subjective—mythical, religious, and judicial—mood of oneself opening to others. The emotional side was a novelty in philosophical scholarship, especially in extreme forms such as his diaries.

Focusing on Wittgenstein from the semiotic doctrine of Peirce requires some clarifying terms of the semiotic doctrine.[6] Thomas A. Sebeok wrote in metaphor that the "*text* constitutes, in effect, a specific 'weaving together' of the linguistic signs in order to communicate something," so that the spider web has "signs that go into the make-up of signs belong to specific *codes*" ([1994] 2001: 7). These codes make text into coded *semiotic signs*. Language is the "agreed transformation of rules in a *code*," because language has "specific kinds of structural properties" (7). But there are the variety of uses of language. One can learn the language and use this as a native work-tool. One can learn foreign languages and use this knowledge as an exploratory or temporary tool to communicate with groups of people with a different code. One can also apply language for the benefit of literature (or any other field) by bending the original code into a different code. These activities require desire, determination, and dedication (the three Ds) of the three-way codification of Peirce's universal categories. The causal series of Peirce's categories includes the quality of "icon" as a sign of firstness, "index" as a sign of secondness, and "symbol" as a sign of thirdness (50–59). The codified principle of Peirce's universal categories correspond more or less with the terminology of Wittgenstein, as studied here. Thus, Peirce's semiotic signs can work as the product of the applied practice to experience the codes in Wittgenstein's "forms of life" (Gorlée 2016b).

Peirce's distinctions of meaning are the evocative icon, the allusive index, and the definitive symbol, they mingle with each other in a semiosis to make sense together. The three-way principle is observed in other "representations" as in "tone," "token," and "type" or, more concretely, the "image," "diagram," and "metaphor" to take care of the "mere idea or quality of feeling" of the human sign-interpreter (Charles S. Peirce Unpublished Manuscripts [MS] 914: 3). The icon refers to the informal pre-sign of feeling, seen merely in itself. The iconic image or picture must have a certain likeness with the original sign referred to, which is called the object. But the likeness can be the mirror image (such as a photo) or may be the copy or imitation of the original sign (such as the caricature of a politician, the smile of a movie star, or the title of a painting) (Sebeok ([1994] 2001: 103–114). The mimetic icon can be the disguise or camouflage of the sign in the "other" world of dreams or fancy. The index consists of the real correspondence in the real world. Subsequently, the index points outside itself to the real sign to find in the close proximity the meaningful sign (for example, smoke points to fire, blushing means shame or embarrassment, a gift is a sign of friendship) (83–101). Finally, the symbol is the "general sign" in language, because the formal sign is ruled by the conventional code without either similarity or contiguity. The symbol gives the formalized "law" between the codes of rules to find the codes of other signs in icons and indices. The final interpretation of the Bible, the Koran, the I Ching, a lawbook, an encyclopedia, a telephone book, technical instructions for practical use are called symbols.

The three categories lead to the active interaction of the three terms. Desire, determination, and dedication—in other words, attention, will, and knowing or even wish, interest, and truth—are Peirce's causal categories of firstness, secondness, and thirdness. The categories are grounded on the "good" (or "bad") principle of Peirce's terms of mixing the indexical "habit of belief" with the iconic "habit of unbelief" (West and Anderson 2016). Peirce's goal was to study the code varieties of the sign to receive the restated, refashioned, reconstructed, and rebuilt statements. He gave the interpreters (consumers of the sign) the space and time to make one, two, or three "interpretants" (receptive signs or reactions to signs; signs that exist to be interpreted and to provide new meanings to other interpreters). The interpretants were sent to receive the interpreter's reaction to the quality of the received sign. The sign was received by the interpreter to enable them to provide the interpretation and translation (Sebeok 1976: 7, [1994] 2001: 6, 34–36).

The emotional, energetic, and final interpretants-signs are those reactor effects produced by the original sign. The task of the new interpreter (inquirer, reader, speaker, translator) is to redefine the meaning of the sign into a new interpretation. If the interpreter understands the sign *standing for* the object, the knowledge enables them to send back the reactor signs produced by the feeling, opinion, or argument to the community of readers or listeners. For example, if the subject is linguistic signs (language), the language speaker may feel, think, and analyze language in three categories of thought, depending on the circumstances of sensation, common form, and law. The infinite process of communicating the received signs points to the fact that Peirce's notion of the interpretant allows no close synonyms to the original signs; it generated the extensional equivalence of creative metaphors transporting the original sign into all kinds of interpretant-signs. One can conclude that interpretation and translation mediates in all ways the original source sign with the new target sign according to the stimulus received by the interpreter to give the ideas, opinion, and judgment to the interpreted or translated sign.

The contrastive, structural, and functional sciences of applied semiotics was based on the habits of linguistic interpretation and cultural translation, both were close to Wittgenstein's style of writing. The linguistic and cultural habits are the reaction to his psychological "forms of life" in the interpretant-signs of his works. Translation was the habit of the symbolic interpretants, in which the language was changed into a new language. Wittgenstein's secret script was the habit of indexical interpretants to compose the quasi-language of his diary. But translation and quasi-language were influenced by the iconic habit of the "sign-maker." Wittgenstein acted as the primary interpreter and secondary translator to give meaning to his works (Gorlée 2012: 17–23). The mirror images do not necessarily make authentic signs, but could be false or fake signs reflecting Wittgenstein's own way of feeling and thinking. Although Wittgenstein's "forms of life" have been reinterpreted and translated to transfer the alien script (from German or, better, Austrian-German) into English script, the "imaginary signs" of his unknown diary remain a mystery. The diary entries are composed in the coded script and must first be indexically transliterated into the one-to-one correspondence in German before being further translated into other languages (Catford [1965] 1974: 66–70).

In the translation of Wittgenstein's texts, the habit of a synonymy between the source term and the target term as the point of strategy must be strictly followed (Gorlée forthcoming a). However, the existing translations have not always been followed exactly (Gorlée 2012: 14–15). My principal goal in this book was to transliterate and translate the "biofiction" (Lackey 2017) of Wittgenstein's diary work. In my translations, the critical discourse can be freed from the debilitating burden of synonymy in language and dangerously become a cultural paraphrase or deconstructive set of homonyms. The translation of Wittgenstein's diary liberates the translator from choices between terms of philosophical reasoning into subjective reasoning. The translation includes the logical sameness of the sense of source and target languages, but when transposed into the different language, the effect could even change the sameness into the emotional reference to something else. Translation must honor the specifications and coherences of the author, but must allow for relevant and definite answers to build on the referential and conceptual identity of the author, in this case Wittgenstein, to maintain the contrast of meaning with other terms of his history.

Formal synonymy is the only appropriate starting point for a philosophical translator to ethically give their semio-linguistic opinion. In the more informal diary genre, other constructive forms of "semantic translation" can create "quite a wide choice of usually equally and indistinguishably imperfect but adequate translations," but these versions are regrettably "no perfect translation" (Newmark 1982: 98). To judge the text in translation is to take a professional risk.

The variety of translated interpretants still remains a slippery art of interpretation, since nowadays it requires not only linguistic knowledge but also, from Peirce's doctrine of signs, cultural intuition to attempt to comprehend the "historical" ideas, thoughts, and arguments of Wittgenstein's "stories." In terms of the semiotic interpretant-signs, my translations will remain personal but build on the systematic versions of semiotics. The emotional and energetic interpretant-signs can in logical semiotics never present a whole or final interpretation. A translation is never a text-sign in isolation but acts in conjunction with contexts and subtexts to give other meanings to the text. The knowledge and intuition of another translator could in fact transpose the source text into another target text with totally different elements and characteristics. It seems that the translator's task is not to integrate word equivalences but to try to translate Wittgenstein's "forms of life" (that is, the situation of the texts with intertexts) from one language into another and to compare it with another culture, making language like a jigsaw puzzle that plays with a variety of meanings (Glock 1996: 197–198). The idea of building a bridge from comparison to representation is the moral task of the multiple processes needed to make correct translations (Gorlée forthcoming a).

Following the classification of the three kinds of signs, Peirce called symbols "laws" and "habits" (Gorlée 2016b). The terminology helps explain how Wittgenstein described the "habits of life" transformed into the "habit of speech" (Kimball 1984: 75–92; Glock 1996: 323–329). Peirce's mechanism of habit was learning the reactive behavior to counteract the moral effects of Wittgenstein's life with the habit of religious virtue (or vice) in right (or wrong) behavior. In Wittgenstein's case, this pointed to the diagnosis of the psychosomatic symptoms he suffered (Staiano 1986: 14, 28). Originally, the symptomatic signs were regarded as open clinical indices that would reveal the hidden signs elsewhere, here Wittgenstein's medical disorder. But the symptom was, for Wittgenstein, the stronger habit signaling the right or wrong side of his cultural and psychological condition. He transmitted the symptoms to the outside world in the coded form and shape of his diary texts. Wittgenstein used the practical term of "signpost" to name the indexical signs, probably to maintain the close affinity with the iconic signs of his own life. The human habits are expressed as sensations or inclinations to save the patient from adversities, and survive the psychological troubles of life. The semiotic notion of habit remains a mixed sign: as individual firstness, it flares up an uncontrollable temper of emotions, but at the same time it predisposed Wittgenstein's action to manifest himself as a patient displaying the symptoms in the reactive habit of keeping the diary.

Wittgenstein's stream of diary entries accompanied his daily task for writing philosophy (secondness to thirdness); but the emotional "habit" (firstness) of writing the diary referred to his events from one day to the other day. The second habit was the habit of writing to learn the habit of emergence situations to "work on oneself"

(Kerr 2008) and gain a "language-game" (*Sprachspiel*) of oneself. For Wittgenstein, the habit of writing was the reaction of change from one "ordinary" situation to the urgent situation calling for assistance or relief. According to Peirce's semiotic terminology, the single habit can be continued into a set of habits, meaning that the habit (firstness) can emerge into repeated habits in Peirce's "habituality" (secondness) in different circumstances. When the victim (patient Wittgenstein) has actually learnt the cultural habits, he can rescue himself from the emergency of life.

At times Wittgenstein felt a victim of urgent necessity, which he uttered in evocative cries for help in his diary. Since the help from others did not come spontaneously, his habitual cries repeated the cries into re-habits. His habituality worked as a continuous force to overcome the troubles of his environment. The sad epiphany of words and paragraphs almost transformed the nervous temperament of cries into the constant routine of Peirce's "habituescence" (thirdness). Further, the syndrome of habituescence seemed to guide Wittgenstein's re-habits to keep his diary alive as an occasional remedy to rescue him from difficulties. The total set of habits helped Wittgenstein's critical mind to skeptically battle to understand the meaning of the "landscape" of his thoughts (*Denkbewegungen).* Wittgenstein's emotional series of habits included in the diary intimate often illogical ideas, "embellished" with the artistic code (as argued in this book).

The sign processes of icon, index, and symbol as well as the synonyms of symbol with the terminology of law in human habit are important to the semiotic argument in this book. For example, consider how Peirce's statement of the universal categories was useful to identify and understand the literary style of his semio-logical writing. Peirce's "rapid sketch of my proof" was, for example, settled in the following fragment from 1906:

> First, an analysis of the essence of a sign, (stretching that word to its widest limits, as *anything which, being determined by an object, determines an interpretation to determination, through it, by the same object*), leads to a proof that every sign is determined by its object, either first, by partaking in the characters of the object, when I call the sign an *Icon*; secondly, by being really and in its individual existence connected with the individual object, when I call the sign an *Index*; thirdly, by more or less approximate certainty that it will be interpreted as denoting the object, in consequence of a habit (which term I use as including a natural disposition), when I call the sign a *Symbol.* I next examine into the different efficiencies and inefficiencies of these three kinds of signs in aiding the ascertainment of truth. A Symbol incorporates a habit, and is indispensable to the application of any *intellectual* habit, *at least.* Moreover, Symbols afford the means of thinking about thoughts in ways in which we could not otherwise think of them. They enable us, for example, to create Abstractions, without which we should lack a great engine of discovery. These enable us to count; they teach us that collections are individuals (individual = individual object), and in many respects they are the very warp of reason. But since symbols rest exclusively on habits already definitely formed but not furnishing any observation even of themselves, and since knowledge is habit, they do not enable us to add to our knowledge even so much as a necessary

> consequent, unless by means of a definite preformed habit. Indices, on the other hand, furnish positive assurance of the reality and the nearness of their Objects. But with the assurance there goes no insight into the nature of those Objects. The same Perceptible may, however, function doubly as a Sign. That footprint that Robinson Crusoe found in the sand, and which has been stamped in the granite of fame, was an Index to him that some creature was on his island, and at the same time, as a Symbol, called up the idea of a man. Each Icon partakes of some more or less overt character of its Object. They, one and all, partake of the most overt character of all lies and deceptions—their Overtness. Yet they have more to do with the living character of truth than have either Symbols or Indices. The Icon does not stand unequivocally for this or that existing thing, as the Index does. Its Object may be a pure fiction, as to its existence. Much less is its Object necessarily a thing of a sort habitually met with. But there is one assurance that the Icon does afford in the highest degree. Namely, that which is displayed before the mind's gaze—the Form of the Icon, which is also its object—must be logically possible. This division of Signs is only one of ten different divisions of Signs which I have found it necessary more especially to study. (CP: 4.531)

Honestly, Wittgenstein did not really believe in Peirce's way of thinking about providing a definitive theory for the capitalized "Symbolide Features" (4.531). His goal was to share and interpret the data without building a theory. Instead, he strongly thought about gaining insight through the practice of pseudo-theoretical messages to guide the human experiences of his philosophy. For present-day research, the logical methodology as science-to-be can be grounded on the methodology of Umberto Eco's *A Theory of Semiotics* (1979) and *Semiotics and the Philosophy of Language* (1984) and the methods of Thomas Sebeok, A. J. Greimas, Yuri Lotman, and other semiotician scholars today. Recently, the methodology was fixed by Karin Boklund-Lagopoulou and Alexandros Lagopoulos in their article "The Role of Methodology in Semiotic Theory Building" (2017). The building of semiotic discourse exists to reimagine and rethink the logical norms, analysis, and techniques to correctly explore the empirical-analytic research of present-day humanities.

Following Jeffrey Di Leo's strong argument to defend the methodological theory of the humanities, the grip on conceptual and methodological theory is summarized in the phrase, "Theory has always struck me as being a living entity," and Di Leo added the motives:

> Perhaps it was because its major figures always seemed so full of life and lively—most of all in their writing. Not staid and static creatures like the philosophers, but dynamic and dangerous individuals who by the power of their personalities and enchantment of their intellect brought to life a body of thought that straddled but was never at home in any of the traditional humanities disciplines. (2014: 2)

Ludwig Wittgenstein remains this living philosopher of language. As the strong and convivial figure with religious and moral principles, his desire was to communicate with others. He secretly announced the postmodern identity of the semiotic discourse to restructure and reconstruct the special identity of his fragments and works. The conclusion is that Wittgenstein's writings, notebooks, and diaries were written for him—but certainly anticipated the meaning of other readers?

The semiotic methodology of my previous book, *Wittgenstein in Translation: Exploring Semiotic Signatures* (Gorlée 2012) will be the starting point for the threefold approach to the mixed bag of Wittgenstein's philosophical manuscripts rhapsodically interspersed with his diary messages. Wittgenstein's works together form the eye-witness activity of the personal coherence of his life events, transliterated by himself into the collective term of "language-game" (Glock 1996: 193–198). The attempt to interpret the "good" laws and "bad" habits of Wittgenstein's discourse eventually would suggest the final symbolicity of Peirce's thirdness.

The problem of facing Wittgenstein's "theatrical" pose as a multicultural author (Barthes [1979] 1983: 480) means that writing in mixed literary genres depends on the self-conscious staging as a player in different roles and different countries. Following the early *Tractatus,* Wittgenstein denied the action of the single self in a narcissistic kind of melodrama, he called it "play-acting" in the language-games (*Philosophical Investigations* [PI]: 23; see Gorlée 2012: 159, 242). Instead, Wittgenstein himself pursued the self-analytic codes of social communication in the philosophy of language, but he imagined his autobiography in the metatalk of his personal details and circumstances. Wittgenstein's duty was to write down the dramatic play-act of his own life (Rotman 1987: 45–46). Planning his autobiography, he seemed to fight an interior battle away from the bourgeois conventionalism of the past century to create the moral unity of something like the prophetic voice of the future. In the present-day stage setting, Wittgenstein was regarded as the general play-actor in different roles as patient, speaker, and interpreter. He spoke out with authoritative opinion (talk and metatalk) as a modern philosopher speaking out to the world. Indeed, his form of reality was for modest wordplay to simply reach out to others (Farb 1974; Goffman 1959, 1981) not in a single identity but in a multiple personality of artistic and non-artistic performance (Wilshire 1982: 217, 230).

In actuality, Wittgenstein merely composed in his works the rough sketch "with ragged edges" (*The Blue and Brown Books* [BBB]: 131), but his real self was not there. One may conclude that Wittgenstein's diaries work in imaginative or critical self-images to write the daily practices of life in metafiction (Waugh 1984: 134–135), but intertextually—like the metaphor of Derrida's political-postal "postcards"—he smoothed out the rough edges to give the readers a quick glance at the informal aspect of his soul (*Seele*). The less formal tone of his diary was written alongside the formal text of his philosophical notebooks. Text and intertext (context and subtext) are the story of Wittgenstein's identity, awaiting the semiotic interpretation to be fully understood by Wittgenstein's readers to comprehend the whole story.

The defining characteristic of Wittgenstein's diaries is based on the semiotic methodology of the three-way interpretation of sign-action to be reasoned in Peirce's unlimited process of "semiosis" in Wittgenstein's language-games. As shall be argued, Peirce's semiotic thought can face the continuum of Wittgenstein's certainty and uncertainty in the *Philosophical Investigations* and later works. Wittgenstein seemed to embrace the interactive "arrangement" of Peirce's *ménage à trois* of the semiotic logic of reasoning labeled as "deduction" (thirdness, going from ideas to ideas), "induction" (secondness, from ideas to things), and "abduction" (firstness, from things to ideas) (Gorlée 2016a: 57–81). To reflect the details of the "forms of life," the reasoning was partly logical and partly non-logical, yet the diary was Wittgenstein's non-logical journal coming from his spiritual soul. He seemed to follow Peirce's man/sign metaphor (CP: 5.310–5.317), in which Wittgenstein worked on himself to become a full (that is, bodily and spiritual) sign in body and mind (Kerr 2008). In the allegorical mirror image of his life experiences, he portrayed, narrated, and reflected the causes, courses, and conclusion of his Catholic background to develop into the modern philosopher acting with the contemporary ideology of progressive and creative religion.

In the cryptographical pages of his diary, Wittgenstein bartered positive sense for negative thinking through the persuasion and remonstrance of the mixed works. The *Denkbewegungen* actualized strange elements to surprise the possible readers. The *disiecta membra* (scattered limbs) of Wittgenstein's diary entries seem to allow him the privilege of virtual cultural diversity, allowing him free entry into writing in different literary genres. Wittgenstein morally and physically wrote the coded and uncoded surfaces in iconic and indexical signs to give the real "forms of life" a pseudo-symbolic place in his kaleidoscope of feelings and power. The fragmentary moments of ordinary life, which he portrayed in common language, deciphered his own emotional code in indecipherable messages into comprehensible passages for other readers. One may conclude that the separate claims of Wittgenstein's diaries may demonstrate how the unwinding chronicles of his personal episodes could intermix with the public, private, and very private games to make the cultural rhetoric of semiotics. The notion of language-games was Wittgenstein's goal in writing and in life. The habits of linguïcultural speech (Anderson and Gorlée 2011) integrate the biological (sexual, medical, religious) features of language and culture, sharing Wittgenstein's own personal information with the reader's other understanding of human relationships. Was Wittgenstein's diary his means of making social communication? (Cherry [1957] 1966).

2

Symptoms

Oznxsvi Ovnhxs rhs ro tznqvn Pvyvn qizng fnw qvnng nfi wzh Tpfxg, wzh wvi ufspg, wvi nzxs pzntvn svugrtun Hxsoviavn vrn lzzi hxsiviaprrhv Hgfnwvn szg. (Vh rhg vrn hvvprtvh Zfuzgovn.)
(Many a man is sick his entire life, and only knows the happiness that he feels when after long and severe agony there are a few painless hours. [A blessed relief.])

(MS 133: 41v-42r, 1946)[1]

Forms of life

As a young man, Ludwig Wittgenstein was not only a deep-thinking idealist but also an old-fashioned patriot of the Austrian-Hungarian Empire. At the outbreak of the First World War, he felt it was his duty to enlist in the army, as most young men of his generation did. He became a volunteer soldier fighting on the front for faith and fatherland (see Wittgenstein's biographies McGuinness 1988: 204–266; Monk 1990: 112–166). Wittgenstein's ugly experiences of the war started with bad news from on the Russian East Front around the city of Kraków.

During the horrors of warfare, Wittgenstein engaged in military activities in enemy territory. In his "leisure" time as a soldier, he started writing an intimate diary, written in the first person. Published posthumously in 1991, the *Geheime Tagebücher* (GT: 11–76) were a collection of his diaries dated from August 9, 1914, to August 19, 1916 (MSS 101–103). Wittgenstein's early diary entries were written together in the philosophical *Notebooks 1914–1916* (TB), in which he sketched the first drafts of the *Tractatus Logico-Philosophicus* (published in 1922). Yet the secret script of the diary was dropped out of the published *Notebooks 1914–1916*. At first unknown, the diary only appeared in Wittgenstein's *Geheime Tagebücher* edited by Wilhelm Baum. The list of the unpublished paragraphs in code, written after the First World War, is available in the working list of the Appendix.

In the spiritual loneliness of the First World War battlefields, Wittgenstein worked as a technical gunner, assigned to the artillery of the river gunboat *Goplana*. The work was heavy and free time for the soldiers was scarce. Beside his military duties, Wittgenstein hardly had a chance to work on his basic research interest, the emerging philosophy of language. He was composing the scientific metaphysics of the logical atomism of propositions, writing progressively the first version of the logical version of the *Tractatus* about the mathematical positivism of the system of language. In the notebook of the "*Prototractatus*," written in pencil on separate pages, Wittgenstein pragmatically used this cahier. He started writing the continuous papers of linguistics intermingled with the entries of the army diary. Then, after a week, he continued with the usual style of writing, namely normal script in logico-philosophical remarks on the pages of the right side and the personal diaries in *Geheimschrift* written on the left side of the manuscript (see GT: 15). The combination between normal and secret scripts symbolized Wittgenstein's shocking reports of the military "forms of life" (*Lebensformen*) (Glock 1996: 124–128) displayed as emotional facts of life in his spoken speech as a soldier.

The first paragraphs written in plaintext during the war were deciphered into the secret script to work out the details of the military environment with psychological profundity. He described, first uncoded, then in code (*Geheimschrift*), that:

> Es geschieht hm ervp wzhh ori vrn gzt hm pzntv emiqmoog drv ernv dmxsv. Yrn tvhgvin afi yvwrvnfnt vrnvh hxsvrndviuvih zfu vrnvo emn fnh tvqzllvign hxsruuv zfu wvi dvrxsvp yvmiwvig dmiwvn wrv yvoznnfnt rhg vrnv hzfyznwv! Vh rhg zphm wmxs nrxsg dzsi wzhh wrv tvovrnhzoov timhhv hzxsv wrv ovnhxsvn zwvpn ofhh. srvwfixs driw zfxs wrv pzhgrthgv ziyvrg afo uimn wrvnhg. Vh rhg oviqdfiwrt drv hrxs wrv ovnhxsvn rsiv ziyvrg hvpyhg af vrnvi szhhprxsvn ofshzp ozxsvn. Fngvi—zppvn fnhvivn zfhhvivn fohgznwvn qmnngv wrv ziyvrg zfu wrvhvo hxsruuv vrnv sviiprxsv tpfxqprxsv avrg avrg tvyvn fnw hgzgg wvhhvn!—Vh driw dmp fnomtprxs hvrn hrxs srvi ort wvn pvfgvn af evihgznwrtvn (zfhhvi vgdz org wvo pvfgnznw wvi vrn tzna nvggvi ovnhxs af hvrn hxsvrng). Zphm rn wvog wrv wrv ziyvrg iviirxsgvn & fnw hrxs hvpyhg fo Tmggvh drppvn nrxsg hrxs hvpyhg eviprvivn!!! Nzsoprxs zo pvrxsgvhgvn evoprvig mzn hrxs hvpyhg dvnn ozn hrxs znwvivn pvfgvn hxsvnqvn drpp.
>
> (It often happens, that days seem like weeks to me. Yesterday I was summoned to operate a spotlight on board of one of the boats we have captured on the Weichsel river. The crew are a band of rogues! No dedication, unbelievable brutality, stupidity, and malice! It is not true, after all, that the common cause *cannot but* ennoble humanity. It turns the most cumbersome chore into forced labor. It is remarkable how people themselves turn their work into unpleasant hardship. Despite—all our external circumstances working on our boats could make for a wonderful, happy time yet instead!—I expect it will be impossible to communicate with the people here [except perhaps with the lieutenant who seems a very friendly fellow]. So just get on with the work with *humility* and for God's sake do not lose oneself!!! For it is easiest to lose oneself, if one wishes to give oneself to others.)
>
> (MS 101: 5r, my translation; see GT: 17, 1914)[2]

There must be an intimate connection between Wittgenstein's informal talk in coded form and the quasi-formal instructions that take place to describe the colleagues serving with him on the front. Young Wittgenstein had emotional things to suffer, and some of what is told has been put into the secret code, presumably to enable the writing to circulate freely without arousing suspicion. The code was supposed to make Wittgenstein's diary above suspicion or hostility from his military superiors.

Noblesse oblige. Ludwig Wittgenstein came from a rich and gifted family in the cosmopolitan city of Vienna. The family had Jewish origins, but the Wittgensteins were baptized as Roman Catholics. His father Karl was a rich iron and steel magnate. The Wittgenstein family were ostentatiously wealthy, like the Krupp family in Germany and the Carnegie family in the United States. The Palais Wittgenstein in the Alléegasse of the city of Vienna became the focal point for the arts, culture, and sciences, inviting musicians, painters, and scientists to come and perform. Coming from a socially prominent and influential family in the *belle époque*, young Ludwig naturally needed to react to the miserable life of the soldier, so extremely different from the luxury of his life in Vienna. The solitary cell, the simple food, the commands of the officers, and the survival of the Russian cannonades around the gunboat left him on arrival with a headache and fatigue (*Kopfschmerzen und Müdigkeit,* GT: 34, 36, 1914).

In between the host of anxieties and fears, Wittgenstein said he suffered from neurotic obsessions. He wrote that he could not free himself from feeling haunted by high temperatures, illnesses, fevers, and other medical symptoms. Later, he psychologically became more or less accustomed to life as a simple soldier, although he often mentioned during the war that he was "very sad and exposed to depression" (*sehr müde und zur Depression geneigt*, GT: 38, 1914, see 43–44, 1914, 60–61, 1915). There was hardly any time or opportunity for writing academic work, which remained his physical drive and emotional passion. Beyond the sensitivity to bodily fears, Wittgenstein felt nostalgia (*Sehnsucht*, GT: 33, 1914) for his home in Vienna. He acutely yearned to see and converse as before with his family members and old friends. After the First World War the deep feelings of "nostalgia-as-illness" were replaced with the sickish, melancholy tinge of "nostalgia-as-therapy" (Macintyre 2016) overshadowing all his works and writings.

Wittgenstein was aware that the nerdy and nervy behavior of being a soldier-and-scholar aroused the criticism of a number of fellow soldiers. They could expose him as a cheat and he could be ostracized by the other officers. Avoiding any gossip about himself to his military superiors, the secret orthography kept Wittgenstein's diary, when it would be eventually found, out of reach to any outsiders. One may perhaps conclude that the early entries of Wittgenstein's diaries could progressively, but in an indirect sense, inform secretly what he wrote in some private remarks to David Pinsent, his dear friend (*den lieben David*, GT: 17, 1914 and further). Pinsent happened to serve during the First World War as an aeronautical volunteer in the British Royal Air Force, on the opposite side of the war. After addressing this close friend, Wittgenstein's diary seems to be directed to his family in Vienna. Trying to reassure his older sister Hermine Wittgenstein (who was fifteen years older than Ludwig), he wrote to her, when he was sent to the front line, with love and irony: "What can I say about myself. I am still alive" (McGuinness, Ascher, and Pfersmann 1996: 38).[3] He attempted to send positive reports to his family, so that they were not preoccupied with his troubles. Beyond the monologue with his family, it may also be possible that Wittgenstein's notes were self-directed, as a kind of quasi-monologue, hoping to survive in one piece the dramatic horrors of the war.

During the war, Wittgenstein repeatedly mentioned the nascent work (*Arbeit*) in progress. His work involves two Herculean habits, putting pressure on him in terms of technical facts (*Tatsachen*) of military life, translated into the framework of actual work in philosophy. One habit was that of a mechanical workman in charge of ammunition. There he hardened himself to bear the "difficulties of *outer* life" (*die Schwierigkeiten des äusserem Leben*, GT: 29, 1914). The other habit was Wittgenstein's scholarly adventure of what has been labeled as the *Notebooks 1914–1916* (TB). New scientific research has uncovered that he added, changed, and reviewed a number of paragraphs of the later *Tractatus* book. One may conclude that the task of the real world *represented* in the military episodes and his *representing* world of the linguistic word or sentence ruled the endless seeking of Wittgenstein's hieroglyphic code-switching of trying to combine scientific text and emotional context (Stankiewicz ([1964] 1972, Alston ([1967] 1972).[4] Young Wittgenstein tried to discover a proper coded "grammar" to find a better behavior of interpretant-signs in his use of language.

The episodic idea of giving meaning to the scholarly life in Wittgenstein's *Tractatus* created the need for advocating the formal meaning, called the "calculus" meaning, which ruled the law of language (Harris 1988: 37, 40–41). Indeed, Wittgenstein's early picture theory (Gorlée 2012: 139–147) was grounded on Saussure's duality of linguistic signs in semiology, ruled by the laws of "value" and "signification" to establish the conventional system of language (Saussure [1959] 1966: 114–117; Harris 1988: 43–45). In Wittgenstein's "grammar" during the First World War, he strongly opposed the preexisting style of "old" philosophy. However, he made it clear in the early *Notebooks 1914–1916* that the novelty of the philosophical work might depend upon the survival of himself—the patriotic soldier, Ludwig Wittgenstein.

Symptoms

The emotional keyword of Wittgenstein's diaries is the multiple "symptoms" felt by his own body and spirit. The concept of "symptom" is explained generally by the *Oxford English Dictionary* as the bodily and mental "phenomenon, circumstance, or change of condition, arising from and accompanying a disease or affection, and constituting an indication or evidence of it," but in modern use symptom seems to refer to the wider use of the "subjective indication perceptible to the patient, as opposed to an objective one or sign" (OED 1989: 17:464).

The symptom is the medical indication of the disease or disorder as noticed by the patient. In semiotic terms, the symptom is considered a wider term referring to the natural sign to point to the medical nature of the patient's physical and psychological body. The patient is the first interpreter giving his own subjective symptoms as the "study material." The symptom transpires through the change of color, pain, fatigue, inflammation, or a higher temperature of parts of the patient's body that prompts the second interpreter, the medical physician, to give the "orthodox" evidence of disease (Gorlée 2014a: 405, 408–409). Sebeok defined the semiotic definition of symptom as follows:

> *A symptom is a compulsive, automatic, nonarbitrary sign, such that the signifier is coupled with the signified in the manner of a natural link* (A *syndrome* is a rule-governed configuration of symptoms with a stable designatum). (1976: 124, see 124–128)[5]

As the successor to Saussure, the diversity of *Denkbewegungen* in Peirce's terms of habituality constitutes Wittgenstein's syndrome of habitual practices to signify the indexicality of repeated symptoms. The repeated habits point to the chronic sign-process of re-habits of Peirce's habituescence. In the symbolic habituescence, the group of signs show the hypothetical real-life habit pointing more than reasonably, but finally, to the specific disease. Wittgenstein's repetition of "nervous" symptoms was his attempt to feel in the diary the *subjective* belief of self-communicating with his own body. He complained as a sign-interpreter (patient) but without examining his body or mind sufficiently as his own patient to be recognized in the specific medical sense of the *objective* diseases and disorders.

Wittgenstein regularly used the term "symptom" in the *Blue Book* (Klagge 2011: 86–88) and later he communicated in the *Philosophical Investigations* the "grammar" of his toothache and other symptoms he suffered. In his "story," the patient holds his cheek and says "I have toothache" (BBB: 24). In Wittgenstein's own words, "Let us introduce two antithetical terms in order to avoid certain elementary confusions: To the question 'How do you know that so-and-so is the case?,' we sometimes answer by giving '*criteria*' and sometimes by living '*symptoms*'" (24–25). Wittgenstein's mixed "grammar" must be the interrelation of syntax (order of words and sentences) and semantics (the meaning of words and sentences) to give pragmatic answers to the symptoms. Pragmatics defines the symptomatic relations of linguistic signs to their interpreters in language (Morris 1971: 28–54; see Hardwick 1971: 52–54). Medical science, however, gives us the criterion of toothache as the "strong thesis," but the patient himself makes his or her personal hypothesis with his own symptom-sign, as a "weak thesis" (Klagge 2011: 87).

Wittgenstein represented the symptom as the vague sign *standing for* the "experience [that] has taught us that it coincided, in some way or other, with the phenomenon which is our defining criterion," but he identified the symptom with a mental purpose:

> In practice, if you were asked which phenomenon is the defining criterion and which is a symptom, you would in most cases be unable to answer this question except by making an arbitrary decision *ad hoc*. It may be practical to define a word by taking one phenomenon as the defining criterion, but we shall easily be persuaded to define the word by means of what, according to our first use, as a symptom. Doctors will use names of diseases without ever deciding which phenomena are to be taken as criteria and which as symptoms; and this need not be a deplorable lack of clarity. For remember that in general we don't use language according to strict rules—it hasn't been taught us by means of strict rules, either. We, in our discussions on the other hand, constantly compare language with a calculus proceeding according to exact rules. (BBB: 25; see PI: 321)

The symptom is not a basic term of the semiotic doctrine, but is often considered as the bodily sign of Peirce's "natural" secondness, relating to the indexical sign (Sebeok 1976: 124–127, 131–134; [1994] 2001: 53–55, 83–101; see Staiano 1986: 3–6, 12, 28). For Peirce and Wittgenstein, the index was for the members of the linguistic community the practical part (or even the fragment) of the original sign to give its meaning (Gorlée 2014a: 408). For Peirce, the index was an *objective* sign of inside and outside reality, while for Wittgenstein, it stood for the *subjective* sign of partly real and partly imaginative "reality" of the work-tool of human language.

The symptom is used throughout Peirce's works, mainly in his later pragmatic period in order to find the "true" sign, which consists of something other than itself in some hidden aspect or quality of disease. The signification of the symptom reflects the most prominent aspect of the sign, directing the sign-interpreter to the meaning. The symptom may also have other details or qualities, which may identify the signification of the sign-receiver. There are several kinds of symptoms, such as linguistic or non-linguistic, natural or artificial, or classified in specific categories. The sign of a symptom is not a single or unique communicator but subject to the cultural transformations of sign and object in medical, biological, psychological, social, political, philosophical, religious, and other areas and fields. A symptom is a mixed sign (CP: 2.273)[6] always present and ready to spring up as a metaphorical twist in a cultural crisis.

In the contribution to *The Meaning of Meaning*, Peirce defined the "*Index* as a sign determining by its dynamical object by virtue of being in a real relation to it" exemplified by "the occurrence of a symptom of a disease" (Peirce quoted in Ogden and Richards [1923] 1969: 283). Sebeok stated that a "sign is said to be indexical insofar as its signifier is contiguous with its signified, or is a sample of the object" (Sebeok 1976: 131, see 131–134). Ogden and Richards proposed in *The Meaning of Meaning* that the imaginative literature of three "sign-situations," including the moral judgment of medical symptoms, happened as followed:

> If we stand in the neighbourhood of a cross road and observe a pedestrian confronted by a notice *To Grantchester* displayed on a post, we commonly distinguish three important factors in the situation. There is, we are sure, (1) a Sign which (2) refers to a Place and (3) is being interpreted by a person. All situations in which Signs are considered are similar to this. A doctor noting that his patient has a temperature and so forth is said to diagnose his disease as influenza. If we talk like this we do not make it clear that signs are here also involved. Even when we speak of *symptoms* we often do not think of these as closely related to other groups of signs. But if we say that the doctor interprets the temperature, etc., as a Sign of influenza, we are at any rate on the way to an inquiry as to whether there is anything in common between the manner in which the pedestrian treated the object at the cross road and that in which the doctor treated his thermometer and the flushed countenance. (Ogden and Richards [1923] 1969: 21, italics added, quoted in Sebeok ([1994] 2001: 67)

The "grammar" of the index gives the "real" sign of the medical facts to be really (factually) connected to the "true" object (like the two wheels which form and shape the necessary and indexical parts of the bicycle). Transposed to linguistics, the index is the "weak" word-sign, which develops the grammatical proposition of the sentence to become the "strong" part of speech in public communication.

Generally, the sign of the demonstrative index (sign of secondness) has a double meaning. The index follows the "soft" state of the single word (or part of the word) as an icon (sign of firstness). The icon vaguely or clearly substitutes the meaning of the individual thing (object) for the sense of the individual speaker (Sebeok ([1994] 2001: 50–53, 103–114; Staiano 1986: 11, 29, 177). But the index can also lead to the "super-hard" state of the symbol (sign of thirdness) (Sebeok ([1994] 2001: 55–59), which gives the true identity of mediation between the icon and the symbol, giving real thought, rules, law, and habit (CP: 1.345f., 1.405f.). The theory of language mentioned in Wittgenstein's early contribution to *The Meaning of Meaning* (Ogden and Richards [1923] 1969: 89, 253, 255) discussed the symmetry of the sign and the object in a mystical language, but the "soft" use (and misuse) of words and sentences brought him away from the logical atoms of the *Tractatus* toward building the "hard" elements of language-games as representing the real modes of life. In Wittgenstein's later works, his aim was eventually to rightly understand one another away from the private monologue to the public dialogue of language-games.

Agreeing with Staiano in her biosemiotic article "The Symptom" (2012), the symptom must not be considered as the genuine index. The symptom can hardly be defined as a natural sign-situation, diagnosing the disease in a clinical sense. Since the symptom is considered the mixed sign and must include essentially private sensations of the patient's psychological background, it must transfigure the genetic symptom into the cultural meaning of the specific sign-interpreter. This would mean that the symptom must be seen as the mixed narrative of Peirce's indexical-iconic sign-event. This means that the self-oriented symptoms of Wittgenstein's diary can be regarded as transforming the physical image of the cultural norm (icon) to represent the usual signification (index) of the linguistic sign. The index is the proximity of the sign with the object, while the icon represents the similarity between them.

The categories of the symptoms consist of weakened or mixed signs. The subsigns are Peirce's "degenerate" signs (Gorlée 1990).[7] The functions of the three categories are not in accurate balance, but shift interactively with new sign situations from genuine to weaker signs. Each function is multifunctional and the sign-activity of Peirce's semiosis of signs moves from one category to the next, extending or narrowing down the true or false meaning of the total message. Wittgenstein's written diary is built on the amalgamation in language of meaningful sounds and sound sequences, corresponding to morphemes, words, word combinations, sentences, paragraphs, and other parts or fragments to give some sense to language. Thus it enabled the transcodification of units and sentences of language into metaphor and simile of language when he wrote about the iconic and indexical "engineering" of meaningful signs. As a tireless symptomatic diarist, Wittgenstein tried to raise the subject and practice of his own symptoms in his diary as well as the purity of language and culture, moving from inside to outside the sign or syndrome.

The stream of thought of Wittgenstein's diary is never finished. It has the inner sense of reality about himself and the world, because the symptom lacks a final symbol of intelligent thirdness in time and space (Sebeok 1976: 136–138). Wittgenstein's sporadic outbursts in the diary continued from his youth to his old age. Organizing his symptoms, they tell the stories of the fixed "habits" of Wittgenstein's psychological codes and sexual customs. According to the *Oxford English Dictionary*, the human habit refers generally to the:

> Settled disposition or tendency to act in a certain way, esp[ecially] one acquired by frequent repetition of the same act until it becomes almost or quite involuntary; a settled practice, custom, usage; a customary way or manner of acting. (OED 1989: 6:993)

Peirce's semiotic development of habit, applied to Wittgenstein's practice of making continual entries in his diaries, suggests that the "nervous" symptoms of physical pain and mental tenderness were transposed into the act of writing his diaries. In Peirce's terms, Wittgenstein instead wrote his story in "nervous" symptoms and the "emotional habits" that continued in his "energetic habits," which were transliterated into uncoded or coded script, but without mentioning the final habit of moral ambiguity to end the history. The nervous symptoms were firstness and secondness, but not yet reaching the stage of thirdness.

Wittgenstein's forms of habit no longer symbolized the law or morality of the right or wrong *cursus* of life. Since he directed his human energy to the straight road of reasoning, he was concerned with biblical behavior to occupy the spiritual and mental "good" conduct. In his late works, Wittgenstein was perhaps influenced and inspired by Freud's "symptomatic action," also called "chance action," in the *Psychopathology of Everyday Life* published in 1901 (Freud 1938: 129–140). The typical "accident" of Freud's symptomatic action refers to the collection of all sorts of typical gestures, such as facial looks or the movements executed with one or two hands. Life is governed by the social collection of firm rules, but the point of making "free" gestures liberated the psychological symptoms, for example, in playing Freud's and Wittgenstein's creative sign games. These games take the form of playing by intuition and grasping by a flash of insight, without thinking, to make "free" gestures. This freedom was associated with the dreamy abandon of Peirce's "musement" to set the neurotic mind at liberty.

Freud's psychoanalysis troubled Wittgenstein's analytic philosophy (Kerr 2008: 70–75). Wittgenstein regarded Freud's philosophy as the work of the speculative dream to sacrifice nature to culture. The treatment happened through long consultations on the couch of psychoanalyst Freud to experience from the interactive conversations what is called the "normal" awareness. Psychoanalysis, in the ongoing debate, was regarded by Wittgenstein as the free association of analyst and patient to reach the scientific directives of psychoanalysts' language for the future. The habit of neurosis gave "patient" Wittgenstein the crisis of self-identity relating to a wider process than following the religious example of prayer. William James's ([1902] 1982: 137–171) personal prayers to God as an omnipresent healer cast out evil demons to feel relieved and to confess. Wittgenstein felt skeptical about Freud's psychoanalytical technique characterized by the suppression of instinctual drives (Gregory 1987: 549–550, 657–658) and other symptoms of neurotic disorders. Wittgenstein wanted to keep his "bad" habits to himself to try to find a self-remedy for his ailments.

Freud's pressing issue was the sensitivity to "bad habits." He wrote that:

> We can undertake a grouping of these extremely frequent chance and symptomatic actions according to their occurrence as habitual, regular under certain circumstances, and as isolated ones. The first group (such as playing with the watch-chain, fingering one's beard, and so on), which can almost serve as characteristic of the person concerned, is related to the numerous tic movements, and certainly deserves to be dealt with in connection with the latter. In the second group, I place the playing with one's cane, the scribbling with one's pencil, the fingling of coins in one's pocket, kneading dough and other plastic materials, all sorts of handling of one's clothing and many more actions of the same order.
>
> These playful occupations during psychoanalytic treatment regularly conceal sense and meaning to which other expression is denied. Generally the person in question knows nothing about it; he is unaware whether he is doing the same thing or whether he has imitated certain modifications in his customary playing, and he also fails to see or hear the effects of these actions. (Freud 1938: 131)

Freud's symptomatic action of playing and healing was, for Wittgenstein, the kind of personal "habit that is maladaptive in a some obvious respect and/or distressing, yet more or less fixed and resistant to modification through the normal processes of learning" (Gregory 1987: 549). Wittgenstein's fluctuating code of symptoms kept away from the fixed criterion of one disease, but in his late years, he was aroused by the psychological aspects of the symptoms, which as strange imaginings needed some therapeutic investigation to be healed.

Despite his resistance to psychoanalysis, Freud's *Inhibitions, Symptoms and Anxiety* of 1926 (Freud 1977) must have influenced the evolution of Wittgenstein's neurotic habits. He felt like a social outcast with neurotic symptoms and must have learned constructive ways of dealing with Freud's theory of neurosis, which causes repression in the patient (Shands 1970: 104–106). Freud's notion of symptom masks the persistent anxiety in two ways. Firstly, the symptom has a strong desire of communicating the internal danger to the patient. Secondly, the real danger is, in actuality, outside but can be internalized to be significant to the helplessness or even the destruction of the patient's body and mind (Hall 1954: 85–89). The signs of a breakdown in Wittgenstein's egocentric (at times narcissistic) behavior was the withdrawal reaction, meaning that the painful memory and feelings of distress of his symptoms were never forgotten but—like the "reagent" signs of interpretants—caused the repressed anger in him to present like a mental patient. The patient (Wittgenstein) tends to develop "weak" or "bad" habits of criticizing the faults of society. According to Staiano's semi-medical book *Interpreting Signs of Illness*, the symptom is the patient's "disguise," i.e., by camouflaging the indexical sign in the organic (neurophysiological) symptom of the general (psychoanalytical) symbol. Staiano emphasized that the repression of the patient's mind provoked the "bad" reactor signs of bodily and mental symptoms generalized in disease, illness, and even death (1986: 5–7).

In *The Last Writings on the Philosophy of Psychology: The Inner and the Outer* (LW2; written in 1948–1949), Wittgenstein was aware that his neurotic troubles were symptomatic signs demonstrating the strong hostility to himself and his world. The repressed symptoms had not disappeared through his own psychoanalysis of his emotions, but they still tempted him into the religious vices of anger and fear. In conclusion, they had to be self-controlled by the patient to allow contact with God to cure them (Schimmel 1992: 92, 131). Freud's therapeutic imagery and ideas for Wittgenstein are clear or hidden "gestures" to treat some medical emotions, but for Wittgenstein these were revised, condensed, displaced, and translated into the linguistic signs of well-being or health which require more complex reactions. Since there are many varieties of emotional feelings. For Wittgenstein, "many meanings, ... they can be true or false" (LW2: 67e), but they have no essence of logic. Such considerations are the central problem of Wittgenstein's private diary, which he repeats in several messages about his anger and fear of the controversial issue to "solve" the playful game by using his own language-games.

In the theory of semiotics, the weak (degenerate) habit of emotional firstness is marked by the genuine secondness of real signs, breaking from subjective (personal) to objective (public) signs. Concretely, the "playful" but neurotic sensations of the patient's habit is a communicative pre-sign breaking through the resistance into the events of life to charge the mental symptoms with deep emotions. The meaning of Wittgenstein's "bad" dream of the reality surrounding him was grounded on the neurotic symptoms of his idea of irreality (CP: 5.493; Gorlée 2016b). When the habits are successfully broken into fragments or pieces (signs or symptoms), the patient needs to put together and rearrange the difficulties into one whole. The rational process of Wittgenstein's ego is steadily undermined by the impulsive outlet of his emotions of anxiety. The routine speech forms cast off the benefits of the unreasonably evil habits into compulsive behavior, to the extent that, outside Wittgenstein's "case," the patients of drug rehabilitation programs even tend to correct the manner of speech they previously used in order to function well—that is, without the burden of anxiety and repression (Cannizzaro and Anderson 2016).

Wittgenstein's neurotic symptoms of anxiety did not lead him to consult a physician or psychiatrist for a medical diagnosis to get better. Nor did he engage in a "technical" visit to heal his body with clinical medications or even psychiatric treatment. Instead, the symptoms led him to heal himself the *objective* habits of behavior, to cure his *subjective* symptoms of unreality, and to regenerate himself into "normal" forms of reality. Wittgenstein's habitual practice, unusual for the end of the nineteenth century when psychiatric diseases were a puzzle (Ginzburg [1986] 1989: 87, 109), was to recompose himself, his mental and spiritual disorder fitting the emotional tone of an energetic remedy to tranquilize his spirit. Thus the flux of repeated habituality was subjected to the hidden rules of good and bad habits, in which Wittgenstein could describe the scientific habits of the "grammatical" structure interspersed with the comments of his own life experiences.

One can conclude that the act of writing in language needs special habits of lifestyle to diagnose the writer's psychological symptoms (Gray 1969: 20–33). Wittgenstein's symptomatology was regarded as the "one-sided perspective on language" (*Philosophical Grammar* [PG]: 68). The style of language needed to place the "notes," "analyses," "remarks," and "reminders" of his life experiences separately in his memoirs (*Erinnerungen*) (see PI: 89–90, 127, 199, 232, 392, 496, 574; PG: 60; Glock 1996: 153). Wittgenstein's diary continued by commenting that the "fluctuation in grammar between criteria and symptoms make it look as if there were nothing at all but symptoms" (PI: 354). Diarist Wittgenstein detected in the description of his own symptoms the peculiar channel to control and self-control his writing habits, that is, he made and remade the sensational habits of firstness and secondness into his remedy to solve his psychological troubles. The enumeration of the symptoms was relativized in Wittgenstein's monologue as a "nonsensical" game; it seemed that Wittgenstein "played" the treatment (or mistreatment) of his "sick" signs as self-therapy to get better.

Read historically and culturally

The diagnostic self-function of the unsteady symptoms of Wittgenstein's body and mind seems to work well in the early *Notebooks 1914–1916*. Here, the symptoms of the informal diary predict and modify the right proposition of Wittgenstein's mental situation to make the formal "grammar" of the *Tractatus* (Glock 1996: 150–155). In the war journals, this diagnosis "heals" the therapy of his symptoms and signs by means of the "protopicture up against reality" (TB: 32). When Wittgenstein found the mirror-therapy of the picture theory to characterize the *Tractatus*, he wanted to discover the magical word, in the biblical phrase "redemptive word" (*das erlösende Wort,* GT: 44, 1914).[8] He wanted to find the right context and accurate phrasing for the philosophy of language. The symptom of the deeper confusion of reality was Wittgenstein's remedy to "heal" the inner symptoms of a serious illness or mental evil, while putting right the simple metaphor of reality into the diagnostic irreality of Wittgenstein's technique, form, and style of writing (Gray 1969: 31).

Wittgenstein's picture theory of thought was derived from Saint Augustine's *Confessions* (Gorlée 2012: 114–147). Augustine embodied the living mirror from the prognostic Word updated to the reality of the twentieth century. Following Augustine, the biblical story enabled Wittgenstein to pronounce his vital sign of the diary to proclaim the up-to-date voice of the revealed Word. Wittgenstein changed the old, even archaic, patterns of philosophical thinking into the right reasoning of postmodernity to attain the truth alive today.

Wittgenstein announced a redemptive science of style to shape modern philosophy. The scientific tools present his individual identity in writing philosophy (Gray 1969: 92), but his selfhood is also mirrored in the inner speech of the diary. The redemption did not work adequately in "ordinary" text, but writing in *Geheimschrift* Wittgenstein's reality showed that he did not see clearly but unclearly. In his words:

> Ovrnv tvwznqvn hrnw ofwv. Rxs hvsv wrv hzxsvn nrxsg uirxs hmnwvin zppgztprxs, msnv pvyvn. Vh rhg zph my vrnv upzoov vipmhxsvn dziv & rxs ofhh dzigvn yrh hrv emn hvpyhg drvwvi af yivnnvn znuzntg. Ovrn tvrhg zyvi rhg ivtv: Txs wvnqv.

> (My thoughts are unhappy. Things do not appear fresh to me but commonplace, lifeless. It's like a flame has been extinguished and I have to wait and wait, until it is rekindled. But my spirit is alert. I think.)
>
> (MS 102: 50v, my translation; GT: 54, 1915)[9]

The biblical nature of the "flame of fire" (Ps. 104:4; Heb. 1:7; Rev. 1:14) and the image of the "flaming sword" (Gen. 3:24) ruled out the vision of Wittgenstein's own redemption to tell him that the promised Word would come true. The enlightening moment inflamed his imagination and passion to provide the figurative or metaphorical meaning as an intermediate spirit of religious faith.[10] The biblical flame relighted the remedy of the inner experience of truth to give the sense of direction and to take responsibility for the mission to think worldwide. Discovering and finding the unmistakable words of the flame influenced Wittgenstein's heart when in fear, awe, or despair during the First World War. Wittgenstein wanted to give the prophetic diaries the biblical oratory of *Heilsgeschichte,* almost the salvation history of formal peace to end the war (Hick [1963] 1973: 62, see 59–60; Lemoine 1975: 203).

Although Wittgenstein was tormented all his life into writing scholarly work on the philosophy of language, he became in his ambiguous style of writing (*Denkbewegungen*) sadly estranged from the cognitive thinking and knowledge of his time. The reason for this suffering was primarily the daily warfare of his immediate surroundings. The dark symptoms of his situation approximated him to the mercy of God to save his soul. Consider, for example,

> Rxs yrn tzna wfnqvpn wzifyvi drv ovrnv ziyvrg dvrgvi tvsvn driw. <u>Nfi</u> wfixs dfnwvi qznn hrv tvprntn. Nfi wzwfixs rnwvo <u>emn zfhhviszpy ori</u> wvi hxspvrvi emn ovrnvn zftvn dvttvnmoovn driw. Rxs ofhh orxs <u>*tzna*</u> rn ovrn hxsrxqhzp vitvyvn.
>
> (I am all in the dark on how my work will proceed. <u>Only</u> a miracle will bring success. Only if <u>something outside of me</u> were to lift the veil from before my eyes. I must resign to my fate, <u>wholly</u>.)
>
> (MS 102: 53v, my translation; GT: 55, 1915)[11]

Wittgenstein's army life was brought into sharpened focus in the diaries written from March 28 to August 19, 1916 (GT: 67–76, 1916). The diaries are full of war events, in which he had to participate. He gained a war medal and was promoted to first class as Austrian military officer. Shell-shocked by his wartime experiences, Wittgenstein became in later life the fugitive and skeptical philosopher that we know from his works and person, and with whom the readers attempt to get acquainted with through the fragmentary, never final nor definitive, scripts he left.

After his time at the front, Wittgenstein was posted to a reserve officers school, away from the conflict. He noted in his diary that, while at war, he had been:

> Emn tvovrnsvrg fotvyvn! Hmpp rn zyhvsyzivi avrg afo qzwvi rnh srngvipznw zytvsvn. Yrn uims wzifyvi. Emn tvovrnsvrg fotvyvn, Tmgg driw svpuvn.

(Surrounded by vulgarity! Will soon be off for officer's training in the countryside. I am glad. Surrounded by vulgarity. God be with me.)

(MS 103: 22v, 1916, my translation)[12]

The very essence of vulgarity (*Gemeinheit*) around him made him feel absent from God's mercy and all alone. He observed that "Yrn wvlirorvig. Zppvrn zppvrn! Tmgg hvr wzn" (Am depressed. Alone, alone! Thank God) (MS 103: 52v, 1916).[13] In the exclamatory prayer, Wittgenstein ended the coded diary (plaintext) of the First World War. From this point in 1916 onwards, he continued with an uncoded dimension of the diary, now saying in plaintext that he was "In pain: on the whole there is some good but more specifically things are bad" (MS 103: 55v, 1916, my translation).[14] The discontinuity of coded paragraphs into the uncoded script, however, did not change the cause of his inner provocation: his inner feeling of isolation, with no real friend to talk to.

From 1916, however, the solitary confinement was relieved by his intellectual friendship with Paul Engelmann in Olmütz (Moravia). In this city, where Wittgenstein attended the Military Officers School (Monk 1990: 147–150, McGuinness 1988: 246–257 and *passim*), he met Engelmann, a disciple of architect Adolf Frege and literary critic and satirist Karl Kraus in Vienna. Engelmann proved to be a listener for Wittgenstein's discourse as he was in the process of writing the *Tractatus*. Engelmann described in his memoir the stories of his walks with Wittgenstein, from his family home to his rooms in the outskirts of Olmütz (*Letters from Ludwig Wittgenstein, With a Memoir of Paul Engelmann* [CPE]).

To feel spiritually safe while surrounded by the traumatic stress of the war, the soldier-philosopher Wittgenstein plunged into reading the moral questions of Tolstoy's *The Gospel in Brief*, written in Russian around 1881 (with preface 1883) (Tolstoy 1896). Composed after the romantic fictional novels of *War and Peace* and *Anna Karénina*, Tolstoy changed from his social and psychological storytelling of figures of Russian history to exploring religious devotion in real practice. He abandoned the Russian Orthodox faith. The pseudo-fictional metatext of *The Gospel in Brief* told of the portents and omens of a spiritual conversion to embrace the love emblematic of Christian belief. He renounced materialism, property, and nobility and became an anarchist, pacifist, and vegetarian. Count Tolstoy came from a Russian noble family, he liberated his serfs, and lived a Rousseau-like simplicity of life. Young Wittgenstein felt Tolstoy to be a progenitor of his religious life.

Although Tolstoy was not a learned theologian, he still raised his voice in warning as a prophet with Christian portents and omens. In *The Gospel in Brief*, the dramatic accounts of Jesus's life included every detail, divided into numerical references to enumerate the biblical verses of the four gospels. Tolstoy's gospels are composed of the partly historical and partly hearsay accounts of the evangelists Matthew, Mark, Luke, and John. The gospels wanted believers to embrace the faith of the historical Jesus transposed to the Russian environment, but the truth of Jesus's prophetic life was elastic and needed the divine seal of approval for the future, in very different circumstances. Through the private purity of confession and penance Tolstoy cured his soul. As he wrote with the sacrament of a religious ritual, he reached the kingdom of heaven from spiritual darkness. Placed between Saint Augustine's *Confessions* and Freud's psychoanalysis, Wittgenstein studied the religious material of the New Testament afresh, taking his soul away from the immediate military context to accept Tolstoy's spiritual love of morality to lead a pure and nonviolent life. In the narrative of the *Tractatus*, Wittgenstein shared Tolstoy's view of the numbered chapters of *The Gospel in Brief* in the style of twelve numbered (and subnumbered) chapters to center the remedy on Christian forgiveness.

Wittgenstein's truer light of God's mercy rested on the love he felt for his English friend David Pinsent (Noll 1998). During the geographical absence from each other, as soldiers on opposite sides of the war, the friends needed to communicate through letters. They had to take into account that all epistolary correspondence had to pass through the military censor. Some letters must have been rejected and disappeared, while the received missives are often short messages, but written with heartfelt sympathy (see GT: 89–104, 1912–1918). For example, Wittgenstein replied to David that "My *dear* Davy! Today I have received your letter of 27 January. I have reached a turning-point. I have started working more" (quoted in Noll 1998: 111, 1915).[15] The goal of Ludwig and David was of course to stay in contact and reunite at the end of the war.

In the coded diaries, Wittgenstein wrote in intimate paragraphs that he often felt deserted and utterly alone. He had the unbearable feelings of despair and depression, sometimes even thoughts about the possibility of suicide (*Selbstmord*, GT: 59, 1915). Scarred by the symptoms of the cultural warfare around him, Wittgenstein was also captivated by the erotic fantasy of the young men around him and testified his sexual desire. His self-reflection demanded his confession to others. In this crisis, he noted briefly, in normal and secret code, that he was more attuned to sensual than the sexual (*sinnlich, sehr sinnlich,* GT: 54–63, 1915) activity, but he felt fastidious about representing the image of maleness. He indulged in the solitary act of the old biblical act of onanism (Gen. 38.9), known today as the habit of masturbation. To decrease the nervous tension, Wittgenstein was, in those days, secretly unhappy with these shameful or sinful acts to become an adult. His unhappiness was shown in the abbreviations of his writings. For example, he abbreviated the first person of the verbal form "onaniere" to the initial vowel "o ..." (GT: 58, 63, 1915). Two years into Ludwig and David's wartime separation, David tragically died in 1918, while flying for the British Army. Wittgenstein was left to suffer the loss of his dear friend and failed to find the closeness of an intimate friendship again during the remainder of his life. Wittgenstein in 1922 dedicated the later volume of *Tractatus* to David's memory. After the war, he presented the book to David's parents.

Beyond the speculative memoirs of old Austria during the First World War, the later diaries emerged at different emotional stages in Wittgenstein's life. Coinciding with the political *Anschluss* of Austria to Nazi Germany in 1938, Wittgenstein was hunted by fascist militiamen who wanted to kill him, as they considered the Wittgenstein family to be unwanted Jews. Wittgenstein's sisters acquired Yugoslav passports for the family's escape from Austria, but since the documents were false they needed to face the financial claims made by the Reichsbank to try to guarantee their prolonged stay in Austria. As a way of escape, Wittgenstein moved abroad to work at the University of Cambridge, keeping him out of the grips of the Nazi regime and enabling him to leave for solitary visits to a simple hut on the Norwegian fjords to work, until the Nazi conquest of Norway (Monk 1990: 254–428).

Private letters and cables between Wittgenstein and his family that were transmitted through the International Red Cross in Geneva were blocked by censors. Intimate news did not get through and there were years of non-communication with family members abroad. Wittgenstein himself moved from the uncommunicative scholar into the sensibly communicative thinker. In the evolution of his personality, Wittgenstein argued freely for the new leftist ideology with the help of political, social, and religious visions. As a radical prophet of language, he argued for the shift from conventional forms of philosophy to an emphasize on the political principle of freedom of speech. He guided the questions and self-questions of language philosophy in lectures and papers to help generate a revolutionary force of writing and speaking from monologue to dialogue.

Within the course of the fluid narrative of language philosophy, Wittgenstein prepared lecture manuscripts[16] (later published as *The Blue and Brown Books* and *Philosophical Investigations*), he used the diaries as interpolated material in the non-patterned fragments of his philosophical writing.[17] The diary entries are mainly short personal episodes sporadically placed within the pages of his language philosophy. The subject of the episodes are Wittgenstein's own "forms of life" transposing the facts of life of human behavior and moral conduct into linguistic words, sentences, and paragraphs in writing to himself and others. Wittgenstein patterned the diaries into a portrayal of his realistic life as a thinker and a man.

Spontaneously experimenting with this self-oriented style, Wittgenstein described in personal details the physical and mental manners of the social, political, and artistic reality in the new time of the future. As argued in *Wittgenstein's Vienna* (Janik and Toulmin 1973), he aimed to explore in his literary style of writing the new philosophical method that would mirror the philosophy the social manners of the twentieth century against the old-fashioned sensibilities of Viennese bourgeois society. In the report of his life, Wittgenstein's style became adjusted to the modern trend of writing in the modern style. Going against British and Austrian law, he accepted male and female partners. Wittgenstein was a homosexual, but the word "homosexual" was a modern term, hardly used in his time. His emotional and social life were not happy. He replaced the crisis of heterosexual friendship with a new ethic of overt homosexuality, trying to measure his sexual habits of religious sin with his own sex.

Wittgenstein had read the novelty of Freudian psychoanalysis unveiling the sexual taboos of the mid-century society (Janik and Toulmin 1973: 46–48). Freud's *Three Essays on the Theory of Sexuality* (1905; Freud 1938: 551–629) had scandalized the Viennese bourgeoisie with the psychopathology of the vagaries of the unsteady *libido* of the patients. Freud's works progressed with the psychoanalysis of neurotic sexuality in the 1920s and 1930s, where the deviations of sexual desire violated the previous limits of patriarchal sexuality into the Freudian polymorphism of free and unattached desires indulging in sexual "perversions." Wittgenstein's logical examination and self-examination of the inner symptoms of the mind and heart were put into writing as a variety of gender symptoms, placing his suppressed and symbolized emotions into open circulation. The disharmony between mathematical jargon and fictional romance was deliberately used by Wittgenstein to understand (and perhaps to misunderstand) the ironic puzzle of his closed and open ideas of sexuality. He moved from the jargon of "conventional" sexuality and "ordinary" moral truth to what was called the sexual deviations.

Following Wittgenstein's death in 1951, the literary executors of his works—the trustees Elizabeth Anscombe, Rush Rhees, and Georg H. von Wright—decided what could be published of his extensive heritage (*Nachlass*) and in what form and under which editor. Initially, the trustees decided that Wittgenstein's personal diaries did not belong to the general readership and had to remain an unknown collection of personal remarks, not to be reproduced for publication. Two decades later, Wittgenstein's trustees—now under the aegis of Elizabeth Anscombe, Georg H. von Wright, Peter Winch, and Anthony Kenny—changed their opinion. They decided that the testament of the coded diaries written in the periods 1930–1932 and 1936–1937 might be edited and published as *Denkbewegungen: Tagebücher* (DB; vols. 1 and 2). The coded and uncoded scripts possessed the qualitative diversity of Wittgenstein's *Denkbewegungen*, picturing the variety of his life experiences to be read and analyzed with melodramatic turns of the diary.

Continuity and progress

In between the paragraphs of *Philosophische Bemerkungen* (PB), Wittgenstein from December 12, 1929, to August 9, 1930, wrote private diaries in plaintext, mixed from December 19, 1929, with text in coded scripts. For the secret entries, he interrupted the philosophical work—called by him in secret script "ovrnv Zig wvh lsrpmhmlsvivnh" (my art of philosophizing) (MS 105: 46c, 1929; cf. CV: 3e)[18]—by confessing the ambiguous troubles of his personal sex life. He became attached to Marguérite Respinger, referring to her in conversation as "M.," "Respi," or "R." However, in the coded diaries written at Christmas time with his family in Vienna, he wrote now in code about his strange way of life:

> Ovrn Pvyvn rhy hvsi hvpgzo! Rxs dvrhh nrxsg drv svpp drv urnhgvi vh rhg. Vh rhg tpvrxshzo szpy svpp, szpy wfnqvp. Ivhlr viqpzigv ori emi vrn lzzi Gztvn, wzhh hrv orxs nrxsg ovsi qfhhvn dviwv dvrp rsi Tvpfhg ufi orxs nrxsg wvizig hvr wzhh vh wrvhvh Avrxsvn ivxsguvigrtv. Rxs yrn nfn wzemn hxsoviaprxs tvgimuuvn fnw wzyvr wmxs uimsprxs. Wvnn vh qmoog wmxs vrtvngprxs wzizfu zn wzhh orxs wvi Tvrhg nrxsg evipzhhg. Wvnn dvnn wvi Tvrhg orxs nrxsg evipzhhg, wznn rhg nrxsgh dzd tvhxrvsg hxsofgart & qpvrnprxs. Rxs zyvi ofhh ervp zfu wvn Avsvnhlegavn hgvsvn dvnn rxs nrxsg fngvitvsvn drpp.
>
> (My life is very strange! I do not know how clear or dark it is. It stays half-clear [and] half-obscure, as it were. Respi told me some days ago that she would no longer kiss me, because her feelings toward me were such as not to justify this token. I am hurt yet happy at the same time. When the spirit does not abandon me, nothing that happens is sordid or petty. But I must tiptoe, if I do not want to go under.)
>
> (MS 108: 24, 1929, my translation)[19]

Living in Viennese culture, which still favored old standards, Wittgenstein focused on reaching his true self; or, better, he attempted to give meaning to his keywords or text-clues in writing, based not on plain sexual behavior but on moral spirituality. He wanted to set new standards for the future, as he could then imagine.

After seeing himself during his youth with the standards of the religious "soul" (*Seele*), Wittgenstein promoted in the introduction of *Philosophische Bemerkungen* (PB:7) the new social and moral "spirit" (*Geist*) inspiring and influencing contemporary Western "mind" to make a manageable civilization (Kripke [1982] 1985): 48–49 fn.). In the paragraphs of his diary, he now saw the spiritual story as a new solution that would provide him with space for his sexual uncertainty in keeping the company of Marguérite. Their relationship moved from friendship to engagement and would probably have ended in marriage. It seems that the psychological and spiritual steps of creating a lasting relationship with a woman brought Wittgenstein both pleasure and anxiety. One should stress that the stories about Marguérite were written by Wittgenstein in ordinary, non-coded plaintext to make the personal remarks public (DB: 1: 19, 23–24, 26–27, 29–32, 37, 41–42, 59–61, 64, 66–68). The plaintext obviously means that, for author Wittgenstein, the anxieties about the alternative and problematic affair did not always deserve the secret text and could even be read by outsiders. The affair with Marguérite did not end well. As biographer Monk observed:

> Though flattered by his attention, and over-awed by the strength of his personality, Marguérite did not see in Wittgenstein the qualities she wishes for in a husband. He was too austere, too demanding (and, one suspects, just a little too Jewish). Besides, when he made clear his intentions, he also made clear that he had a Platonic, childless, marriage in mind—and that was not for her. (Monk 1990: 258)

Abandoning the bourgeois culture of conventional marriage, Wittgenstein's vulnerable "spirituality" kept him in touch with his sensitive self and what he desired with the religious "soul." Premeditating on the crumbling sensuality of the complex adventures with Marguérite, which ended after the Christmas vacation of 1931, Wittgenstein felt deeply hurt facing a life of celibacy, starting his alternative life.

Wittgenstein's anxiety about his spirituality created two differing sexual sides to the problem. The intellectual and cognitive features of the right hemisphere of the brain represent the "male" qualities of reason and logic. The right hemisphere was completed with the affection and love inspired by the "feminine" glow of the immediate and intuitive side, coming from the left hemisphere of the brain (Jakobson 1980). The paradoxical process in his friendship with Marguérite brought Wittgenstein the emotional awareness of sexual desire and erotic love, but from the right side of the brain, and he abandoned the left side. Beyond the form of sexual pleasure, the deep and lasting affair realized the *force majeure* to overcome the emotional and bourgeois anxieties of the bourgeois standards of civil requirements. The traditional code excused him from the fulfillment of a marital contract with her, but the complex affair with Marguérite made it difficult to focus on his scholarly work. Yet during the affair with

Marguérite, Ludwig found even and uneven alternatives to giving form to his sexual self in acting with his critical "selves" (Colapietro 1989).

The spirituality of honest and actual experience thickened with the apocalyptic symptoms of Nazi ideology, threatening the life and survival of the Wittgenstein family in Austria. In the strange era of European society in the 1930s, the annexation to Germany meant that Wittgenstein's fear of being considered as having Jewish origins fortified him to try to seek political survival elsewhere. Since he had abandoned Vienna and returned to teach at the University of Cambridge, he was beyond the reach of the Nazis. After his return to Cambridge in 1929, Wittgenstein earned a PhD for his thesis, the *Tractatus* (1929), and the very next day was appointed as fellow of the University of Cambridge (Schimmel 1992: 26–54). There was no commentary in his diaries, since Wittgenstein's attention was elsewhere.

Wittgenstein's real attention was focused on writing his main work, the *Philosophische Bemerkungen*. At the end of April 1930, he presented a proposal to Bertrand Russell for a research grant to stay in the safety of the University of Cambridge. In the introduction of the *Philophische Bemerkungen*, Wittgenstein stressed that he wanted to devote the book to the honor of God (*zur Ehre Gottes*), but the metaphor of the political atmosphere made this religious remark a rascally trick (*eine Schurkerei*) (PB: 7). He later found an administrative alternative for his political security by becoming a British citizen.

In his diaries, still in uncoded script, he said that he felt like a satirist of his era (*der grosse Satiriker dieser Zeit*) (DB: 1:33, 1930), while paradoxically he tried to be taken as honest and credible. Wittgenstein wrote in German (rarely in English) that his life felt like living in a "more raryfied atmosphere" (DB: 1:48, 1931) out of contact with others. He typified the strange self-centeredness by the knack for aphorism and parable. As a teacher, Wittgenstein's true tale included more than philosophy, namely the sense of dreamlike visions as well as poetic or biblical epigraphs (DB: 1:48–54; see Chambers 2010: 198–199). As a good teacher, Wittgenstein was still inspired by Tolstoy's mystic universe to see how the world changed from bad to good. But, as a false teacher, he infused the hidden harmony of style with his own self-critical misery. Indeed, Wittgenstein acted with the voice of a damned soul from Hell (*ein Verdammter aus der Hölle*) (MS 183: 96, 1931, DB: 1:51), writing that he fully deserved divine punishment. The negative perspective of death was what Wittgenstein considered his punishment for being proud. His new project was writing his autobiography with the identity of a humble person. Wittgenstein's public confession in the "private" diary was the journal meant for the anonymous readers of "public" family and friends.

Considering the variety of the mental thought-movements (*Denkbewegungen*) he lived in, Wittgenstein confessed in the diary that (in plaintext) "I am somewhat in love with my kind of movements of thought in philosophy. (And perhaps I must leave out the word 'somewhat.')" (MS 183: 100, 1930; DB: 1:53).[20] Then, he affirmed that "This does not mean that I am in love with my style. I am not" (MS 183: 101, 1930).[21] He changed the material for the diary, continuing with the troubles of losing the intimacy with Marguérite Respinger, which remained closely on his mind and in his heart, together with the misrepresentation of living alone without her company. Wittgenstein's isolation confirmed him in his dedication to pure scholarship. He had been appointed research fellow at Trinity College in Cambridge (1930–1935) and embarked on the project of lecturing to advanced students. He dictated the manuscripts of *The Blue Book* (1933–1934) and *The Brown Book* (1934–1935). He used the questioning-and-answering technique on himself and the students, which activated the interpretive method of the *Big Typescript* [BT]. The assemblage of manuscripts was the first attempt at his principal work, the *Philosophical Investigations*.

Wittgenstein spent the summer holidays of 1931 with his family at the Hochreith estate in the Austrian countryside. Staying at a woodman's cottage, on the edge of the villa grounds, he worked at the re-readings, editing, corrections, and revisions sketched out for a sturdy volume, *The Big Typescript*, which included the *Philosophical Remarks* (PR), *Philosophical Grammar*, and other typescripts (Monk 1990: 319). The warm climate in the Austrian Alps troubled Wittgenstein's delicate spirit and body. In June and July 1931, he complained in *Geheimschrift* about his grief for his own weakness in correct orthography, the high bodily temperatures, and mainly the misfortune of the dangerous insects plaguing him every day of the summer season (MS 110: 208, 226, 240, 1931). He desperately tried to brave the warmest season of the year but felt like an agonized victim.

Wittgenstein explained the psychological disposition of body and soul away from the horrors of his everyday life into the cryptogram of the "yvpvrtv Pvyvidfihg" (noxious liverwurst) (MS 110: 247, 1931; comp. CV: 13, 13e).[22] In the humorous (or tragic) metaphor, Wittgenstein turned the popular saying inside out: the sausage was cut open to poison/intoxicate Wittgenstein's mind.[23] When revealing the voluminous exercise of compiling the *Big Typescript*, he commented on the possibility of publishing his works. Ironically, he confided secretly, in coded script, that stuffing the liverwurst was the symptom representing the mental disorders inside the pork sausage: "Vh rhg yvhxszovnw hrxs zph pvvivi Hxspzfxs avrtvn af ofhhvn, wvi nfi emo Tvrhg zfutvypzhvn driw" (It is humiliating having to present oneself as an empty tube only inflated by the mind) (MS 11O: 242, 1931; CV: 13e).[24] The liverwurst announced Wittgenstein's horror of his human person; as a religious man, he turned pride into emptiness. The cultural symptoms given to the devilish name of the pork sausage were stuffed with spiced meats with many shades of political, folklorical, and religious meanings.

The shape of the liverwurst represented in medical terms the caricatural image (icon) of shameful symptoms, seen and analyzed as medical diagrams (index) to spread the symbolic metaphor to the community of readers.[25] Wittgenstein's "infection" of the metaphorical twist revealed stigmas of the Jewish code, in which the dietary regulations prohibited eating or touching flesh of pigs and insects as they were considered pure parasites there to infect his body. He imagined, or unimagined, them giving him the ritual impurity of drugs and indigestion (Douglas [1966] 1979: 29–323). In Cambridge, Wittgenstein felt a polluted immigrant but lacked courage to fight the moral battle in his philosophical writing. His ailments were discussed secretly in the coded diary.

For Wittgenstein, this paradox of serious threats to life and limb became the cultural symptoms of the summer of 1931. He suffered emotional distress during the months he passed with his family in the Hochreith, but even in the company of family members he was unable to improve or ease the stress around him. In his diary,

Wittgenstein continued to note that he felt depressed about his abortive efforts to write an autobiography. The confession was a personal plan but meant for failure (MS 110: 252–253, 1931). Of course, Wittgenstein was a courageous citizen, independent of mind, but he was not an emotionally hardy person. He pictured himself as an eccentric man who needed spiritual comfort from his environment: "Af wvo wvi wrxs nrxsg ozt, tfg af hvrn, viumiwvig nrxsg nfi ervp Tfgofgrtqvrg hmnwvin zfxs ervp Gzqg" (To treat well somebody who does not like you requires not just great good nature but great *tact* too) (MS 153a: 29v, 1931; CV: 13e).

The coded paragraphs of 1931 ended with the growing image of becoming "blind" (*Blind*) (MS 110: 290, 1931; Gorlée 2012: 205). Rather than "growing blind" (*verblinden*), that is "near-sighted" or "short-sighted" (*kurzsichtig*), Wittgenstein foresaw that he would at some age turn totally blind. The meaningful catchwords modified Wittgenstein's sign-word of "blindness" (*Blindness*), substituting the intellectual inability of a man who was born blind for a spiritual blindness. Wittgenstein expected no miracle, but gave a new vision to the blind man's darkness and light (Jn 9; Lk. 11.33). The plot of blindness started with the short-sighted man, blinded by seeing real facts but circumscribed the word by giving them an actual name or proposition in his quasi-language. Instead of observing real things, the blind man could merely observe some aspects or details of the object, extending their meaning into his alternative linguistic code that he could imagine with his cerebral mechanism. Wittgenstein announced in plaintext the impossible logical similarity between the names or propositions. Then he wrote in parenthesis the English aphorism "Every symbol is what it is & not an other symbol," adding in secret code these particular points:

> Vh rhg hxsdvi vrnvo Qfiahrxsgrtvn vrnvn Dvt af yvhxsivryvn. Dvrp ozn rso nrxsg hztvn qznn "hxszf zfu wvn Qrixsgfio wmig 10 Ovrpvn emn fnh fnw tvs rn wrvhvi."
>
> (It is hard to tell someone who is shortsighted how to get to a place. Because you can't say "Look at that church tower ten miles away over there and go in that direction.")
>
> (MS 105: 85c, 1929; CV: 3e)[26]

The true-false remarks of the possible and impossible truth function as the truth of the blind man. Wittgenstein's personal act of belief now turned into a objective proposition (Glock 1996: 58–63). The biblical picture of darkness and light pulled Wittgenstein, when he was under stress, away to suffering "mental and physical strain" (BBB: 133, 1934–1935). His sensualistic psychology of the blind man enabled him to observe the world around him in "some kind of abnormality" (BBB: 139, 1934–1935). Wittgenstein was not a blind man, but certainly he play-acted the language-act of being blind. In the indexical language disturbances, he "translated" the words into the coded mechanism of quasi-language (Gorlée 2012: 159, 242).

Notes for Lectures on "Private Experience" and Sense Data offered Wittgenstein the opportunity to lecture from 1934 to 1936, the book was then revised and expanded with lecture notes taken by Rush Rhees (Wittgenstein 1993: 200–367). The blind man expanded into providing examples of the general behavior of blindness (218–219,

232–233, 285, 290, 300, 360). Wittgenstein did not dispute the direct facts in his own way but experienced them indirectly as the dramatic "meaning of blindness *for him*" (218). It seemed that the privacy of meaning "stands or falls with its usefulness" (285) signifying the rules of the game to relate word and object for the "mechanism" of the blind man. Yet to give blindness its own sense of real blindness, the play-act has its own interpretant of being a quasi-blind person. The interpretant dramatizes the traumatic event itself for all speakers in his private word game (454). Being blind differs from the play-act of being quasi-blind.

Wittgenstein's phrase "Every symbol is what it is & not an other symbol" signified that the "description made sense only if it was to be understood in a symbolical game of 'I follow the rule *blindly*'" (PI: 219, see 281). Instead of real blindness, the game appeared in the metaphorical "picture of blindness as a darkness in the mind or in the head of a blind person" (PI: 424). The self-game becomes the as-if utterance to express quasi-blindness as the action of make-believe in nonsensical games. The private game can also become "blind to the *expression* [*Ausdruck*] of a face" (PI/PPF: 232) and included not only the linguistic aspect of the facial expression but also the psychological aspects of seeing the face (or other objects). These private games are comparable to the mental and non-mental aspects of "colour-blindness" (*Farbenblindheit*) (PI/PPF: 257), in which Wittgenstein named "aspect-blindness" (*Aspektblindheit*) with the "anomalies of *this* kind [which] are easy for us to imagine" (PI/PPF: 257–260; Glock 1996: 39–40).

Finally, Wittgenstein's manuscript 110 (1931) referred to the problems of the as-if procedure in regard to expressing the true image (*Bild*) as separate from false ones with hardly having any sense. Wittgenstein exclaimed his own troubles regarding his own blind spot, writing in code that "Ovrn Tvsrin driw driw dmsp vrnozp tpvrxshzo emi Zpgvi viyprnwvn. Zyvi nrxsg fnyvwrntg vihg, dvnn rxs ervp zpgvi yrn zph rvgag" (My brain will probably grow blind with age. But not necessarily, only when I am much older than I am now) (MS 110: 290, 1931, my translation).[27] Regrettably, he already felt old at that age, as he noted now in the uncoded phrases: "I appear to myself as an old man … One could imagine a person who from his birth to his death is either always sleeping or lives in some sort of half-sleep or daze. This is how my life compares to that of someone who is truly alive" (DB: 2:134–136, my translation).[28] Wittgenstein's phrases are half personal and half public speech, appearing in monologue and dialogue.

Through lack of sleep, the symptoms of depression continued. While in 1930 Wittgenstein introduced the notion of "dzsnhrnn" (*Wahnsinn,* that is, madness), he manipulated his nervous irritability to handle life with uncertainty. Although his academic work continued as usual, Wittgenstein felt ill and worthless. In 1931, Wittgenstein put an end to the entries in secret code, stepping into plaintext. He stopped using secret code halfway down the cover page of notebook X in the *Philosophical Grammar*. The following phrase appears in the title:

> In the case of my death before hmppvn ovrnv Zfuavrxsnfntvn uiztovngzirhxs evimuuvngprxsg dviwvn fngvi wvo Grpvp:
>
> "Lsrpmhmlsrhxsv Yvoviqfntvn"
>
> fnw org wvi Drwofnt:
>
> "UIZNXRH HQRNNVI aftvvrtnvg"

—Vi rhg, dvnn wrvhv Yvoviqfnt nzxs ovrnvo Gmwv tvpvhvn driw, emn ovrnvi Zyhrxsg rn Qvnngnrh af hvgavn, zn wrv Zwivhhv—: Girnrgb Xmppvtv Xzoyirwtv.

([In the case of my death before] completion or publication of this book my notes should be published as fragments under the title:
"Philosophical Investigations"
and with the dedication:
"to FRANCIS SKINNER"
—If this comment will be read after my death, he is to be informed of my work, at the address—: Trinity College, Cambridge.)

(MS 114: iv, 1932, my translation)[29]

Is this a public or a private notice? It was probably not meant for Wittgenstein's friend, the young mathematician Francis Skinner, whose practical advice about Wittgenstein's work had come to an end (Monk 1990: 331–335). Wittgenstein probably addressed the forward, to the future editors, correctors, translators, and cryptographers of his total works revised again in some "fragmentary" forms of life for the students at Cambridge (331–335 and *passim*).

The same process of fragmentary revision happened on the cover page containing notebook number three of the *Philosophical Remarks*:

Wrvhvh Yfxs qznn zppviwrnth tvqfiag dviwvn, zyvi vh rhg *hvsi* hxsdvi vh irxsgrt af qfiavn Wrvhv Yvoviqfnt yvarvsg hrxs nrxsg zfu wvn—"Evihfxs vrnvi Foziyvrgfnt."

(This book could be shortened, but it is *extremely* difficult to shorten it properly. This comment does not regard the "attempt at a revision.")

(MS 115: iv, 1933)[30]

Beyond these historical examples, what stopped Wittgenstein was the psychological fact that the diaries continued not as before in private paragraphs but modified into normal (that is uncoded) speech reflecting the lecture collection of the future monograph, *The Blue and Brown Books*. Considering Wittgenstein's interest in social communication, were the private diaries perhaps destined for "everyone"?

Language-games

Perhaps one can conclude that Wittgenstein had eventually found the "redemptive word" (*erlösende Wort*) of the definition of language when he formulated the final term of language-games. In the 1933–1934 lecture notes of *The Blue Book* (BBB: 1–74), Wittgenstein presented how the language speaker can play-act with communicating in public language. The ordered and systematic forms of native language had to come and be understood by other speakers in Wittgenstein's notion of language-games. Thus, he wrote:

> I will give someone the order: "fetch me six apples from the grocer," and I will describe a way of making use of such an order: The words "six apples" are written on a piece of paper, the paper is handed to the grocer, the grocer compares the word "apple" with labels on different shelves. He finds it to agree with one of the labels, counts from 1 to the number written on the slip of paper, and for every number counted takes a fruit off the shelf and puts it in a bag.—And here you have a case of the use of words. I shall in the future again and again draw your attention to what I shall call language-games. (BBB: 16–17)

Wittgenstein added on the language-game of shopping that:

> The study of language-games is the study of primitive forms of language or primitive languages. If we want to study the problems of truth and falsehood, of the agreement and disagreement of propositions with reality, of the nature of assertion, assumption, and question, we shall with great advantage look at primitive forms of language in which the forms of thinking appear without the confusing background of highly complicated processes of thought. (BBB: 17)

The language-game of shopping was reduced to a child's task of learning the private "activities, reactions, which are clear-cut and transparent," in which the language-game described the forms of life of the social (tribal) environment with the general aim of "building up the complicated forms from the primitive ones by gradually adding new forms" (BBB: 17). The language-games were Wittgenstein's diagnostic word in the saga of man's heroic enterprise of using the human equipment of language—a long saga, gaining with its essential craftsman's tools the series of episodes narrated by all kinds of interpreters and speakers in various circumstances of life. Now, Wittgenstein was en route to quote the groundless language-games extending beyond the simple fairytales of a child to learn objects and numbers and to perform the specific games we played with the tools of language.

The entries in *Geheimschrift* are missing, suggesting that Wittgenstein's possible troubles were kept to himself in 1936. In that year, the end of his research fellowship in Cambridge brought him no further income, no rooms at Trinity College, and no company of friends, colleagues, and students in Cambridge. Heavy on Wittgenstein's mind and heart were the risks of the hazardous political situation of the Nazi government in Germany if he traveled to see his family. He felt left alone and prepared a remorseful confession as an act of challenge to fight his pride (*Stolz, Eitelkeit*), hoping to illuminate his soul into the virtue of devote modesty (*Bescheidenheit*). Wittgenstein's confession was a secret message addressed firstly to his closest friends, including Francis Skinner and Paul Engelmann, and secondly to his friends in Cambridge, including the philosopher G. E. (George Edward) Moore (Monk 1990: 367–372). The "unhealthy" sins haunting Wittgenstein's soul were his bisexual behavior, his Jewish origins, and the sad circumstances of having beaten a pupil when he was a schoolteacher in the Alpine village of Otterthal. The confession of guilt was Wittgenstein's cure through penitence to regain the path of righteousness.

A long trip to Skjolden in Norway provided a new opportunity for the isolation to write the manuscript of the *Philosophical Investigations*, but Wittgenstein still felt unhappy about life. During the emotionally charged trip in August 1937 to work in absolute solitude (Monk 1990: 373, see 361–384), Wittgenstein traveled alone from England to Bergen (Norway). On the ferry, he wrote in between the pages of his "ordinary" work in philosophy, in secret code, about his troubles:

> Vrnrtvh tvziyvrgvg. Fnw wmxs rsg ovrn Tvrhg nrxsg 'wholeheartedly' yvr wvi Ziyvrg. Wzsrngvi hgvsg wmxs vrn eztvh Tvufsp emo Limpypvo wrvhvh ovrnvh Pvyvnh.
>
> (Been working a bit. And yet I cannot keep my mind wholeheartedly on the work. At the back [of my mind] lurks a vague sense of the problem of this life of mine.)
>
> (MS 118: front cover, 1937, my translation)[31]

Three days afterwards, Wittgenstein spoke to himself about his anxieties:

> Zfu wvo Hxsruu nzxs Hqrmpwvn. Hxsivryv ovsi mwvi dvnrtvi zfh pzntvi dvrpv. Rxs ufspv: <u>rxs givryv</u>. Vrgvp, tvwznqvnpmhm znthgpr. Rxs dfnhxsv rvg. Rxs dfnhxsv rvgag wfixszfh nrxsg, zppvrn af pvyvn. Ufixsgv, dviwv yvwifxqg hvrn & nrxsg ziyvrgvn qmnnvn. Rxs omxsgv rvgag rvoznwvn dmsnvn. In wvi Uifs vrn ovnhxsprxsvh Tvhrxsg hvsvn.—Znwvihvrgh yrn rxs rvgag drvwvi hm <u>evidvrxsprxsg</u>, wzhh vh ervppvrxsg tfg dziv zppvrn hvrn af ofhhvn. Yrn rvgag zffhhvimiwvngprxs evizxsgprxs. Wzirn wzhh rxs wzh hxsiv prvtg nzgfiprxs vrnv Fndzsisvrg.—*Szpgpmh.*
>
> (From the ship to Skjolden. Am writing more or less because I am bored. I feel: <u>I am adrift</u>. Vain, thoughtless, anxious. I wish now not at all to live alone. Fear that I will become depressed and unable to work. I would now like to live with someone. To see another's human face in the morning.—Still, I have now become so *pathetic* that perhaps it would be good that I am alone by necessity. Am now utterly wretched. Writing it is of course the untruthfulness.—*Unhinged.*)
>
> (MS 118: front cover, 1937, my translation)[32]

Once he had arrived at his hut in the Norwegian fjords, he continued:

> Rn Hqrmpwvn. Ufspv orxs fyvp. Fntpfxqprxs, izhgpmh & tvwznqvnpmh. … Fnw wz qzo ori drvwvi Yvdfhhghvrn, drv vrnart Francis rhg & fnvihzgaprxs. Und drv dvnrt rxs wmxs wzh dvrhh dvnn rxs org rso yrn.
>
> (In Skjolden. Feeling poorly. Unhappy, helpless, and thoughtless … But then I remembered again how unique Francis is, almost irreplaceable. And how little I am aware of this, when I am with him.)

> Yrn tzna rn Qpvrnprxsqvrg evihgvxqg. Yrn irigrvig, wvnqv nfi zn orxs & ufspv wzhh ovrn Pvyvn vpvnw rhg, fnw wzyvr szyv rxs zfxs tzi qvrnv Zsnfnt, drv vpvnw.
>
> (Am completely entangled in pettiness. Am irritable, think about myself only, and feel that my life is miserable, but have no idea how miserable it really is.)
>
> (MS 118: 1r, 1937, my translation)[33]

Wittgenstein's formal brain rejected the truth of his life, but he mainly remembered the "untruthfulness" (*Unwahrheit*) of his unstable heart. In the first-person experience of the diary, Wittgenstein moved from the self-referentiality of the monologue to a narcissistic kind of half dialogue, attempting to embody the fictional reality around him without the closeness of the friendship with Francis Skinner. Wittgenstein felt alone and sick, writing that "Yrn rvgag driqprxs qizng. Fnqvipvryhxsoviavn & gvolvizgfi" (I am now really ill. Abdominal pains and hot temperature) (MS 118: 9v, 1937, my translation).[34] Wittgenstein's symptoms seemed to be his stories of both exile and existential angst.

Wittgenstein's "sick soul" (in the terminology of Peirce's friend, the psychologist and theologian William James, see James [1902] 1982: 137–171) had the "romantic" spirit flowing in the thought and form of his sad diaries. In his diary Wittgenstein expressed the circumstances of his life experiences, but he equally associated his morbid suspicion to the tone of his philosophy. Short evocative sentences "solved" some of his personal problems (bad sleep, fatigue, dreams, worries, or pain), but these sentences were uttered as words of wisdom to survive. For example, during August 28, 1938, Wittgenstein wrote the text of the *Philosophical Investigations* but encouraged the stream of his logical thoughts in his coded imperative:

> Ziyvrgv dvrgi & hrvs, dzd driw! …
> Dviwv rxs rv zworg af Iznwv qmoovn? Ziyvrgv dvrggv dvrgvi & fyvipzhh vh wvi Hxsrxqfnt! …
> Zfxs Tvwznqvn uzppvn oznwsozp fnivru emo Uzfo.
>
> (Continue the work to see what the future brings! …
> Will it bring me to the edge? Continue working and leave it to fate! …
> Thoughts, too, occasionally fall unripe from the tree.)
>
> (MS 118: 34v-35r, 1937, my translation)[35]

Perhaps the solution can lie in his diary entries two days earlier (August 27, 1937), when he switched from first-person script to the second-person, announcing for himself and for everyone the virtue of the "forms of life"? He switched from monologue in code to the half-communication in uncoded plain script:

> Wrv Pmhfnt wvh Limypvoh, wzh Wf ro Pvyvn hrvshg, rhg vrnv Zig af pvyvn, wrv wzh Limypvoszugv afo Evihxsdrnwvn yirntg.
>
> (The solution to the problem, which you see in life, lies in living in a way that makes the problems disappear.)

> The fact that life is not without problems means that your life does not fit the forms of life. You must change your life to fit the form to let the problems disappear.
> Or should I say: that who lives rightly, feels the problems not as *sadness*, meaning full of problems, but rather as a joy, as a thin ether surrounding life, instead of a doubtful background.
>
> (MS 118: 17r, 17v, 1937, my translation)[36]

In this "mixed" message, Wittgenstein appears to draw from the cosmological image of the Star of Bethlehem. The falling star crossed the heaven with the starry tails. The Star of Bethlehem symbolized the birth of the mysterious life. Viewing the bright star, one can make a wish, but the stellar spectacle aroused no fear nor anxiety. For Wittgenstein, this star announced the coming of a new universe (Gorlée 2015c: 169).

If we gather the symptomatology of Wittgenstein, the clues in his diary are grounded on the confessions of our sins to God. Wittgenstein wanted to elevate his soul to obey the biblical virtues. He constantly subjected himself in his diary to the humility of self-observation, self-examination, self-delusion, and self-criticism (Colapietro 1989). After returning to Cambridge, Wittgenstein was not really aware that he was a recognized philosophical genius of his time. Following Moore's resignation, Wittgenstein applied for the post of Professor of Philosophy at the University of Cambridge, and on February 10, 1939, he was elected (Monk 1990: 414–415). The chair brought him no happiness in his philosophical life; rather, it brought him unhappiness about the degree of intellectual success he had achieved (415).

Envy or selfish desire had never been Wittgenstein's game. This vice came to nothing in the terror of the Second World War, which brought suffering for Wittgenstein in the German *Blitz.* He was aware that "Envy is something superficial ... farther down passion has a different colouring. (That does not, of course, make envy any less real)" (MS 162: 21v, 1939–1940; CV: 40e). Perhaps Wittgenstein reached up from generosity to genius. As he explained in uncoded text:

> Genius is not "talent *and* character," but character manifesting itself in the form of a special talent. Where one man will show courage by jumping into the water, another will show courage by writing a symphony. (This is a weak example.)
>
> (MS 162b: 22, 1939–1940; CV: 40e)[37]

Then, he defined in secret code that "Ozn qmnngv hztvn: 'Tvnrv rht Ofg ro Gzpvng'" (One could say that: "Genius is courage with talent") (MS 117: 152, 1940),[38] meaning in English and German *Geheimschrift:*

> Nmg ufnq yfg ufnq xwnkfvivw rh dszg rh dmigsb mu zworizgrmn & ozqvh pruv wmigh szernt yvvn prevw. Wvi Ofg, wrv Tvhxsrxqprxsqvrg; nrxsg vrnozp drv Rnhlrizgrmn, rhg wzh Hvnuqmin, wzh afo timhhvn Yzfo volmi dzxshg.

> (Not funk but funk conquered what is worthy of admiration and makes life worth having been lived. Courage, not cleverness; not even inspiration, is the grain of the mustard seed, which can grow into a big tree.)
>
> (MS 117: 151, 1940, my translation; cf. CV: 43e–44e)[39]

Wittgenstein attempted to evade the dangers of arrogance and success, in writing:

> Zfuhvrnvn Pmiyvivn zfhafifsvn rhg hm tvuzsiprxs, drv zfu vrnvi Hxsnvvdznwvifnt zfhifsvn. Ozn hxspzug Wf nrxqhg brn & hgriyhg ro Hxspzu.
>
> (Resting on your laurels is as dangerous as resting during a walk in the snow? You do not You fall asleep and die in your sleep.)
>
> (MS 162b: 42v, 1939–1940, my translation)[40]

The mixture of monologue and quasi-dialogue transports the talk to an acceptance of his personal failure, which did not deter him from trying to write the dialogue again. Wittgenstein deleted "Ozn hxspzug" (One sleeps)[41] without describing the dramatic effect, but he responded to the sinful idea by answering positively. He spoke about the "language-game" of the grain of the mustard seed. The plant grows, almost miraculously, into a tree so that the birds of the air can shelter in its branches (Mt. 13:31–32; Mk 4:31–32; Lk. 13:18–21; see Jeremias 1963: 146–151). For Wittgenstein and his readers the moral lesson of the gospel parable was to compare the kingdom of God with the final stage of human life. Wittgenstein's work to receive the philosophical Word provides an explanation of the psychological crises of his life. His life was burdened with spiritual symptoms, difficult to survive as a whole person. The reasons were not only his charitable contribution to the war effort but also Francis Skinner's unexpected death of poliomyelitis in 1941, at the young age of twenty-nine years. The friendship had broken down earlier but Skinner's death again left Wittgenstein with guilt and remorse (Monk 1990: 425–428).

Despite these troubles, Wittgenstein had an active period in which he continued preparing the preliminary manuscripts of the *Philosophical Investigations* (Pichler 2006: 137–143). Between Fall 1939 and 1943, he revised, rearranged, and reworked by hand the early manuscripts to be printed together with the rearranged version of the *Tractatus*. This double project of "telling" and "showing" was abandoned later, but kept Wittgenstein working during the outbreak of the Second World War. Wittgenstein was kept safe by his British citizenship, but he worried about the horrors of Nazified pressure applied against his sisters in Vienna. Working became an almost impossible duty. He struggled each day with an outburst of medical symptom-signs of "nervous" diseases. In June 1940, he wrote each day in code, abandoning the philosophical notebooks to work on his diary instead, to calm down his mood. His nervous disorders were caused by the constant lack of sleep, anxiety, a weak pulse, and all kinds of pains (MS 117: 271–272, 1940). Given the clinical problems, that repeated in later years, Wittgenstein described in his diary these bad moments of going through a nervous breakdown with no way out.

At the age of fifty-one, Wittgenstein left his chair at Cambridge to contribute to the war effort. He served "anonymously" as a porter in Guy's Hospital in London, and later as a laboratory assistant in Newcastle (Monk 1990: 431–436, 447–454). From this period, Wittgenstein's use of the *Geheimschrift* increased in his diaries, intensifying his emotionality. Perhaps this change was also motivated by his interest in reading Freud's new theories of the human psyche and his stay in hospital. Wittgenstein had an inflammation of the gallbladder and in code he briefly mentioned the symptoms of pain (MS 120: 56r, 1937; MS 120: 71r, 1938). Following an acute attack of pain he was operated on at Guy's Hospital in 1942 to remove gallstones (cholecystectomy) (Monk 1990: 436), patient Wittgenstein merely described in code the hospital room seen from the outside, but unfortunately he did not give any details of his sickness:

> Ro Qiznqvnhhp, dzigv zuf wrv omitrtv Plvizgmn, Vh hxsvrng vrn vxsg zyhhxsvfprxsi Mig. Zfhhvi Oznnvin hrnw zfxs vrn lzzi qiznqv Qrnwvi wz, vrnvh droovig fnnzfusmiprxs. Vh rhg aftrt fnyvkfvo & fntvofgprxs. Fntvofgprxs zfxs wrv Luptvirnnvn.
>
> (In the hospital place, waiting for the operation tomorrow. It is an altogether hideous room. Populated by men and a number of sick children, one of them whimpering all the time. It is drafty, uncomfortable and unpleasant. Unpleasant too are the nurses.)
>
> (MS 125: 58v, 1942, my translation)[42]

Almost intertextualizing the horror of the hospital room, Wittgenstein described the dictatorial attitude of the hospital staff (see Klagge 2011: 116–117; Rhees 1984: 154, 223 fn. 40) but without giving any physical details or personal intimacies about his medical situation. As Rilke notes, he "told" but did not "show" the details. Then he continued in plaintext (now without code) speaking in third-person indirectly about his fears:

> A man is *trapped* in his room, when the door is not blocked, it opens inwards; but it does not occur to him to pull instead of push.
>
> Bring the man into the wrong atmosphere and nothing will function as it should. He will seem unhealthy in all parts. Bring him back to the right element, and everything will unfold and become healthy. But what if he is in the wrong element? Then he must accept to resemble an invalid. (MS 125: 58v-58r, 1942, my translation)[43]

Wittgenstein felt symptoms of alienation from his self, but after a week he had recuperated somewhat and added in code that:

> Ovrn Fntpfxq rhg hm qmolpvc, wzhh vh hxsdvi af yvhxsivryvn rhg. Zyvi dzsihxsvrnprxs rhg wmxs <u>Evivrvrnhzofnt</u> wrv Szflghzxsv.
>
> (My unhappiness is so complex that it is hard to describe. But perhaps <u>isolation</u> is most prominent.)
>
> (MS 125: 58v, 1942, my translation)[44]

This description of his isolation, confined to the hospital ward to treat his psychosomatic illness under the guard of medical professionals. Without a friend to take care of him, Wittgenstein uttered the sensitive cry for help. He did send positive cables to the Wittgenstein sisters, not to worry them. But although the sisters saw that "you were in a very bad state of health [but your news from the hospital] sounded just as reassuring" (McGuinness, Ascher, and Pfersmann 1996: 177, my translation). In Nazified Europe his sisters were unable to travel to England to help him. Wittgenstein acutely felt that he as a lonely person was misunderstood and misdiagnosed. From this point, he broke down in fear in the role of a social outcast:

> The balance between the construction of realistic illusion and its deconstruction gives way; the metafictional tension of technique and counter-technique is dissolved, and metafictional elements are superseded by those of surrealism, the grotesque, randomness, cut-ups and fold-ins. (Waugh 1984: 130)

The effect was an alternative to rejecting a simplistic concept of *mimesis* (the belief that verbal construction can somehow directly imitate non-verbal ones) is to assert the opposite narrative pole of *diegesis:* "'telling' instead of 'showing'" (130). The fabrication of fictional things, such as the diagnostic experiment of Wittgenstein's language-games, could exist to create the existence of the social world, but beyond the uncertainty to try to communicate with others, Wittgenstein was "a lone Creative Figure busily inventing and constructing, producing the text from His [*sic*] position in the Real World" (130). His performance was useless and worth nothing. As he said in the metaphor, "rxs dzi vrn Urhxs & yrn vrn Urhxs tvyrvyvn" (I was a fish and will remain a fish) (MS 125: 59v, 1942, my translation).[45]

Fallen angel

Wittgenstein was surrounded by imaginary fear. This neurotic habit was determined by his constant emotions and vague intuition. This nervous breakdown was Wittgenstein's form of anxiety, developed when he must have been, according to the medical terminology of *Black's Medical Dictionary* [BMD] "in a state of persistent anxiety and worry, 'tensed up,' always feeling fatigued and unable to sleep at night. In addition, there are often complaints suggesting some physical disorder: e.g., palpitation, flatulence or headache" (1987: 491). His symptoms did not reach the stage of obsessional neurosis, developed in Freud's symptomatic action to make ordinary life almost an unbearable habit. But the borderline between anxiety neurosis and obsessional neurosis "may be far from clear, but in the latter the obsession interferes much more with ordinary life of the patient" (BMD 1987: 491). Wittgenstein's ordinary life—still writing on the philosophy of language—was the main duty of his mind and kept him clear of psychoneurosis, but the psychosomatic sickness changed his personality.

During Wittgenstein's convalescence from his gallbladder operation in London, he could not work and wrote no entries in his diary. However, he had new friends, although he may have missed the intellectual fellowship of academe? Wittgenstein's notebook of MS 127, written from early 1943 to 1944 with a total of 237 pages, covers the verbal material of mathematics and logic, but has only one entry in *Geheimschrift*:

> Wrv Prvyv szg hmaf hztvn advr Gvolvizgfivn: vnvn Srgavtizw vr nvn Dziovtizm.
>
> (Love has two temperatures, as it were; one is the heat temperature and the second is the body temperature.)
>
> (MS 127: 120, 1944, my translation)[46]

Wittgenstein's reason associated the first with the second (Schulte 2001: 183–184). He had an agonizing uncertainty, even impatience and nausea, at the idea of living again in the city of Cambridge. He wrote that

> Zppvh rn wvo Mig hgmggf orxs zy. Wzh Hgvruv, Qfnhgprxsv, Svpyhgtvuzpprtv wvi Pvfgv. Wrv Fnrevihrgvruvm Zgomhlsziv rhg ori vqvpszug.
>
> (Everything here [in Cambridge] repels me. The rigidity, the artificiality, the self-satisfaction of the [English] people. The atmosphere of the University makes me sick.)
>
> (MS 132: 85, 1946; see Monk 1990: 493)[47]

At the university's request, Wittgenstein had to return to Cambridge in the fall of 1944 to resume his philosophical lectures to the new students (included Elizabeth Anscombe) and his plan to continue the second part of the *Philosophical Investigations*.

With agony, Wittgenstein questioned himself about the why and how of "wzh Tvufsp wvi Zysznttrtqvrg" (my feelings of dependence) (MS 130: 292, 1946).[48] His dependence on the professional duties of his professorial status seemed to subordinate his self, at the moment when his intellectual pride had been forgotten and abandoned to humility. He wrote in ordinary plaintext that the mixture of vice (pride, arrogance) and virtue (humility) shifted between extremes of emotional dependence and independence. The "value" depended on the good or bad situation to affect his pragmatic standing in society. Any "request, reward, punishment, etc., does not entirely depend on the image but rather on the specific situation" (MS 130: 292, 1946, my translation).[49]

Wittgenstein wanted to alleviate the situation of the less fortunate. The disasters of the Second World War including the fire-bombs on Dresden, the horrors of the concentration camps, the atomic bombs on Japan, and many other human catastrophes, left him with depression. In the post-war period he changed his political views to the Left, identifying himself away from conservative religion to the future reconstruction of Europe along Marxist lines. In this period, Wittgenstein also fell in love with Ben Richard, an undergraduate student of medicine at Cambridge. Despite this new friendship, Wittgenstein's was woefully homesick. Since the *Anschluss* of Austria, he missed the intimate visits to his family. The essential loneliness and nostalgia was Wittgenstein's mental and emotional stress.

Against the symptoms of "Wrv Znthg, wvi Advruvp, wrv Hvsnhfxsg, wrv Yvqpvoofnt" (the anxiety, the doubt, the nostalgia, of being imprisoned), he only "gizxsgv vrtvngprxs nfi wvn Dzsnhrnn emn ori uvinafszpgvn" (tried to keep madness away from me) (MS 131: 41, 46, 1946, my translation). Wittgenstein felt like a fallen angel or bad demon, mediating between pride, ambition, and success. He continued in plaintext about himself as a lost sheep "tricked by an evil spirit but encircled by pleasant and green pastures" (MS 131; 38, 1946, my translation).[50] The biblical epitaph explained that Wittgenstein wandered alone in the wilderness in search of the good shepherd (Jn 10:11–18). He must have had visions of fighting off demons attacking him as he entered fresh pastures. In search of spiritual nourishment in Cambridge, he had little opportunity to listen to musical performances to relax from nervous anxiety (McGuinness, Ascher, and Pfersmann 1996: 188, 189), as had been his habit in Vienna prior to the Second World War.

Perhaps Wittgenstein's wandering soul was musing on the "green pastures" of the Psalms (Pss. 22:2; 74:1; 97:13; 100:13) to give him a resting place. Perhaps he retold the story of the well-known hymn *Jerusalem* (1804), written by Wittgenstein's favorite English poet, William Blake (1757–1827). Blake's mythical vision of a "green and pleasant land" evoked, for Wittgenstein, memories of the darkest days of the First and Second World Wars, liberated in the ultimate truth of God's arms:

And did those feet in ancient time
Walk upon England's mountains green?
And was the holy Lamb of God
On England's pleasant pastures seen?
And did the Countenance Divine
Shine forth upon our clouded hills?
And was Jerusalem builded here
Among these dark Satanic Mills?
Bring me my Bow of burning gold!
Bring me my Arrows of desire;
Bring me my Spear! O clouds unfold!
Bring me my Chariot of fire!
I will not cease from Mental Fight,
Nor shall my Sword sleep in my hand,
Till we have built Jerusalem,
In England's green and pleasant Land.

(Blake quoted in Barr 2002: 21)

Philosophy and religion were unconnected doctrines going their separate ways in life, for both Wittgenstein and Blake (Monk 1990: 540). This separation signified that philosophical truth did not influence religious truth, and religious truth did not inspire philosophical truth. Indeed, Wittgenstein had not found the Holy Grail in England, but he vividly remembered "those feet in ancient time," marching on European soil. Maurice Drury's wish—"Yvprvev rn Orizxpuh!" (Believe in miracles!) (MS 131: 221, 1946, in English)—inspired teacher Wittgenstein's yearning for order in the world. He heard God's answers to his prayer, saying that "Omtv wzh Sviadvs orxs afi irxsgrtvn

Sznwpfnt ufsivn" (May the heartache be healed by the right *action*) (MS 131: 26, 1946, my translation).[51]

Wittgenstein's future involved changes of life and environment. Instead of taking the chair at Cambridge as the crowning achievement of his scientific life, he choose in 1947 to abandon the chair and work on his own in Ireland, the United States, and Norway, and to visit his family members in Austria. Instead of the impossibility of thinking (*Denkunmöglichkeit*) (MS 131: 39, 1946) about the imitative notions or procedures of good and evil, Wittgenstein, mentally transformed down to his very being, sought the radical essence of a new philosophy—without uttering religious dogmas and far away from the accepted opinion of his colleagues at the university. In this radical sense, Wittgenstein's traveling (*Wandlung*) created the anarchistic manifesto of exile as a medication to get better (Klagge 2010). He needed this proviso to create his own *Lebensraum* (living space) in order to compose the spiritual opportunities to write from his real self.

Even when Wittgenstein was together with Ben Richard, he felt lonely, tired, and unwell (MS 133: 76, 81, 1946). He felt hopeless about his medical condition and station in life. In the last part of his life, he wrote Part II of the *Philosophical Investigations*. Part II was separate from Part I and investigated the modern-day philosophy of psychology within language. Part II is named "A Fragment" (PI/PPF: 1–372; see Monk 1990: 544–550). In his last years, in small notebooks he wrote the first-draft material of his final work *On Certainty* (OC; discussed in Moyal-Sharrock 2007; Gorlée 2012: 273–317), in which logical certainty in philosophical truth was radically transformed into doubt and uncertainty.

Wittgenstein's symptoms became those of an older man, complaining in the last years of his life of being lonely and unwell:

> Rxs ufspv orxs nrxsg dmsp, dvrhh zyvi nrxsg ivxsg dzifo. Rxs yrn viofwvg; ufspv orxs uivow rn wvi Dvpg zph vrn Uivowprnt. Dvnn wrxs qvrn Yznw zn Ovnhxsvn & qvrn Yznw zn Tmgg yrnwvg, hm yrhg wf vrn Uivowprnt. ... Qznn dvtvn hxspvxsgvn Hxspzuvh & Ofwrtqvrg.
>
> (I am not feeling well, do not really know why. I am fatigued, feel a stranger in this world. When you have no ties to people and no ties binding you to God, you are a stranger ... Because of sleep loss & fatigue, I cannot work.)
>
> (MS 135: 110, 115, 1947)[52]

The pathological states returned Wittgenstein to his usual exclamation "Tmgg yvdziv orxs emio Dzsnhrnn!" (God preserve me from madness!) (MS 136: 60a, 1948).[53] The nervous explosion triggered memories of mourning and guilt. To combat the demonic spirit, Wittgenstein prayed frequently, turning to God for a better life (MS 137: 71a–71b, 72b, 1948). To his sister Helene, he wrote as usual that he was totally healthy and had no further news (McGuinness, Ascher, and Pfersmann 1996: 186–187).

During his final years (1949–1951), Wittgenstein's worldwide intelligence and linguistic statements shocked and astounded his readers. As an individual, he "turned into a slippery customer; if one door is closed to it, it finds, or even breaks, another entrance to the world" (Langer [1942] 1948: 69). Wittgenstein turned into the unspeakable "citizen of no community" (Monk 1990: 551–575). With no income, no possessions, and no home, he stayed with his friends and disciples to work on his philosophy. His discussions stimulated the further works of his hosts—Norman Malcolm in Ithaca (USA), Georg H. von Wright as his successor in Cambridge, and Elisabeth Anscombe in Oxford. Wittgenstein discussed philosophy in *On Certainty*, where he wrote on Goethe's spectrum of colors, but the symptomatic feelings of poor health and weakness continued. He asked himself with every symptom "My wzh ovrnv pvgagv Qiznqsvrg rhg?" (Could this be my last disease?) (MS 138: 11b, 1949).[54] Wittgenstein went to consult a physician and after the examination wrote "Dzi yvro Ziag, ori uvspv nrxssgh Vinhgvh, nfi Tzhgirgrh. Rxs tpzfyv vi szg ivxsg, evigizfv zyvi hvrnvi Gsvizlrv nrxsg" (Been to the doctor, who says I have nothing serious, just gastritis. I think he is right, but do not trust his therapy) (MS 138: 12b, 1949).[55] These symptoms came to his readers "in the form of metaphysical and artistic fancies" (Langer [1943] 1948: 70) or were they real life?

Returning to Cambridge, the inflammation of the stomach was found to be cancer of the prostate, which had no cure. When Wittgenstein spent Christmas with his family in Vienna, both he and his older sister Hermine had cancer, and Wittgenstein also had to spend part of the day in bed. He was comforted by being together with his family and listened to the usual musical performances he enjoyed at home—but he did not tell the Wittgenstein family that he had cancer. Back in Cambridge, he wrote his last diary in code on March 24, 1950:

> Tvhgvin emn Drvn afifxg. Wznzxs qmoog ori Pmnwmn ufixsgyzi gifyhvprt emi. Wrv Miwnfnt hvpyhg rhg srvi vqvpszug, Wrv Ovnhxsvn hrnw emn wvn Yvwfiunrhhvn hvpyhg tvgmgvg, Rvwvi Hxsdfbt rhg,hg, drv wfixs vrne fntvsvfiv Ivryfnt, tznaprxs zfhtvavsig.
>
> (Returned from Vienna yesterday. After that, London appears to me woefully miserable. The orderliness is sick-making. The people are killed by their needs. Drained of all zest as if by infinite friction.)
>
> (MS 173: ii, 1950)[56]

Wittgenstein lived only a few months longer and during this time he wrote in several notebooks (MSS 173, 174, 175, 176, and 176) with ordinary script. The last entries of philosophy were about turning from certainty to uncertainty, and in the last paragraph he addressed himself as a patient to relieve the certainty of his pain. In quotation marks, he induced the uncertain dream state under narcotics, writing that:

> If someone believes that he has flown from America to England in the last few days, then, I believe, he cannot be making a mistake.
>
> And just the same if someone says that he is at this moment sitting at a table & writing.

> "But if I cannot be mistaken in such cases—I could even be drugged?" If I exist & if the drug has affected my consciousness, I do not really talk & think. Now I can guess seriously that I am not dreaming now. If the dreamer says that "I am dreaming," the expression in language is as true as when he said in a dream "It is raining," when indeed it was raining. Also if his dream actually connects itself with the noise of the rain (MS 177: 10v-11, 1951, my translation; cf. OC 89e–90; see Gorlée 2012: 315–316)[57]

The last sentence is unfinished. The effects of narcotic drugs is translated as "drugs" meant to anaesthetize the pain. The depersonalized effects on mental functions is known from Freud's literature about speech in dreams. "The would-be dream interpreter [would] not accept the overt lexical meaning of these 'utterances' at face value," Gedo writes, but "Freud pointed out that these sonic manifest contents are associated with unconscious latent thoughts in an associative manner" (Gedo 2000: 42). Deprived of the force of human consciousness, life is reduced to Wittgenstein's vague "dream" weakened to Peirce's pre-sign of firstness—that is, the simplicity of feelings with quasi-automatic reactions and no real habits. Wittgenstein's dream was his emotional interpretant perhaps combined with his energetic interpretant, but not reaching anything in the sense of logical interpretants. Wittgenstein's would-be dream is, it seems, imaginary and not real. The dreamer Wittgenstein could wake up and make a hypothesis that he was dreaming; or he can hope for God's judgment that he has not misread nor mispronounced life's experiences.

Ludwig Wittgenstein died on April 29, 1951, in the company of his closest friends, Ben Richard, Elizabeth Anscombe, Yorick Smythies, and Maurice Drury (discussed in Monk 1990: 575–580). Wittgenstein was given a Catholic burial to give him rest and peace. One can conclude that the multiple symptoms of clinical depression were Wittgenstein's extreme signs of honesty and credibility fighting against the dangers of his environment. The symptoms were embodied in the personal sadness and unhappiness of what the world had to offer him, but they were grounded on the religious principles of virtue and sin. Wittgenstein's honesty was applied to the generalities of moral principle and actions, because he did not want to accept the amoral mode of conduct and tempers of mind around him. The negative virtue of honesty brought together the goodness, uprightness, and integrity needed to combat the evil of oneself and that of society.

Wittgenstein's argument for real honesty started with the reversals of fortune he suffered. Firstly, the physical environment of the military front, where he worked as young volunteer in the First World War, changed his life of nobility into the environment of conflict and war. Then, Wittgenstein's sexual orientation unsettled his life, separating him from the majority around him. Wittgenstein's idea of a sexless marriage had no success with his female partner, and finding a male friend for life remained a troublesome affair. His dismissal from Trinity College, when he was writing the *Philosophical Investigations*, brought mental disorder, keeping him unsettled. Wittgenstein's Jewish ancestry became dangerous in the horror of the Nazi occupations. At a later date, abandoning his professorate at Cambridge, Wittgenstein was again in bodily pain. He had problems with his arm and walked with a cane. Finally, he was weakened by cancer, from which he died.

The criticism in the empirical approach to the symptomatology of Wittgenstein established "indicative (*endeiktika*) and scientific (*epistémonika*) signs" of medical symptoms, but the signs lacked the prominence of the "scientific precision [to turn into] conjectural (*stochastika*)" symptoms (Sebeok 1986: 1: 280). The stochastic signs repeat the culture-bound signs of illnesses or troubles generating no genuine solution but making indeterminate habits with variants and invariant symptoms, as described in the anthropological and religious examples of this chapter. The analysis of Wittgenstein's bodily and mental symptomatology acts on the degenerative process of Peirce's interpretant-signs to judge reality in the personal form of how he observed "reality." The symptoms display the semiotic *sign* itself as:

> The First which stands in such a genuine triadic relation to a Second, called its *Object,* as to be capable of determining a Third, called its *Interpretant,* to assume the same triadic relation to its Object in which it stands itself to the same Object. (CP: 2.274)

Wittgenstein's personal interpretation assumed the habit and habituality of his symptoms, which could not give a final meaning to solve his neurotic anxieties.

Peirce's three interpretants are the similarity, proximity, and finality of the semiosis of signs, called immediate, dynamical, and final interpretants. The personal interpreter generated emotional, energetic, and logical interpretants. Wittgenstein's habits consisted of the feelings of his emotional interpretant (firstness) followed by the activity of the energetic interpretant (secondness) to write the coded scripts. The continuity of Wittgenstein's diary came from his mental belief of keeping his own diary. The desire (firstness) and determination (secondness) cultivated the habit into the re-habits of habituality, but unfortunately no logical solution (thirdness) was possible for him. For Wittgenstein the habit was not the spare-time hobby of writing but the close observation of his heart. But it did not bring Peirce's final habituescence (thirdness) to his mind. Although Peirce's process of mixed interpretants has been open to debate, he marginally used a number of other alternatives given without definition—such as explicit, suggestive, ejaculative, imperative, usual, destinate, and normative forms of interpretants. These interpretants transform the private monologue addressed to himself into self-playing the public dialogue to utter the scientific language-games. Yet Wittgenstein's diary remains a mysterious habit with obscure rules and unrules.

3

Cryptography

I never more than half succeed in expressing what I want to express. Actually not as much as that, but by no more than a tenth. That is still worth something. Often my writing is nothing but "stuttering."

(MS 154: 1v, 1931)[1]

Coded messages

Behind Wittgenstein's mental image of a secret code lies the larger question about code-switching from natural or native signs to the cultural quasi-sign of secrecy. The touches of strangeness in Wittgenstein's quasi-language were his secret habit of "speaking thinking" (Putnam 2008: 31–33) in codes. The code is "an agreed transformation, or set of unambiguous rules, whereby messages are converted from one representation to another" (Sebeok 1984a: 29). While encoding is a "transformation, whereby, by operation of code rules, a source alters a message from one representation to another," decoding must be a "transformation, whereby, by operation of code rules, a destination alters an incoming message from one representation to another" (29). The keyword of the code is the transformation from source text and target text in forms of translation (Gorlée forthcoming b). In his diary, Wittgenstein's unseen ideas are encoded into the written codes of the German language. The decoding process for Wittgenstein's students is threefold: confronted with the written codes they first need to know the code; second, they need to decode the written code into German; and third, they have to decode the German into English. In these transformations of post-coding and interpretation, there must be loss of information. The diary is a multimessage with different meanings depending on the time and place of the reader (Sebeok 1984a: 30).

The coded message with the alien dimension of the secret code estranges the possible readers from understanding the real message of Wittgenstein's diary. The hypothetical code *stands for* Wittgenstein's inner body and mind to relate the experiences of his life back to himself as his auto-control. When the written words are translated to the strange and distant code system, they seem to detach from author-diarist Wittgenstein to become the task of the readers, and they have a life of their own. Is it true that the broken-down message of language and codes can be translatable (or retranslatable or even untranslatable) without the trouble of interpreting the other signs? Are the code and Wittgenstein's thoughts the transformation between synonymous systems? Did Wittgenstein's code record correctly or incorrectly what transpired in the coded message? Wittgenstein's shibboleths of the activities of speaking and thinking can break the formal word game of the early *Tractatus* to learn that the password of cultural uncertainties (the codes) can provide the entrance into the social and political word games of less formal messages in coded words, sentences, and fragments.

Breaking through the "romantic interest in secret code" (Sebeok 1991b: 15) of the adventures of spies and double agents to defeat enemies on the secret battlefield, Roman Jakobson pointed out that the inquirer approaching a totally unknown language becomes the *cryptanalyst,* different from the decoder of language. The cryptanalyst "must break this code through dexterous manipulation of the language ... until, through a gradual breaking of the code, he is finally enabled to approach any messages in this language like a native decoder" (Jakobson and Halle [1956] 1971: 28–30). David Kahn's *The Codebreakers* concerned the mode of cryptological expression of the secret communications of the intelligence in the Second World War, revealing how the Germans deciphered most of the British codes at the beginning of the war. But the British, in turn, broke the U-boat codes and won the war. Cryptography does not conceal the presence of a secret message but renders it intelligible to outsiders. The technical secrecy of cryptography has two basic transformations:

> In *transposition*, the letters of the plaintext are jumbled; their normal order is disarranged. To shuffle *secret* into ETCRSE is a transposition. In *substitution*, the letters of the plaintext are replaced by other letters, or by numbers or symbols. Thus *secret* might become ... XIWOXY in a more complicated system. In transposition, the letters retain their identities—the two e's of *secret* are still present in ETCRSE—but they lose their positions, while in substitution the letters retain their position but lose their identities. (Kahn [1968] 1974: xi, original emphasis)

Wittgenstein's cryptography was not political, but his cryptography came from his imagination to surprise the readers of his diary, but urging the ideal readers to be cryptoanalysts and learn the full range of the code. As informants of the code system, the readers decode the mystery of the manipulation to see the information and the reasons behind Wittgenstein's double thinking in code or without code. The form of secrecy enabled the cryptoanalysts to explore the "hidden essence" of the silent imagination of his thoughts. The readers of the diary go through the stages of the preliminary work. With this preliminary effort they learn the educational habit needed to understand the atypical process of Wittgenstein's habit of thinking and writing. The learning process is not about general information delivery, but the delivery of the actual teaching built on the close relationship of Wittgenstein with a group of students. Like any good teacher, Wittgenstein believed that the students were possible readers and should learn the code system to understand his encoded writings. In semiotic terms, Wittgenstein's readers move from the immediate and emotional interpretants to try to build the dynamical or energetic interpretant. Progressively, they hope to achieve the final or logical interpretant of understanding Wittgenstein's inner thought-signs.

Wittgenstein's teaching program shows that the secret speech was the word-by-word literalism of the original thoughts to comprehend the reverse transliteration, in which he had defamiliarized the native language (German) into the strange speech (Catford [1965] 1974: 66–70; Anderson and Gorlée 2011). In the lexical transliteration from familiar plaintext to the set of unfamiliar words and artificial sentences, the context and the equivalents of the graphological translation have supposedly remained the same, but Wittgenstein wrote that other propositions can weigh and balance the values of linguistic and cultural diagnosis by the symptomatology of source and target texts. Wittgenstein's forms of cryptography consist in the synonymy of possible beliefs in other statements of linguistic reasoning, and possibly in Wittgenstein's usual example of the quasi-language in exclamations and interjections (Gorlée 2015b). Let us inquire into Wittgenstein's meaningful code-signs to break the clues, myths, and symptoms of the code and decipher the dramatic storytelling of his diary (Ginzburg [1986] 1989, 1990).

The transformation of the cryptographical speech intermeshed Wittgenstein's imagined words, sentences, and fragments to the apocalyptic puzzle written in single "ciphers" (McGuinness, Ascher, and Pfersmann 1996: 41), as was the name of the code in Wittgenstein's time (Pratt 1939: 16–18). Later, the term "codes" came into use to construct encoded messages which need decoding to understand the message. In Sebeok's words,

> Encoding and decoding imply a code, a set of unambiguous rules whereby messages are convertible from one representation to another; the code is what the two parties in the message exchange are supposed to have, in fact or by assumption, totally or in part, in common. (Sebeok [1994] 2001: 31)

The semiotic system of the code of word-signs would depend on Kahn's "thousands of words, phrases, letters, and syllables with the codewords … that replace those plaintext elements"; but Kahn specified the quality of code into a sweeping study of two semiotic codes, subtly intertwined into code and message. He wrote that "In a sense, a code comprises a gigantic cipher alphabet, in which the basic plaintext unit is the word or the phrase; syllables and letters are supplied mainly to spell out words not present in the code" (Kahn [1968] 1974: xii–xiii).

Wittgenstein's diary was obviously a more complex artifact than merely adding ornamental speech composed into a strange chain of random letters addressed to surprise the readers. He substituted the anagrams of the linguistic units into the linguïcultural sensitivity of religion and philosophy to arouse the curiosity of unpracticed readers and to suggest to them unfamiliar shapes and forms. The formal meaning of letters and interpunction already showed the rule-directed forms of the construction of Wittgenstein's "grammar" (Glock 1996: 150–155). But it was clear that the interrelations of the formal string of linguistic units build the grammatical construction of the logical syntax and semantics into unfamiliar code words belonging to another linguistic system. The enciphered mode of writing was the two-layered explanation/interpretation of Wittgenstein's double thoughts to show the transition of the original German text transfiguring through the method of the cryptography into the exotic alphabet.

The practical exercise of Wittgenstein's coded wordplay (Farb 1974) was used to project the educational program for students (and other readers). It demonstrated the image of unblocking the coded messages and using it to project the magical process of the secret code transposed into daily language. Israel Scheffler in *Of Human Potential: An Essay in the Philosophy of Education* (1985: 58–63) argued that the reader (listener, student) could in such a program become a *potential* student by taking active part in the demythologizing process to grasp in this case the codes of Wittgenstein's diary (91–97). In the policy-making role of teacher, Wittgenstein had introduced in the curriculum the mythological play of his secret script to display the ability to go beyond the technical knowledge and read the human aspects of Wittgenstein's "absurd" self or selves. The task was to reformulate them in applied linguistics to understand the cultural contexts of the theoretical constructs and special notations belonging to the secret script.

Scheffler's exploratory model went beyond the actual "books in the library [which] are opaque physical objects" to enter upon understanding the cultural "ideas they contain [which] cannot be acquired merely by intention and effort" (86). Scheffler notes an intriguing story about:

> [A] professor at an American university, lecturing in Russian, who became annoyed that several people in the audience arose to leave shortly after he had begun. "Why are you leaving?" he asked. "We do not understand Russian," they replied. "You must concentrate!" thundered the professor. Reading, like the general case of acquiring a language, opens doors to learning, otherwise sealed. With a knowledge of spoken Russian, concentration indeed enables leaning of the oral Russian message. With ability to read, one may learn the contents of a library volume by striving to do so, thus expanding access to stored messages beyond the local context. (86)

The personal choice to learn the strange language through effort and will works in the same way as Jewish education teaches the believer to understand God's mysterious words by reading and learning (Neville 1996). This happens by explaining, commenting, and expounding the tradition of the Jewish law from oral Torah to the written Talmud (Bamberger 1981: xxix–xxxi; Putnam 2008: 14–15). The reader of Wittgenstein's diary must become stronger than Kahn's political codebreaker, believing that the object of study must be highly relevant for learning more than the curriculum as a rigid body of knowledge in all religions. The curriculum must be negotiated in classrooms by teachers and students. The silent speech of the diary is not sealed off from Wittgenstein's lectures of philosophy but can, with some effort, be translated into ordinary language (Isa. 29:11). The diary is seen in itself as a critical paraphrase to observe Wittgenstein's control and self-control to compose the writing in cryptography.[2]

The educational program develops through presenting the sense of the wordplay to make the readers engage in creative thinking to understand the double game. Wittgenstein's game marked the dissection and growth of his own revelation of the language in sealed words to encourage the students to attempt to learn the code. As usual, Wittgenstein himself learned to speak when he was a child (Isa. 29:12–13), but through the "transition from simple imitation to meaningful imitation" (Hardwick 1971: 95, 127) the child in the learning process will recognize the cultural meaning of the single word (and later the sentence and so on). The child does not take the word or sentence in utter isolation but takes account of the comprehension of meaning in the social reality around them. Later, the child will learn the use of language simply through the tone and token of the voice of their parents to associate the non-formal word game with the formal facts of life around them. The meaning arises from the appropriate object or situation to enter the cosmology of "naming" to give some "form" to objects in the world (126–137). Thereby, if the child grows up to be one of Wittgenstein's students, they become stimulus-seeking learners doing different assignments to learn their own language-game using the words and sentences of their native language. They work as individuals and as teams to build the basic material to construct their knowledge through questions and answers.

The "primitive" practice of the language speaker allows the students to gradually learn the human practice of language by observing its fixed and flexible boundaries and by attempting to build their personal form of identity (self) in the secret words. The goal of the word game is to play the private game of language—denominated by George Steiner as "playing the game of *solitaire*" (1975: 167)—to let the word game grow into the native language to build a variety of "language-games" (Glock 1996: 193–198). The language-games they play code the collective behavior into a social language, made from old rules and new rules. Old rules are developed and forgotten, while new rules are formulated for use by all the speakers of the native community to practice to communicate socially or publicly with each other (Steiner 1975: 91).

The physiological and psychological aspects of the child code was illustrated by Wittgenstein in the dramatic statement formulated in the opening paragraph of the *Philosophical Investigations*. By quoting Saint Augustine's *Confessions* in the original Latin language, Wittgenstein exemplified the "primitive" codification of the memories of his childhood, as follows:

> Cum ipsi (majores homines) appellabant rem aliquam, et cum secundum eam vicem corpus ad aliquid movebant, videbam, et tenebam hoc ab eis vicari rem illam, quod sonabant, cum eam vellent ostendere. Hoc autem eos velle ex motu corporis aperiebatur: tamquam verbis naturalibus omnium gentium, quae fiunt vultu et nutu oculorum, ceterumquo membrorum actu, et sonitu vocis indicante affectionem animi in petendis, habendis, rejiciendis, fugiendisve rebus. Ita verba in variis sententiis locis suis posita, et cerebro audita, et crebro audita, quarum rerum signa essent, paulatim colligebam, measque jam voluntates, edomito in eis signis ore, per haec enuntiabam.
>
> (When grown-ups named some object and at the same time turned toward it, I perceived it, and I grasped that the thing was signified by the sound they uttered, since they meant to point *it* out. This, however, I gathered from their gestures, the natural language of all peoples, the language that by means of facial expression and the play of eyes, of the movements of the limbs and the tone of voice, indicates the affection of the soul when it desires, or clings to, or rejects, or recoils from,

> something. In this way, little by little, I learnt to understand what things the words, which I heard uttered in their respective places in various sentences, signified. And once I got my tongue around these signs, I used them to express my wishes.)
> (PI: 1 fn. 1; Gorlée 2012: 136–137)

Use of this Latin language was no pointless verbiage for its own sake. Wittgenstein wanted to show that learning a strange language must arise from the emotional and sensuous desire to master verbal and non-verbal communication. The student must master the energy to learn their own native language—but equally to learn foreign languages. The free will, attention, and effort to learn language was, for Augustine and Wittgenstein, the child's own decision to imitate what was shown by the adults as the native model of language including paralanguage to make the language-games of the community.

Augustine's informal example of his childhood described the simple way of individuation of objects and things, which became a form of activity to give a model of learning through experience the native function of language. The point that is stressed is that the child's mind is still fresh and spontaneous, not yet fixed in rigid patterns like that of an adult. The "childlike" identity corresponds to Peirce's emotional interpretants of learning single words to build the energetic interpretants of full sentences and so on. Since the child has not (yet) reached the learning, experience, and knowledge of the adult person, they could easily climb the intellectual ladder to mount from a single habit to the habitual use of the learning, and from native language to foreign languages.

The Wittgenstein children led a sheltered life in the splendid isolation of a wealthy family in the *belle époque* of Vienna. They did not go to school and their parents hired private tutors for their instruction. The siblings had no outside friends to confide in and were very close to each other. One of their games was sending coded messages in their *Geheimschrift* to each other (Immler 2011: 80). The family code was for the Wittgenstein children the family ritual of handling, manipulating, and fabricating the secretive codes with ease to shape their private thoughts and communicate in secret writing with each other (Monk 1990: 267). This analogy or allegory from language to quasi-language signified that the secret code for the Wittgenstein children, and also for Wittgenstein himself, was not the final and definitive act of writing the intellectual sign of language (final interpretant) but rather the open sign of their creative thrill of friendship and love in generating the play of secret messages in the interpretant-signs of the emotional icon and the energetic index.

Learning the password to the secret code challenged Wittgenstein's resistance to the mechanistic validity of theory indulging without problems in the experience of writing. He hardly believed in scientific method. For him, the dynamic and energetic activity of learning was the open activity of attempting to grow into understanding the philosophical; transformations of language. Wittgenstein's calling was guiding the students into the "right method of philosophy" (TLP: 6.53) performed in the play-act of retranslating the abstract method into the habitual practice of human language. The absurdity of Wittgenstein's emotional silence is his maxim, "Whereof one cannot speak, thereof one must be silent" (TLP: 7; Gorlée 2012: 42, 73–78). Behind this hidden silence, the maxim did not establish the readiness of giving "meaning to certain signs in his proposition" (TLP: 6.53); instead, the silence was applied to alert the students to the unknown language to make an energetic translation of the code, to learn to overcome the mediative silence, and finally to enter from linguistic half-communications and misreadings to understand the total communication in open reproductivity.

Wittgenstein explained the ascending and descending of philosophical understanding with the metaphor of the effort to climb a ladder. The biblical ladder (Gen. 28:12) connected the lowest truth with the highest celestial light. The ladder of heaven to earth inspired Wittgenstein's learnability of philosophy:

> My propositions are elucidatory in this way: he who understands me finally recognizes them as senseless, when he has climbed out through them, on them, over them. (He must so to speak throw away the ladder, after he has climbed up on it.) (TLP: 6.54; see CV: 10e, 1930; Kishik 2008: 66–68)

The secretive code requires the readers reading or listening to Wittgenstein's frame of mind not just to feel the emotional interpretants but also requires their isolated efforts to attempt to reconstruct the energetic interpretants to break open the final mystery of the ciphertext. One should never walk underneath a ladder but attempt to climb up to learn philosophical arguments. In Wittgenstein's words, the unpracticed outsider must, "surmount these propositions; then he sees the world rightly" (TLP: 6.54). The truth of the reader's effort is to understand the ruled system to signify the going up and down of the ladder. The alien outsider could be gradually transformed into the native insider.[3] In the stages of the learning process, Wittgenstein's silence can become "grammaticalized" to translate the private code (monologue) into the open benefit of social communication (dialogue).

Wittgenstein's cryptography consisted of the relatively simple method of an alphabet cipher or "*substitution cipher*," in which the original letters are "replaced by letters, figures or symbols" (Pratt 1939: 16). Wittgenstein's code weakened the method into the "*simple-substitution cipher* … in which one letter [of plaintext] is represented by one, and always the same, letter, figure or symbol of the cipher" (16). Wittgenstein's code employed this alphabetical arrangement, replacing the separate letters of the one-alphabet cipher from German into the coded script. The code effect created the unfamiliar scripture.

Much later, on March 23, 1937, Wittgenstein illustrated the definition of the family code, when he responded to the personal mood in the letter of his brother-in-law Max Salzer, married to his sister Helene. Max Salzer wrote to Wittgenstein that he wanted to receive from him "any friendly words (or perhaps some strong words *à la Luki)*"[4] (McGuinness, Ascher, and Pfersmann 1996: 156, my translation). In his letter of response, Wittgenstein's joke greeted Salzer with the coded and half-coded "My old *Hxszhrn!*"[5] (157, my translation). Wittgenstein referred to his sister Helene for the decipherment or decoding of the family catchword. The punch line of the language-game was the word "*Hxszhrn*" (Schasian), which was speculated on by Schulte, but remains a vague and open word without specific content (2001: 178–179). This word "*Hxszhrn*" is probably a family in-joke, but the proper name must remain full of confidence and free of self-pity. To grasp it, the word could be the affectionate "cursing" of the brother-in-law denominating him by a wicked name; or perhaps he used the pseudonym of his name Salzer with the double use of "*h*" to "s" and the single "*z*" to "a"? Or perhaps the mysterious designations of "*Hxsvhxszhxs*" (German: Scheschach) could convert it into a religious and political word as the half-synonym of Babylon described in Kabbalah quasi-language? (This is unlikely for the Wittgensteins' in-joke.)

To grasp the outlines of Wittgenstein's secret script, it was clear that the possible readers must have the intellectual ability to learn the password and to master the diary code. Each letter of the start of the alphabet was replaced by a special letter of the end of the alphabet, replacing German "a" for "z" in secret code, "b" for "y," "c" for "x," and so forth. The monoalphabetic reformulation of Wittgenstein's German "grammar" into the code alphabet yields the following model to explain the system of rules:

a = z	f = u	k = q	p = l	u = f	z = a
b = y	g = t	l = p	q = k	v = e	
c = x	h = s	m = o	r = i/j	w = d	f with *Umlaut* = ü
d = w	hh= ss/ß	n = n	s = h	x = c	m with *Umlaut* = ö
e = v	i = r	o = m	t = g	y = b	z with *Umlaut* = ä

(Somavilla quoted in DB: 1:13–15; Pichler 2006: 143–144)

Beyond the transformation of the letters (except "n" which remains the same in both plaintext and code), the visual signals of figures and symbols in the German punctuation, capitalization, underlining, numbers, commas, brackets, paragraphs, lines, and sections (including the final point) are unchanged in Wittgenstein's code to give the coded messages somehow the "normal" surface.

Seen in terms of translation theory, as the applied science of general linguistics, Wittgenstein's decoded message was the mixture of interlingual translation happening inside the same language, or extralingual translation between two languages. The source language is Wittgenstein's *lingua franca* of Austro-German language, but the code-switching recorded his own idiom into the technical code of the target language. This would mean for Wittgenstein's diary that the primary concept of oral language does not exclude the written code as secondary code, which can be translated into other languages to provide the tertiary code. The difference between the primary natural language and the secondary written code is that the artificial language felt "like coding, and reading like decoding" but the rules between both are "much more complicated than the rules of any cryptography" (Freudenthal 1960: 3). With the tertiary code, the algebraic codes "multiply astonishingly" (CP: 4.309) into new codes, making information a problem.

While cryptography was the secret manner of writing, cryptology was logically based on a secure system of syntactical and semantical codes, handled in terms of simplicity and regularity, with no exceptions to the mathematical and statistical rules (Van der Lubbe 1998). Often cryptoanalysis embraces the dual fields of cryptography and cryptology. For example, the mathematician Hans Freudenthal in 1960 designed the logistic language of Lincos (abbreviation of "Lingua Cosmica") to create the "cosmic intercourse" (Freudenthal 1960). The constructed ideal of generating this "cosmic" language was successful in the technical generations of the analytical and artistic formulas as enacted in the artificial quasi-languages of Volapuk, Esperanto, Lincos, and Klingon (Gorlée 1998: 79–81). But these universal models of one-world language (Nuessel 1996) were of little use in cross-cultural communication worldwide, because the English language became in the Western universe the common tongue of worldwide internationalism for all language speakers.

Cryptography as the art of linguistic writing included "translation" and "translating" accompanied by the interpreter's presence in the "translatability" or even the "untranslatability" of the possibility of signification (Gorlée 2004a: 123–124, Anderson and Gorlée 2011). The act of translating is not the symbolic replacement with a new language but the real index of coding and decoding to formally replace the oral with the written code, from language to quasi-language. In the transcription of natural to unnatural language, the interpreter's mind acts as the simple translator (interpreter, speaker, agent) transporting as sign-maker linguistic text into coded text. The translatability of the translator's knowledge integrates the formal (technical, statistical, mathematical) rules without linguistic troubles for the reading of the new interpreters. In the concept of translation, the translator "secretly" gives the coded language their own cultural insights to comprehend the signal with its own message. The interpreter (translator) acts with the human "quasi-mind" (CP: 4.536; Gorlée 2004a: 66–67, 129–132, 148) to replace the coded language to the formal substitution into the quasi-speech (idiom or dialect). Without the evident learning of the codes, the untranslatability of the coded text faces the readers with some alienated expression of quasi-codification, which can be more complex than ordinary cryptography.

In Peirce's universal categories of tone-token-type, the source language is more than Wittgenstein's inner voice but unheard by the readers. The inner voice is the "indefinite significant character" of the "tone of voice" (CP: 4.537), which has disappeared from writing. Wittgenstein's internal voice would be the "tone" of the translatability of the original thought in German language, but the hidden translatability of Wittgenstein's iconic voice has evaporated in the untranslatability of the language code. Reading the documentary record is the open sign serving as the "token" of Wittgenstein's translatability, but can have for uninstructed readers the hidden meaning of untranslatability. Wittgenstein emphasized that the quasi-linguistic type of the secret code would integrate the cultural type of his personal identity. The indexical combination of language and code makes the mixed metaphor of language and code the attractive sign, but Wittgenstein emphasized that the code must first be learnt to be cryptoanalyzed and to make sense. After this instruction, the "type" can be reapplied to the linguistic and cultural framework (Anderson and Gorlée 2011) to give the double meaning of the diagram system to have the signification. Any translation creates a record of the social and political events that serve as the cultural background to the target version. With the arrival of the new translation, the old source version is left dissected, broken down into simpler pieces to help the textual and contextual analysis for each of the main items involved.

Language has a semiotic system in which the linguistic signs are regarded as a theory of meaningful (or even unmeaningful) codes (Nöth 1990: 237–239, see 229–239). The rules of the codes build Wittgenstein's notion of "grammar" with the double articulation of language, since they share the order of syntactic messages with the meaning of semantics to communicate the varieties of the use of language (Hardwick 1971: 49–53). Sebeok wrote that semiotics of language is concerned with the "generation and encoding of messages, their propagation in any sensorially appropriate form of physical energy, their decoding and interpretation" (1979: 36). Sebeok even claimed that if the "subject matter of semiotics is, quite simply, messages—any messages whatsoever" (37) in natural and unnatural languages, the verbal codes are signs of encoded messages in quasi-language. Semiotics promoted empirical or analytical linguistics to the status of the "pilot science" (37) including the theory of codes and non-codes into languages. Indeed, the codification of language dominated the semiotic oeuvre of Peirce, Saussure, Morris, Eco, and other semioticians (Nöth 1990: 237–239) and will be central in the analysis of Wittgenstein's diary.

Language and code are not merely considered as the semiogenetic translation of the human "brain" to deal with the delay between the incoming auditory message and the outgoing response language tool (Nöth 1990: 236). Instead, language and code derive from the biological roots of biotranslation (Kull and Torop 2003; Gorlée 2004b, forthcoming b). The anthroposemiotic system of translation improves promiscuous—or perhaps better: parasitic—messages of language with fixed codes. The "serial strings, as in speech, or writing, or gesturing" (Sebeok 1984a: 8) have been cultivated in Wittgenstein's symbiosis of language transported into the secret code. The double articulation between internal and external message systems is not the effect of genuine semiosis but the degenerate activity engaging in quasi-semiosis (3). Generally, human speakers (translators, interpreters) tend to weaken their ideal linguistic idea-thought to generate the human paraphrase of encoded messages.

The botanical parasite attempts to form a code but is condemned as an "evil" organism having a dependent relationship with another organism (here, language). Parasites are merely target outsiders, with no vital function except finding nourishment and refuge from predators in the host source. The target parasites may even cause disease or deformation in the source specimen (source text), short of terminally undermining its substrate host. The parasitical plant or animal can survive as a target organism at the expense of, and harmful to, the natural species. Instead of the "hard" sense of parasitism with target intruders invading a source prey, the "soft" reproductive system is perhaps a more useful association to spread out from the source to the target of Wittgenstein's specialized form of semiotranslation, the combination of semiotics and translation theory into transduction (Gorlée 2015c:11–12; see Sebeok 1984a: 30; Gorlée 2011: 177–178 and forthcoming b).[6]

The parasitism of the code in Wittgenstein's diary repeats the translated copies of the non-verbal sign of his voice. The emotional verbal messages grow in the soft plasticity of the fertile soil to give obvious branches and leaves. That was Wittgenstein's memory. The multiple copies can harden into a final cause for the future, such that the original source channels of the code's information are the hidden memory of Wittgenstein's tone as a forgotten thing of the past. The parasitical elasticity of both sides of translating and translation will reconvert the brain. The recoding and encoded messages lead to the learning effect of decoding the semiotic transformation of the closed cryptograms to make cerebral sense to the readers (Nöth 1990: 239).

Cryptography

Learning by heart was the central memory of Wittgenstein's laboratory of cryptography. The historical background of language and codes in communication (Cherry [1957] 1966: 32–41) was the tradition of "Caesar's script" used by Roman general and consul Caesar (Gaius Julius Caesar, 100–44 BCE) to gain victory in his military campaigns of the Gallic Wars. Caesar even stressed the education of learning the Celtic tongue handed down by the illiterate memory of the Druids. Caesar mentioned that "With almost all men it is so, that through the help of letters they lose attentiveness in learning and their memory" (*On the Gallic War* [*De Bello Gallico*] 6:14, quoted in Jensen 1970: 20 fn).[7] Caesar was strongly inclined to learning other languages to understand other peoples' way of being. In Roman antiquity, the memorizing ability of the wild "barbarian" tribes outside the Roman world aroused the Romans' attention to learn, not only to brutally conquer their Gaulish lands but also to learn the ceremonies spoken by the magical brotherhood of Druidic priests. Ignorant of the standard development of written records, the Druid priests circulated the wisdom of their worship not by writing sacred texts but by transmitting them orally to be learnt secretly through the memory (Heller-Roazen 2013: 100–101).

Suetonius (Gaius Tranquillus Suetonius, *c.* 69–*c.* 140), who was the "gossip columnist of ancient Rome" (Kahn 1968 [1974]: 77), wrote a biography of Caesar in his "Deified Julius" (*Divus Iulius*), which was Part I of *The Lives of the Caesars* (*De Vita Caesarum*). Suetonius noted that, during the history of brilliant campaigns and political memoirs, Caesar's personal secretary-slave applied to the correspondence what is now called "Caesar's shorthand." Suetonius reported that:

> Some letters of his to the senate are also preserved, and he seems to have been the first to reduce such documents to pages and the form of a note-book, whereas previously consuls and generals sent their reports written right across the sheet. There are also letters of his to Cicero, as well as to his intimates on private affairs, and in the latter, if he had anything confidential to say, he wrote it in cipher, that is, by so changing the order of the letters of the alphabet, that not a word could be made out. If anyone wishes to decipher these, and get at their meaning, he must substitute the fourth letter of the alphabet, namely D, for A, and so with the others. (§ 56: 6 in Suetonius [1914] 1920: 78)[8]

Caesar's military records were not only abbreviated and reduced by Suetonius, they were also arranged in columns written separately on several sheets, bound together in the book form, the Latin *codex*, like a modern-day calendar. Like the sketchbook of the *Denkbewegungen*, Wittgenstein's notebooks fold together the philosophy of language with his diary to construct the emotional states and cultural thoughts of what he called the "album," offering merely the "picture of the landscape" (*Landschaftsbild*) but not the real thing, in what he called the "imaginary landscape" (*Phantasielandschaft*) (PI: 398). Caesar wrote, according to Suetonius, formal reports in secret code to the Senate and military generals of the Roman Army; and he also applied the secret code in confidential passages of private letters to his friends, such as the great Roman orator Cicero (Marcus Tullius Cicero, 106–43 BCE) (Heller-Roazen 2013: 95). While never mentioning Caesar as the source of his shorthand, Wittgenstein used Caesar's substitution as the simplest and least secure system of his cipher alphabet (Danesi 2002: 55–58).

Unlike Suetonius's anatomy of military and private texts (Toporov 1977), Wittgenstein's auto-communication in cryptography (Lotman 1990: 20–35) did not associate with magical prophesies or auguries received from the ancient oracles. Nor did he, as Caesar, imagine technical tricks to withhold information from foreign enemies in wartime—particularly the secret intelligence of the Second World War and the Cold War espionage between the United States and the Soviet Union, at the time when the skills of cryptography and cryptoanalysis reached political heights of international paranoia and conspiracy (Kahn [1968] 1974; Hastings 2015). For example, the political narratives between the United States and Japan and between Germany and Britain brought a flow of secret information about developing the atom bomb and breaking the U-boat codes to win the Second World War. To ensure military secrecy of signals intelligence, enciphering machines were developed. At sea, the war was controlled by the Admiralty in London and the US Navy, who even employed Navajo speakers making up deceptive codes in the unknown language of the North American Indian tribe to assure the strictest secrecy of their speech. The scrambled speech of military messages was conglomorated with Navajo language, American slang, and military terminology. Today, the secrecy is reserved only for political and military messages, and applied to medical and financial files, automatic banking, videophones, polling data, and global computer networks to give the sense of security (Van der Lubbe 1998).

Beyond the political cryptography, one could learn the code alphabet to employ it in international espionage work or in the private correspondence of secret love. Yet Wittgenstein's secret business did not keep any amorous intrigue confidential from hidden lovers in his diary, but he tried to avoid including unwanted information for outsiders (McCormick 1980). Wittgenstein's technical magic of the secret code pointed to the "everyday oblique" experience of ordinary life (Blake 2010: 241–264). Using "normal" cryptography as his "usual" speech, Wittgenstein gave to the possible readers of his diary the political (or even dramatic) clues of his life (Sebeok 1988) unveiling the events in a "secret" way. He expected to be an ironic, sarcastic, or even a playfully abusive user of cryptotypes. But revealing to the readers the "ordinary" craft of decryption, he addressed the messages in indirect rather than direct modes of metalingual discourse in digital code. A reference manual for the computer-linguistic analysis of Wittgenstein's *Geheimschrift* is, with critical entries, useful to read Wittgenstein cryptography with more understanding (Krey 2016).

Wittgenstein's grammar and lexicon are based on the linguistic and literary art of writing messages to transform examples and create an individual manner of writing. As mentioned, Wittgenstein restricted himself to reading the creation story of, for example, Saint Augustine's memoirs, who reminded him of wanting to learn his native language in his childhood. As previously noted, he had thoroughly read Tolstoy's ethical confession, but also Keller's political notebook and Rilke's detached cryptograms (see Chapter 4). These historical readings used familiar and unfamiliar words as "normal" word types, inspiring Wittgenstein with vagrant thoughts, accidents, or even adventures. Also he modeled his diary on Samuel Pepys's stenographical diary. Stenography was the cryptosystem of words abbreviated into coded microdots and pictographical arrangements. In Wittgenstein's time, the future of "cryptographic culture [has] led to a cultural mythos that associates cryptographic culture with the disembodiment, self-transcendence, and fetishization of communication" making the present-day technology of "electronic communications on the Internet reproduce features of cryptographic identity" (Rosenheim 1997: 15; see 171–197, 247–248 fn. 76).

One can stress that the art of Wittgenstein's reversed cryptography, encrypted in his diary as mainly short messages, was to characterize the messages as a "political" game of explanatory notes, but without "satisfactory methods for systematically collecting and describing word uses" (Posner 1980: 91). Instead of elaborating on his theory about cryptography, Wittgenstein imagined his art of cryptoanalysis as a simple word game not fabricated by himself but representing the cryptoanalytic practice of language and quasi-language to tease and surprise the readers. He wanted the readers to understand his minute observations of, say, the email entries of his diary. The readers should benefit from Peirce's habits of emotional and mental attention to spare them the pain of learning the strange code; they would learn about Wittgenstein's subject of his medical symptoms to be able to project the secret code into science fiction for future generations (Gorlée 2015b).

In linguistic terminology, the alphabetical translation of Wittgenstein's cryptography belongs to the special writing systems of human language, divided into: (1) orthography as the writing system in standard everyday use, which consequently attracts most study; (2) stenography as a system that enables writing to take place at speed, as in other methods of shorthand; (3) cryptography as a method devised to keep a written message secret, (4) paedography as a method devised to help children to read in a natural situation; and (5) technography as a method that enables a specialized field to perform its various functions, such as phonetic transcription, chemical notation, cartography, or computer coding (Crystal 1987: 194).

In the early linguistics of the 1930s, phonetic linguistics started the technical analysis of the practical use of language. Later, the emerging linguists put the adventure of phonetic words aside to advocate the counterpart, the quasi-linguistic behavior of phonemics (Pike 1947), introducing cultural behavior to linguistic signs. The separate examples of Wittgenstein's secret notations displayed the technique of transposition into the hypothetical language, now called quasi-language. This procedure was, at least for Wittgenstein himself, the manipulation to transform with his familiarity the German letters into the secret script. The problem of the readers was to give sense to the alien alphabetic writing, which systematically used many unused letters, such as the sequence of "x," "q," "v," and "z," contextualized and highlighted by Wittgenstein in the secret transcription of the thought-movements (*Denkbewegungen*) to make sense of an unfamiliar and exotic scripture for Western readers. Their duty did not easily follow

Wittgenstein's spontaneous procedure to comprehend his strange phonetics. When the readers followed the step-by-step procedure of traveling from phonetics of language to the phonemics of Wittgenstein's secret code, the cultural remarks complicated the vocabulary with the readers' social speech (Anderson and Gorlée 2011) to make any sense.

In Wittgenstein's time, language was defined by linguist Bloomsfield as the analysis of *phonetics* and *semantics*:

> *Phonetics*, in which we studied the speech-event without reference to the meaning, investigating only the sound-producing movements of the speaker, the sound-waves, and the action of the hearer's ear-drum, and *semantics*, in which we studied the relation of these features to the features of meaning, showing that a certain type of speech-sound was uttered in certain types of situation and led the hearer to perform certain types of response. (Bloomsfield [1933] 1967: 74)

Ironically, Bloomsfield stated that "our knowledge of the world in which we live is so imperfect that we can rarely make accurate statements about the meaning of a speech-form" (74). Linguistic messages are infinitely varied in form and continuous in shape, so that understanding their meaning becomes a complex or unpleasant task. Bloomsfield noted that:

> To recognize the distinctive features of a language, we must leave the ground of pure phonetics and act as though science had progressed far enough to identify all the situations and responses that make up the meaning of speech-forms. In the case of our own language, we trust our everyday knowledge to tell us whether speech-forms are "the same" or "different." ... In the case of a strange language we have to learn such things by trial and error, or to obtain the meanings from someone that knows the language. (77–78)

Through the entrance of complex kinds of messages, the old acoustic form of alphabetic writing was abandoned. Bloomsfield obviously recognized that human communication must depend on the clues of phonetics with the component of cultural phonemes to judge the "difference with other phonemes between this configuration and all the other phonemes of the same language" (128). The solution to the problem of phonemes lies "entirely in the habits of [native] speakers," but Bloomfield confronted the strange quasi-language as the innocent speaker who "has no way of knowing" which features are or are not significant (77, 84). Each feature of the phoneme becomes a distinct unit of the phonetic transcription and can in different situations have different meanings in alphabetic writing. First, the meaning was mostly religious and spiritual, then redefined into mental linguistics. The modern awareness of Wittgenstein's time was focused on psychological and sexual problems, treated by Freud's psychoanalysis.

Phonetics demonstrate the clue of how the phonetic letters of the alphabet can serve to synchronize the relative frequency of the actual occurrence of the letters. This frequency of lettering is observed in "normal" texts. Pratt's general survey, made in

Wittgenstein's time (1939), placed the groups of letters of the German language from most usual to rare occurrences, as follows:

I. e
II. n, i
III. s, t, r, a, d
IV. h, u, g
V. m, c, l, b
VI. o, f, k
VII. w, v, z, p
VIII. j, y, x (modif. Pratt 1939: 256)

In Wittgenstein's code these groups of letters were substituted as the following groups from high to low frequency:

I. v
II. n, r
III. h, g, i, z, w
IV. ss/ß, f, t
V. o, x, p, y
VI. m, u, q
VII. d, e, z, l
VIII. r, a, b, c

Pratt took care of the phonetic writing of the German language by, for example, placing the *Umlaut* of the vocals "a," "o," and "u" into "ä," "ö," and "ü." The distinctive character of the double "m" (mm = *oo*) is frequent, as is the double "s" or "ß" (ss = *hh*). The combination of "sz" (*ha*) is also usual in the German language. The special frequency of "c" (*x*) is evident in the usual German diphthongs "ch" (*xs*) and "sch" (*hxs*).[9] Pratt's phonetic division was sufficient to replace the lexicon of the alphabetic script, but since he was considered an "early" linguist, Pratt's background was rather insufficient to give sense to the analysis of discourse. He commented on or underlined the surface structure with the large body of the different activities, but Wittgenstein's varieties of philosophy and diary was for him a step too far.

Wittgenstein's special code alphabet fabricated the cipher script into the rhetorical manipulation of the known linguistic combinations of "*v*," "*n*," "*h*," and "*r*," but aroused semantic curiosities about the rhetorical abundance of the low-frequency action of the letters "*w*," "*x*," "*y*," and "*z*." The reversed sequence of Wittgenstein's "grammatical" alphabet in the phonetical script dealt with the distinctive speech sounds in the total message, but the reader needs significant clues to handle not the unmarked technical speech sounds but the marked message of the text (Jakobson 1972). The phonetic clues concern themselves with the practical significance of vocal sounds corresponding to the symmetrical ideal to transform the rough source material into a one-to-one equivalence of the target material.

Further, the measurable validity of the sounds in phonetics is referenced through the system of phonemics. Phonemics illustrate the meaning of both cultural interpretations, which fluctuate in time and space from oral source to written target texts (Pike [1943] 1961, 1947, [1952] 1972). In the sense of Pike and Jakobson, the cultural function of written messages moves away from the linguistic terminology of English to the quasi-linguistic transcription of the alien "dialects," as in Pike's "Kalaba-X" (1947: 68–158, 241; 1957–1958: 348–360). Kabala-X was denominated by Pike as hypothetical or artificial language (here called quasi-language) allowing access through translation to the cultural and social meaning of native English (Pike 1947: vii, 239; 1967: *passim*; see Gorlée 1998: 79–81; 2015b; Gorlée and Anderson 2011). For the coded "dialect" of Wittgenstein's diary, the readers must first judge the phonetics to be able to study the phonemics of the hypothetical (artificial) code-text.

In *Fundamentals of Language* (Jakobson and Halle [1956] 1971), Jakobson described phonemes as signs of Otherness, removed from the natural phonetic code to the unnatural cultural code. While most phonemes lack "individual, particular signalization," they always function on their own, in relative isolation to other phonemes, to share some linguistic elements, correlating the "speaker's code with the own code of features," so that the reader may readily "infer the origin, educational status and social environment of the sender" (22). If the phonemes are code-restricted, the whole can also become a vague and overlapping text with an usual meaning creating an unusual sense for the other culture. Some phonemes may take a non-formal approach including fictional or literary roots, some have formal perspectives such as Jakobson's algebraic references to the spelling system. But in Jakobson's time, literary works of science fiction tend to use formalized artificial language. This fictitious diction became highly fashionable in political messages to identify the cryptographical fantasy of the Cold War and justify the political survival of Western languages and culture. The concept of hypothetical languages also became, for the Christian missionary Pike, the problem of analyzing the linguistic differences between different native languages to solve the dilemmas about including cultural items unknown in tribal societies (Gorlée 2015b). While most interpretations are for the reader (and the translator) decoded messages (translatability) with uncoded interpretation (untranslatability), the readers of Wittgenstein's secret code include the decoding of his oral thoughts (translating) transposed in the written cryptography (translation) (Jakobson and Halle [1956] 1971: 22–28).

Cryptoanalysis applies the quasi-linguistic code system to generate the natural and spontaneous code to clarify the cryptography of strange messages. The term cryptology broadens cryptography, signifying the solving and unlocking of dark signals to solve the alien meaning. The secret communication of cryptography must have linguistic and extralinguistic aspects determining the biological, sociological, psychological, and cultural codes coming from the outside world. The transition of the statistical source of the cryptographer to the trend of social communication highlighted the cryptographical trend of coded words to generate the secrecy of quasi-languages. This development into contemporary telecommunication means that cryptoanalysis corresponded to the encoding and decoding activity of written, visual, or pictorial messages depending on sensory, acoustic, visual, gustatory, and olfactory codes (Eco

1979: 9–14). These multilayered messages are technically transformed into visible and invisible means of political cryptology (Kahn [1968] 1974: 455). The quasi-linguistic puzzle of cryptograms has been developed as partly linguistic and partly mechanical and arithmetical theory of codes as one of the primary branches of semiotics (Eco 1979; Kahn 1986; Danesi 2002: 53–59; 2014: 25, 78–89).

In "*A Theory of Semiotics*" (1979), Umberto Eco proposed a general introduction to the field of semiotics to act as the semiotic research model of human communication. For Eco, social communication would mean that literary communication must include the cryptography of "written languages, unknown alphabets, secret codes," while social communication was situated between "formalized languages" and "natural languages" (11). Eco's model produced the meta-codes of the signals of conventional symptoms and unconventional clues allowing the readers to decipher both of them. The code is explained as the unmarked sign of possible communication to or between human beings (8–9). It points to the object in a neutral way, like Peirce's pre-sign offering pure "suchness"[10] giving the "airy nothingness" (CP: 4.241) of simple language. However, the code also points to non-communication (or half-communication), since real communication depends on which secret codes with special insights have been applied as the key.[11] The meta-code is the metalinguistic or analytic activity marked by the code to give the literary work the novelty of creative power—as observed in the linguistic and cultural Otherness of science fiction (Gorlée 2015b).

The signification of the code comes from the interpretive transition to the meta-code of the reaction of the readers—reflecting the emotional and energetic effects of Peirce's interpretants to upgrade or upshift them into the literary meta-sign. This "translation" means that the reader (interpreter, translator) can transform the simple code into the complex rule of a strange signal with combinatorial or oppositional meaning (Eco 1979: 20). The literary sign is not considered the fixed term from writer to reader, but can assume a false or deceptive reaction in different codes. The physical symptoms and cultural signals give the art of physical, mechanical, and creative possibilities to the code in literary messages (16–19, 20–21). The cultural motives of the traditional signs and symptoms come from the traditional cultures (subcultures), but the improprieties of the alternative signal liberate the signs and symptoms to violate the rule and freely explore the aesthetic nerve of literary speech in cultural strangeness (262). Echoing the personal fragments of his life, Wittgenstein's driving power of literary signs suggested the integration of fresh impulses from Saint Augustine's diary genre, Keller's political and cultural autobiography as well as Rilke's fictional, metafictional, or nonfictional universe of free verse in prose, to reach the variance of styles and quasi-styles of the *Denkbewegungen*.

Peirce's figure of the interpreter, who receives, replicates, and reconstructs the sign to extract the significance and express the interpretant(s), becomes the human agent, organizing and disorganizing Eco's sign-process of semiosis (1979: 314–317). The messages are personal or privileged signs in open or secret channels of communication, but since the interpreter is not an empirical subject but the acting human subject, genuine semiosis is almost impossible for human communication. The human interpreter must be considered to be the living sign using other living and non-living signs for human semiosis. Semiosis reproduces a circularity of signs (firstness, secondness, and thirdness) interacting with each other, but the result of these complimentary steps remains a circle or spiral of signs without reaching the final interpretant.

Eco wrote, however, that no genuine semiosis can reproduce the final or logical interpretant. Sebeok responded to Eco's problem, adding that human sign-action stays behind in what he called "quasi-semiosis" with qualitative or structural similarity of signs and symptoms (Sebeok 1984a: 3). To organize and structure the sign puzzle, the "quasi-interpreter" uses the degenerate habits of the "quasi-mind" to find the ways of "quasi-thought" lying behind cultural messages (Gorlée 2004a: 66–67, 129–130, 145, 147–148, 206). In a positive sense of culture, quasi-semiosis adopts the human code for the practical purpose of successfully (not always truthfully) interpreting the meaning of external signs. But in the "negative" sense, quasi-semiosis can possibly weaken human subculture by adopting self-destructive misreadings and misinterpretations against those compulsive and even addictive behaviors impossible to remedy into "normal" readings (Cannizzaro and Anderson 2016).

If the code of the rule of quasi-semiosis is the blind belief in the degenerate action, it must come from pure intuition (CP: 5.213–5.214) to reveal the human version of truth. Intuition is the human impulse working out of ordinary cognition (with no final sense of habituescence) to feel the simple acceptance of the "internal authority" of the "education, old associations, etc." (CP: 5.214–5.215). Intuition trusts the personal habit of its own code, but perhaps, in the conflicting sense of habituality, it can prophesy the religious "divination—which utilizes codes with a restricted distribution" (Sebeok 1991b: 16). Peirce's belief in the immediate intuition of habit is the same as Wittgenstein's skeptical code of the confusions made in language use; both grow to change into the dynamical habits of culture (and subculture). But Wittgenstein's cryptotypical confusions stressed the importance of human quasi-semiosis, giving it the paradoxical sense of the cryptography, which defies ordinary analysis but still refers to the real nature of language. Secrecy has transformed the original subject into the hypothetical puzzle, signifying the "implied proposition ... is thought in some cryptic sense" (CP: 4.52). The cryptoanalyst reasons the "cryptograph" as the maker of the "statistical syllogism to the other premiss" and tries to answer the questions "Why is this?" and "How is this" (CP: 2.716) to explain the secret code.

Cryptoanalyst Kahn's recent contribution to the *Encyclopedic Dictionary of Semiotics* (Sebeok 1986b) emphasizes the secret non-communication of written messages with parallel codes used in military and political messages. Kahn divides the secret code of cryptology into the semiotic features of quasi-semiosis, writing that "If the messages are written, either in ordinary language or in those of computers, the methods are those of *cryptography*; if the messages are spoken, the methods are those of *cryptophony*, if pictorial or gestural, those of *cryptoeidography*" (Kahn 1986: 155). Sebeok referred quasi-semiosis to the older wisdom of the folk sagacity of the North American Indian tribes (1991b: 16–18; see Umiker-Sebeok and Sebeok 1978: 1–437). The Indian system of signs followed the pictography of sign language among the (Siouan) Dakota Indians of the Great Plains. As cryptosemioticians, the Indians worked out a system of signaling with mirrors, blankets, and other devices. The Plain Indians used the pantomimic Plain Sign Language to make their (inter)tribal communication possible for their inter-communications. The significant gestures of hand and arm were "perfected" in other signals, such as the pictographic use of signals of smoke, fire, or signals made by waving blankets. The semiotic gestures and expressions of the Indian tribes were their secret mystery until Mallery's compendium and guide (Mallery 1972; discussed by Sebeok 1991b:16–19).

Instead of returning to the old secrecy of the mythic world, Kahn was politically oriented to argue the future of the code system in the intellectual habit of espionage work. He warned about including activities that appear to be cryptologic but are not, such as the:

> Kabbalah, gematria, and the "discovery" of the signatures of Francis Bacon in Shakespeare's plays educe ambiguous messages: all persons will not achieve the same results, as they would in solving or decrypting a true cryptogram. Rebuses, riddles, and crossword and other language puzzles and games involve a secrecy that is intended to be penetrated. The "decipherment" of lost languages likewise is not cryptologic because no secrecy was intended (though cryptoanalytic techniques may help in the decipherment). For the same reason, Morse code, semaphore, code flags, though they convert a message into a different alphabet, are not cryptologic because no secrecy is intended; the same holds for artificial languages.
>
> On the other hand, the use of language to obscure meaning, as in politicians' speeches and allusive references by confederates, may be regarded as cryptology, although, because of its lack of rigid prearrangements, as marginal. Voltaire's comment that "Men use … speech only to connect their thoughts" is a statement—though barely—in cryptology. (Kahn 1986: 156)

Kahn's reasons of exclusion are diverse, but it always seems that magical formulas can solve the secret code but without finding the epistemological reply. Puzzling language with quasi-language must necessarily keep the secrecy of the code; if not, the mystery disappears (Danesi 2002: 38–70). Some languages, such as the spiritual tradition of the Jewish Kabbalah, have historically enigmatic codes, and can be considered as quasi-language to keep their secrecy. The Kabbalah specialists trust in the secret codification of this old faith, since the "veiled" access to the code is limited to the Kabbalists and not to outsiders. Other cipher codes need measures of secrecy to function by professional scholars. Imagine Wittgenstein's double picture of the rabbit-duck (PI/PPF: 118, see Gorlée 2012: 22–23), which will be discussed further in this book. Cryptography was seen by Wittgenstein on a more personal and popular level as the literary method of substitution of language. The half-secret analysis of verbal and non-verbal communication were forms of human quasi-semiosis. The secrecy of the puzzle picture still remained for the general public, but the secret puzzle must be experienced as happening in the particular situation of reading and learning (or just visualizing) the diary text, experiencing with all the senses Wittgenstein's behavioral attitudes, and reacting accordingly to this experience. (PI–PI/PPF: 119–240; see Hick [1963] 1973: 61–62)

The double relationship of puzzle pictures deals with their differences in opposition to their similarities—reading in semiotic terms the variation/invariance within the context of markedness/unmarkedness of the strangeness of the puzzle figures. For Jakobson, language consists of both contradictory and self-contradictory signs, that is positive and negative symptoms (or signals). He realized that:

> The presence of the special attribute ("markedness") in contraposition to its absence ("unmarkedness") displays the hierarchical arrangement of [O]therness, that ... follows the same principle of marked terms superposed upon the corresponding unmarked terms. (Jakobson 1972: 76)

The double interplay of puzzle figures is Wittgenstein's mediating bridge, helping him through its very puzzles to read the marked quasi-language modeled by his unmarked habit changes. Danesi, in his argument about recognizing the signs of crime (2014: 37–38), remarked that the reader would normally expect Wittgenstein's unmarked German language, but surprisingly they receive the marked retranslation of hybrid variations written in the fragmentary paragraphs of the quasi-signs. The marked verbal code stimulates the readers to interpret the infinite number of cultural messages to enable them to form and develop what can be called Wittgenstein's alternative communication in his talks, comments, and notes.[12]

Shibboleth

As an instrument for his message, Wittgenstein's secret speech, as the charismatic gift of speaking in strange tongues, was influenced by the translation of the sacred writings. The Bible translator must aim for full intelligibility of the translation but often struggles with difficult interpretative passages to make an acceptable translation instead of the figurative extensions of exocentric idioms (Nida 1964; Crystal 1987: 384–385). For Eco, the interpretation of language was considered "not *glossolalia* but *xenoglossia*, that is, polyglotism—or, failing that, at least a sort of mystic service of simultaneous translation" ([1995] 1997: 351). Wittgenstein's code system arose from the biblical story of the Tower of Babel (Babylon), in which the non-communication of strange languages came into actual existence to confuse the citizens of the city. In the early tradition of Christianity, the charismatic confusion of languages was the quasi-automatic speech of the tongues of men and angels.

The history of the confusion of languages referred to the earlier event of the Babylonian exile learning the Hebrew alphabet. The prophet Jeremiah spoke about the secret speech to denominate the local name of the city of Babylon in the foreign word "Sheshach." According to translator Saint Jerome (*c.* 347–*c.* 420), who produced the *Vulgate* translation or standard Latin Bible, but was involved in theological and scholarly controversies, the secret script of "Sheshnach" was used as an exercise to teach the "elementary practice in learning the Greek alphabet, i.e., *alpha-omega, beta-psi*" (Demsky 1977: 20). The practice to modify the ordinary word "Babylon" to the transcription of "Sheshnach" can be traced back to the old Kabbalistic-Jewish etymology starting during the Babylonian exile to teach the Hebrew alphabet. Jeremiah's rabbinic commandments rebelled against the situation of Jewish exile to change their life by moving back to Israel, to make their own Jewish future (Bamberger 1981: xxxi).

Wittgenstein was essentially a Bible-oriented believer—or better, a virtuous, but somewhat skeptic, believer who yearned to receive the gift of Christian spirituality to spread the acts of creativity. Perhaps through his Hebrew origins, he almost felt the attitude of skepticism of the "punished" believer living in various religious faiths. When facing relevant political issues such as the power of human signs, Wittgenstein chose "his" private devotion, modeled on his own style of life. He disregarded any principles and conventions, broke the rules, and, in his work, he led the readers down into the unexpected devotional life of mystical feelings, mostly during the early days of the First World War (Glock 1996: 251–253). Mysticism was one of Wittgenstein's habit-like "addictions" endured in hard times to open the emotional signs and non-signs of belief in the aphorisms of his diary, but far from the mythical themes of the *Tractatus*, where Wittgenstein's mystical side was conventionally rooted (Glock 1996: 251).

Moving out of the self-control of genuinely symbolic logic, Wittgenstein embraced the quasi-semiosis of not acknowledging the total experience but rather obeying his own "quasi-experience" of work and life (252). Doing that, his quasi-mind did not reveal the biblical truth but envisaged how the hidden script of the facts of life was seen and felt by other interpretive readers. The secrecy of the function and dysfunction of single words can be repaired to serve as separate word-tools in Wittgenstein's diary. The desires and dreams in his diary played an educational game to teach the readers to take part in his adventure: without fear, he used the translation or paraphrase of quasi-language to give a strange form to the original language. For Wittgenstein, as a secret diarist, the true task of philosophy was the bitter work of freeing his mind from the familiar habit to learn the unfamiliar code of the translation to clearly see the magical meaning of the thought process (*Denkbewegungen*).

The early Wittgenstein was bewitched by the mystical pages of "Tolstoy, Kierkegaard, and Tagore" (251). The formal break of language in Wittgenstein's *Tractatus* created the logical order of general propositions (according to Peirce's interactive semiosis). Wittgenstein wrote in an optimistic sense that "Everything that can be thought at all can be thought clearly. Everything that can be said can be said clearly" (TLP: 4.116).[13] Simultaneously, the formal truth of meaningful propositions left the inner dimension of words and sentences in the intellectual disorder of strange and unknown codes. The sense and thought of propositions transformed into pseudo-propositions (*Scheinsätze*) (TLP: 6.2), moving out of God's reality, but they were unable to escape from the "weak" nature of quasi-semiosis to ruin him (Glock 1996: 315–319).

In the *Tractatus*, Wittgenstein balanced the logical atomism in his scientific theory (Peirce's secondness moving to thirdness). But he ended with the secrecy of unspeakable words, which were set apart as the emotional "silence" of non-communication (Peirce's firstness). The evident impossibility of single words transcending the ordinary boundaries of our minds made no sense and stayed silent. He wrote that "Whereof one cannot speak, thereof one must be silent" (TLP: 7).[14] Wittgenstein's concept of silence as a non-productive alternative to productive speech must be regarded as *Tractatus*' paraphrase, before the opening of the last seal of the

Bible. We have to face the profound "silence in heaven for the space of half an hour" (Rev. 8:1) before the apocalyptic trumpets sound for real communication. Starting an emotional silence restores what Wittgenstein wanted from his broader moral: the creation of the educational tool of a silent experience until the time of eloquent speech arrives (Gorlée 2012: 42).

Nevertheless, the interpretation of the sense of language described the sense of the facts of life in Wittgenstein's "nonsense" world, in which he suggested the "Stoic moral ideal of [his own] mystical experience" (Glock 1996: 253; see James ([1902] 1982): 366–413). Beyond the actual world, Wittgenstein stated that "There is indeed the inexpressible. This *shows* itself; it is the mystical" (TLP: 6.522).[15] Behind the meaningful propositions of formal philosophy (Glock 1996: 252), his mystical program "would be unsatisfying to the other [readers]—he would not have the feeling that we were teaching his philosophy—but it would be the only strictly correct method" (TLP: 6.53).[16] During the early *Tractatus* period, Wittgenstein seemed to play-act the formal notion of language, but used this as the antidote to the informal vagueness of the secret messages. The *Geheimschrift* consisted of the "cosmic" nature of illogical concepts formulated in words to build free scriptures, since the cryptographical writing was free from meaning in itself. In semiotic terms, the quasi-language enlightened the ideal sign as God's judgment (symbol), but during the logical game of religion Wittgenstein treated his bodily symptoms as playing the symbolic trick of his mystical language moving out of the expertise of writing—illustrative of real semiosis weakened into his own quasi-semiosis.

In later years, the non-technical illuminations and illogical revelations of the mystical condition did not disappear from Wittgenstein's writings. While Wittgenstein "neither developed nor criticized his earlier mysticism" (Glock 1996: 253), he did indeed give lectures about religious belief in 1938 (*Lectures & Conversations on Aesthetics, Psychology and Religious Belief* [LA]: 53–72). Throughout his life Wittgenstein was guarded by religious sensitivity. The various similarities between Wittgenstein's philosophical statements are mediated by the prophetical riddles of Zen-Buddhism (Glock 1996: 253). Zen-Buddhism seemed to cure his symptoms into creating his new self-identity. Indeed, Buddha's moral lessons are similar to the meaning of Wittgenstein's description of "philosophizing" in his diary (Powell 1982: 128–132). For both Buddha and Wittgenstein, the stream of life would be full of misery and frustrations, but the pains of the "disease" could be cured by the mind or reason. Let us stress that in Wittgenstein's time psychotherapy as psychological religion was considered the central teaching for inner transformation (Capra [1976] 1985: 105, see 105–112).

To escape from the sickness of life, we cannot cling to the medical or psychological symptoms to be fully healed. Buddha and Wittgenstein sought logical justice not in the theory of religious dogmas nor in the religious dogmas of rituals, but rather in the personified explanation to seek one's own absolute righteousness of the true facts of life. All prophets commanded that to make the heart pure, one must eradicate the other side, the domain of evil desire (pleasure, hatred, jealousy, and others) moving away from egoism and stupidity into the mystical experience of the mental liberation in ultimate freedom. Nothing less than Buddha's meditations repaired oneself for the calm state of mind in peace, goodness, and wisdom. Thus, salvation with love, reparation of good will, and justice can detect the climax of Buddhist thought to achieve the full truth of Heaven in Buddha's Nirvana.

The four phases of Buddha's meditative exercise are reformulated into William James's Christian words as follows:

> The first stage comes through concentration of the point upon one point. It excludes desire, but not concentration or judgment: it is still intellectual. In the second stage the intellectual functions drop off, and the satisfied sense of unity remains. In the third stage the satisfaction departs, and indifference begins, along with memory and self-consciousness. In the fourth stage the indifference, memory, and self-consciousness are perfected. … Higher stages still of contemplation are mentioned—a region where there exists nothing. ([1902] 1982: 387; for Buddhist terminology, see Capra [1976] 1985: 107–108)

For both Buddha and Wittgenstein, the correct path to reach the plenitude and fullness of Nirvana does not arise from religious belief nor the logical epistemology, but from the private and personal ethics with moral disciplines to cope with day-to-day life. In other words, not through theory but rather in terms of daily practice and activity, in which the formal analysis is substituted with prayer to reach personal happiness and wisdom.

The creative effects of Wittgenstein's cryptograms are formulated by asking questions:

> "What is the color of the number three?" "Can a machine have a toothache?" "How can you hang a thief who doesn't exist?" "How do we think with our feet?" These questions were posed in order to baffle, insult, cajole, or kick our minds into a clearer perception of language and thus reality. (Powell 1982: 129)

The ideal and humor of Wittgenstein's riddles, dialogues, parables, and other intentional game words questioned the doubt of the language-users (now Wittgenstein's students). The questions were an analysis of their discourse to constitute the ideal language-game. Breaking down the false belief and ego-oriented "jargon" of daily speech (Wittgenstein's concept of nonsense), the cryptograms are decoded and encoded in the social language-games to approximate the humor and happiness of daily communication. Wittgenstein's full attention of the philosophy of language included the mystical meditation about the cryptic decodification of the bilingual—empirical and grammatical—translation of the forms of life to create the spiritual job of making sense to the metaphysical substitution of the alphabet, preserving the same logical identity of subject, substances, and structure (Alston 1964: 1–4).[17]

The Jewish (and Christian) problem of communication and understanding of languages within the native group was promoted by Wittgenstein's notion of dialogue games, accentuating the rhetoric of cultural traditions in the multicultural universe of the highly organized civilization. Wittgenstein seemed to follow the mystery story of the Tower of Babel:

> Hitherto, the world had only one way of speech, only one language. And now, as men travelled westwards, they found a plain in the land of Sennaar, and made themselves a home there; Here we can make bricks, they said to one another, baked with fire; and they built, not in stone, but in brick, with pitch for their mortar. It would be well, they said, to build ourselves a city, and a tower in it with a top that reaches to heaven; we will make ourselves a great people, instead of scattering over the wide face of the earth. But now the Lord came down to look at the city, with its tower, which Adam's children were building; and he said, Here is a people all one, with a tongue common to all; this is but the beginning of their undertakings, and what is to prevent them carrying out all they design? It would be well to go down and throw confusion into the speech they use there, so that they will not be able to understand each other. Thus the Lord broke up their common home, and scattered them over the earth, and the building of the city came to an end. That is why it was called Babel, Confusion, because it was there that the Lord confused the whole world's speech, and scattered them far away, over the wide face of the earth. (Gen. 11:1–9)

The luxury, skill, and arrogance of the Mesopotamian people was paid back in God's punishment, the destruction of their communication with others. The history of the oldest city of the world started as the story of a nomadic population, living in simple tents in the desert. After God flooded the rivers of Mesopotamia (Tigris and Euphrates; Gen. 7.6), the Mesopotamians wanted to attempt a military uprising and build a genuine city with public buildings and private houses. Learning the skills of masonry, they worked together to build the stonework of the old settlement of Babel, and also the cultural city of Nineveh, on the Tigris river, with the famous ornament of the royal hanging gardens. The new Mesopotamian Empire flourished with the pride and vanity of military victories, especially after reaching its height with the captivity of Babylon. The strong general and king Nebuchadnezzar (*c.* 634–*c.* 562 BCE) stormed over the desert to capture Jerusalem and deported the Hebrews as exiles to Babel. For the Hebrews the exile brought expatriation from their language and culture. For the Mesopotamian immigrants, the captivity brought the confusion of polyglotism. Both felt a linguistic strangeness, as they were unable to easily communicate with each other.

The national unit of native and exiled inhabitants provoked a mixed confusion of languages and a mingling of religions; indeed, the confusion prompted the radical difference of power and authority over the city of Babel. Not only was the deity Baal of the Mesopotamians unacceptable for Jewish believers but the citizens of Babel were unable to understand the varieties of languages spoken in the Mesopotamian country. Indeed, the Mesopotamians and Hebrew immigrants struggled with the cultural confusion of the secular and sacred tongues and their mystical interpretations. Despite God's punishment to judge man for his pride, the sacred text of the Tower of Babel remains the ultimate mystery to learn the crime of the Mesopotamian builders. The controversy between the community of Babel, together with the dilemmas about Baal and God, provoked psychological and causal stories associated with the resistance or acceptance of the multiplicity of languages. The xenoglossolalia led to the ultimate confusion for the mixed population of learning alien and foreign tongues to survive the confusion.

Derrida explained the "double" proper name of the "single" city of Babel. The name Babel was explained literally and religiously as "Gate of the Gods." When translated into the Sumerian and Akkadian (Babylonian) cuneiform alphabet, Babel satirically referred to the "confusion" of God's criminal sanction. In the names of this double confusion, Derrida stated that "Babel is untranslatable" meaning that unfortunately, "God weeps over his name" (1985: 184). Derrida stated that the "Truth would be the *pure language*" (196). The proper name of Babel was for the anxious xenophobes transformed into the double mystery of translatability (meaning: sanctity) causing havoc with the untranslatability (meaning: sanction) of the unintelligible name. Derrida radically questioned the semantic unity to stabilize the "incompletion, the impossibility of finishing, of totalizing, of saturating, of completing something on the order of edification, architectural construction, system and architectonics" of the form and name of Babel (165).

Similarly, Wittgenstein wrote in his early *Tractatus* that the name Babel is a "simple sign," which says *how* it is and the meaning can be "completely analysed" (TLP: 3.201). But the outward simplicity can be analyzed in the "state of affairs" of the proper name to state *how* Babel really is, "not *what* it is" (TLP: 3.221). The "constant" untranslatability of the name can become actually translated into the variable" translatability of all kinds of definitions and notations (TLP: 3.312). The "different symbols" of the name Babel and the "variable name" must refer to a common sign but signifying "in different ways" (TLP: 3.321–3.323). In Wittgenstein's early *Tractatus*, they must form a "logical form [or] logical prototype" (TLP: 3.314–3.315).

In 1934, Wittgenstein's lectures from the *Brown Book* (1934) refigured the same image into the construction of the reference to the "language-game" as the building of a brick wall by a team of builders (BBB: 77–81; see Gorlée 2012: 155–156, 179, 241–244; 2017). There, Wittgenstein told the details of the "*demonstrative* teaching of words" (BBB: 77) to assist and instruct the work of the builders to do a good job of building the brick wall together. From real language, the builders used their own quasi-language in the single names of "cube," "brick," "slab," and "column." Such names are repeated as elliptical quasi-sentences in words, meant to create the tool of propositions or sentences necessary for this language-game. For Wittgenstein, the word "brick" seems to function as "a cultural shorthand for the proposition or sentence 'Bring me a brick'" (BBB: 78). The real language and the variable verbal translations apply a partly linguistic and partly quasi-linguistic rule of psychology as translated in gestures, movements, and other signs of body language to speak to the team members about organizing the combinatorial movements of the building materials. Wittgenstein articulated this language-game as the general teaching tool of learning a quasi-language: namely, to interpret (or paraphrase) the builders' habits of feelings and thoughts by translating from ordinary language into coded quasi-language to transmit the shorthand name.

Between Babel (Old Testament) and Pentecost (New Testament), the mystery of the Bible's cryptotext narrated the story of the charismatic gifts of the High Spirit. The High Spirit donated the talent to pray, speak, sing, and even dance with the strange confusion of the languages given to Babel. After Jesus's death, the apostles gather in the builders' team to pray with the crowd of Christian believers about the future of their apostleship. The mystery happens by a miracle:

> When the day of Pentecost came round, while they were all gathered together in unity of purpose, all at once a sound came from heaven like that of a strong wind blowing, and filled the whole house where they were singing. The appeared to them what seemed to be tongues of fire, which parted and came to rest on each of them; and they were filled with the Holy Spirit, and began to speak in strange languages, as the Spirit gave utterance to each. Among those who were dwelling in Jerusalem at this time were devout Jews from every country under heaven; so, when the noise of this went abroad, the crowd which gathered was in bewilderment; each man severally heard them speak in his own language. (Acts 2:1–6)

All languages were involved in this miracle of the High Spirit, so:

> When the noise of this went abroad, the crown which gathered was in bewilderment; each man severally heard them speak in his own language. And they were all beside themselves with astonishment; Are they not all Galicians speaking? they asked. How is it that each of us hears them talking his own native language? There are Parthians among us, and Medes, and Elamites; our homes are in Mesopotamia, or Judea, or Cappadocia; in Pontus or Asia, Phrygia or Pamphylia, Egypt or the parts of Libya round Cyrene; some of us are visitors from Rome, some of us are Jews and other proselytes; there are Cretans among us too, and Arabians; and each has been hearing them tell of God's wonders in his own language. So they were all besides themselves with perplexity, and asked one another, What can this mean? (Acts 2:6–12)

The disciple Peter, the traveling companion of Jesus, addressed the crowd of men and women in these words:

> In the last times, God says, I will pour out my spirit upon all mankind, and your sons and daughters will be prophets. Your young men shall see visions, and your old men shall dream dreams; and I will pour out my spirit in those days upon my servants and hand-maids, so that they will prophesy. I will shew wonders in heaven above, and signs on the earth beneath, blood and fire and whirling smoke; the sun will be turned into darkness and the moon into blood, before the day of the Lord comes, great and glorious. And then everyone who calls on the name of the Lord shall be saved. (Acts 2:17–22)

In the early Christian Church, there was confusion about the spiritual gift of speaking in tongues (Samarin 1972, 1975). The goal was what Wittgenstein formed and named the language-game, which was to have the sense of revelation or conversion through translation.

Different from the xenoglossia of the story of the Tower of Babel, this paralinguistic phenomenon of translation was named glossolalia. Glossolalia inflamed the human habits with the emotional passion of speaking, singing, and even dancing to the joy of divine gesticulation with gestures and body language—these sign games correspond with Peirce's emotional and energetic interpretants that are needed to reach the final interpretants. Glossolalia is not explained as literary confusion of natural language but, influenced by the power of the High Spirit, it serves as the sign of prophetic conversion to strengthen the faith of believers. The charismatic gifts of the early church are demonstrated by the testimony of prayers with inarticulate "groans beyond all utterance" (Rom. 8:26). The prophecy of the gestures was for the early Christians and contemporary Pentecostals the center of their religious worship, in which the speakers entered or heard the divine message of God to bring them to the ecstatic expression of speaking in strange tongues (Kydd 1984: 34–36, 38–39, 45, 53, 61; Lawless 1994: 273–278, 291–292).

Glossolalia seems to transform Wittgenstein's personal silence of signs (TLP: 7), so that he is able to communicate through the social discourse of language-games. The interjections of the verbal and non-verbal gestures were considered a class of words but without name and without any grammatical description (Gorlée 2015a). In ordinary linguistics, the tongue-speaking experience is considered the activity of spontaneous speech emitted in any "marginal" language without code and without serious signification. Despite this failure, the disorderly language phenomena of uncoded speech have generated interdisciplinary questions to give the role of language the interdisciplinary form and function to act "properly." Glossolalia can be explained by the spiritual and mystical implications of religion, anthropology, and sociology as well as medical semiotics (Roch Lecours, Nespoulous, and Viau 1986). It seems that the mystical experience of prayer can break forth in cheers and dances, when the historical or social structures of the unknown tongues makes clear the rejoicing of the revelation or the expectancy of receiving the High Spirit. Against the strong trend of heretical beliefs, the driving wind and the flames of fire coming from the High Spirit build up, for thousands of Christians, the mystical mediation between God, the High Spirit, and the unknown languages to create a real miracle.

The written crypototext of Wittgenstein's secret speech came from the evil message of Jeremiah (*c.* 645–587 BCE), the political prophet who warned the Jews in Babel with threats and terror to follow him. Jeremiah wrote the autobiographical *Book of Jeremiah*, with his lamentations about the "jeremiads," against the sinful behavior of the Jewish people living in Babylon. Jeremiah's cries of terror wanted to obey the voice of God to transform the Jewish people to accept the good news with God. As their prophet, Jeremiah described his prophecy on a crucial moment, when:

> The Lord put out his hand, and touched me on the mouth; See, he told me, I have inspired thy lips with utterance. Here and now I give thee authority over nations and kingdoms everywhere; with a word thou shalt root them up and pull them down, overthrow and lay them in ruins; with a word thou shall build them up and plant them anew. (Jer. 1:9–10)

During the Babylonian exile, Jeremiah's plan was to reconstruct Palestine creating the new Jewish state. He boldly announced to the Jewish flock that:

> I would have you build yourselves houses of your own to dwell in, plant yourselves gardens of your own to support you ... grow numerous, that are now so few, there in your land of exile. A new home I have given you; for the welfare of that realm be ever concerned, ever solicit the divine favour; its welfare is yours. And this warning he sends you, the Lord of hosts, the God of Israel. (Jer. 29:5–8)

In his prophetic life, Jeremiah complained about the calamitous future of the exiled Jews. He foresaw the explosive dynamic and the future destruction of Jerusalem by the Babylonian army, and predicted how the false gods could even be worshipped by the exiled Jews who shared their captivity in Babel. To disentangle the confounding image of politics, his narrative discourse promised divine help to return to Palestine. Jeremiah's disasters came true: Jerusalem was taken by Nebuchadnezzar (586 BCE) but the prophet Jeremiah, despite the leadership of the Jewish people, was unable to lead the Hebrews back to the kingdom of God. The priests and the Jews themselves were deaf to his constant pleading and blind to his laments. Despite his martyrdom, the prophecy of Jeremiah was cursed with an unfortunately end. Charged with treason, Jeremiah was stoned to death.

Wittgenstein's late colleague in the United States, Oets Bouwsma, recalled him as "the nearest to be a prophet I have ever known. He is a man who is like a tower, who stands high and unattached, leaning on no one" (1986: xv). Wittgenstein himself probably did not feel like the prophet of his time (PI: 461). Unlike the figure of the prophet Jeremiah, who spoke the voice of God, Wittgenstein embodied the voice of his subcultural countertrend, commanding him to live strictly by the simple word in the sacred writings. Despite many differences between him and the historical figure Jeremiah, the lip service paid to Jeremiah's prophetic life is the cup of bitterness in Wittgenstein's life experiences, described by him in his biofictional diary (Matt. 29:8; Isa. 29:13).

Jeremiah's pictographic code word "Scheshach" turned the proper name of Babylon into the Kabbalistic-Jewish version. The mystical cryptogram referring to the "king of Sheshach" in the verse 25:26 was repeated in 51:41, and the double name of "Sheshach" led to confusion. The secret name stands for the local name of Babylon but was formulated to the alphabetic lettering of the early Kabbalah (Kahn [1968] 1974: 72–73). The Kabbalistic translation stands within the Hebrew text of the Old Testament, but the name "Sheshach" is absent from the old Greek version of the Book of Jeremiah (*c.* 600 BCE) (Steiner 1996). The strong inclination to translate the catchword has remained a political mystery (Noegel 1996) of the combination of translatability with untranslatability.

The Kabbalistic version of the local name of Babel created for "Sheshach" the double identity. According to Eco, this name speculated on the literal image of the proper name to attempt to build the perfect language of mysticism ([1995] 1997: 126–128). However, the double identity must be a more complex name. The Kabbalistic rite of "putting on the name" created the prophetic way to reach through the proper name the divine truth (Farber and Gandelman 1993: 24–25). Jeremiah's oral works were written down not by himself but by his amanuensis Baruch. Secretary Baruch took care of the oral exposition of the prophetic writing to guide the assembled Jewish people (Jer. 36:10, see 43:3). In similar fashion, Wittgenstein employed some of his students (called "pupils" by him) as go-betweens with co-writers and editors of his works. They codified his oral work and lectures into the written "albums" to be read and interpreted by the anonymous public of readers.

The instructional use of the catchword Babylon translated into the Hebrew "Sheshach" substituted the original word with a number of historical, literal, and political reasons during the Babylonian exile. The parallel synonyms of the translation made clear that:

> At the time this verse was inserted it was dangerous to speak of the fall of Babylon in plain language, or because the writer [Jeremiah] had the apocalyptic fondness for mysterious designations. In view of the freedom with which Babylon is mentioned in prophesies of its downfall towards the close of the exile, and especially of the use of Babel in the same breath with Sheshach in [Jer. 51:41], the former motive seems not to have operated. We may accordingly assume that it was chosen with the latter impulse, but also because the name contained in itself a congenial suggestion. To the Hebrew ear the name would suggest "humiliation." (Freedman [1949] 1966: 30 fn. 26)

The Kabbalistic name seems to actually foresee and foreordain the future of the fall of the city of Babel, showing through mentioning the proper name how the city would probably be attacked and disappear from the earth. In Jeremiah's dangerous times, the exiled Hebrews were acutely aware of how the commercial and religious city of Babylon was seen as the luxurious metropolis of "New York" (Keller [1956] 1980: 287, see 287–293), jeopardizing the honest life of the old Jewish world into luxury. The proper name meant that the fall of the glorious Babylon was regarded as a secret plan for a terrorist attack against the high status of the Babylonian king and the world politics of the Mesopotamian Empire. Jeremiah's politicized caution (as formulated in Baruch's discourse) secured the personal and tribal safety of the Jewish immigrants but was inscripted in the unknown code of Jewish Kabbalah.

The Kabbalistic practice rests on the Jewish tradition of shibboleths, the system of mystical codes revealed by God. The prophets hand down God's normative but sacred words into the words of wisdom handed down from generation to generation. Rooted in the educational tradition of Greek *paideia*, the Jewish process of instruction meant the systematic practice of lessons to learn the divine teaching as the Jewish tradition, to make direct communion with God, and acquire knowledge of God through the cultural means of learning and instruction of the religious sources. The cultural teaching of the Jews includes more than learning by heart the spiritual comments of Moses's Torah into the rabbinic commentaries of the Talmud. The drafting of the Bible was the esoteric operation of learning the spiritual lessons by setting out the metaphysical law of Jewish existence in the specialized Kabbalah language. The mystical idiom of the Kabbalah uses the quasi-language Atbash, in which the monoalphabetical substitution of the last letter of the Jewish alphabet has been substituted for the first, the penultimate for the second, and so on (later called Caesar's code; see Blake 2010: 117; Heller-Roazen 2013: 95–107). This mystical cryptogram of the proper name "Sheshach" standing for Babylon was the ecstatic prayer with emotional urgency coming from the message of prophet Jeremiah to the Jews. In his lessons, Jeremiah (or his scribe Baruch) avoided calling Babel by its true name and instead used the secret quasi-language of Kabbalah (Steiner 1996: 80–84).

Jeremiah's language-game was addressed to the Judean community. He transliterated the language-game into the rarely used Atbash code.[18] The word-puzzle of "Sheshach" unveiled the political meaning formulated in the how and why of the alphabetical code (Hoskisson 2010). The exiled prophet made clear that God struggled against Babylon itself, proclaiming that he would raise up against the city. The Atbash system was a practical code for communication, since it was not understandable for the Babylonians and could not be translated into other languages. Jeremiah's cryptography was meant "to be more than the extension of the spoken idea: they possessed the substance and form of that idea" of the prophet, meaning that "once spoken, [his] words were capable of affecting the observable reality" (Noegel 1996: 83–84). Semiotically, Jeremiah's clue words acted not as the fixed symbols of language but behaved as living signs of icons and indices to express the sensible and dynamic symptoms of the historical reality of the exiled Jews (Sebeok [1994] 2001: 46–59). Jeremiah was not trapped in the city of Babylon, but his prophetic voice protested the luxury of Babylon to teach the Jews to build their Promised Country elsewhere.

Wittgenstein was a religious thinker all his life, although he was an undogmatic and skeptical believer. He followed a disciplined train of life to discover the critical thinking of God's voice. The spiritual struggle, when he lived in the anti-religious cultures of the European countries occupied by the Nazis, became for him, with the cultural background of the vanished Habsburg Empire, the path to find the appropriate understanding of religious faith. He wanted to attain the moral perfection for himself and the world around him to survive. Wittgenstein's Jewish "textual" perspective on the prophecy and authorship of the philosophy of language was the clear message of sharing his thoughts. Despite his Jewish ancestry, Wittgenstein's religious essence was not that of the "Jewish philosopher" (Putnam 2008: 9). He did not follow here and elsewhere the old tradition of the Jewish shibboleth, meaning the "flow of stream" or "ear of grain" (Judg. 12:1–4). The Hebrews had their dialects and could not pronounce the word properly. At that time, native clue words were used instead. Wittgenstein strongly believed in the religious fact of Jewish dialogue (or the Christian incarnation) between man and God, requiring the human activity of quasi-semiosis to put the spiritual intention into human effect. In reading the human language of Wittgenstein speaking parables, the readers see that the "Verb becomes Flesh in exactly the same proportion as Man becomes Text" (Farber and Gandelman 1993: 28).

Wittgenstein created the symbolic signs of writing in dialectical conflict with the coded use of the quasi-sign (Faber and Gandelman 1993: 12–23). In the pictographic substitute of language with the quasi-language of the parables, Wittgenstein wrote in the tradition of the semiotic man/sign metaphor (CP: 5.313–5.317). Like the semio-logician Peirce, Wittgenstein wanted to become a man-shaped symbol, inseparable from the logical symbol of language; but he also became himself a sign with the informal symptoms of emotional and energetic interpretant-signs. For Wittgenstein, the cryptography was not a point of controversy in relation to the truth of the gospel or the authenticity of the Bible. His mission of text and language was that of the practical layman in search of the theological imperative between Judaism and Christianity, or even Eastern thought. Wittgenstein found the truth of life and philosophy in the mystical operation of interreligious theology. The dramatic backstory of the Wittgenstein family prepared him for the ideological approach of his critical, or even skeptical, hermeneutics representing the variety of forms or facts of his life in his "quasi-textual" wishes to form an imaginative model to write from his emotional beliefs.

The Wittgenstein family was utterly assimilated to the usual customs and behavior (Peirce's habits) of the wealthy citizens in the Viennese population. They were Catholics living in the economical laissez-faire of the Austrian state religion, while the "same paradoxes were reflected equally in its politics and its mores, its music and its press, its Imperial aristocracy and its workers" (Janik and Toulmin 1973: 37). The Wittgenstein household in their Viennese *Palais* followed the old formal tradition: the parents lived their own social and cultural life, while, separated from them, the children grew up together informally in the nursery and the garden. Wittgenstein's parents hired private tutors for the children's instruction; but there is no reason to suppose that they had any rabbinical training during their childhood. At home, Wittgenstein learned the Roman Catholic wisdom of religious language, but it seems that the Jewish inner voice carried out the uncoded instructions for creating the symbolic herald of God's language.

The Wittgenstein children grew up within their own world under the guidance of nannies and servants. Their intellectual and cultural identity was inspired by their father's talent in the engineering industry and their mother's musical talents, but each of the children developed freely their own spontaneous hobbies and crafts, such as playing the piano, carpentry, painting, and so on. The Wittgenstein children together formed the strong attachments as siblings, which assured their survival in the difficult times ahead. It would be natural to guess that the *Geheimschrift* was their own language to communicate intimately with one another about the family secrets. The preparatory work of learning was seen "not as doctrine but as activity" to challenge Wittgenstein in his later life as a metaphorical "enigmatic master-spy" (Nordmann 2001: 157–158). The cryptography was the myth of not thinking textually about real life but according to the intertextuality of translating the coded messages. The children's cryptography in early days did not produce fictional truth but expressed the metafiction (or even nonfiction) of their reality as children to think magically and mythically about their own narratives pronounced in secret code. Finally, the secret writing was not the made-up story of the childish quasi-language. The Wittgenstein children never broke with the emotional (iconic) habit of writing to each other in the secret code. The family worked as a cultural unit of brotherly and sisterly love. They pronounced the shibboleth properly as the comfortable sign of their survival (Neville 1996: 39–41, Hackett 2001: 460).

Hieroglyphic puzzles

Wittgenstein's sources for cryptography encode the superficial meaning of the symptoms in the secret code. The style of artistic literature printed in short paragraphs with pictographic shapes were rewritten to illustrate the scientific subject of his radical philosophy of language (Gorlée 2007), but the emotional and bodily side of the diary was the deep interpretation hidden by Wittgenstein. For example, the creative enigmas and solutions of short stories, written by such authors as Edgar Allan Poe and Sir Arthur Conan Doyle, had brought the criminal genre into fashion. This new literary genre exemplified cryptography and pictography to entertain present-day readers with the quasi-science fiction of horror and crime. In the Victorian era, this popular genre of literature was no longer published in actual books but rather in periodical journals. A myriad of magazines published articles about literature and art. Edited serially in weekly or monthly "sketches," these magazines appealed to the literary culture of the up-and-coming middle class. In the cryptographical fragments, they recalled Wittgenstein's idea of writing in fragmentary "thoughts as remarks, short paragraphs, sometimes in longer chains about the same subject," so the writing becomes "really just an album" containing no genuine book but "marked by all the defects of a weak draughtsman"—the total work was "a number of sketches ... approached afresh from different directions and new sketches made ... to give the viewer an idea of the landscape" (PI: 3e-4e; see Gorlée 2012: 43–44).

Edgar Allan Poe (1806–1849) introduced himself as an Anglo-American cryptographic writer, fitting himself within the scientific framework of rationalism at the end of the nineteenth century. His cryptograms and anagrams were a forerunner of the Sunday newspaper puzzles. Instead of being an intellectual or poetic book in the traditional fashion, Poe's cryptographical puzzles explored the magic of public entertainment in short stories with political, literary, and artistic themes. Poe contributed jigsaw puzzles as novelties in magazine fiction, to be published serially as "sketches" in weekly or monthly novels. Readers were eager to be amused and entertained by the miscellaneous information and light entertainment offered by Poe's sets of magazines.

In his later years, Poe worked as the literary editor for some magazines. He created a vogue with his article "A Few Words on Secret Writing" (1841) in *Graham's Magazine*. Two years later, he published the prize-winning mystery story "The Gold Bug" ([1843] 1993: 1–30) and other criminal stories to be read by the membership of modern ladies and gentlemen. Poe's trivial literature was aimed toward ordinary readers in a style of writing removed from the literary convention of the "learned" readers of the English nobility and clergy. Magazine articles focused on contemporary subjects to interest the imagination of the readers. The magazines gave a real taste of the new problems of the social, political, and cultural reforms of the up-and-coming middle class. Poe's stories in themselves were sentimental and didactic enigmas, but they were encoded in secret ciphers, symbols, and other codes, and were refitted into romantic stories. After the Egyptian hieroglyphics were deciphered by Jean-François Champollion in 1824 and attempts were made to transliterate other alien scripts (Pope [1975] 1999), Poe's hieroglyphic contributions made him a popular and fashionable writer; but, the cryptographical side of Poe's work was the unanalyzed aspect of his poetic literature.

Wimsatt's early article "What Poe Knew About Cryptography" (1943) challenged Poe's cryptographical skills as limited to rational hocus-pocus. Wimsatt stated that the historical information was drawn from the *Encyclopaedia Brittanica* (Wimsatt 1943: 756, 768–771) and he simply reduced Poe's knowledge of cryptography to the manipulation of one-alphabetic substitution ciphers (as used in Wittgenstein's secret script). Wimsatt thought that to be a real codebreaker the creative intelligence to undertake the complex study of the seven-alphabet cipher was required. He put Poe down as a magician: "To study Poe at work on ciphers is to find not a wide knowledge and intricate method of procedure, but rather a kind of untrained wit, an intuition which more quickly than accurately grasped the outlines of cryptic principle and immediately with confident imagination proclaimed the whole" (Wimsatt 1943: 765).

Despite the modern scientific terminology used by Poe in his cryptography, such as "hieroglyphical," "enigmatic," "puzzles," and "cypher," Poe was judged by Wimsatt to be "entirely self-taught" (767) and an amateur cryptographer. Nevertheless, when Poe wrote the cipher tale "The Gold Bug," Wimsatt changed his dogmatic opinion. After the classical "The Gold Bug," he judged Poe by his romantic merits as a professional expert in cryptoanalysis and he thought Poe added to old "cryptography the glamour of illusion" (768; see Gray 1969: 9–13, 78–80). In "The Gold Bug," Poe found the key to the buried treasure through the cryptoanalysis of simple alphabetic substitution. Poe combined his two inventions—literary cryptography and the detective story—into the *entrée* of his trademark, the mystery story. In the new genre, he combined magic and religion into a matter of sensible evidence and intellectual demonstration of legal proof. Poe even set the model for later cryptographers during the intelligence of the Second World War and the Cold War (Kahn [1968] 1974: 416). Poe's cryptographic writings are discussed by Rosenheim in *Secret Writing from Edgar Poe to the Internet*, who remarks that Poe's deep interest in the future of cryptography was driven by the "intellectual and cultural consequences of his invention, which required the immediate development of commercial telegraphic codes and of ciphers to protect the diplomatic and military traffic of nations" (Rosenheim 1997: 88–89).

Poe seems to have been one of Peirce's favorite writers (CP: 1.251, 6.400; MS 689 [undated]; MS 1539 [undated]). Judging from his references to Poe's *The Murders in the Rue Morgue* (1841), Peirce was fascinated by Poe's detective stories (Sebeok in Eco and Sebeok [1983] 1988: 50). Peirce also made a pictography of Poe's literary poem *The Raven* (1845) in his *Art Chirography* (MS 1539; see Brent 1993: 329). Peirce believed that Poe's detective stories were structured by the secret code of the unrealistic romance (emotional interpretant) to attract the ladies, but was also intermingled for the gentlemen with scientific fact to substantiate the fictional "reality" in the short story (energetic interpretant). Poe attempted to reach the prophetic model of Peirce's logical interpretant in the experience of giving the law to provide the truth. Poe was not mentioned in Wittgenstein's works, but Poe's quasi-model followed the model of the immediate habit to build through the cryptographical script of his diary the dynamical style of his secret code. Following the habit of the addresses in writing in code, Wittgenstein guided the philosophical path of his readers to break into the definitive meaning of writing in cryptography.

In the narrative of "The Gold Bug," the protagonist William Legrand was stationed in the wilderness landscape of Sullivan's Island, near Charleston, South Carolina. Poe knew the scenery of the island, since he had been a soldier there at Fort Moultrie from 1827 to late 1828. Legrand was figured as a naturalist and, investigating the natural phenomena of Sullivan's Island, he found the specimen of a scientifically unknown beetle in Latin *scarabaeus*. The beetle was ornamented with "two round black spots near one extremity of the back, and a long near the other" and the "scales were hard and glossy" (Poe [1843] 1993: 7).[19] Poe was a Southerner, coming of age in a slave society. His conventional prejudices about white and black were realigned in "The Gold Bug" with the "pidgin" speech of Jupiter, Legrand's black servant. Jupiter said that his master Legrand had been bitten by the bug, which was made of solid gold. Deranged by the mental madness affecting his brain, Legrand thought that there was a hidden treasure waiting for him on the island. Legrand's hallucination was not a mental illusion but reality.

During Legrand's nightly exploration, Jupiter, and the author (Poe), find the treasure in a wooden chest "subjected to some mineralising process—perhaps that of the bichloride of mercury"—which also contained a "heap of gold and of jewels" (16). The secret of the buried treasure was written in invisible ink and hidden in the golden *scarabaeus* and a skull. Legrand unraveled the jigsaw puzzle, decoding as a professional cryptoanalyst the random substitution of the letter-to-symbol ciphers. Legrand's exposition of the cryptology revealed in a romantic sense the "apocalypse of signification, in which the opaque materiality of the world reveals its symbolic organization" (Rosenheim 1997: 89). The detective story "The Gold Bug" was not a moral tale; the high drama described the encryption of signs in quasi-language to tell the science fiction of Poe's narrative (Gorlée 2015b).

Sir Arthur Conan Doyle's (1959–1930) was influenced by Poe's detective stories (see *A Study in Scarlet* [1887] 1953: 1:14). He extended Poe's stories into the legend of the private detective Sherlock Holmes, whose sportive task of consulting detective was to solve the enigmatic murder cases in nineteenth-century London and the surrounding counties. Holmes had the "cunning ability, that bewitching semiotic illusion to decode and disclose the profoundly private thoughts of others by incarnating their unvoiced interior dialogues into verbal signs" (Sebeok in Eco and Sebeok [1983] 1988: 10). Sherlock Holmes reasoned in a rational problem of deduction (renamed as abduction). The cryptographical mystery was the central element of the stories of Sherlock Holmes such as *The Adventure of the Dancing Men* (Conan Doyle [1903] 1953: 2:593–612; see Kahn [1968] 1974: 416–420; Eco and Sebeok [1983] 1988; Sebeok 1991b: 15–16; Rosenheim 1997: 54–56).

Holmes's client, who visits him in his famous rooms on Baker Street in London, is Mr. Hilton Cubitt of Riding Thorpe Manor in the County of Norfolk. The gentleman reports that his wife, Elsie, became upset when she received several notes with drawings of figures of dancing men penciled on them. The code of the drawings consisted of "little stick figures with their arms and legs in various positions" (Kahn [1968] 1974: 416). Holmes went about deciphering the two-step cipher illustrated with the method of the "hieroglyphs." The slips of paper with the dancing men had to come from Abe Slaney, the American gangster from Chicago, who was in love with Elsie Patrick before she married Hilton Cubitt a year earlier. Slaney came to Norfolk and killed Cubitt with three fatal shots through the heart. After the tragedy, Holmes spoke about his full knowledge of cryptography to solve the strange case:

> I am fairly familiar with all forms of secret writings, and am myself the author of a trifling monograph upon the subject, in which I analyze one hundred and sixty separate ciphers, but I confess that this is entirely new to me. The object of those who invented the system has apparently been to conceal that these characters convey a message, and to give the idea that they are the mere random sketches of children. (Conan Doyle [1903] 1953: 2:606–607)

Holmes's inquiry became a deadly serious enterprise; he deciphered the code system of the polyalphabetic substitution of a two-part code into one solution (Kahn [1968] 1974: xii–xiii). The code consisted of the alphabetic cipher moving into the pictography of the collection of dancing men. There were two sets of human characters, ones with and ones without flags. The characters holding a flag in one hand mark the last letter of the words. The last letter of the last word may or may not have a flag. Holmes noticed in the first message that out of fifteen human figures, four were the same. He identified "15 dancing men, of which four are in an ecstatic spread-eagle position and three have their left leg bent" which he identified as *e* "with some confidence" (417–418), so it was reasonable that the repeated letters *e* represent for detective Holmes the proper name "Elsie" (Doyle [1903] 1953: 2:607). Instead of deduction, the reasoning of the cryptograms has jumped from deduction to induction.

After the detention of the criminal Abe Slaney, Holmes asked him about the history of the code system he used. Slaney replied that:

> There were seven of us in a gang in Chicago, and Elsie's father was the boss of the Joint. He was a clever man, was old Patrick. It was he who invented that writing, which would pass as a child's scrawl unless you just happened to have the key to it. Well, Elsie learned some of our ways, but she couldn't stand the business … and got away to London. (2:611)

Conan Doyle's code of the dancing men was a clear sign of criminal behavior, opposite to the family ritual of the Wittgenstein children to rewrite their ideas in secret code. The emotional interpretant of the children's reality was suggested by the cozy sense of their humor. Naturally, the children's monoalphabetic code was that of simple amateurs of cryptography *sans peur et sans reproche* (Shipley 1972: 94). Instead of the detection of the emotional interpretant in the children's amusement, the criminal thrill gambled for the excitement of playing with the polyalphabetic code, upshifting the emotional interpretant of play into the energetic interpretant of solving the real crime (Wouters 2000). The detective solves the perfect crime of threat and murder in real-life situations, which are fictional, not reality. The crime is based on factual narratives but is now pure fiction.

Wittgenstein did not mention the literary authors Poe and Conan Doyle in his work. But he stressed that, for relaxation in his later years, he enjoyed reading full-blooded detective stories. Wittgenstein consumed murder mysteries of the hard-boiled Wild West variety, which he sent to his friends to read (Monk 1990: 422–423, 528–529). Maybe he found some intellectual justification for the soft "addiction" to the snappy diction and popular style in the postmodern crime detective. His favorite tale was *Rendezvous with Fear*, written by Norbert Davis, later called *The Mouse in the Mountain* ([1943] 2001). The plot tells the adventures of Doan, the private detective in Los Angeles, who was sent to Mexico to convince a missing refugee from the law to remain there. In Mexico, Doan is followed by three murders and an earthquake in Los Altos. Davis's story is written in the simple language of popular fiction, full of short answers and replies in the punk lyricism of the day (Gorlée 2015a: 78).

Wittgenstein's work was beyond the ephemeral stories of detectives. In 1947, following the horrors of the Second World War, Wittgenstein resigned from the University of Cambridge. In his final years, he imagined the aphorisms of *Vermischte Bemerkungen* [VB], in which he described the philosophical language-game as building a mystery novel, to discover the detectable meaning in the fictitious material to learn and understand the experiences of life (MS 137: 78b, 1948; see VB: 142 [in German]; *Letzte Schriften über die Philosophie der Psychology* [LW1]: 4e; CV 85e). The outsider (the police "detective") is asked to "read" the "faces" of, for example, the persons in the court room to give a glimpse of their inner life. However, the rules of the police "detective's" legal language-game for the "obvious suspect" (MS 167: 8v, 1947–1948) deals with critical problem-solving related to past experiences. The questions are not a philosophical revolution but are strictly limited to the received style of the legal case to come to the formal judgment to punish the criminal (Scheffler 1985: 117–126).

Legal language is a socially constructed institution in its own right (Stygall 1994: 4) but far removed from Wittgenstein's language-game. Wittgenstein raised two questions: "What is the primitive reaction that starts the game of language?" and "Which can be transformed into words?" (MS 167: 9r, 1947–1948).[20] Playing the "social" game in the courtroom, Wittgenstein applied logical "philosophy" to accurately "read" the faces of the protagonists in the courtroom. Yet, he realized that each person brings an inner character and life experience—the cultural form of life—to mark the clues of their individual language-game. In the eyes of Wittgenstein as a "private detective," the formal and informal surroundings of forensic criminology build "the uncertainty in the 'thrill' of many detective stories" and he remarked "perhaps this is the foundation for all problems of the detective story?" (MS 167: 23R, 1947–1948).[21]

Samuel Pepys

From 1929, Wittgenstein worked at the University of Cambridge. In between the plaintext of the *Philosophische Bemerkungen*, he wrote the coded part of his diary. Mixed with the uncoded text, the coded script was transformed into an educational and moral task in itself. Wittgenstein briefly explained the "historical" influence of writing in two genres in coded text:

Vnghliznt vh afo Gvrp wvo Nzxszofnthgirvy (rxs szggv Qvppvih Gztvh Gztvyfxsvi tvpuhun) Gvrp wvo Yvwfiunrh wmxs vgdzh emn ori nrvwviafpvtvn. Vh dzi zphm afo timhzvn Gvrp Vrgvpqvrg. Afo Gvrp uivrprxs zfxs drvwvi wvi Vilzga ufi vrnvn Ovnhxsvn wvo rxs orxs znevigizfvn qmnngv. Hlzgvi orhxsgv hrxs wzaf zfxs Nzxszofnt wvi Lvlbhhxsvn Gztvyfxsvi. Uivrprxs rhg vh, drv roovim hxsdvi, srvi tvivxsg af hvrn, wvnn vh dzi nzgfiprxsvh & vrgpv Yvhgivyfntvn hgziq eviorhxsh.

(I was inspired in part by the instinct to imitate [having read Keller's diaries], and in part by the need to make a record of my life. Vanity, mostly. Although partly also a substitute for someone in whom I could confide. To this came later the imitation of the Pepysian diaries. But, as always it is difficult to be fair, as natural and vain aspirations are strongly intertwined.)

(MS 107: 74, 1929)[22]

Wittgenstein confided in code that he followed the secret script of the "Lvlbhhxsvn Gztvyfxsvi" (Pepysian diaries) (MS 107: 74, 1929). But he let it be known that he was not merely creating his thoughts of what transpired into the unifying collection of secret paragraphs, but that he copied the characters of Pepys's shorthand, at least to a certain degree.

Samuel Pepys (1633–1703) was the son of a London tailor, but, thanks to scholarships, young Pepys was educated at Magdalene College in Cambridge. Pepys was an ambitious and intelligent man, eager to advance himself. He started as an officer of the Royal Navy and rose to the highest rank of Secretary of the Admiralty. He entered Parliament and was elected President of the Royal Society. Living in the time of the art, manners, and fashion of King Louis XIV, the *Roi-Soleil* of France, Pepys was a man of elegant fashion with good taste in food, wine, and theater. He had the right contacts within the aristocracy and wealthy society to advance his political abilities, mainly after the Restoration of the English monarchy under King Charles II (1660–1685). After the death of Cromwell (1658), who ruled Britain as Lord Protector, Pepys reformed the navy. Charles II reigned in an unstable balance with the landowners and merchants of the Parliament. Pepys mediated in domestic intrigues and intervened with foreign policy, hoping to pacify the economic rivalry with Holland to benefit from commerce with the East.

Despite his high position, Pepys's principal claim to fame is his diary, written between 1660 and 1669, when he had to abandon the work because of the onset of blindness. For "ordinary" eyes, the diary was an unreadable script. After Pepys's death, his private library and his diary came together in the *Bibliotheca Pepysiana* housed in Magdalene College at Cambridge. Pepys's diary was not easily deciphered; the puzzle was resolved only in 1815 around the same time as the deciphering of the hierographic mysteries of three languages in the Rosetta Stone found in Egypt. Pepys's English shorthand followed the rules of Sheltonian cryptography. The diary is a vivid and picturesque record of public and private life in London during the Restoration period. He commented on the outbreak of the plague in 1665, the Great Fire of London in 1666, as well as the political unrest caused by the Dutch fleet invading the harbor of London, the intricacies of the court life of Charles II, and administering the Royal Navy.

For example, Pepys was an eyewitness to the Great Fire of London, and he commented in secret code (translated into English):

> Everybody endeavouring to remove their goods, and flinging into the River or bringing them into lighters that lay off. Poor people staying in their houses as long as till the very fire touched them, and then running into boats or clambering from one pair of stairs by the waterside to another. And among other things the poor pigeons I perceive were loath to leave their houses, but hovered about the windows and balconies till they were some of them burned, their wings, and fell down.
>
> Having stayed, and in an hour's time seen the fire rage everyway, and nobody to my sight endeavouring to quench it, but to remove their goods and leave it all to the fire; and having seen it get as far as the Steeleyard, and the wind mighty high and driving it into the city, and everything, after so long a drought, proving combustible, even the very stones of churches … I to Whitehall with a gentleman with me who desired to go off from the Tower to see the fire in my boat—to Whitehall, and there up to the King's closet in the chapel, where people came about me and I did give them an account dismayed them all; and word was carried in to the King, so I was called for and did tell the King and Duke of York what I saw, and that unless his Majesty did command houses to be pulled down, nothing could stop the fire. They seemed much troubled, and the King commanded me to go to my Lord Mayor from him and commanded him to spare no houses but to pull down before the fire every way. The Duke of York bid me tell him that if he would have any more soldiers, he shall; and so did my Lord Arlington afterwards, as a great secret. (Pepys 1985: 660, written September 2, 1666)

That evening Pepys and his wife Elizabeth went out on the River Thames and they:

> Walked to my boat, and there upon the water again, and to the fire up and down, it still increasing and the wind great. So near the fire as we could for smoke; and all over the Thames, wth one's face in the wind you were almost burned with a shower of Firedrops—this is very true—so as houses were burned by these drops and flakes of fire, three or four, nay five or six houses, one from another. … and there stayed till it was dark almost and saw the fire grow; and as it grows darker, appeared more and more, and in Corners and upon steeples and between churches and houses, as far as we could see up the hill of the City, in a most horrid malicious bloody flame, not like the fine flame if an ordinary fire. … We stayed till, it being darkish, we saw the fire as only one entire arch of fire from this to the other side of the bridge, and in a bow up the hill, for an arch of above a mile long. It made me weep to see it. The churches, houses, and all on fire and flaming at once, and a horrid noise the flames made, and the cracking of houses at their ruine. (Pepys 1985: 662, written September 2, 1666)

Behind the attractive account of Pepys's "journalism" to tell the political story of the professional events, Pepys's diary is full of sexy stories about his amorous escapades. Chasing other women was the light pastime outside Pepys's married life. Pepys was a womanizer who wanted to satisfy his constant lust. Actually, sexual desire was, after political work, his favorite entertainment. As a married man, Pepys wanted to keep secret his adventures in politics and primarily his secret love affairs. He chronicled that the hidden code could not reach his jealous wife and others (McCormick 1980: 27–32). To ensure the absolute secrecy of office politics and private adventures, Pepys's six volumes of diaries were written in the new code system, described in the pamphlet "A tutor to tachygraphy, or short-writing," written by Thomas Shelton (1642) and published with the Latin version "Tachygraphia" (1647) (for a modern reprint, see Shelton [1642–1647] 1970). Shelton's method of codes did not sketch the abbreviated diagrams derived from the writing of the alphabet but, rather, something different in the composition of the graphic design in microscopically small characters with points, angles, and curves. The coded handwriting was modeled on this new "design cipher which no one had yet looked at it could interpret" (Pratt 1939: 151).

In the years of the Restoration, Shelton's cipher system was a popular method of rapid shorthand writing, officially approved by the university authorities and mainly used to copy letters of business and legal writing. In Shelton's presentation, the swift-writing had a sign for every letter of the alphabet in the set of twenty brief signs. A few abbreviated forms of Shelton's extraordinary "alphabet" did not contain any letters of the alphabet, but the words were transcribed into the simple lines and curves reserved for consonants. Vowels were indicated by dots, the position of the dot determining which vowel was meant. Unfortunately, Pepys had omitted his vowel dots, making the characters vaguely imprecise with regard to vowels. Imagine the following troubles Shelton had with Pepys's graphological problems:

> No one can be sure whether Pepys had a "bit" to eat or a "bite"; it is equally impossible to be certain which of the forms of "have"—"has," "hath," "have," "had"— is represented by the symbol which stands for them all; neither is it possible to be sure whether Pepys meant "see" or "saw," "come" or "came" as past sentence. (Matthews's editorial remarks in Shelton [1642–1647] 1970: vii)

For vowels in the middle or at the end of words, Pepys seemed to use two methods:

> A medial vowel is represented by putting the following consonant-sign (disjointed and written small!) in five positions about the preceding consonant-sign. These five positions symbolize *a, e, i, o, u*, and the system makes do with these five to represent all the long and short vowels and diphthongs that are used in English speech. The following examples will show the method in its simplest form. The consonant *t* is represented by a short straight line running down obliquely from right to left; the consonant *m* is represented by a similar line running from left to right. If a small form of *m* is placed above *t*, the total symbol represents *t-a-m*; if it is placed on the right side of *t*, near the top, the symbol represents *t-e-m*; if it is placed right-center, the symbol represents *t-i-m*; if it is placed right-bottom, the symbol represents *t-o-m*; if it is placed under t, the symbol represents *t-u-m*. End-vowels are represented by dots placed in the same five positions, and their value is the same. Since each of the five vowels makes do for the long and short

> forms of the same vowel and also for the related diphthong, the word-symbols clearly have several possible meanings: *t-a-m* can mean "tame" or "Thame" and possibly "team"; *t-e-m* can mean "teem" or "team" and possibly also "theme"; *t-i-m* can mean "Tim," "time" or "thyme"; *t-o-m* can mean "Tom," or "tome" or "tomb"; and *t-u-m* can mean "tum" or "-thume" as in "imposthume." (Matthew's editorial remarks in Shelton ([1642-1647]1970: v)

Pepys's tachygraphy only distinguished between five vowels, meaning that:

> One symbol may often represent several words: "on," "one," or "own"; "stripped" or "striped"; "sit," "site" or "sight" and so on. Symbols for different words are sometimes so similar that they are virtually indistinguishable: thus, "your" and "great," "go" and "give," "will" and "answer," "breath" and "width," "present" and "promise," "though," "thou," "through" and "thought" share symbols that are neither the same for both words or groups of words or are so similar that they might be confused by a transcriber. (Matthews's editorial remarks in Shelton [1642–1647] 1970: vi)

At the same time, Pepys used other systems and devices available to English shorthand writing, leading to further confusions about the transcription of the pictographic and arbitrary characters:

> Some consonant groups, particularly *wr, br, sk, sb*, are symbolized by short fusions of the basic consonant symbols. Some 300 quickly written arbitrary symbols are provided for the mostly commonly-used words, prefixes, and suffixes. Thus, a small cross symbolizes "Christ" and "-ture," and a colon represents "owe" and "oh!" … The signs which when joined represent *kl* also arbitrarily represent "it" and the suffix "-fication." The same arbitrary symbol sometimes signifies different things: "-temal" and "which," "mess-" and "what," and so on. (Matthews's editorial remarks in Shelton [1642–1647] 1970: v–vi)

Subsequently, some characters form entire words, such as "'carpenter,' 'congratulate,' 'reimbursed' [for words that] are so long that it might be almost as easy to write them in longhand—Pepys in fact sometimes does write a few words in longhand" (Williams in Shelton [1642–1647] 1970: vi). Finally, Pepys frequently mixed French and sometimes Spanish words with the English to record in mixed languages the stories of his amorous adventures for their linguistic secrecy (McCormick 1980: 28–33).

The translated vocabulary of Pepys's flirtations and love-making with one of his mistresses, Doll Lane, who worked in a wine-house of London, in an "English" transcription reads as follows:

> So to the Rose tavern, while Doll Lane came to me and we did *biber* a good deal *de vino, et jo* did give *ella* 12 *solidos para comprar ella* some *gans* for a new *ano*'s gift. I did *tocar et no mas su cosa*, but in fit time and place *jo creo que je pouvais fair* whatever I would *con ella*. (Pepys 1985: 710, written January 2, 1667)

Another time Pepys annotated that he went:

> To the Hall and there walked a while, it being term; and hence home to the Rose and there had Doll Lane *vener para me*; but it was in a *lugar* mighty *ouvert*, so as we *no poda hazer algo*; so parted and then met again at the Swan, where for *la misma* reason we *no pode hazer*, but put off to *recontrar anon*, which I only used as a put-off. (Pepys 1985: 764, written May 1, 1667)

Another example of his mixed use of languages is as follows:

> After dinner away ... by coach to Westminster, where to the Swan and drank; and then to the Hall and there talked a little, with great joy of the peace; and then to Mrs. Martins, where I met with the good news *que esta no es con* child, she having *de estos* upon her—the fear of which, which she did give me the other day, had troubles me much. My joy in this made me send for wine, and thither came her sister and Mrs. Cragg and I stayed a good while there. (Pepys 1985: 710, written July 3, 1667)

Shelton's abbreviated version offers, despite the popularity at the time of the Restoration, the indicated errors and ambiguities of graphological problems, such that Pepys's relative or weak art of tachygraphy is extremely hard to follow. Moreover, at the beginning tachygraphy gave the number of three hundred arbitrary symbols that the beginner must learn by heart and use (Matthews's editorial remarks in Shelton [1642–1647] 1970: v).

Wittgenstein, who had rooms at Trinity College, lived in immediate proximity to Magdalene College, both being on the banks of the River Cam. Wittgenstein must have seen Pepys's books and diaries exhibited in Magdalene College. He had observed Pepys's pictorial characters and probably noted the transcription into English. Wittgenstein was fully aware of the differences between the ambiguous kind of shorthand used by Pepys and the simple system of the monoalphabetical substitution he used in his diary. Despite the differences, Wittgenstein imitated the secret speech of the "Pepysian diaries" (MS 107: 74, 1929), written in secret code as "Lvlbhhxsvn gztvyfxsvi." Wittgenstein's coded text seemed to be a "caricature" imitation of what happened in Pepys's actual scene, yet the scenarios of Pepys and Wittgenstein were totally different.

In semiotic terms, Wittgenstein wrote indirectly (in iconic-indexical images) about the possible likeness of his diary with the "Pepysian diaries." For Wittgenstein's educational game of art, the secret code is in itself the imaginative expressiveness of a certain "playfulness" to render the signals secure in the cipher alphabet, but the real truth of Wittgenstein's diary would play a minor role. Wittgenstein did not directly mention the real "work" of Pepys writing in the linguistically relevant circumstances of the bourgeois etiquette of his time. What he wanted was to give the metaphor, simile, or analogy of Pepys's diary, to create a dramatic background to the less formal sign of his diary. In the secret messages, Wittgenstein gesticulated to the representational model in Pepys's quasi-messages, but he did not communicate his arrangement to shift language into Pepys's secret quasi-language. The secret expression of Pepysian diaries would serve as Wittgenstein's pure icon, but the *imaginative* sign of creating his fictional identity was upshifted to the real *representational* model of the indexical system of translating the linguistic words into the secret system of quasi-language.

Wittgenstein had observed Pepys's shorthand, but he reacted in a bitter form of irony: contrary to Pepys, Wittgenstein modeled his own quasi-language on Caesar's cipher alphabet. The icon is a pure image bearing an intrinsic resemblance to the object it designates, while the index is an automatic rule of conduct with a purely sensual but also non-sensual connection with their referent. Indeed, Wittgenstein did not imitate Pepys as an iconic model. Wittgenstein's secret expression automatically "reproduced" the secrecy of the Pepysian diaries, but he selected the iconic part of cryptography to write in the open *Zeitgeist* of indexical writing. Wittgenstein did not recede in the historical source to produce an intrinsic mirror image or some algebraic formula with no information. After all, he gave an abstractable likeness with artistic effort to tell the differences of his language-game from Pepys's code system. Wittgenstein's secret code was considered to represent in code his life in "normal" shorthand, different from Pepys's object of sexual adventures; but he did not pass on the critical opinion about the comparison with Pepys's cryptic language-game.

Wittgenstein's simple reverse-alphabet of Caesar's code was surely no imitation game of the stenographic report of Pepys's shorthand illustrated with pictographical drawings. The similarities between Pepys and Wittgenstein include that they both wrote their diaries using the persona of a cryptographer. Both diarists were trained and schooled as writers, authors, or journalists to engage in the creation and deciphering of secret codes. By appealing to the feelings or emotions described in the pages of a diary, the themes of politics and love can find a melodramatic place in composing chronicles, parables, sermons, news reports, and journalistic articles. The cryptographical code can become a clever disguise for popular and official, romantic and business-like reports, as well as the secret paragraphs describing the diarist's private life. Pepys and Wittgenstein used differing methods and tones for their diaries. The journalistic case of Pepys glows with good humor and vitality in his version of shorthand, meant for quick writing about the sexual caprices and the clever manipulation of politics. By contrast, Wittgenstein's diaries are deeper cryptotypes of good and bad facts of the religious aspects of life, hidden with dark spots of sorrow beneath the half-cheerful appearance.

The approval or disapproval led to guide the conflicting estrangement of Wittgenstein's secret code. He detached himself from the secret analogy between cryptographical art and analytic analysis. He did not use the complex abbreviations in the pictorial characters of Pepys's code system, which kept Pepys busy writing the many untranslatable and hardly translatable characters. Pepys's writing was not a leisure activity but hard labor in which translation failed and errors were easily made. Wittgenstein's translatability had no graphological problems at all, and it was a relatively simple lingo to learn. Without problems, is was a swift application of "perfect" translation from his ideas to the coded words and sentences. Wittgenstein reached toward the paradigm or practical experience (no theory) by using technoscientific methods to describe the coded game of language (Catford [1965] 1974: 93–103). But did Wittgenstein turn the sad story of the coded text into the cynical virus infecting him with the neurotic disease to personal strangeness?

4

Cryptomnesia

A confession has to be part of your new life.

(MS 154: 1r, 1931)[1]

Crypto-autobiography

Within the philosophical pages of the notebooks, Wittgenstein was a radical thinker. He went against the conventionalism of the belle epoque to guide the direction of modern (or postmodern) future generations. In terms of semiotic signs and symptoms, Wittgenstein was in search of moral truth given the examples at practical work to the exposition of language as the "first thoughts" of scholarship. At the same time he went deeper into "second thoughts" to relate developments in the political, social, and religious world. Subsequently, the autobiographical sketches illuminate the "third thoughts" of Wittgenstein's personal narratives originating from his self as a human individual to form the inner thoughts of common language. In the simultaneity of the discontinuous and informal narratives, Wittgenstein assumed responsibility for the "first thoughts" in abstract philosophy to claim the deeper "second thoughts" of a social nature and to challenge the intimate "third thoughts" to reveal his own cultural self. Wittgenstein mixed his concrete, non-philosophical crypto-experiences with his dialectic of work and life (Markoš 2012). The literary form, shape, and content of the series of detached notes in the diarial remarks decorated the active passages of Wittgenstein's fusion of work and life. Yet the unsolvable puzzle had a part iconized by living pieces to decipher the indices of Wittgenstein's intimate thoughts, since he brought out the worst and the best of private remarks to make *his* shape of social realism available to other readers.

Wittgenstein's personal observations never quite fitted with the sociopolitical doctrine of public history books, while his diary turned actual events into internal remarks that addressed his own life. Wittgenstein's day-to-day diary of wartime events was illustrated by the moment-by-moment narrative of the catastrophic events he had to live through. Each episode has a special date and place, but the freedom of the emotional impressions stays hermetically sealed in the real intimacy of the diary extracts, without flowing over into the formalist textuality of philosophy. The sociological, ideological, and sexual shock of being different in religion, class, and gender transfigured Wittgenstein's personal attitude into the prophetic exclamation of a wandering pilgrim, standing on alien soil. Through spiritual exile, he observed the failures of his environment while secretly determining a new path to face the future (Klagge 2011; Hick [1963] 1973: 62–63).

Wittgenstein's diaries are considered broader than the definition in the *Oxford English Dictionary* as the "daily record of events or transactions, a journal," specifically used as a "daily record of matters affecting the writer personally, or which come under his personal observation" (OED 1989: 4:612). Wittgenstein's biography seeks for his ideas and thoughts to be comprehended by "outsiders," and to enrich not only his philosophy but also his person (Monk 2001: 3–4). The melancholy temper of Wittgenstein's journal is not actually based on the realism of his daily life but has been "retranslated" into a new form of autobiography in the elegiac memoir of details of his personal life. In his autobiography he interpreted the personal and social events around him, discovering in the "pilgrimage" of his life the identity of his role in modern life (Bauman 1996: 18–23). His political exile forced him to express misleading statements of society, almost contrary to the truth but fully integrated into the platform of Wittgenstein's various *Denkbewegungen* in his mind.

Wittgenstein's crypto-autobiography is chronicled in his evocative cries for help, invocations, and prayers (Pichler 2006: 144). In the non-logical signals of life, Wittgenstein tried to psychologically control and self-control the dramatic challenges of the changing world in the First and Second World Wars, while trying to remain a genuine human being. According to many observers Wittgenstein frequently behaved like a "strange" alien, and at times they were even unable to talk with him. The crypto-autobiography of his diary invested the emotional and mental habits of thought needed to survive his political diaspora. In his own biofiction (Lackey 2017), Wittgenstein was transfigured as an exiled person. With Jewish origins and plagued by a mental illness, he felt in dire straits. He survived the Nazi annexation of Austria by moving to work in Britain, meaning that his conversations and lectures opened him up from speaking Austrian to English. He even changed the style and content of his philosophical writing without a distinct, conscious division between the objective and subjective sides of his project. In doing so, he even opened up the literary fragments of his vision of realism into the metafictive accounts of his personal thoughts (Waugh 1984). In a mixture of literary genres he wandered around the train of events in his life and even talked about his reclusion and retirement from the environment around him.

The discontinuous pages of Wittgenstein's philosophical work contained the anecdotes and excursions of diary entries. In a double vision, he attempted to collect and rearrange the realism of the political challenges with a human face. The dissonant process of integrating macro-ideas into micro-thoughts and back again were told in both plaintext in the philosophy and coded text in the diary. Wittgenstein's stories were able to create the "secondary, derivative literary creation" of the "metalinguistic (analytical) activity" (Popovič 1975: 12) imposed on him as a writer and philosopher. Wittgenstein's grand life narrative was not only an attempt to understand the thoughts of language philosophy but also, through his own metanarrative ideas, a means to cope with the cacophony of the events taking place around him (Gorlée 2012: 55). The psychological and cultural behavior of uttering the anagrams of speech or talk were the secondary concern of his diary (Gorlée 2008a: 351–360; 2012: 48–58; 2015b). His emotional reply to the changes was the "reaction and remedy" (Goffman 1981: 218), which allowed him to take individual action and even theatrical liberties to think freely in reality and irreality.

Wittgenstein's diary does attend to series of sad events but observes the satirical stimulus to respond to the "different" ideas and thoughts. The agreement and controversy (Popovič 1975: 13) of the "forms of life" shaped the creative movements of the "facts of life" in his mental *Denkbewegungen*. In terms of the patent transition between the first movement of philosophical thought, suspended by the second meaning of the allegorical parts, and the third part of the autobiography, one may conclude that Wittgenstein's total narratives, read between the surface story, still remains unclear. The harmonization between the actual meaning seems on the surface comprehensible and accessible, but the slippery narrative of the first language together with the metaphors of second or third speeches fabricates the cumulative dialogue of various undertexts or subtexts, giving an estranging effect of reality. The whole amounts to a dramatic artifact into which readers must be initiated by observation, to discover the rules and codes of Wittgenstein's personal life reworded in the crypto-autobiography.

On Christmas Day, 1929, Wittgenstein wrote in coded text this confession:

> Rxs yrn vrn Hxdvrn & wzyvr yrn rxs wmxs nrxsg fntpfxqprxs. Rxs yrn rn wvi Tvuzsi nmxs hvrxsgvi af dviwvn. Omtv Tmgg vh evisfgvn!
>
> (I am a swine yet not unhappy. I am in danger of becoming even shallower. May God forbid it!)
>
> (MS 108: 38, 1929, my translation; cf. Monk 1990: 281).[2]

By describing his medical and spiritual selves in the image of "liverwurst," Wittgenstein makes a heartfelt cry in a religious and biological metaphor (MS 110: 247, 1931). Wittgenstein saw himself as a gross and sensual beast, whose animal appetite became associated with the biblical sense of an evil man living alone in filth and dirt. Since he also alluded to the metaphor of "swine" three days later, the bestial form turned into the intestinal background of himself as a forbidden pig. He explained the code word "Hxdvrn" (*Schwein*) as follows:

> Rxs ufspgv wzhh rxs vrn Hxdvrn yrn dvrp rxs zfxs vxsgvh org fnvxsgvo orhxsv. Omxsgv ori Tmgg Ivrnsvrg & Dzsisvrg hxsrxqvn.
>
> (I feel that I am a swine because I also mix the real with the false. May God send me purity and truth.)
>
> (MS 108: 47, 1929; see Stern 2004)[3]

The word "swine" was probably spoken with tongue in cheek. In a letter to his sister Hermine the elements are minimized in a veiled allusion. He mentioned his future plans to carry out his bracketed "(confession etc.)," and he added ironically that "I should be happy that I have been a lucky swine, that there will be many opportunities for me to worry about it. If my worries had not been so superficial, there would have been improvement" (McGuinness, Ascher, and Pfersmann 1996: 131, my translation).[4]

The biblical term "swine" (or pig) in the Old Testament meant the unclean animal that was forbidden to be eaten (Lev. 11:7–8), while the New Testament spoke of those who love only worldly riches and not spiritual gifts (Mt. 7:6). The "swine" became the center of later passages, in which Wittgenstein's image was beset with troubles and ideological prejudices to condemn himself as a "fallen angel." He remained nervously apprehensive of being an evil spirit with a devilish soul who could not appreciate the pearls of God. Not accepting the interplay of his racial culture nor the totemic nature of his Jewish origins, he was unable to accept his own sexual deviation from the norm. Wittgenstein's plan for survival was to write his own kind of autobiography. As a religious man, he wanted to tell his possible readers how he avowed his own acts and the truth of who he really was. In moments of pain, doubt, or uncertainty, he felt different from other people and wanted to inspire awe of his complex feelings. Wittgenstein's moral confession must be acknowledged as a sincere desire to express his real purity and truth (*Reinheit und Wahrheit*). His mental instability inclined him to circulate this cryptic confession to his nearest friends. His self-examination became similar to the judiciary's avowal to obey all religious values. Wittgenstein wanted to change his psyche from evil to good (Foucault 2014).

In the occasional diary of the notebooks he confesses his struggle against his moral behavior to obey the mythical, religious, and social meanings for himself and society. In the diary, he speculated that:

> The spirit in which one can write the truth about oneself can take the most varied forms; from the most decent to the most indecent. And accordingly it is very desirable or very wrong for it to be written. Indeed, among the true autobiographies that one might write there are all the gradations from the highest to the lowest. I for instance cannot write my biography on a higher plane than I exist on. And by the very fact of writing it I do not *necessarily* enhance myself; I *may* thereby even make myself dirtier than I was in the first place. Something inside me speaks in favour of my writing my biography, and in fact I would like some time to spread out my life clearly, in order to have it clearly in front of me, and for others too. Not so much to put it on trial as to produce, in any case, clarity and truth. (MS 108: 46–47, 1929; see Monk 1990: 281–282)[5]

However, the crypto-autobiography did not turn into any kind of legal trial for him. Instead, the entries in coded messages meditated on his own self-reflection. The freedom of his spirituality went beyond rumors and hearsay. His traditional Jewish origins as well as his auto-erotic orientation were alleged by Wittgenstein. But, as a radical thinker, he was devoid of the politically sensitive workings of the ideological imperatives and totalitarian guilt as they seemed to flourish in the Nazified ideology of the 1930s. In his crypto-autobiography, he wanted to wash away the spot and stain of immorality to reach the genuine truth.

Wittgenstein's autobiography achieves the harmony of the artistic fact of writing about himself to avoid the disharmony of fragmentary metafiction (Gorlée 2009:

220–222). He expressed his life by writing about his personal memories and fragments of life, creatively illustrated with dreams and fantasies as images and wishes for the future. In return for the personal *Erinnerungen* (memoirs), he even revived the actual meaning of gospel "parables" into his own making. To imagine the novelty to create new meaning in his words and sentences, Wittgenstein stated that: "Vrn tfgvh Tpvrxsnrh viuirhxsg wvn Evihgznw" (A good parable refreshes the brain) (MS 105: 73, 1929; see CV: 3e).[6]

The renovation of Wittgenstein's biography is basically to give him a new narrative, written by someone else, to add objective documents (for example, given in McGuinness 1988), but the perfect parable can include illustrated material or photographed pictures to become photojournalism and to reveal the truth (Monk 1990; Nedo, Moreton, and Finlay 2005; Waugh 2008; Nedo 2012). With the synthesis of the sources of the philosophical work and individual memories, the biography seems to tell the many-sided story of Wittgenstein's artistic, dramatic, and/or intellectual history. The life of the biography forms the emotional, actional, or logical guideline for the uninvolved readers, contributing to the individual learning or social recreation by reading the exemplification of Wittgenstein's way of life. The biography is often transposed into the autobiographical "novel" giving no special attention to the routines or rules of writing life experiences but rather to the special efforts of the embarrassing personal facts of one famous individual, often composed after their death to disclose them as a nuanced or complex personality. Instead, Wittgenstein's iconic-indexical plan of writing his own autobiography was thought of as his "spiritual duty" (Monk 1990: 312). He wanted to transform his own personality into a spiritual spirit to encourage his readers to see his reckless and negligent behavior. It seems that Wittgenstein's symbolic idea was inaccurate for a young man of thirty-nine with all his life before him.

To reveal the direction of his crypto-autobiography, Wittgenstein wrote on July 1, 1931, about embracing the unheroic nature (*unheldenshafte Natur*) of what he called the "beggar"'s biography. The parable (*Vergleich*) appeared secretly, in code:

> Dvnn vrn "Hgizhhvnqmgvi" hvrnv Yrmtizlsrv hxsirvyv, hm yvhgffbwv wie Tvuzsi (a) wzhh vi vngdvwvi hvrnvNzgfi evipvftnvn, mwvi (y) vrnvn Tinw zfhurnwrt ozxsvn dfiwv zfu hrv hgmpa af hvrn, mwvi (x) wrv Hzxsv hm wzihgvppgv zph hvr wrvhv hvrnv Nzgfi vrnv nvyvnhzxsprxsv Zntvpvtvnsvrg. Ro vihgvn Uzppv pftg vi, ro advrgvn zsog vi vrnv ufi wvo Nzgfzwvp nzgfiprxsv Vrtvnhxszug, wvn Hgmpa nzxs wvi vrn ergrfo hlpvnwrwfo rhg wzh vu vyvnhmdvnrt driqprxs yvhrgavn qznnm drv vrn qifllvpszugvi Qmilvi nzgfiprxsv Tizxrv. Ro wirggvn Uzpp ozxsg vi tpvrxshzo wrz hmarzpwvomqizgrhxsv Tvhgvm wrv wrv Yrpwfbt fyvu wrv imsvn Vrtvnhxszugvn wvh Qmilvih hgvppg, zyvi zfxs wzh rhg vrn Yvgift. Rhg dzh vi rhg wzh rhg aftpvrxs drxsgrt & yvwvfghzo zyvi qvrn Tifnw afo Hgmpa znwvihvrgh roovi Tvtvnhgznw wvi Hvpyhgzxssgfnt. Rz rxs qznn wvn Zwvphhgmpa wvh Znwvin & hvrnv Evizxsgfnt ovrnvi Nzgf znviqvnnvn, wvnn rxs viqvnnv rz wzwfixs nfi ovrnv Nzgfi zn & wvn znwvib wvi afi Fotvyfnt ovrnvi Nzgfi, wrv Dvpg, wvivn Orggvplfnqg wrvhvi ervppvrxsg szhhprxsv Tvtvnhgznw, ovrnv Lvihmn, thg.

(If a street loafer were to write his biography, the danger would be that he would either (a) deny that his nature was what it is, or (b) would find some reason to be proud of it, or (c) present the matter as though this—that he has such a nature—were of no consequence. In the first case he lies, in the second he mimics a trait of the natural aristocrat, that pride which is a vitium splendidum and which cannot really have any more than a crippled body can have natural grace. In the third case he makes as it were the gesture of social democracy, placing nature above the bodily qualities—but this is deception as well. He is what he is, and this is important and means something but is no reason for pride, on the other hand it is always the object of his self-respect. And I can accept the other's aristocratic pride and his concept for my nature, for in this I am only taking account of what my nature is and of the other man as part of the environment of my nature—the world with this perhaps ugly object, my person, as its centre.)

(MS 110: 252–253, 1931; cf. Monk 1990: 311–312)[7]

Wittgenstein did not become a beggar, but one may come to the conclusion that the fidelity of his biography was transformed into the authenticity of his autobiography and displayed the philosophical text by throwing light on Wittgenstein's hindrance of pride (*Stolz, Eitelkeit*). The religious sin of pride was derived from his personal souvenirs, words, letters, and photographs to elevate himself as an intelligent thinker. The social provenance can also include the assistance of first-hand information, interviews with family members and friends, and conversations with colleagues, and can become the collection of documentary biographical appurtenances of materials from the archives and the press. In a biography, the individual is often considered to be an experienced, wise, and aged hero. It expresses the day-to-day narrative of the events in time and transactions located within the space or the historical events in which he played a role. The life described can be a personal life of a well-known individual, engaging in a positive sense the occupation and temperament as well as the milieu and field of endeavor of the honoree. However, an autobiography can be different in spiritual mood to a biography, and can be influenced by the author's personal emotions about their own life and the nuancing of personal remarks in a positive sense.

The goal of a biography is the joint combination of the experiences and activities rescued from oblivion and forgetfulness to highlight the crypto-biography, in which autobiography-as-fiction was transformed into fiction-as-autobiography interrogating himself as formulated by the initials "R.B." (as used by Roland Barthes). Barthes wrote in his autobiography that:

I do not say "I am going to describe myself," but "I am writing a text and I call it R.B." … I myself am my own symbol. I am the story which happens to me: freewheeling in language. I have nothing to compare myself to; and in this movement, the pronoun of the imaginary "I" is *im-pertinent*; the symbolic necomes literally *immediate*: essential danger for the life of the subject: to write oneself may seem a pretentious idea; but it is also a simple idea: simple as the idea of suicide. (Barthes 1977: 56; quoted in Waugh 1984: 135)

Wittgenstein's crypto-autobiography narrates the choice of the events or episodes of his life. The choice is made freely by the diarist himself to manifest his present or absent document-of-his-own-life. Wittgenstein's autobiography rested on his choice of events to shape the cultural "forms of life" or "facts of life" (*Lebensformen*) as literary clues reflecting his life. But the truth of his autobiography can be far removed from Wittgenstein's own (self)portrait. It can present reports of all sorts, with uncommon adventures and alternative thoughts and ideas coming from the diarist. The movement of Wittgenstein's crypto-autobiography does not necessarily reflect the real truth but demystifies the personality of its maker (or self-maker) by avowing the individual he wanted to be or become: a respected and loved person. Wittgenstein's nervous disposition was in a state of chronic ill-health, but readers were ignorant of his facts of life in his diary. Wittgenstein wanted to acknowledge the pressure of his physical and mental pain, so that he could bear the pain better and actually feel less pain.

Confession

Instead of the novelesque evocation of the diary, one may call Wittgenstein's noble aspiration to compose the autobiographical confession as the *auto-da-fé* or "act of faith" (translated from Latin *actus fidei*). The *auto-da-fé* was the Spanish Inquisition's ceremony of public confession and penance of condemned heretics who opposed Catholic dogmas during the later fifteenth and sixteenth centuries with "new" beliefs and opinions coming from Judaism, Islam, and later Protestantism. Wittgenstein's attempt to recover, through the activity of writing, the unremembered and unheralded episodes of his personal life expressed in solemn oaths the "judicial 'act' [of the] sentence of the Inquisition" (OED 1989: 1:803). Usually, the public procession of the Holy Office would be followed by an execution, the ceremony of the "burning of a heretic" (1:803). In Wittgenstein's era, in which the statutes of the Spanish *limpieza de sangre* (purity of blood) were again in full force in Nazi ideology, he seemed to mistreat himself on the self-charges of being an alien and unwanted individual. Historically counted as a racial *converso* belonging to the *judaizante* belief, Wittgenstein knew himself to be a *marrano* (swine). The pejorative connotations implied that there was no escape from the contemporary prejudice of the Nazi laws on race. The secret terror was that he would be arrested and tortured, and eventually condemned by the ultimate punishment by fire.

The intensity of ideological and racial persecutions of the *auto-da-fés* caused a religious crisis in Wittgenstein's religious self-reflections. Both in the *Lecture of Ethics* pronounced in 1929 in Cambridge (Wittgenstein 1993: 36–44) and particularly in the early diaries written from 1929 to 1932, he graphically pictured a contemporary version of the seven deadly sins. Pride, envy, anger, lust, gluttony, greed, and sloth were represented as contemporary religious vices (Schimmel 1992: 11–18). In his auto-psychoanalysis, he highlighted his own battle against the sensual temptations which he had to confront in his own lifestyle. The battle was not of a materialistic nature, such as theft or gluttony, but was devoted largely to his own spirituality in contemplating the truth of moral feelings of goodness and badness. Wittgenstein was too honest a person to indulge in neurotic lust, academic covetousness, criminal negligence, and other escapist longings or yearnings of religious sins. He trusted that his peccadilloes would be forgiven after his *auto-da-fé*, and hoped that his defects would be glossed over as minor weaknesses.

In *Denkbewegungen* Wittgenstein criticized the agonizing spiral of meanings as his "method, which is in essence the transition of the question [problem] from truth to his sense" (MS 105: 46c, 1929; see also CV: 3e).[8] The clear meaning, which he wrote in the misrepresented sense of his journals, revealed his narcissistic feelings of guilt. His diaries placed an emphasis on the quasi-Freudian resistance to the conflict embracing the "conventional" truth. Wittgenstein's intellectual focus in those years was not on writing the original work but on the critical commentaries of the translation of the *Tractatus*. Officially the translation from German to English was made by Ogden, but in actuality it was translated by Frank Ramsey (Wittgenstein 1973; discussed in Gorlée 2012: 27–29; Monk 2016). Wittgenstein's sentimental problems were elsewhere, still involved in his friendship with Marguérite Respinger; he had enjoyed the lust of sexual appetite as ancillary to true love (Schimmel 1992: 111–137), but his diary shows that he was overcome by sexual fears of intimacy and hesitated to give in to the guilt of moral sensuality with her. The effect was sensory deprivation in the sense of "disorientation, depersonalization, loss of identity, and mental blankness" (Walker 1977: 259).

Wittgenstein's panic ascribed the bad luck of producing good work to having missed the mark of good humanity. He had given in to physical laziness in the biblical sense of indolent behavior, feeling in himself the apathy of a cold and phlegmatic temper. The vice of sloth gave him larger-than-life depression, anxiety, and even despair, driving him to consider suicide (Schimmel 1992: 191–216). Wittgenstein experienced in his own mind and heart that the "sin of sloth has two components: *acedia*, which means a lack of caring, an aimless indifference to one's responsibilities to God and to man, and *tristitia*, meaning sadness and sorrow" (193). Wittgenstein seemed to suffer both of these traumatic situations, evoking in his spirit evil troubles of life, and he hoped the divine would dissolve his moral troubles and cares.

Wittgenstein's anxieties to think and write philosophy made him overcome the pleasurable vices of arrogance, indiscipline, and other amusements. His duty to further the interest of his scientific work was hindered by the moral pain (*Schmerz*) and anger (*Wut*) he suffered daily. He complained that:

> Rxs hzyv 14 Gztv pznt nrxsh tvziyvrgvg. Nfn dmppvn dri hvsvn my vh drvwvi tvsvn driw. Rxs yrn nmxs nrxsg afi Ifsv tvqmoovn. Fnw ovrnv Tvwznqvn upzggvin fo wvn Tvtvnhgznw svifo.
>
> (I have not worked for 14 days. Now let us see if the work will proceed. I have not yet come to rest. And my thoughts keep circling around the subject.)
>
> (MS 105: 105, 1929;[9] see Wittgenstein 1993: 194, 195, 2005: 431; Pichler 2006: 131).

Wittgenstein constantly overcame the personal disillusionment of not being ripe for demanding work. Yet the poor condition of his "philosophizing" seemed to transpire in a spiritual vacuum. He repeated the despair of doing nothing, in the uncoded words "I like to dawdle. Perhaps less so now than before" (MS 183: 9, 1930;[10] see DB: 1:21; 2:9). He even attempted to control the slippage of the evil desires beyond the study of the real subject (studying, thinking, and working), hoping to solve the problematic affair of doing nothing. In acute conflict with the traditional biblical vices, he seemed to transform the vice into something like a virtue. As a spiritual guide of soul and body, he almost engaged in the modern-day *charisma* of becoming a prophet living alone in the wilderness, which was associated with the persuasive voice coming from wild nature.

From 1929, Wittgenstein felt unwell and wrote many diary entries to reconcile himself to his fate. To explain the diary, he recapitulated the history of the war diaries of 1914–1916:

> Vh rhg pvoqdfiwrt wzhh rxs hvrg hm ervpvn Rzsivn uzhg nrv ovs wzh pvrhvhgv Yvwfuynrh volufnwvn hzyv Gztvyfxszfuavrxsnfntvn af ozxsvn. Rn wvi zppvrvihgvn Arg rn Yviprn zph rxs wzorg znurnt zfu Avggvp Tvwznqn fyvi orxs zfuafhxsivryvn, wz dzi vh vrn Yvwfiunrh. Vh dzi ven ufi orxs drxsgrtvi Hxsirgg. Hlzgvi vnghliznt vh afo Gvrp wvo Nzxszofnthgirvy (rxs szggv Qvppvih Gztvh Gztvyfxsvi tvpuhun) Gvrp wvo Yvwfiunrh wmxs vgdzh emn ori nrvwviafpvtvn. Vh dzi zphm afo timhzvn Gvrp Vrgvpqvrg. Afo Gvrp uivrprxs zfxs drvwvi wvi Vilzga ufi vrnvn Ovnhxsvn wvo rxs orxs znevigizfvn qmnngv. Hlzgvi orhxsgv hrxs wzaf zfxs Nzxszofnt wvi Lvlbhhxsvn Gztvyfxsvi. Uivrprxs rhg vh, drv roovim hxsdvi, srvi tvivxsg af hvrn, wvnn vh dzi nzgfiprxsvh & vrgpv Yvhgivyfntvn hgziq eviorhxsh.
>
> (It is remarkable that for so many years I have not had even the slightest inclination to write entries in my diary. When I was first in Berlin and started jotting down thoughts about myself, it was a need. An important step for me. Later I was inspired in part by the instinct to imitate (having read Keller's diaries), and in part by the need to make a record of my life. Vanity, mostly. Although partly also a substitute for someone in whom I could confide. To this came later the imitation of the Pepysian diaries. But, as always, it is difficult to be fair, as natural and vain aspirations are strongly intertwined.)
>
> (MS 107: 74, 1929)[11]

Wittgenstein's tormented spirit wanted to heal in plaintext (uncoded text) the habit of arrogance by continuing the vital habit into the habituality of pursuing the diary of his life events.

Abandoning the extremes of a crumbling bourgeois model, Wittgenstein needed to compose a new genre of work in his passionate quest for a private subjectivity. He continued the diary notebooks but made contact with the traditional meaning of the autobiographical diary to refresh the attention of his readers. The speculative story of Wittgenstein's diary points toward his short paragraphs extended to the movements of thought (*Denkbewegungen*)—following the literary tradition of writing the events, but moving from the day-to-day toward the move-by-move or moment-by-moment genre. He needed other "forms of life" in his diary to move the reader from the abstract nature of the philosophical *Denkbewegungen* to a concrete interest in Wittgenstein's autobiographical "forms of life." Wittgenstein's diary confessions are a mixed bag of hardly verifiable facts, seemingly with no goal in themselves. The episodic structure of the events are described in the motive power of his cognitive thought; written in the first person, but Wittgenstein's thoughts convey the emotional stimulus to survive the trials and tribulations of his individual identity as a private person.

In the preface to his principal work *Philosophical Investigations,* Wittgenstein explicitly stated that his literary endeavors were not directed at composing a genuine book but, as he explained in plaintext, as "really just an album" (PI: 3e-4e; see MS 130: 22, 1946; for Wittgenstein's "album," see Gorlée 2012: 68–70). The experiment in the flow of short sketches does not form a whole book but the collection of rather fragmentary aphorisms to probe the semiotic exploration of new "shibboleths" in his literary style. Wittgenstein's "album" was the forerunner to the modern-day summary of separate manuscripts (Pichler 2004; Gorlée 2012: 68–69, 82, 187, 228). The written "sketches" were possibly an early codex bound together in the loose-leaf pages of Wittgenstein's notebook. For him, the "album" was the portable summary of his manuscripts, but for the readers it served as a volume or handbook, suited to the "mission" of the philosopher. As can be ascertained from the *Oxford English Dictionary,* the sketches transcend the superficial "rough draught or design" patterns (OED 1989: 15:593) shifting to the causal series of Wittgensteinian's fragmentation in writing.

In the (uncoded) preface of *Philosophical Investigations,* Wittgenstein prepared the details for his preliminary study to become the large outline of his work:

> The same or almost the same points were always being approached afresh from different directions, and new sketches made. Very many of these were badly drawn or lacking in character, marked by all the defects of a weak draughtsman. And when they were rejected, a number of half-way decent ones were left, which then had to be arranged and often cut down, in order to give the viewer an idea of the landscape. Thus this book is really only an album. (PI: 3e)

The notion of an album showed the interdisciplinary and intertextual lines of the "landscape" of Wittgenstein's knowledge, including the questions and answers for readers (students) to use to answer their own doubts significantly, that is, informatively and imaginatively.

As a writer Wittgenstein acted as a humble sinner seeking an antidote to intellectual pride (Schimmel 1992: 27–54, esp. 36–48, 50–54). The radical humility of his vulnerability in going from imperfection to perfection means that Wittgenstein's notion of an "album" is regarded as a pejorative term for the medley of condensed paragraphs, dealing with a number of logical functions in arithmetical or mathematical terms (Barton 1990: 215). When his album implies personal illustrations of the content in his philosophical text—in the form of "autographs, memorial verses, original drawings, or other souvenirs" (OED 1989: 1:298)—it allows Wittgenstein's intellectual problems to reveal to readers a certain tenderness in him when understanding his crypto-confession. The personal illustrations are grounded in Wittgenstein's reading of the traditional confession genre, but the historical reading reflects Wittgenstein's own "journey from self-deprecation, sorrow, and guilt, through firm resolve, to a feeling of cleansing and purification, culminating with repose and joy in God's grace and love" (Schimmel 1992: 236).

Wittgenstein's memories refer back to the long-forgotten experiences of the books he must have read during his youth. From the plan, structure, and shape of these books he harbored a subliminal awareness of "forgotten" memories. When Wittgenstein thought, worked, and wrote, these dreams and prayers directly emerged from illiteracy to freshened consciousness. In his psychological and psychiatrical works, Carl Jung named such hidden memory "cryptomnesia," when the reader acted in the new role of author ([1964] 1979): 36–38). Unaware of the old ideas and thoughts, the author retranslated similar passages into individual instances with fresh ideas. The cryptomnesia was revived by the reader's nervous shock of a new understanding. The effects of the hidden memory in Wittgenstein's informal diary with the diagnosis of signs and symptoms arose from his formal wordplay as the interplay of language philosophy, lectures, letters, and diary (Farb 1974: 192).

Firstly, Wittgenstein's important historical source must be the memoir of the early Christian bishop Saint Augustine (354–430). In 397–398, Augustine wrote the personal *Confessions* ([1961] 1974), where he described his birth, his early belief in Manichaeism, his baptism into Christianity, and the death of his mother, Monica (later, Saint Monica). Augustine's memoirs, written when he was forty-three (with thirty-three years to come) is a statement of faith and belief and shows no trace of guilt. Augustine went from heresy in Hippo (North Africa) to the leadership of the emerging Christian Church in Rome. His conversion announced the transformation of the pagan Roman Empire into the center of Christendom. Augustine described his Christian conversion as his high drama in the *Confessions*, in which he narrated in lyrical Latin how the spot and stain had been washed from his person by God's mercy. After an agonizing inward conflict, Augustine started the *Confessions* by telling his religious episodes from his time in Africa up until his conversion to Christianity. The story included the events of his sexual life, since he had a son with a Carthaginian woman. Moving to Rome, he cleansed his life to seek absolute wisdom from God. Giving up sex and other bodily temptations, in the pages of his diary Augustine told of how by God's grace he found the spiritual way of life. Augustine's movement from sin to sainthood was followed by Wittgenstein (Gorlée 2012: 5–9, 114–128, 133–139, and *passim*).

Wittgenstein considered Saint Augustine's *Confessions* as "the most serious book ever written" (Rhees 1984: 90). In search of an ethical dimension, Wittgenstein struggled with the same moral battle as Augustine, fighting in the wilderness of contemporary politics. Augustine brought to prominence the philosophical and psychological concepts of a man with a personality and authority (Henry 1960: 1). Augustine's personal testimony brought vital ideas to Wittgenstein's mind and heart. His model Augustine shaped the Christians in their devouring desire to find rest or peace. Augustine's revelation of the *libido* as the forbidden sexual force did not examine the difference of his own concept of sin, but the same happened with Wittgenstein, who did not critically evaluate his erotic lust replete with the ambivalence of heterosexual and homosexual relationships. These forms of relationship were charged in Wittgenstein's bourgeois society with the evils of bourgeois prejudices, legally betrayed by the public judgments of decency. Wittgenstein's religious revival of Augustine is clarified in the references at the start of the *Philosophical Investigations* (PI: 5), where Wittgenstein discusses the education of language in children, as well as in *The Blue Book* and *The Brown Book* (BBB), when he introduces the "ideal" of the language-games (Gorlée 2012: 136–138). The first masterpiece of Augustine's *Confessions* gave Wittgenstein a fresh impulse toward self-thought and self-scrutiny rephrased in his philosophy and his diary.

The other historical sources of Wittgenstein's diary stories are scarcely mentioned. It seems that, according to psychiatrist Jung, the "information we obtain from our patients ... is seldom complete ... We ourselves do not find it at all easy to remember where some of our own ideas come from" ([1956] 1976: 313). Instances of cryptomnesia can happen with half-forgotten stories that guide the spiritual transformation of a person's identity, which start in secret forms in a political or religious pilgrimage. Wittgenstein's literary source could have been the confessional and skeptical statements of Michel de Montaigne (1533–1592), who first used the new literary form of an essay. Montaigne's *Essays* ([1580, 1588] 2005) were not meant as early "autobiography—the events of his life were too insignificant, he thought—but a revelation of his 'fantasies,' his imagination, his whims, his ideas" (Rosen 2008: 48). The form of Montaigne's essays assigned the characteristics of formality to the objectivity of the systematic and technical exposition of the essays, but, surprisingly, they are (as in Wittgenstein) drafted in the informal tone of intimate subjectivity with himself (Shipley 1972: 140). As an impromptu and even playful genre of literature, the concept of Montaigne's essays discussed a variety of topics but was finely arranged in the old tendency of moral journalism, seen today in political and cultural editorials, articles, interviews, and even book reviews.

After a busy life as a noble landowner, lawyer, and mayor of the city of Bordeaux, Montaigne withdrew totally from public life when the plague and religious wars between Catholics and Protestants broke out in France. At the age of thirty-nine, Montaigne, who had a Spanish-Jewish mother but a firm *converso* to Roman Catholicism (but with a respect to Protestantism), retired to his estate to live and work in freedom. He composed the famous *Essays* in personal isolation, aloof from the political and religious revolts of France. For him, the new term of "essay" was the fragmentary and even playful self-portrait arranged in Latin prose to reach the meaning of his life. The *Essays* were of moderate length, could treat any topic of conversation, and were in Montaigne's time a free project of autobiographical narratives, written to communicate, instruct, and even entertain the readers (Blanchard 1980). Wittgenstein's discussion in short paragraphs followed the new trend to transport his ideas of thought (*Denkbewegungen*) far away from traditional (religious) narratives to generate the mixed (formal and less formal) type of stylistic experiment. Montaigne's and Wittgenstein's essays remove the cultural certainty of oneself—which provides readers with a defense against uncertainty and doubt—whilst reflecting on the speculations and irony of their times (Rosen 2008: 51).

Montaigne, like Wittgenstein, was a skeptic thinker with signs of criticism and despair. Their backgrounds and attitudes were, bridging the ages, more or less alike in scientific attitude, but their approach to life was different: Montaigne was a conservative statesman, while Wittgenstein was a revolutionary critic. Both agreed that human knowledge hardly exists, as most knowledge is merely relative and a fleeting form of information. Montaigne's *Essays* are provisional trials or tests of reality, implying not an admission of guilt or regret, but a dogmatic desire for sermons and prayers to clear the habits of self-judgments in life. Man is no angel, no animal, but observed by Montaigne as an honest and good brother with the physical, mental, historical, philosophical, and religious gifts of God to man. Man was not regarded as an individual but seen as a member of society and institutions, such as family, city, state, and church. Although in the Roman Catholicism of Montaigne's time women were regarded as possessing no rational thought, Montaigne's stepdaughter Marie de Gournay edited the laborious revision of the *Essays*, with indications of inserts and variants in her hand.

Freedom, equity, and brotherhood constituted Montaigne's motto. These ideas could be discussed with close friends, in the nineteenth century this meant male friends. In the essay "On Friendship" (Montaigne [1580, 1588] 2005: 83–101) Montaigne described the personal story of his friendship with the young lawyer and humanist Étienne de la Boëtie. After five years of intense friendship, de la Boëtie died in 1563 at a very young age. Montaigne was deeply grieved without his comrade. He wrote that they had an exclusive friendship "which we cherished, as long as God willed it, so perfect and entire, that surely the like of it is seldom read of, and no sign of any such friendship is to be seen in the men of our day" (84). Compared to the love of Achilles and Patroclus (Gorlée 2012: 184), Montaigne romantically wrote that "In the friendship I speak of, our souls blend and melt so entirely, that there is no more sign of the seam which joins them. If I am pressed to say why I loved him, I feel that I can only express myself by answering, 'Because it was he, because it was I'" ([1580, 1588] 2005: 90–91). Montaigne's suggestive remarks are similar to Wittgenstein's air of romance in his friendship with David Pinsent. In his diary and letters Wittgenstein called him "dearest David" (*den lieben David*, GT: 17, 1914 and further; see Noll 1998). David Pinsent, a British soldier, died a martyr's death in the First World War. The *Tractatus* was "Dedicated to the memory of my friend David H. Pinsent" (TLP: 25) with Wittgenstein's love.

In the *Essays*, Montaigne's implied his answer by the highly sensitive—that is, religious and sexual—symbolism of friendship. In his essay "Of Ancient Customs" (Montaigne [1580, 1588] 2005: 149–155; see 14–15), the sign of greeting among men was pointed out as the affectionate and enthusiastic gesture of body language following the habit of ancient philosophers:

> When saluting or proffering a request to a great person they touched his knees. Pasicles [of Thebes] the philosopher, brother of Cratis [of Thebes], laid his hands on the genitals instead of on the knee. When a man he was addressing rudely repelled him he replied: "What, is not this yours as well as the knees?" (151–152)

Instead of men grasping each other's arms or hands to embrace, the Greek convention was to use this auto-erotic (or homoerotic) game, separate from and beyond normal language, to make sense. The dirty joke seemed to amuse the readers to agree or disagree with these old customs (Arango 1989: 119–122). But touching someone's genital organs in public is a religious and social taboo, but it can also turn into a secret pleasure of the neurotic individual struggling between the hostility of the *super-ego* and the *ego* (see Freud's argument of patients in *Inhibitions, Symptoms and Anxiety* [1904] [1938: 48–49]). Writing an educational book without the modern intake of psychology or psychiatry, Montaigne made the point that the cultural code will change with fashion.

The moral stories of Montaigne told the history of a religiously exemplary man, living in society with peace and dignity. Focusing on the romantic return to the simplicity of the "noble savage," the American Indians were seen by Montaigne as the virtuous simplicity of "cannibals" or even "slaves," but also as truly free men, not (yet) corrupted by Western civilization. Following Montaigne's freedom, Jean-Jacques Rousseau (1712–1778) also considered primitive humans to be free animals "wandering in the forests, without industry, without speech, without domicile, without war and without liaisons" (quoted in Masters 1986: 2:837)—as seemed to happen to Wittgenstein in his final years without home and work.

Rousseau's autobiographical *Confessions* ([1781] 1973) and *Reveries of the Solitary Walker* ([1782] 1982) did not tell the "external" story of Montaigne's general citizen of society but insisted the guilt and regret of Rousseau's "internal" life as an unwanted intellectual citizen. A native of Geneva, Rousseau had a troubled youth and was—like Wittgenstein—self-taught in German *Wissenschaft* and French *science*, including not only natural but also cultural and historical sciences (*Literaturwissenschaft, sciences humaines*). In his works, Rousseau became famous through his sharp criticism of society. But as a diarist, he was, after Saint Augustine, a thinker on contemporary man working as an authentic writer, revolutionizing the diary into a complex kind of person-oriented speech.

Wittgenstein pointed to the critical distinction of Rousseau's "contract sociale" (MS 115: 40, 1933; MS 213: 196v, 1932–1933). This contract was not the social pact of bringing together free citizens to give the "general will" of the majority and political equality for everyone. Often, the social contract created political tyranny through the bold experiment of the individual citizen to be naturally and primitively free from others, even enslaving others for their own welfare. For Rousseau man's promise is by nature good, but human civilization becomes the alienation of the single citizen in the absolute obedience to the king and government. Both Montaigne and Rousseau must have influenced Wittgenstein's acute feeling of pessimism in his autobiographical works, unhappy as he was with the political development of the Nazis enslaving European countries, yet wishing for a better life for future generations. Wittgenstein stressed in 1932 that "the occurrence of the paradigm and the class of symbolism does not signify that a special sentence of the symbolism must be true"; but, significantly, he added, more to himself, that "Rousseau had an almost Jewish nature" (MS 154: 20v, 1932, my translation; see CV: 17e).[12]

From the 1930s, Wittgenstein fully realized that the theoretical multiplicity of symbol and sign generated troubles in open political life. The life-and-death symptoms created dangerous thoughts with no solutions. Wittgenstein wanted to subject the citizens to new meanings to change their ideological sovereignty to personal subjectivity (following Peirce's interpretants). Under the Nazi regime, however, ideological and political signs were practically applied in the symbolic use of evil signs against humanity, meaning the Nazi's large-scale tyrannical crimes against humanity.

For the Jewish population racial, sexual, political, and religious crimes had the mortal effects of servitude and slavery. According to Nazi ideology, Wittgenstein was counted as a Jew, meaning he was their victim. While the divine Word of the Torah carried the truth as flesh of God, this Word was totally dismembered in the crimes against humanity. The Jewish law and the Talmudic tradition celebrate the endless publications of the rabbis in their commentaries, summaries, debates, marginalia, and other glosses of the Holy Script. Their task was spreading the wisdom of truth, which is basically an incomprehensible lesson subject to God's hand, not human government or society.

Wittgenstein stressed that "It is typical of the Jewish mind to understand someone else's work better than he understands himself" (MS 154: 15v, 1932). Rousseau's self must have had the same relatively uneasy and critical temperament, tastes, and manners as Wittgenstein's self to rightly comprehend the old law and tradition. For Rousseau the Jewish emphasis on compassion and justice meant that the primitive elements of the good and egalitarian citizen merely brought exterior freedom. It seems that Rousseau and Wittgenstein were haunted by the illusion that they were persecuted by everyone; they were forced to search for spiritual refuge to survive in one piece as a whole person. Wittgenstein was always in exile (Klagge 2011) and should have perfectly understood Rousseau's lack of spirit in desperation (Marks 2010). In their private autobiographies, both of them described the loss of identity as the enslavement of the escapism of the private self.

Following the iconic models of Saint Augustine, Montaigne, and Rousseau, Wittgenstein's problem throughout his life was the indexical intention to write his language philosophy. He accepted the misuse of the rule (*Ordnung*) of language as the primary source to try to communicate human or psychological confusion (*Unordnung*) in communications with other language speakers. After the logical forms of the *Tractatus*, the *Brown Book* attached value to "primitive" words and rudimentary sentences, exemplified in the simplicity of tribal languages. The cultural Otherness of "primitive" beliefs and practices is understood according to Wittgenstein's different standards of what the weak type of "primitive" logic can *stand for* (BBB: 93–148; see Gorlée 2012: 99, 171 with fn. 1, 243–250, 292, 295).[13] Returning to the early *Tractatus* (TLP: 3.326), in which Wittgenstein considered linguistic signs (propositions) to be the Augustinian image of reality (Gorlée 2012: 139–152), he distinguished between "primitive" signs (*Urzeichen*) "which cannot be further analyzed by definition" and "articulate" signs which are "defined, and the definitions show the way" (TLP: 3.26, 3.261) of understanding them. Simple signs were easy, but the meaning of articulate signs was not. The definition merely symbolized ("named") the meaning, but the symbols themselves "cannot be taken to pieces by definition (nor any sign which alone and independently has a meaning)" (TLP: 3.261). Although "At first sight it appears as if they were also a different way in which one proposition could occur in another" (TLP: 5.541), the symbols remain as they are, unsolved signs.

For Wittgenstein, symbol and sign are firmly connected terms, but different from Peirce's thoughts. This would mean that for Wittgenstein the symbol defines and conditions ("names") the meaning of the verbal sign (Glock 1996: 345–348). Differing from his earlier works in accordance with the Saussurean tradition of the certainty in formal philosophy, Wittgenstein's late works (ending with the last volume of *On*

Certainty) were derived from the notion of uncertainty. This is the same as Peirce's quasi-semiosis, in which the uncertainty of human interpreters generates the infinite sign-action of semiosis (Sebeok 1984a: 3). Wittgenstein reproduced emotional and energetic interpretants to give the form of signs their meaning. Wittgenstein expressed serious doubt about giving logical consistency to naming prefixes, words, and sentences (Gorlée 2012: 273–317; 2015a: 63–80). The uncertainty was resolved by the practical use of the language-games, which invented the collective signs of language to give meaning. While Peirce's "symbol" was specifically the logical or formal sign of thirdness, for Wittgenstein the term "sign" was the semiotic genus for all types of signs, including interpretant-signs. These could be emotional, energetic, and intellectual interpretant-signs (firstness, secondness, and thirdness). But for Wittgenstein the symbol had many meanings both in reality and in the metaphorical sense of "reality." In Wittgenstein's work the symbol is an essential sign but far away from his practical experiences with the surplus of irrational or vague symbolism (Nöth 1990: 118–120).

Wittgenstein's iconic sources of practical insight were the models in conventional classics. The history of the diary genre was in a sense announced by his primary symbols—Saint Augustine, Montaigne, and Rousseau. The dream symbols of the historical diarists were Wittgenstein's "forgotten" cryptomnesia (Farb 1974: 74–75). At the same time, the questions and spiritual replies of Wittgenstein's diary pointed further than his philosophical work to the "traveler's" diaries of his contemporaries Gottfried Keller and Rainer Maria Rilke, who served as Wittgenstein's secondary sources to contribute to his poetic "pilgrimage." The third source of Wittgenstein's diary was not the literary or romantic genre, but the technical codification. The code entries were probably modeled on Samuel Pepys's shorthand, although Wittgenstein's truth lies elsewhere.

Gottfried Keller

Wittgenstein revealed in plaintext (MS 107: 74, 1929) that his source of insight was reading the diary of Gottfried Keller (1819–1890), the Swiss novelist and poet of the Realist school. In his diary Keller recalled the fond memory of his youthful years as a student abroad in Munich (from 1843). The story of Keller's diary carved him out as an international student of the Royal Academy of Fine Arts at Munich. The autobiographical memory of the young traveler later inspired a fellow traveler, Ludwig Wittgenstein (McGuinness 1988: 34, 56, 251, 272).

Keller, as a young student of painting, was something of a hippie. As a radical opponent of the conventional politics of his time, he supported the popular reforms of the European revolution of 1848. The middle class wanted to establish complete democracy, threatening the established privileges of the well-to-do. The goal of the socialists was to unite the German princedoms into a single unified Germany. However, this new socialism was a highly controversial principle of politics, since it pointed to the newly published theory of Karl Marx (1818–1883), which wanted to reform the social order to end noble privileges and formal inequalities, and to guarantee the cooperation and mutuality of different political parties from the nineteenth century onward. Socialism found an alternative in the political climate of communist and anarchist parties (Williams [1976] 1988: 286–291), and Keller became an ideological radical of socialism, who rebelled against the inequalities of the political order to establish social justice. Despite Marx's communist program, to lead society from capitalism to communism, the ideological claims in Western Europe became the social revolution that gave the national consciousness of separate groups living together the common feeling of military nationalism. The chronic unemployment and financial scandals grew into political unrest. The new political parties eventually became German National Socialists and rapidly gained power in Austria.

Keller's radicalism changed from the dreams of a student into active involvement with the real political party of the Socialist movement. In memory of the bitter pessimism of the *Tagebuch* (Keller 1942: 27–58), written in 1843, the poet Keller looked back in an autobiographical act at his revolutionary period with a certain nostalgia for his younger days. When Keller had to return home to Zürich, he abandoned his political dreams and romanticized about life in his *Traumbuch* (written 1846–1848) (Keller 1942: 61–99). In his later years, Keller found conservative pleasure in writing a number of fragmentary sketches, far away from the revolutionary battle-cry of his earlier student days. The sexual fantasizing of romantic dreams was in the past; he was now engaged in organizing Sunday excursions to the mountain Zürichberg, to improve his sister's health, and in arranging meetings with the celebrities of his day.

Wittgenstein was fascinated by Keller's first diary of 1854. It served as the model for writing the iconic and indexical aspects of his own diary according to his own shape and form. Keller's short *Tagebuch* was taken by Wittgenstein as a sign of honesty and credibility, written when he moved from early boyhood into adulthood. Wittgenstein followed Keller's beggarly mood to become a diarist. Keller wrote that:

> A man stops being a man when he no longer watches himself and always seeks restoration and nourishment outside himself. He loses his posture, his steadfastness, his character and once his spiritual independence is gone, he turns into a miserable wretch (*Tropf*). Yet he can only preserve his independence by constant self-contemplation and the best way of doing this is by keeping a diary. (Keller 1942: 27, my translation)

Keller explained his diary as a vade mecum to build his ideas of his good and bad life as a traveler in foreign lands. His diary created a fresh life away from the fixed course. Keller continued saying that:

> When a young man goes out into the world, he is given a wanderer's journal (*Wanderbuch*), with a colored string looped through the pages, affixed to the last page with a seal. This diary will be my wanderer's journal, which I will present to my highest tribunal, my conscience, at every new station in my life, and the connecting green thread is hope, and the seal holding this green thread is death depicted as eternity. (Keller 1942: 31–32, my translation)

Keller's silky cover was a metaphor for the green bijou ornamenting what he considered his treasure box that held his private diaries. Although the luxurious cover of the green notebook offered no "vanity" for the schoolboy-like record of his day-to-day adventures, the authentic confession would remain the truth of Keller's alternative youth in arts and politics.

In the pages of his diary, called *Der grüne Heinrich* (*Green Henry* [Keller 2003]; written in 1854–1855), several times Keller implied the symbolism of the color green, meaning hope or better, provoking the emotions of nostalgia he felt for his native hometown, Zürich, different from his dynamic connection with the city of Munich. He wished to return but had no means to do so, as he described in *Green Henry*. Despite his suffering and poverty, Keller had turned into a beggar. Unable to find any prospective buyers for his paintings, he followed the creative idea of moving his career in a new direction by keeping a diary: "Suddenly I bought some books of writing paper and began, in order to make my development and character clear once for all to myself, an account of my life and experiences up to that time" (Keller 2003: 542).

He transformed the unsuccessful art of painting into writing an autobiographical novel with more success with the public. After completing the process of writing the novel, Keller took the packet of pages to:

> A bookbinder to have them clothed in my personal colour, in the shape of green linen binding, and to have the book to keep in my chest. Some days later, I went there before dinner to fetch it. The craftsman had misunderstood me, and made the binding far more elaborate and elegant than I ever dreamed. Instead of linen, he had used silk, he had gilded the edges and supplied metal clasps to close the book. (Keller 2003: 543)

In fact, poor Keller was starving, but he could not resist the beauty of the superbly bound green notebook. He enjoyed the elegant "feeling of respect for the orderly logical consequence of things, where everything followed so beautifully" but he "pondered my life over again in spite of the green silk book which lay on the table, and remembered my sins" (543).

Simplicity but criticism competed as Wittgenstein's personal motto. His diary was also written in a simple cahier (*Taschennotizbuch*). Secretly, he believed that his academic success was a dangerous business, since it would actually cultivate hostile feelings of rage, envy, greed, lust, and mainly vanity (Schimmel 1992). Vanity put the moral basis of genius in danger of gaining or losing touch with Christian humility. Wittgenstein was fully aware that the blank pages of his diary could grow into a wide assortment of new ideas and creative incidents, which could give his thoughts the virtue of Keller's hopes and expectations for the future. But Wittgenstein's vanity was kept in check by the ethical standards he constantly defended to give moral sense to his life.

For Keller and Wittgenstein, writing a diary was the troubling and ridiculous act of giving personal confession to others, even strangers. By publishing their diaries, the autobiographical record can be judged in a public trial of the real truth of their lives (Brooks 2000). Since both Keller and Wittgenstein felt themselves betrayed and alienated, their private diaries were almost a spiritual asylum, affording them the shelter of intellectual safety against all kinds of political, religious, and ideological anxieties threatening their mercurial existence. Without the gift of spiritual refuge, Keller confirmed that one can easily become the biblical "philistine" (1942: 30, 35), thereby announcing the same pejorative catchphrase "philistine" used by Wittgenstein to signify the evil-disposed mob of popular people ending the fate of humanity (1 Sam. 5, 6; Judg. 16.3; see Gorlée 2012: 210–212, 232).

Wittgenstein seemed to follow Keller's wanderer's journal (*Wanderbuch*), when he wrote in secret code that:

> Wf ofhhg vihg zfu wrv Dznwvihxszug tvsvn & wznn qznnhg wf rn wrv Svrozg afifxqqvsivn & wznn drihg wf htv znwvih evihgvsn.
>
> (You must first go out into the world [*Wanderschaft*] and after returning to the homeland [*Heimat*] you can understand it differently.)
>
> (MS 107: 114, 1929)[14]

When Wittgenstein traveled abroad in his younger days, he certainly missed the good company of his family, but he also lacked friends to talk to, particularly in difficult moments, for example, when facing enemies in the First World War and during his exile as a prisoner of war. Wittgenstein's loneliness strongly evolved in his letters mainly directed to his oldest sister Hermine, to whom he always felt very close (McGuinness, Ascher, and Pfersmann 1996: 20–22, 23–49). Their affectionate care for each other made their letters intimate messages filled with love. Usually, Wittgenstein's correspondence was marked by the correct formality characteristic of the nineteenth century. A friendly letter, as written to his beloved sister Hermine, was an unusual message. It could be a creative letter but was more or less an exotic present in those days. Despite the formal correspondence, Wittgenstein's originality had, for real intimacy with his friends, informal ideas to communicate with special emotions. Perhaps his route to happiness lay in the personal remarks written on postcards, stressing that his bitter unhappiness was caused by the horrid idea of his diary entries.

One can conclude that Keller's writings anticipated Wittgenstein's autobiographical diary (Brouwer 1986: 54–55). Complementing the romantic, ironical, political, and even humorous form of Keller's traveler's *Tagebuch*, Wittgenstein followed Keller's "wandering thoughts" ([1960] 2003: 544–545) to achieve the philosophical truth of his life. In his confessional diary, Wittgenstein upshifted Keller's journal entries to a different period with other social and political commitments communicating creatively the problems in the *Denkbewegungen*. Wittgenstein's modern thoughts bear the postmodern flavor of the contemporary mixture of language and culture (Anderson and Gorlée 2011). Wittgenstein's diary entries were spontaneously embodied in the framework of his philosophical texts. Since the lives of Keller and Wittgenstein were not the same, they referred to differing historical traditions and sociohistorical contexts. The interaction between them is the possible correspondence of gaining a new identity of the "semiotic self" (Sebeok 1979: 263–267). The painter and the modern philosopher struggled against the cultural episodes of their time, but this cannot be transposed into any close working relationship between their real works.

The psychological content of Wittgenstein's diaries explains the moral or spiritual goal of his autobiography. His neuroses brought him to indulge in bad habits but always with the yearning for good habits, in Peirce's moralistic sense (Gorlée 2016b: 14–17, 23–24). Writing a confessional diary was Wittgenstein's way of healing the vulnerable personality of feeling the miserable life of the "beggar." In secret code, Wittgenstein wrote that:

> Hmdvrg wzh Gztvyfxshxsivryvn nrxsg hvpyvi pvyvn rhg, rhg vh rn ovrnvo Uzpp hxspvxsg. Wvnn vh driw ufi orxs, drv zpph dzd rxs ozxsv yvrnzsv hrxsvi afo Znpzhh wvi Vrgvpqvrg & rv dvnrtvi Avrg rxs szyv orxs zfu vrgpv Dvrhv hvpyvi af yvhlrtvpn, wvhgm yvhhvo. Wzh Pvvyvn avihgivfg, eviypzhg zo yvhgvn wrvhvn Izfxs & vi rhg zfxs hvnn vi ypmh emifyvitvsvnw tvwzxsg driw sziopmhvi.
>
> (To the extent that keeping a diary is not life itself, it is a bad thing, in my case. For to me, like everything else I produce, it almost certainly becomes a reason for vanity and the less time I have for vain self-reflection, the better. If this smoke will be diffused, paled by life, it will be more harmless when keeping it for just a few moments.)
>
> (MS 107: 74–75, 1929)[15]

Wittgenstein's feelings of guilt longed to cleanse him of his vanity. His personality traits were related to the "traditional sin of pride, which retain their negative sense, such as *arrogant, haughty, conceited, egocentric, narcissistic, insolent, presumptuous*, and *vain*" (Schimmel 1992: 37; see 27–54). It seemed that Christian sin was what Wittgenstein mostly feared for himself.

Courageously, Wittgenstein explained the dramatic openness of his autobiography, but he continued in secret code to taste life:

> Rxs ofhh zfh ovrnvo Gztvyfxs, dvnn vh rn Miwnfnt hvrn hmpp kfzhr vyvn rnh Uivrv—rnwzh Pvyvn—givgn & dvwvi drv zfh vrnvo Qvppvipmxs znh Prxsg hgvrtvn, nmxs drv emn vrnvo smsvivn Mig drvwi zfu wrv Viwv svifngvihlirntvn ofhhvn.
>
> (To make it right I just have to emerge as it were from my diary into the open—into life—neither like coming out into the light from a dark cellar, not like coming down to earth from a higher place.)
>
> (MS 107: 75, 1929)[16]

The event of Wittgenstein's skill consists of the reconversion of feelings of isolation and the sin of pride into the "real" life of a human individual. If pride "gave birth to his desire to publish, it also prevented his doing so" (Monk 1990: 414). By writing his secret diaries, he acquired the humility and intimacy of a spiritual confidant to comfort him with blind trust. Although Wittgenstein had many friends in Cambridge and elsewhere, he still felt alone. His academic and individual insularity caused him to lack the warm friendliness he had with personal friends in Austria. His warmth was there, because:

> Dm Dziov rhg wz qznn wiv Vrgvpqvrg nrxsg tfg tvwvrsvn. Dzh wrv Znwvivn emn ori szpgvn yvhxszugrtg orxs roovi zfhhvimiwvngprxs ervp.
>
> (Where there is warmth, vanity cannot thrive. I am always extraordinarily concerned with what others think of me.)
>
> (MS 107: 75–76, 1929)[17]

Perhaps he thought back to the intellectual company of his army friend Paul Engelmann. Engelmann was Wittgenstein's close confidant, listening carefully to his first reasonings of the *Tractatus* during the First World War (Wittgenstein 1967; Lemoine 1975: 174–177; Nedo 2012: 148–149; Gorlée 2012: 73).

The episodic art-form of writing paragraphs was reconstructed and redefined by Wittgenstein's fresh ideas that arose with alternative states of mind. He transformed the conventions of realism into the political, religious, and didactic flow of new ideas put into unclear or incoherent forms of literary styles. This stream of new consciousness conveyed different styles of writing amalgamated together into a fresh genre of literature. The secret anagrams give an idyllic variety to Wittgenstein's habit of writing romantic fragments, in which he used different varieties of language side by side in his album, without approaching the format of the genuine book. Wittgenstein observed in plaintext his obstacles to writing in this way:

> I do not quite know how to begin a book that is because something is still unclear. For I should like to begin with the original date of philosophy, written & spoken sentences, with books as it were. And here we encounter the difficulty of "Everything is in flux." And perhaps that is the very point at which to begin. (MS 110: 10, 1930; CV 11e; see Gorlée 2016a: 49, 55)[18]

Wittgenstein's diaries, composed alternately in coded and uncoded forms, observed in words, sentences, and even punctuation the unanalyzed fantasy of his *Denkbewegungen* circling around in his mind and heart. In the descriptive form, thematic shape, and mythical patterns of the journals, Wittgenstein seemed to speak to the *alter ego* deep within himself. But it seems that the literary autobiography also painted a self-portrait that contained intimate thoughts addressed to a confidant. The iconic structure of the mixed metaphor was the narrative between the "systematic ambiguity of such concepts as *identity* and *self-identity*" (Singer 1984: 2), meant to reflect Wittgenstein's inside and outside views about his alternative ideas of realism and "unrealism." The moral search of Wittgenstein's diaries symbolizes his *auto-da-fé*, which only emerged in a paradoxical nature throughout the pages of his language philosophy, but with more emphasis in writing the diaries (Monk 1990: 413).

Rainer Maria Rilke

In addition to the diary of traveler Gottfried Keller, who moved abroad to Germany with the aesthetic and political goal to discover the strangeness of living in a foreign country, Wittgenstein incorporated the early works of the Bohemian-Austrian poet

Rainer Maria Rilke (1875–1926). Rilke had a Jewish mother, but he was baptized as a Roman Catholic. He was born in Prague, and his first language was German, like that of the Jewish minority of Czech population. Wittgenstein greatly admired Rilke's early work including his diary. In 1914, Wittgenstein left Rilke 20,000 crowns as a gift from the patronage of his father, Karl Wittgenstein (McGuinness 1988: 206–209; Monk 1990: 106–110). Wittgenstein felt close to the "confession" of Rilke's early work, but he wanted to add to Rilke's depression and passivity to create his own literary style.

As a young man, just married, 24-year-old Rilke portrayed a poet or novelist as an insular and nostalgic person, yet who still lived an imaginative life in the cult of youth. Rilke had received a poem from Franz Xaver Kappus, who was a 19-year-old officer cadet in the Bohemian-Austrian Army but anxious to become a poet. He sought Rilke's epistolary advice on how to gain an education and become a literary artist. Rilke produced ten letters during their correspondence between 1903 and 1908, but the letters were only published posthumously in 1929, under the title *Briefe an einen jungen Dichter* (*Letters to a Young Poet*; Rilke 2012), and without Kappus's letters. The late publication in 1929 meant that Wittgenstein was unable to read Rilke's sensible advice to Kappus, announcing the artist's trajectory of poetry and life.

Rilke's source of the genius for literature seemed in those days split into two stories. In one story, Rilke had received a poem written by Kappus and replied in 1903 from Paris, commenting to Kappus, that "your verses have no style of their own, although they do have silent and hidden beginnings of something personal" (Rilke 2012: 13). To personalize this criticism, Rilke added a positive formulation: "There is one thing you should do," namely "Go into yourself" (14). In his letters, Rilke explained to Kappus the iconic model of his style of writing, encouraging him to:

> Describe your sorrows and desires, the thoughts that pass through your mind and your belief in some kind of beauty—describe all these with heartfelt, silent, humble sincerity and when you express yourself, use the Things around you, the images from your dreams, and the objects that you remember. If your everyday life seems poor, don't blame it; blame yourself; admit to yourself that you are not enough of a poet to call forth its riches; because for the creator there is no poverty and no poor indifferent place. And even if you found yourself in some prison, whose walls let in none of the world's sounds—wouldn't you still have your childhood, that jewel beyond all price, that treasure house of memories? (15–16)

In the second story, Rilke went quite unconventionally against the social tensions of the time to describe in his letter his own misfortunes of marital life. He compared his present crisis to the traditional code of the day which would have required that sexual life had to do away with "the artist's experience [which] lies so unbelievably close to the sexual, to its pain and its pleasures, that the two phenomena are really just different forms of one and the same longing and bliss" (26). Rilke suggested to young Kappus that the traditional role of male sexuality is to preserve the male's selfish or perverse qualities, and that sex for men is a trivial amusement, whereas marriage works against the creative activity of love and art. Rilke wrote that:

> Instead of a completely ripe and pure world of sexuality, sex finds a world that is not human enough, that is only male, heat, thunder, and restlessness, burdened with old prejudice and arrogance, with which the male has always disfigured and burdened love. Because he loves only as a male, and not as a human being, there is something ... wild, malicious, time-bound, uneternal, which diminishes his art and makes it ambiguous and doubtful. [Since the art is imperfect], it is marked by time and by passion, and little of it will endure. (But most art is like that!) (27)

Rilke concluded that "Sex is difficult; yes. But those tasks entrusted to us are difficult; almost everything serious is difficult; and everything is serious" (31). Sexuality was for him a trouble (indeed, both iconic and indexical trouble). Rilke was frightened by the stiffness of society and dismissed sexual friendship as a rigid and uncaring activity, preferring to be alone. Rilke wrote that the solitary person bears no hardship of sexual intercourse but feels intensely the sadnesses (*Traurigkeiten*) of life:

> With greater trust than we have in our joys. For they are the moments [of tension] when something new has entered us, something unknown; our feelings grow mute in shy embarrassment, everything in us withdraws, a silence arises, and the new experience, which no one knows, stands in the midst of all and says nothing. (58)

During the *rite de passage* of the correspondence of man (and woman), Rilke urged young Kappus to educate himself into adulthood, but at the same time he treated him as a puerile *voyeur* of his sexual topics.

Rilke's diary, *Die Aufzeichnungen des Malte Laurids Brigges* (*The Notebooks of Malte Laurids Brigge*; written 1904–1910; Rilke [1910] 1988: 7–208), is written in an unconventional style. Rilke treated the subjects of the diary entries as belonging to the aristocratic milieu of the different countries and cities he visited, emphasizing that he had escaped from the traditional bourgeoisie to live in the early "existentialism" of the deviant life and anonymity of the big metropolis of Paris. In the loss of personal existence, young Rilke encountered the mystery of nothingness immersed in his "anthropological" lifestyle of a *voyeur* observing the culture of alien countries.

Acting in the diary as a romantic "pilgrim," Rilke observed the spiritual dislocation with the strangeness of the critical outsider (Bauman 1996: 23–26), but he was hardly there as an identical person, who can read the environment. To "read" the variety of non-linguistic symbols functioning in society, Rilke used miscellaneous impressions gathered from his intellectual glance at morphological features of images and inscriptions of Paris. These inscriptions were taken directly from the buildings, gates, doors, and store windows of the city, but Rilke did not decipher the French names to be understood in native German, the language of his diary. Language was for him the discursive scheme of random notations in strange inscriptions, which need no explanation to be understood. Rilke's anthropological tricks included simple iconic and indexical signs to reveal the strange *ego* of his complete isolation embodied in his fictional *alter ego* of his diary, Malte Laurids Brigges.

During his stay in Paris, Rilke's diary analyzed his pilgrimage in terms of free space and in real time as a number of crypto-autobiographical letters. In the flow of separate snapshots, Rilke seems to divide the "*fragmentation* of time into *episodes*, each one cut from its past and from its future, each one self-enclosed and self-contained," setting forth the Heraclitean observation that "Time is no longer a river, but a collection of ponds and pools" (Bauman 1996: 25). Semiotically, Rilke moved from pure firstness of iconicity into the secondness of indexicality. Rilke is now embodied into a lonely young Danish nobleman sauntering slowly and aimlessly about Rue Toullier in Paris. Moving in a void, he passed the time by abstracting the world of sight into numbers, atoms, or assertions. Through the experience of visual semiotics, he imagined the good and mainly bad habits of his nextdoor neighbors. As a subject for his diary entries, Rilke visited the Bibliotèque Nationale to look at the readers and read a book of French sermons. He observed the patients of the Salpêtrière hospital and visited other public locations to wander the city and observe the citizens. He created a new form of urban art.

Rilke had the unbalanced and sexually ambivalent presence of the figure of the impersonal artist. He meditated as a solitary "stroller" (Fr. *flâneur*), a term invented by Charles Baudelaire but vividly imagined by Walter Benjamin's anecdotal sketches when he walked through the *boulevards* and *passages* of Paris at the end of the twentieth century (Benjamin 1978: 150). In the spiritual diary of urban art, both Rilke and Benjamin wandered as strangers in meditative absence through the streets of this city (Bauman 1996: 26–28). Their *flânerie* missed the real world of Paris and their random excursions had no fixed itinerary. The stroller Rilke lost himself in the streets of Paris in an attempt to fill the emptiness of his life. In real time but away from the crowds, the *flâneur* offered the urban life of Paris a way of time by describing the crimes as a detective. Rilke observed and described the details of the painful incidents suffered by the citizens.

The Rilkian story narrated a nameless universe of travelers, migrants, and vagabonds. He painted the crisis of the complexities of modern urban life stylized in the new zone of writing about people's disasters observed not from the inside of the pain of human reality but merely from the outside surface. The first page of young Rilke's diary related his prose in verse-structure to depict his version of the street scenes of Paris in 1906:

> Here, then, is where people come to live, I would have thought it more a place to die in. I have been out. I have seen: hospitals. I saw a man who staggered and fell down. People gathered around him, which spared me the rest. I saw a pregnant woman. She pushed herself heavily along beside a very hot wall, sometimes touching it as if to make sure it was still there. Yes, it was still there. And behind the wall? I looked at my map: Maison d'Accouchement. Fine. To be delivered—and give birth. Further on, in rue Saint-Jacques, a high building with a cupola. On the map, Val-de grâce, Hôspital militaire. Old knowledge, but good to know. The narrow street began to stink heavily. It was the musty smell of iodoform, of the grease of pommes frites, of fear. All streets smell in the summer. Then I saw a house strangely blinded, not on the map, but over the door stands the secret name: Asyle de nuit. Next to the entrance were the prices. I read them. It was not expensive.
>
> And further? A child in a standing pram: had a thick greenish eruption breaking out on the face. The wound was healed and did not itch. The child slept, the mouth was open, breathing iodoform, pommes frites, fear. And that's life. The main point is that one is living. That was the main point. (Rilke [1910] 1988: 7, my translation)

Rilke was a poet, but he rarely wrote in prose or prosaic verse (*Prosagedicht*) as in the diary sketches of *Die Aufzeichnungen des Malte Laurids Brigges*. While Rilke walked the streets of Paris, he only observed the surfaces of the exterior side of the city. He wrote down the series of letters, labels, and titles of the nude particles to build the "grammar" of the city buildings, leaving the citizens with hardly the space to live a decent life. He mentioned plaques, gravestones, and doorplates to discover the "names" to baptize the outside world, but the untitled signs of numbers, their proportions and names had no sculpture and no content. Rilke was a connoisseur of façades catching the rhapsodic experience of the lonely walker. He conveyed a sense of privacy in the alibi of writing to avoid the glance of the public audience. He recontextualized the theory of the human cosmos through reading the anxious signs of the "things" around his inward life of loneliness.

Rilke's diary can be regarded as the metafiction of short prayers and longer sermons reflecting the fictional world of the minimalist civilization of surfaces (Hofmann 2015). He acted not as the inner observer but rather stayed the outside *voyeur* observing the:

> [Inside misfortunes of alien] events without past and with no consequences. It also means rehearsing meetings as mis-meetings, as encounters without impact: the fleeting fragments of other persons' live the stroller spun off into stories at will—it was his perception that made them into actors, let alone the plot of the drama they play. (Bauman 1996: 26)

In Rilke's hermetic fragments, he discredited the vibrational effect of poetry with rhythm and meter to show the new and somewhat puzzling indexical signs of disembodied verse-prose. But the strong style of enumerating separate words between prose and poetry was also furnished with the imagined and impassioned diction of strange and foreign words, metaphors, and other ornamental variants to furnish the strange icons in Rilke's *Aufzeichnungen* (*Notebooks*). The sketches could include epitaphs, aphorisms, evocations, exclamations, citations, and other fragmentary notes (Gorlée 2007) to mythologize and de-mythologize the "things" of disorder into Rilke's strange order.

Rilke's iconoclasm of the world wanted to escape from everyday life to render the alien life of Otherness—away from feeling lost in the aristocratic ways of bourgeoisie in the intellectual knowledge of literature. He used the *demimonde*, directing it to his cultural stereotypes and taboos to indexically create a fresh sense of human habits around himself as a contemporary author. Rilke almost followed the logical thought of Wittgenstein's philosophical analysis written in short paragraphs and fragments, with the aim to criticize the logical and linguistic mistakes and confusions around him and, for the readers, to promote deep emotions. Rilke wanted the emotive spirit of words and sentences to change his prose from ordinary prose into an iconic playpoem, in which he aimed to evoke "any specific deviation (peculiar kind of diction, or sound-structure, or meaning, etc.)" (Shipley 1972: 312). The ideal of the language-games of Rilke and Wittgenstein was to construct afresh the modern *lexis* or verbal texture of poetic prose to clarify in their new style the dim view of the world around them.

In his semi-autobiographical diary, Rilke also remembered his sexually ambivalent life as a boy, with the Danish countess Sophia (Phia) Öllegaard Skeep (representing the figure of his mother, Sophia Rilke). The tragic death of his sister Ingeborg transformed his life completely, and:

> Maman wanted me to be a little girl and not this boy that I always was ... When I entered [her room] (dressed in a small girlish house-dress I wore with rolled-up sleeves) I became Sophie, Maman's little Sophie, busying herself about the house, her hair plaited by Maman, she looked away from the bad boy, should he ever return. (Rilke [1910] 1988: 82, my translation)[19]

Wearing the girl's garments must have upset the boy Rainer Maria in a touch of sexual mutilation, revealing his personal wishes in the bisexual orientation of being both male and female. Despite the metafiction of encoding the events in his diary, the latent homoeroticism was certainly a true fact in the realism of young Rilke and Wittgenstein; but at this point their sexual orientation was a secret intention and considered an illegal feeling, a moral problem, and an evil influence which the public interest did not allow to stand.

Rilke recalled the impact of his sexual emotions in his early mythical poems, written in 1907. He displayed the naked figure in his poem about Saint Sebastian ("Sankt Sebastian"; 1955: 507–508). In the poem he romantically attempted to martyricize the vulnerable body of the early Roman Christian, who was shot with arrows to die as a Christian martyr. In the sculptural poem "Archaischer Torso Apollos" (Archaic torso of Apollo), written in 1908 (1955: 557), and other early poems, Rilke also depicted male beauty in the Rodin-like sculpture of the dazzling young Greek gods. Since he worked from 1902 as the secretary and biographer of Auguste Rodin (1840–1917), the sculptural images served Rilke as seductive word clues to depict his sexual pilgrimages in poetic style (Siegel 1996: 118).

Rilke ended the poem "Sankt Sebastian" with an existential line to himself: "You must change your life," but he added "to see it *better*?," meaning to change your life from a dramatic play for others to following your own sexual impulse (Wilshire 1982: 131–132). Rilke speculated with extreme sensibility to create his style, changing the sounds and rhythms of the male emotions detached from the usual style of the belle epoque. He wanted to make his spiritual work better than just composing the conventional "study of Carpaccio, which is bad, the drama 'Marriage' to piece together false evidence with ambiguous arguments, and some verses" (Rilke [1910] 1988: 18, my translation). The literary style was Rilke's adventure of creating a novel style.

The obscure scene of Rilke's (and Wittgenstein's) criminal behavior was healing his intellectual sorrow and the emotional pain of his "unhealthy" mind and body into a "healthy" life. Young Rilke in his literary works attempted to find free access to enter the so-called "degenerate" life of homoeroticism (argued by Siegel 1996), yet at the age of twenty-five, Rilke had been married for some years to the sculptress Clara Westhoff. He also had a long-standing affair with Lou (Louise) Andreas-Salomé, a married psychoanalyst from Russia. Lou acted as Rilke's mother-figure as well as his poetic muse. His marriage to Clara Westhoff did not work and Rilke became a "virtuoso of absence" (Hofmann 2015: 43). Rilke's loss of love was beset by troubles in the aristocratic circles he moved in, as his bourgeois friends were blind to see the reason for Rilke's sexual problems. His absence from home gave Rilke the room to develop his "feminine persona" (Siegel 1996: 114), when he became (dis)entangled in liaisons with a set of women artists (Hofmann 2015; Siegel 1996).

To escape the unattached feelings of his *libido,* the dubious longing for a partner, and the passionate yearning of sexuality marginalized from his life, as well as criticism, Rilke traveled extensively. In the company of Lou Andreas-Salomé, Rilke visited Russia to meet Tolstoy, the Russian "god" of literature. Rilke's wandering life took him to many countries including Italy, Spain, Tunisia, and Egypt. The life of Rilke as a *demimonde* artistic figure was disrespected by the bourgeois society to which he socially belonged. His social circle disliked the liberty of his lifestyle and the sexual freedom of aesthetic art circles. But the unfreedom was the reason that he had to distance himself from his wife, his family, and religion to work alone. The same distancing from family members and friends happened to Wittgenstein, who traveled from society's bourgeois rigidity to think and write alone, "philosophizing" his life in relative isolation.

Rilke was a fugitive poet, who struggled to restore the self-delusion of his *ego* to build his real self-identity (Colapietro 1989: 40). Wittgenstein traveled to Norway and Ireland in what he called his "pilgrimages" to work alone. One can conclude that both Rilke and Wittgenstein were in search of erotic roots in the most moralistic terms of life. Rilke possibly moved away from hidden homosexuality by overcoming his inhibitions by having many liaisons with women. As discussed, Wittgenstein had a liaison with Marguérite Respinger, which did not work. These liaisons never satisfied Wittgenstein's "head *or* heart, reason *or* emotion" transforming him into "reason *with* emotion, head *and* heart" (Wittgenstein 1967: 89). Unfortunately, Rilke never found a lifelong male companion to support his skeptical self in authentic friendship ([1910] 1988: 97). Like Wittgenstein, Rilke was formally a Catholic, but in reality he was a non-practicing, even skeptical, believer. In those days the ethics of religion restricted sexual activity to the Roman Catholic institution of marriage, since the moral problems of other forms of sexuality were totally marginalized as unlawful activities of erotic intercourse, since for the church they were not intended for the procreation of children.

Following the death of his parents, Rilke's *ego* and *alter ego* described in the fictional figure of Malte Laurids Brigge how he badly lacked his ancestor's home, property, and nobility. In poverty, he turned into himself as a writer and poet, complaining about his ordinary life. But Abelone, Maman's youngest sister, and other women friends comforted Rilke as a prophetic angel (Rilke [1910] 1988: 102, see 163–165, 198–200). The figure of the angel was not the memory of mother or father to child, but the magical choir of female angels singing with masculine voices. The mixed message of the angels could elevate Rilke's spirit to the "further elevation (or is it purification?)" (Bauman 1996: 27), saving Rilke's soul from the agony of good or evil with their male voices. The female angels upon masculine angels acted as Rilke's prophetic brothers and poetical muses.

The pure poetry conveyed by the guardian angels moved Rilke from sad thoughts of death (emotional interpretants) into the activity of writing literature (energetic interpretants) (Rilke [1910] 1988: 131). The angelic role of rhythmic messages accompanied the sound and music of Rilke's spirituality from passive thoughts of failure into the art of life, affection, and love, moving from energetic to logical interpretants. A similar procedure of semiosis also happened to young Wittgenstein, who tirelessly kept his diary to avoid the fatal significance of death or the inner thoughts of suicide; in this dynamic process, Wittgenstein elevated himself to accept the active rhythms of work and life. The diary message serves the diarist as a first antidote to the neurotic symptoms of real life, enabling him to pass through the danger of accident and the awareness of death to the sense of spiritual conversion.

Drawn from death into life, the diary of Rilke (and Wittgenstein) returned metaphorically to his home. After the voluntary confession, Rilke felt the homecoming of the biblical parable of the "prodigal son" ([1910] 1988: 200–208; see Lk. 15.11–32). The teachings of Jesus seem to justify and possibly consolidate the misinformation through information of the autobiographical confession. The public was informed of the (mis)adventures of the prodigal son, who secretly hoped for unconditional mercy and abounding love. Rilke and Wittgenstein formulated their way of life, in which they wanted to reveal the naked identity of the ambiguous and contradictory feelings against the bitter struggle with ultimate randomness, depression, and even suicidal thoughts. Both split the difference in sexual opinion with others to a degree. Both searched to comprehend the grim problems of the horrors they suffered. Both had been voluntaries in the First World War, and after the mortal effect of bombs and trenches, they became brain-damaged patients. Both returned home as creatures of the wounded healer expressing as confessees the authentic utterances of death and life.

Young Wittgenstein made himself explicit during the war in writing the *Tractatus Logico-Philosophicus*. By writing, he created the logical forms of the systematization of language. The tacit logic of Wittgenstein's thought-movements (*Denkbewegungen*) was capable of a diversity of literary meanings—logical, analytical, intuitive, and irrational—but his strategy moved out of the "ordinary" conventions to adopt the philosophical method. Rilke wrote *Die Aufzeichnungen des Malte Laurids Brigges* ([1910] 1988), describing the material world as a guardian of secrets, requiring patience and attention to understand the meanings of his pseudo-autobiography. There was a near relation—"although not a close one" (Lemoine 1975: 25)—between early Wittgenstein and Rilke. Their sensitivity and emotionalism directed both to the purifying view of language: both Rilke as a poet and Wittgenstein as a philosopher showed their style of life in the meaningful propositions about dealing with logical and other aspects of their works, but they also emphasized in their own way the poetical and religious qualities of their lives (Lemoine 1975: 35, 77–78, 138–139, 141–143).

Ten years later, after surviving the horrors of his military service in the First World War, Rilke compiled his epistolary fragments into *Das Testament* ([1921] 1974). The "nonsensical" words of his diary notebook were even intensified to suggest the absolute finality of what Rilke really desired with his "last will" (33–34). Starting with the words:

> Silver pleasure rawness roundness *loos* dearest
> infusion sand wherefore never attention
> ambush down envy glutton blessing mania

gnawer path twig deepens hedge legend simplicity
wasp heart cinema (child) mourning dewdrop.

Rilke ended two pages later with:

Hindrance *Niefeln Hieber* heart's-ease
Ichthys nomenclature *Beinung* judge
Regulus gallows militancy teasel spool
plays slowly but no music reaches
the round dance *Naumann*. (33–34, my translation)[20]

Rilke's translatable words and (in italics) untranslatable words can be compared to Wittgenstein's plan to confess. The word types were probably taken out of his quasi-habit of speech, condensed in the iconic indices of talking in evocations, interjections, or exclamations (Gorlée 2015a). The continuum of loosely joined words without punctuation and without fixation to any object pointed to the absent sentences with visual sounds, shapes, images, lines, and color, but without meaning. The real spirit of the words had become superfluous without any disagreement with the speech they came from (Bouwsma 1986: 72).

Rilke's testament was briefly noted in the "small notebook, bound in blue leather, which I took with me on the trip to account for my wretched condition" (Rilke [1921] 1974: 33, my translation). Following Rilke's series of unfamiliar and untranslatable word types, Wittgenstein's notebooks equally include the writing of indexical signs to accentuate the poetical value of the iconic "initials" (here symbolically translated into English). Imagine the loose enumeration of words without any sense in any significant language in:

mendicant
aphid
Schönbern
Kleborn
Bornemouth
Valborn
Friborn
Kalblusen
Klobasen
Kleebon (MS 152: 56, 1936, my translation)[21]

Wittgenstein's quasi-language emphasized that the obscure "meaning of these word-signs will in the language-game" be progressively organized to "fix the meaning through the indicative explanation" (MS 152: 56, 1936, my translation).[22] The fragmentary indices of nameless words are a rough draft in short forms of some quasi-language, but the poetic prose is presented without context and without information. The half-synonyms shared the quasi-rhythm at the end or the repetition of the initial consonant, but the sense remains unknown.[23] Wittgenstein's word games only mention some unclear words as non-signs (or pre-signs), which were hardly recognized to mean anything. He progressively gave the words some definitive meaning as logical sentences to fit into his social game of language. The technical language-games intensified the communicative function of indexical signs to illustrate in a negative sense the use of quasi-language instead of real language.

Rilke's testament of life was not written as his last work, but surprisingly (like Wittgenstein's confession) at an early age, in 1921, when he was only forty-five. In Rilke's anti-novel, *Das Testament*, he confronted the final escape from the unhappy adventures of the sensuality of love with a woman partner, deciding now to write alone ([1921] 1974: 39). *Das Testament* was his *auto-da-fé* of the narcissistic self-love of the romance with the female painter Baladine Klossowska (called by him "Merline" or "Mouky"), which had become a difficult judgment for Rilke to endure (48). In the pages of *Das Testament*, he gave up love altogether to become a lonely writer. In metaphorical figures, he saw himself disguised as the "Russian pilgrim or one of these Bedouin nomads" trying to live in the bleak and arid soil of the "steppe and the desert" (36, my translation). In the metaphorical refuge of being a pilgrim, Rilke discovered what was his personal truth.

Keller's green notebook and Rilke's blue notebook may point the way to Wittgenstein's many notebooks for writing his philosophy with a diary. The notebooks were published as *The Blue Book* and *The Brown Book* as a preparation for writing his main work, the *Philosophical Investigations*. Wittgenstein was also in search of the roots of his pilgrimage to reach his own spiritual reality, writing on the correct use of public language to introduce the private notion of language-games. While the young Keller was influenced by the philosophy of literature and social developments, he created his own political universe. Wittgenstein's interests were the social and political developments of his day, but he moved away from his earlier style of philosophy to assemble his scholarship and diary together in the *Denkbewegungen*. He created an ambiguous and fragmentary "collection" of surprises in style and content.

Rilke's literature owed much to Rodin's sculptural art. The incomplete or schematic art of empty "surfaces" or "initials" externalize themselves in the pages but the game was not to be understood. Rodin's sculptures of human figures leaves the imagination of the spectators intellectually and emotionally dependent on the movements and gestures of the human figures (Perl 2016: 30–32). Rilke's fragments spontaneously brought to the surface the social context with a lack of premeditation or insight to guess their own freedom to interpret. In doing so, he raised burning questions about the real things to question and self-question, leaving his readers to reflect on their ethnic, religious, sexual, and other cultural habits. The revolutionary aspect of Rilke's and Wittgenstein's works was their break with tradition, making changes in perspective a real possibility for their readers and listeners. The final difference between them may be that Rilke was more oriented to the goodness of his heart, while Wittgenstein more to that of his mind.

In the examples of half-remembering (cryptomnesia), Wittgenstein had not forgotten the hermetic prose of Rilke's model as the cryptogram of obscure word-signs including codes with hardly any meaning. Rilke's and Wittgenstein's diaries shared the word clues of pseudo-autobiography, suggesting the practice in which the cultural milieu of the bourgeois age could abandon the emotional response to diagnose afresh the non-meaning of mental illness and much else. The autobiographical works devitalize the emotional and energetic preference for political revolution or sexuality and bisexuality. Rilke's cryptogram leads further toward Wittgenstein's life-model, in which he depicted the personal experiences in the coded script of quasi-language as the main topic of his book. As Wittgenstein indicated (MS 107: 74, 1929), his crisis of cryptomnesia would probably lie in pursuing an autobiography like that of the classic Samuel Pepys, but written in a different genre: not about transcribing trivial love messages but setting the serious example of the unfinished novelty for future generations.

In Wittgenstein's coded fragments, the verbal material world appears as the canny guardian of his secrets, requiring patience, caution, practicality, and knowledge to decipher the quasi-messages. After the reader's intellectual effort of deciphering the code system, Wittgenstein fastened the readers on his own anguish of being an absolute stranger in this world. Wittgenstein's meanderings were not the pure and simple voice of the pilgrim on the way to find God, but were weighed up and down by the religious sign-burden of his human passions. Wittgenstein was possessed by evil and original guilt, but also he felt rejected by society. In the diary he reflected on himself, spelling the subjective self out in the structure of his works. The episodic structure of the events he describes are more than the motive power of his thought but, written in the first person, work as emotional counter-moves to read Wittgenstein's philosophical content as a social and public work. The diaries convey the emotional stimulus to yearn for prayer and moral eternity, but highlighting the miserable side of Wittgenstein's fragmentary life.

5

Fact or fiction

Nmg ufnq yfg ufnq xwnkfvivw rh dszg rh dmigsb mu
zworizgrmn & ozqvh pruv wmigh szernt yvvn prevw.
(Not funk but funk conquered what is worthy of admiration
and makes life worth having been lived.)

(MS 117: 151, 1940)

Denkbewegungen

Wittgenstein's *Denkbewegungen* are the movements or transitions of his thoughts on the "degenerate" varieties of his ideas. These thoughts crossed Wittgenstein's brain to effectively communicate the philosophical and autobiographical genres to others and to enable him to function in society. The writing was unusual, in ordinary language or in secret quasi-language (see Chapter 1). Sometimes Wittgenstein was considered a researching scholar, scientific mathematician, or critical reader; often, he acted as an aesthetic poet in a metaphoric extension of the philosophy of literature; at times, he was a neurotic patient, needing clinical or psychological treatment to cope with his fears and anxieties (Gray 1969).

The *Denkbewegungen* are the palimpsest of many layers of dreams or memories of the "historical" symptoms of war and peace. With time and place, these symptoms are supposed to lessen the pain and guilt. Since Wittgenstein's philosophy and diary were written over a period of many years, the fictional pages were often intermingled with nonfiction in a self-conscious metafiction (Gray 1975: 59–65, 191–194, 205–210; see Waugh 1984). Reading the emotional and social processes of Wittgenstein's thoughts gives readers the bizarre combination of concrete and literary genres pressed into one whole continuum. The *Denkbewegungen* is not a history of myths or legends. The episodes were remythologized into the self-image of Wittgenstein's real facts of life, into his reconstruction of his bold experiments to play the game of free speech acts written in daily language.

Fiction means the communication of concrete art in creative or artistic literature, while nonfiction contains an abstract argument, including formal reasoning, inferring, assuming, and concluding, as in philosophy (Rundle 1993). After the old Habsburg Empire vanished, the new trend was for an aggressive style of writing scraps of memory

(Perloff 2016). At the expense of facts and fancy, the territories of fiction and nonfiction can be exchanged for the neologism of metafiction, a blend of literary narrative used in the scraps of memory of both fictional reality and nonfictional irreality. If Wittgenstein's philosophy can be presented as a "parody" of pseudo-literature and factual events, his concept of:

> "Family resemblances" is seen to be meaningful ultimately because the notion of family has been established, so it is that pseudo-history depends on the understanding of history, and non-fiction novel depends on an understanding of novel. (Gray 1975: 204–205; see Glock 1996: 115–120, 120–124)

With Wittgenstein's variety of family connections in writing, the new "pseudo-novelistic" construction was more playful than truthful, because it included the "opposition" of diary entries and philosophical pages. In this mixture of feeling and logic, the demonstrative meaning of the *Denkbewegungen* suggested with the diary entries the troubled ambiguity of Wittgenstein's own family connections forming a literary meta-family of his private and public games.

For Wittgenstein, the double allegiance to the open implications of the subjective symptoms—the inner signs (*Innenwelt*) attached to his emotional world—functioned as objective symptoms, but he wanted to heal his defects in the outer signs of his work and lectures to work in his environment (*Umwelt).*[1] There is no excess on one side or the other. In the integration of matter and form, Wittgenstein was cast in the scientific role as his own "physician" (Barthes 1972: 38; see Sebeok 1976: 124) to heal the traumas, wound, or injury (PI: 255). The natural link between the contrastive pair of *subjective* roles was inspired, and even activated, by the *objective* reality of the outer world trying to piece together the alternative narrative of Wittgenstein's illness with his metafiction (Sebeok [1994] 2001: 33–34, 76, 100–101, 144–145; Glock 1996: 174–179).

Wittgenstein liked to air his personal grievances and to openly explore the philosophical beliefs and desires of his own "pain" with his readers, as can be seen in many of his writings. The environmental *Umwelt* goes beyond the evidence of him as a helpless refugee escaping from political danger to the textual metaphors that provided him with a remedy to work psychologically on healing his own mind. He textualized the multiple textures of his life philosophy in his work, and he recontextualized the secrecy of his private situation by adding the coded script in his diary. The final outcome was the cryptotexts written in his "secret" diary, which puzzled the minds of his readers.

The philosophical thought-movements (*Denkbewegungen)* were not composed in book-length volumes but in the sketches of Wittgenstein's "album," in which his philosophical paragraphs were sporadically parted by his diary entries (PI: 3e). While Wittgenstein's philosophy contained his formal perspective on the correct use of language, his diary provided the less formal facts about his personal "forms of life." The rearrangements of Wittgenstein's fiction and nonfiction notebooks document the adventurous quality of the "album" of his ideas and thoughts. Wittgenstein's ideas and thoughts can be regarded as a laboratory experiment, in which his passages of certainty were constantly rewritten in the abstract forms of cognitive meaning, while his intermittent diary entries gave the concrete facts of his private uncertainty. His diary paragraphs were sometimes written in plaintext but mainly rewritten in secret code. The code aroused the reader's thoughts, shifting them from being an outsider, through the self-awareness of the inner activity of learning the code, to an insider of Wittgenstein's works. In conclusion, the abstract and concrete forms of Wittgenstein's different meanings proposed a *va-et-vient* alternative to fiction and nonfiction. The literary alternative of Wittgenstein's *Denkbewegungen* was to deny the logical necessity of two choices to tell the story in definite and indefinite signs with open borders and outlines.

For example, the philosophical progress of Wittgenstein's language of "pain" (*Schmerz*), started in the early lectures of *The Blue and Brown Books* (BBB: 73, 1933–1934), become one of his "favorite" topics. The series of symptoms about his sensation and reactions to the symptom of "pain" was first pronounced in his own speech as an iconic patient. To seek out the indexical signs of pain, Wittgenstein cried out for an explanation of the iconic messages in the sensational forms of "thinking, hoping, wishing, fearing, and so forth" (Rundle 1993: 46; see 57, 75). The speech of the patient represented Wittgenstein's own jargon to express the emotional sensation of his personal pain, but it seemed that Wittgenstein's jargon was different from the expression of the language-game of "pain" used by other speakers. The psychosomatic "pain" was a lonely cry of one patient, remaining a shadow world for others in the environment.

The private speech nuanced the ambiguity of the patient's existence from the iconic "self" into indexical "selves." Wittgenstein seemed to agree with the duality of Peirce's "reagent" signs to others:

> A scream of help that is not only intended to force the mind the knowledge that help is wanted, but also the will to accord it. It is, therefore, a reagent used rhetorically. Just as a designation can denote nothing unless the interpreting mind is already acquainted with the thing it denotes, so a reagent can indicate nothing unless the mind is already acquainted with its connection with the phenomenon it indicates. (CP: 8.368 fn. 23; see Sebeok [1994] 2001: 86)

Wittgenstein meant that his "*descriptions*" of "pain" were merely "instruments for particular uses" (MS 124: 33, 1941; PI: 291, 1944).[2] They were taken from his own experience but they were unable to reach the thoughts of the community around him. The screams for help were his individual signs, but the collective explanations of "pain" were unable to give the "slightest guidance" (*geringsten Führung*) (MS 124: 256, 1944 [unmentioned in PI]). The general therapy of what "pain" could eventually *stand for* in public (Sebeok [1994] 2001: 71, 78–79) was embodied in the scream of "pain." The fine line between fiction and fantasy explained how Wittgenstein's "pain" was thematically actualized. But he replaced the individual habit of "pain" to carry it further indexically into the public setting, as Peirce pointed out. The indexical signal of the symptoms would be the first groundwork of the logical and unlimited "grammar" of Wittgenstein's language-games.

A case in point of Wittgenstein's "pain" is the metaphorical story of the "beetle" (*Käfer*), which is trapped in a jar (Gorlée forthcoming a). The message-in-a-bottle tale concerned Wittgenstein's language of pain and told the sad story of an insect left alone without an escape from the enclosed situation. As Wittgenstein wrote in the *Philosophical Investigations*:

> Let's assume that everyone had a box with something in it which we will call a "beetle." No one can ever look into anyone's else's box, and everyone says he knows what a beetle is just by looking at *his* beetle.—It would then be quite possible for everyone to have something different in his box. One might even imagine such a thing constantly changing.—But what if the word "beetle" used by those people had a use nonetheless?—If so, it would not be as the name of a thing. The thing in the box doesn't belong to the language-game at all; not even as a *something*: for the box might even be empty.—No, this thing in the box can be annulled; it cancels itself out, whatever it is. (PI: 293; translation by Anscombe, Hacker, and Schulte modified, discussed in Gorlée forthcoming a; MS 124: 256–257, 1941–1944)[3]

Wittgenstein was a biological magician when he produced the beetle story from his hat. He was no entomologist, so he transported his attention away from reality into the mythical irreality of the animal setting, in which the insect was metaphorized into the fairytale of the beetle (Gorlée 2015a: 53–54).

The beetle is a physical creature with biting mouth parts and, standing out from the insect's head, two tufted antennae. The beetle has six walking legs and hard horny forewings to cover its membraneous flight wings. The shaggy eyebrows scared human observers and the beetle is often regarded as a horrid, filthy insect. But in folk belief and tales, it is regarded as a supernatural spirit. The beetle can, as a magical amulet, protect a human person against a fever or headache to bring good luck (Leach and Fried [1972] 1984: 131). The physical "thing" of the beetle has the possibility of being both a mythical and magical figure.

The image of the beetle is a bold experiment of metafiction which Wittgenstein used as a narrative game in his philosophy. The "beetle" with the lack of meaning and emphasis of quotation marks can convey the private "thing" but trapped in the creative stasis of the invariation of Darwin's derivative meaning of evolution. The present-day beetle is often no longer observed as the paleontological treasure of the old fossil, but the bug in amber is seen as the art object or as a cameo manufactured by a jeweler. The insect encased in the handmade rounded stone has become a fashionable jewel with the rise in the appeal of precious "natural" gemstones. But the "natural" ingredient of the insect with the gas bubbles of the crystals enclosed the "artificial" objects of bracelets and brooches. The "artificial" jewelry pieces are merely enjoyed as decorative amusements, in complete ignorance of the insects involved.

Wittgenstein extended the meaning of the insect to protagonize the fairytale of the beetle for all readers. He provoked the impossible story away from the private non-communication of the cry for help. Wittgenstein prophesied of strange "things" to come in the real communication of half-"natural" and half-"artificial" language-games to be shared equally by all language speakers. It seems that the hybrid of positive and negative qualities of the insect can be viewed as a psychological niche to emotionalize the human emotions of fear, hope, and strength. The merging of human symptoms can be considered as synonymous with the semiotic signs of firstness, secondness, and thirdness *standing for* fears and anxieties. Wittgenstein's sensation upgraded the story of himself as a patient with mental disorders into his decision to heal his symptoms.

The secret symptoms of the beetle scene are enclosed in the hidden message of the box to keep the captured insects alive, called the "killing jar" by entomologists. The glass jar was hermetically sealed and forbidden to be opened. But when opened, the evils flew out, spreading as an agonizing "black box" over humankind. The beetle's box buried the demonic spirits, like Pandora's box, filling the human spectators with suffering and disease, lies and theft, and even criminal behavior. When the cover of Pandora's box lifted itself and the wordplay of Wittgenstein's "pains" scrambled out, he suffered and screamed for help. The afterlife of the beetle's troubles showed that the magical word was a logical form of argument to get beyond the particular case of the message-in-a-bottle to become the paradigm of broadening its wings to learn about the world (Donnellan [1967] 1972): 41–42).

The pain description was confined to the private speech of Wittgenstein's own sensations. As happens to personal words, the word "pain" was a shibboleth. The mispronounced idea of a public language-act let other speakers know his unhealthy situation (Posner 1980: 98). But if the personal expression of "pain" can grow from the literal meaning from one speaker further into the public expression of Wittgenstein's language-game, it will in scientific research express the collective behavior of "pain" to refer to all language-games. The inability of non-communication could perhaps over time transform into the ability to speak with the rules of the language-game of other humans (see Cherry [1957] 1966). This purely logical goal was Wittgenstein's analysis of the mystery story, which he needed to use to test his life and prove himself to be a true philosopher.

The connections between personal speech and public language-games are shaken about in a triangle: firstly, variability (the literal meaning with its content elements exchanged for new meaning with new content elements), secondly, cancellability (the literal meaning supplemented with positive additions to annul the negative suggestions), and thirdly, non-detachability (instead of the literal meaning, another formulation is chosen) (Posner 1980: 99–100). Wittgenstein furnished the individual meaning of human "pain" several times as a word clue, but as a method he foregrounded the "grammatical" speaking of the rhetorical language-game. In the 1980s, Wittgenstein revealed his "modern" method, which involved the movement of the verbal speech-act into the theory of textuality, speech coherence, and interpretability (Gray 1977).

In the composition of Wittgenstein's speech-act, his private monologues had been changed into lectures for a number of interlocutors (probably students). He also defined the experiment of the solitary "pain" in the "grammatical" experience of interactive speech-communication to other readers, telling them about the story of painful behavior in what Bateson named the multilogue ([1972] 1985; discussed in following chapters). In Wittgenstein's discourse analysis, the nonfiction of philosophy is used to cancel the fictional speech of the autobiographical diary. To illustrate the transition from abstract to concrete, in the narrative of the beetle-in-the-box Wittgenstein used ordinary plaintext, without touching the secret script for eventual privacy of the information (PI: 293; discussed in Gorlée forthcoming a).

The ordinary speech-act describes the close analysis of Wittgenstein's "fairytale" of the insects. The integration of the beetle-text inside the pages of the *Philosophical Investigations* is the mirror image of Wittgenstein's philosophical experiment, in which the physical texture of processing the verbal text *and* verbal and non-verbal contexts is further "philosophized" into the speech-act story taken from history, literature, and his own life. The connectedness of Wittgenstein's private sense points to the *Denkbewegungen* embedded from iconicity in the web of indexical connections. In the same way, the cohesion and coherence of text and contexts or subtexts points to the meaning of his lectures or his diary. The original text presented the unfinished work, but it needed close contextuality to be correctly interpreted in a wider sense (Schulte 1990: 146–148). Intertextuality or contextuality is the practical experience of understanding the first text of the beetle-in-the-box. Thus the text must be transformed not by the author but by the reader into the "painful" influx of unexpected inter- and contexts to create a web of stories about the beetle. Sebeok wrote that "A *text* constitutes, in effect, a specific 'weaving together' of signs in order to communicate something," so that "the signs that go into the make-up of texts belong to specific *codes*" (Sebeok [1994] 2001: 7; see Sebeok 1985a).

Textuality is defined as the ordered system of linguistic codes to rule a work in progress. But when Wittgenstein's private language is held together by his use of cryptography, as he did at many moments in his diary, the combination is turned adrift by mixing private and public codes. Sebeok looked for the comprehension of the semiotic code in textuality:

> Clearly, a text bears no meaning unless the receiver of the text knows the *code(s)* from which it was constructed and unless the text refers to, occurs in or entails some specific *context*. The *context* is the environment—physical, psychological, and social—in which a sign or text is used or occurs. ([1994] 2001: 8)

Wittgenstein's history of textuality is ruled by codes in contextuality and intertextuality. As an illustration, the story of Wittgenstein's beetle was inspired by the secondary passages of Poe's "The Gold Bug" or Kafka's *Metamorphosis*, but may also be understood as a renewed version of the Old Testament book of prophet Joel. The plague of noxious locusts (replaced by Wittgenstein's beetles) had destroyed the country of Egypt, the grass, corn, and the trees were fully devastated. The invasion of the hostile locusts signified that the day of the Lord affected not only Egyptians but the fugitive Israelites, who were living in Egypt. Prophet Joel summoned up arguments to save the lives of the Jewish immigrants. In the days of darkness, Jewish cries to God were the apocalyptic signs of their repentance, which would with God's grace spare the lives of the true believers (Joel 1:2). The occurrence of the locust plague compelled the Egyptians to let go of the cheap supply of forced foreign workers.

The chronologically arranged "open" signs of the text can spin out into a web-like contextuality with a closed variety of secondary texts to reconstruct Wittgenstein's text with revised and reconceptualized threads of history. These separate threads of text and context give the inter- or subtextuality (Sebeok 1985a) the free play of sameness and "difference" as is usual in works of art and the humanities (Derrida

1973: 132). To reimagine the linguistic culture of Wittgenstein's textuality, his texts were diversified in the signification of three varieties of "differences" to guide the readers along the linguistic and cultural way of understanding the philosophy and diary medium of his *Denkbewegungen*. As argued by Moyal-Sharrock (2007), beyond the primary text of philosophy there is the combination of contexts written in common text—see Wittgenstein's lectures, notes, typescripts, dictations, revisions, reviews, correspondence, and other shorter writings—and the subtexts of the diary written in code. The possible "differences" relate to the role of the receivers, who are not thought of as passive persons reading other's works but must convey active interpretants to give meaning to Wittgenstein's works.

The private thoughts of sub- and intertextuality were Wittgenstein's usual habit of writing energetic and emotional interpretant-signs. Transliterated into the secret code of his private text, the emotional habit was the open texture to speak about his personal life, in which he spoke to himself. The monologue of private remarks was secretly transformed into the hidden energy of "outside" readers. Manifested for quasi-public communication, the quasi-dialogue struggled with Wittgenstein's mental products of writing for others. With good intentions, his works were intended as an educational way to learn the code. Yet to generate the troubled ambiguity into an energetic interpretant (and even approaching something like a final interpretant), the coded habit must be confronted and juxtaposed with the continuance of habit to refine it into the re-habit, meaning the habituality of various contexts and subtexts. Wittgenstein redefined the same thought experiment into alternative ideas with radical meanings to receive at a later date the final meaning not from himself, but from readers, students, and so forth (Gorlée 2016b: 24–31).

Wittgenstein's habit of textuality and the re-habituality of contextuality and intertextuality is splendidly exemplified in his philosophical story of the beetle-in-the-box, to give the grammar of this story an attractive surface meaning, but it requires that readers of the coded diary are good or bad readers. For uncertain readers, the deep meaning of coded and uncoded sentences remained a mystery, giving them the vague idea of the randomness of the insect story. For interested readers, however, the secrecy of the code led to the breakthrough of how to arrange their minds differently into what was intended by Wittgenstein as the communicative way to learn the code and understand his whole work including the underlying background (Glock 1996: 86–92).

Wittgenstein's beetle story was repeated in the same year in the next notebook (MS 129: 59, 1944). As usual, the revision (habituality) gave the same words and sentences, but could possibly be rearranged to suit different contexts relating the same story but with different endings (Segre 1986). Wittgenstein jumped from the secrecy of the voyeuristic code of the beetle-in-the-box to the systematic set of the "grammatical" re-habits of his language-games. The paragraphs of co-text in context and subtext remain variants of each other, but although MS 124 was the spiritual and anthropological text—almost a fairytale—it seemed that MS 129 turned into the pragmatic and social context. At the end of MS 129, Wittgenstein did not compose the conclusion (habituescence or final interpretant), but he practiced the sense of the rule or instruction to use the experiment with additional readers. The difference between the two manuscripts lies in the reformulation of Wittgenstein's idealism of MS 124 which is reduced to the realism of MS 129; in this process of thought, the contextual history has changed from certainty into the feeling of uncertainty. The repetitions of the beetle story (habituality) demonstrate that the contexts were more or less synonymous messages, but were carrying different interchangeable names of words with different meanings. With this method of examples and quasi-explanations, the conclusion is that Wittgenstein's thought process went through the motions of impossible exercises of quasi-communication to catch the meaning.

Wittgenstein was a practitioner of the grammatical tension of words and sentences, but he was certainly opposed to writing the final moral of the story. Instead of attempting to write something like the tentative conclusion, he gave in the notebook of MS 129 the practical rule (*Regel*) of the syntactic and semantic experiment. In the beetle experiment, he hoped to find the social rule of generality (*Allgemeinheit*) from the biodiversity of the rules to introduce as the solution the remedy of the language-games, but he was aware that this puzzle would mean uncertainty for the readers. In Wittgenstein's words,

> If one would construct the grammar of the expression of feeling by the model of—"word and object," the subject is taken out of the equation as irrelevant. And what kind of sentence is "I just know my own case …" anyway? An experiential proposition?—No.—A grammatical one? (MS 129: 60, 1944, my translation)[4]

Could Wittgenstein explain in actual practice the technical or mathematical perspective of Saussure's structural linguistics? (Saussure [1959] 1966). Could Saussure's formal directions explain the real tension between the "grammatical" rules and the language-games? Wittgenstein seemed to feel differently about the elastic body of symbol and referent. He must have had serious doubts about the possible truth of language when he acquired Saussure's intellectual system of rules (Gorlée forthcoming b). For Wittgenstein, human pain plays the game of the spontaneous cry of himself responding to others for help; but this method is not a final and definitive rule, but comes from the heart and pulse of Peirce's emotional and energetic interpretants. Wittgenstein wrote that:

> I'm also thinking: Everyone says he only knows what pain is from his own pain. Not that people actually say that or are even prepared to say that. But <u>if</u> everyone would say so, well that could be like a cry of some sorts. (MS 129: 60, 1944, my translation)[5]

Wittgenstein's pain was overcoming the gnawing fear of war. The emotional feeling of discomfort crossed his path several times and made him desperately search for comfort to heal the eternal pain. Asking him personal questions was, even for his friends, an impossible activity. Wittgenstein was a closed individual who did not partake in the lives of others (see the memory of Fania Pascal in Rhees 1984: 22). The darkness and terror of Hitler's totalitarian regime (Snyder 2015) left Wittgenstein as a refugee with Jewish origins exiled from Austria in England: he saw how his mental habits were regarded by others as those manners of an émigré following his station in life from his occupied homeland.

Overall, Wittgenstein felt a prisoner in England and tried as hard as he could to "forget" the personal evocative of nostalgia. Yet the "pain" sensations were also his own arduous struggle, since he as a sick patient had to deal philosophically and medically with his situation. The direct emotion of "pain" was not the metaphor or analogy of illness, he seriously reflected the tangible and total truth to survive alone, as a strange insider, in another country. Instead of feeling merely like a sick patient, Wittgenstein returned to being a whole man indulging in the good habit of secret prayer or confession to heal himself. In this case, the religious belief was Wittgenstein's habitual practice of writing his personal diary to make himself the agent of self-therapy in his emotional and energetic interpretants.

In dangerous times, Wittgenstein was aware that "pain" can sometimes be moved out of a private habit to show a crisis that demands action. The pain habit can be transformed through Peirce's rest and tranquility into the habituality of the dynamic motion of learning the habit of a social code. Wittgenstein's exclamatory interjections had used the human communication of his cry of "pain" to address the other members of the human family signaling the potential danger to all. The reactive sign of the alarm call signified that the language-act to other individuals of the tribe can enable the security of each person (or animal, including the unhappy story of the beetle) to move around safely through their natural habitat, without risk of peril and danger (Gorlée 2015b: 40 and throughout). The discomfort of Wittgenstein's private sensation of "pain" was reaching the comfort of the language-games to help him as a tribe member to get better.

Wittgenstein's sadness regarding his life changed for the better during his summer visits to Swansea, where holidays were turned into the busy action of writing. Wittgenstein felt immediately better, as his "confusions" of words and sentences could be "taken out of language to send it for cleaning—& then you can put it back into circulation" (MS 117: 156, 1940; CV 1998: 44e; Gorlée 2012: 61).[6] It seemed that strange material should be abandoned, rejected, and removed. But after going through the "dry-cleaning" process, language and quasi-language seemed to be a better instrument for communicating good instead of bad ideas.

After doing hospital work as a war volunteer in London and Newcastle, Wittgenstein was called back to Cambridge to lecture. Instead, he wanted desperately to finish the text of the *Philosophical Investigations* and needed some time to work on his own to complete it. Wittgenstein's leave of absence from his duties as professor brought him on a long visit to the seaside city of Swansea. He enjoyed his working stay in Wales and found the people of Swansea more natural and congenial than the stiffness of Cambridge's academic society. In the summer of 1944, while staying in Swansea, the direction of his philosophical writing changed permanently (Monk 1990: 458–470). The positive "dry-cleaning" out of the secret code must have been one of the reasons why he wrote the story of the beetle-text in ordinary plaintext, separating the cultural transfer from the coded language.

In 1944 Wittgenstein shifted the methodology of his later works. Shaken with the cold emotions of the battles of the Allied invasion against Nazi Germany, Wittgenstein's thought-transference of his mind (*Denkbewegungen*) abandoned the "old" certainty of mathematical philosophy to focus on the uncertainty of the "new" branch of psychological philosophy. This shift divided Wittgenstein's work of the *Philosophical Investigations* into old and new parts. In the revised edition (PI [1953] 2009), after the mathematical text (PI: 1–693) there is the "Philosophy of Psychology," consisting of a long "Fragment" including a number of psychological manuscripts (PI: 1–372). In Wittgenstein's approach to the emerging discipline of psychology, the hypothetical description of the beetle-in-the-box was no more than a hypothesis. For this reason, the beetle story was not repeated again in Wittgenstein's psychological narrative—*neither* in plaintext *nor* in coded text.

Within the new notion of psychology, Wittgenstein did not follow the "fashion" of psychoanalysis. He stayed permanently ambiguous about Freud's instinctive search for the sexual meaning of his patients to discover the unconscious dreams, anxiety, repression, and secret guilt, the central concepts of Freud's theory (Hall 1954: 54–57). Instead of Freud's unconscious pathology, Wittgenstein's "therapeutic positivism" analyzed Freud not as a psychiatrist but as a scientific or cultural scholar. The feelings of pain or pleasure were the pragmatic use of the conscious minds of all speakers. In this perspective, Wittgenstein was treated as a patient. He stressed the potential danger of the inner and outer world, transforming his painful experiences into a nonpathological and unconscious habit of action. Doing something with real feeling or genuine activity in the world kept him off of the psychoanalyst's couch. Wittgenstein's psychic energy followed the rational-emotive therapy of Peirce's pragmatism, in the reformulation of William James's psychological works—*Principles of Psychology* ([1890] 1950) and *Pragmatics: A New Name for Some Old Ways of Thinking* ([1907] 1981) as well as *The Varieties of Religious Behavior: A Study in Human Nature* ([1902] 1982) (Mounce 1997: 70–125). James took Peirce's practical will to take the voluntary actions of religious faith to remedy "abnormal" patients. The conscious habits of doubt and guilt continued in Peirce's index as habituality, embedded in the routine speech forms of habituescence to transform the patient's unconscious behavior into conventional or "normal" behavior (White [1955] 1983: 135–173; Gorlée 2016b: 24–31).

In Wittgenstein's era, the political opposition to the tyranny of Nazism spread their propaganda in the circulation of literary parodies. Arguing against the rise of Hitler's ethnic clichés regarding man as an animal (Snyder 2015), Franz Kafka's novel *Die Verwandlung* (*Metamorphosis* [1916] 1992) bewildered readers' minds for a long time. Wittgenstein never met Kafka (1894–1924), who lived in the Bohemian capital of Prague, but he recognized Kafka as himself, the German-speaking author with Jewish origins. He must have read Kafka's short story *Die Verwandlung*, but his perspective was against the skepticism of the conventional Habsburg Empire to begin afresh with radical answers to existential questions. In an anarchy of style, Kafka's surrealist story explored the hallucinatory process of the human condition involved in the metamorphosis from man to animal. The protagonist Georg Samsa, a traveling salesman, changed overnight into a giant beetle. First Kafka introspectively imagined the real insect with the febrile denomination of a "gigantic insect" (*ungeheures Ungeziefer*) (9). But the metamorphosis into a monster, with the bestial attributes of a segmented body, mobile structures, and antennae on its head, was a story about the dark emotions of an uncommon man who becomes an insect.

Kafka's fantastic "reproduction" from a man to a beetle tried to make the most of the strange bodily forms and shapes to survive. The negative "uncertainty" (*Ungewissheit*) and "uncomfortableness" (*Unwohlsein*) was Samsa's discomfort (*Unhöflichkeit)* to deal as a human with the unfamiliar body of an animal. The discomfort was miraculously transformed by Kafka into the good fortune of doing something (positive action) to accustom oneself to an animal body. The anatomy and physiology of the insect seem to overcome the metamorphosis of the body without the help of the façade of human "comforts" (*Wohlbehagen*), adopted for life and work. Paradoxically, Wittgenstein's beetle story shifted the positive sense into a negative one, settling into the uncomfortable world of the animal, far away from the world of the human body, but with the hope to speak "real" language playing through the uncertainties of animal self-identity.

Exploring the delusions of body and mind in the total loss of his self was expressed by Wittgenstein, especially after he ended his friendship with Marguérite and remained alone. In the same period Wittgenstein enjoyed, first in Austria, then in Cambridge, academic discussions with the mathematician Frank Ramsey, during the period when Wittgenstein wrote *Philosophical Remarks*. Sharing intense communications with Ramsey, Wittgenstein ended his formal analysis of the *Tractatus* to start a philosophy of the twentieth century using the new style of *Denkbewegungen* (Monk 1990: 309–327; Monk 2016; Klagge and Nordmann 2003: 3–256). The exchange from one style to the next meant that in Wittgenstein's later works the deception and self-deception of his real identity caused the disorder of truth and reality. Wittgenstein brought therapeutic insights to philosophy, but the effects were too vague to order the irreality of life into the philosophical sense of certainty (Hardwick 1971: 15–32).

The diary questioned and self-questioned the falseness of Wittgenstein's own *Gestalt*, which represented the illusion of other "mimetic" effects of what happened in the world. Wittgenstein wrote that:

> If to protect it against air raids a canon is painted to look like trees or stones from above so that its real contours are unrecognisable and have been replaced by false ones, how difficult would it be to appraise this thing. One could well imagine someone saying: "all of these are false contours so this thing has no *Gestalt* at all." And still, it has a real *Gestalt* but cannot be appraised with the usual means. (MS 183: 112–113, 1931)[7]

The delusions of body and spirit twisted not only Kafka but also Wittgenstein into telling the beetle stories. These fictional games embraced not merely the physical, biological, and even psychological evolution of insects, but played the cultural evolution to speak language as a comfortable tool in primitive language. Man's association of expressing himself in animal language reprocessed confusions of animal speech into human language, like the uncertain way of the emotional, dynamic, and formalized interpretant (Sebeok 1984a: 16). The technical word was Wittgenstein's human language-game.

Charles Darwin's *On the Origin of Species* ([1858] 1958) centered the cultural *mimesis* away from the ordinary social convention of animals and plants into the derivative extensions of metamorphic survivals. Darwin did not speak about natural men, but mainly about the life and survival of animals. The insects, who live in difficult circumstances and try to survive, "often resemble for the sake of protection various objects, such as green or decayed leaves, dead twigs, bits of lichen, flowers, spines, excrements of birds, and living insects"; but although the "resemblance is often wonderfully close," the metempsychosis of human souls into malignant animals was "not confined to colour, but extends to form, and even to the manner in which the insects hold themselves" (206). In Darwin's evolution, the generality of the survival of animals and plants mattered more than the formalized specimen of the culture of one human individual. Wittgenstein's quasi-language with the secret code was perhaps the reconstruction of animal communication (Sebeok 1972: 34–83) specialized by Sebeok as "zoosemiotic language" (1985b).

In 1931, Wittgenstein returned to the memory of his sister Gretle (Margarethe Stoneborough, née Wittgenstein). She sent a message to her brother Ludwig during his military service in the First World War. Gretle had read the *Essays* (1910) of Ralph Waldo Emerson, the forerunner of transcendentalism and lover of nature. She was impressed by Emerson's conversation with his friend, the biologist Henry Thoreau, author of *Walden* (Gorlée 2015c: 139–171). The reason was that Thoreau wanted to abandon his city life in Concord, Massachusetts, and live outside, in the wilderness of the North American nature. He built a wooden hut and a vegetable garden to live alone in tranquility and work in isolation. Gretle compared Thoreau's desire for isolation and seclusion to that of her brother, then a young soldier, foreboding the paths of his future life in a fjord-side hut to survive the Arctic winters. Wittgenstein felt the natural game of mimesis in himself, when he wrote: "What a game of Nature!—What a game of Nature, when the beetle looks as a leaf, but is a real beetle & not an artificial leaf of a flower" (MS 183: 113, 1931, my translation).[8]

Wittgenstein secularized the military practice of formal logic into trying to find in the darkness the magical light. The story of the beetle sealed in a pottery jar held him enclosed in his own fly-bottle (*Fliegenglas*) of life (MS 117: 61, 92, 1937–1940; MS 118: 44v, 71r, 1937; MS 228: 105, 1937). He revisited this self-image from Poe's "The Gold Bug" and Kafka's *Metamorphosis*, when he was working at the workman's cottage of Hochreith during the summer of 1931. Plagued by insect bites, Wittgenstein avoided becoming their next target. As a contemporary prophet Joel, he exclaimed that:

> Vy ofhh wzaf, tpvrxshzo, wfixs wrv Wvxxqv, wvn Lpzumnw, fngvi wvo rxs ziyvrgv, fyvi wvn rxs nrs nrxsg hgvrrtvn drpp, vrn Prxsg wfixshxsroovin.
>
> (Through the cover, the ceiling of my work, I must now elevate myself to see the light shining through.)
>
> As the insect buzzes around me so I will be enlightened by the New Testament.
>
> (MS 183: 168, 1931, my translation)[9]

Opening the fly-bottle, the clamor in insects showed the good way out of the darkened room to see the light. He allowed the magical spirit to grasp the "geometry showing you rather the new dimension of the space" (MS 117: 60–61, 1939; see MS 118: 44v, 1937).[10] After the mention of Darwin's *mimesis* of leaf and flower, Wittgenstein's game of biological stories pointed to the "grammatical" speech-act with "non-grammatical" and "grammatical" dimensions to use language correctly (MS 118: 44v, 1937; see MS 118: 71r, 1937).

Wittgenstein's beetle experiment transformed the cultural "thing" of concealing language into quasi-language by showing the mirror image of the disguise into the "natural" behavior of language. He wrote that

> In the correctly written sentence a particle gets detached from the heart or brain and appears on paper as a sentence. I believe that my sentences are descriptions mostly of visual images that come to me. (MS 183: 114, 1931, my translation)[11]

Wittgenstein's textual vision of meeting philosophy was the exploratory or temporary structure to construct the backstage of how "things" can behave in their natural environment (*Umwelt*). The description of Wittgenstein's texts attempted to catch the reasonable context of these "things," but the play of contextual and subtextual news brought many modalities of meaning to the surface. This secondary information was useful, since it was compared to the texts, repeated correctly (*Umarbeitung*), and revised or was, if incorrectly used, lost and forgotten.

Wittgenstein remarked in his 1933 lecture that "we learn in *certain* contexts" (BBB: 9). We learn from facts giving shared "forms of life," but we must take care of judging the half-truth of metaphorical stories. Taking contexts as inspiration of the text, the puzzle of the text has disparate meanings. Cavell warned that we "learn words in certain contexts and after a while we are expected to know when they are appropriately used in (= can appropriately be projected into) further contexts" (1979: 169; see 105). Textually the beetle-in-the-box turns out to influence Wittgenstein's aesthetic idea of providing new thoughts to be able to suffer his "pain," but Wittgenstein's formal logic also changed by reading Kafka's contextual story of metamorphosis. The beetle sealed in a glass jar was not only Wittgenstein's logical experiment of thought but also aroused his readers to learn the full fact of the secret code to magically survive as "philosophers." Textually and contextually, the beetle story was a literary fiction to see the mythical light of linguistic wisdom. The beetle story was Wittgenstein's own speech-act, but also it attempted to communicate the story to possible readers.

Fictional games

In later years, Wittgenstein's diary entries mingled together coded text with uncoded text (plaintext). The private language tory of the beetles was written in plaintext. It seems that Wittgenstein's diary was transformed from the intertext of philosophy to the alternative subtext of the coded diary. Textually and intertextually, the main philosophical genre was the technical discourse of the public text, while the subtext of the diary transcribed the private text into the secrecy of the Wittgensteinian code. In the transcript, Wittgenstein reproduced and reimagined the "facts of life" into something like conversational "forms of life." The secret code reflected Wittgenstein's psychological temper for dealing intertextually (that is, contextually and subtextually) with the pensive, playful, or angry moods of his reflexive monologue to form an educational "dialogue" with readers (Lemberger 2015). As argued, the readers were expected to receive their silent or written contexts and give their interpretants of the original text. The interaction between the text and the subtext signified the changes of Wittgenstein's diary and code to courageously face the serious problems of communicating with the trick of using his "fictional games" in his philosophical work.

While staying in Swansea in 1944 and during the summer holidays of 1945 to 1947, Wittgenstein felt relatively happy in his new environment. Thus he wrote notebook after notebook in common text without feeling the need to transcribe paragraphs into secret code. In the notebook of MS 127, where he wrote *Mathematik und Logik*, he shaped the concept of "following a rule." Firstly, he remarked that the habit of learning public rules had the expectation that they be followed blindly; he meant that in the case of teaching arithmetic to school children, the teacher speaks alone. Secondly, he argued that the examples were not mechanical but seemed to follow the public rules of his own codes. The readers (students, observers, interpreters) are not behind the scenes but take part in the scenery to follow Wittgenstein's new rules to understand the examples from mathematical philosophy. But the truth of the logical work depends on the lack of rules. In Wittgenstein's words, the uncertainty created an irrational and non-logical code system, exchanging the psychological truth for the magical spell of untruth. This was certainly the case with Wittgenstein's "family" of fictional games, situated halfway between private and public speech.

Wittgenstein interrupted the plaintext of philosophy with the private subtext in code: "Wrv Prvyv szg hmaf hztvn advr Gvolvizgfivn: vnvn Srgavtizw vr nvn Dziovtizm" (Love has two temperatures, as it were; one is the heat temperature and the second is the body temperature) (MS 127: 120, 1944, my translation).[12] Philosopher Wittgenstein subscribed to the physical truth of philosophy but avoided the specter of failure in the abyss of untruth of the surrounding world. Turning back to common text, Wittgenstein bitterly wrote in the next sentence: "Can I please make an observation" (MS 127: 127, 1944).[13] He wanted to imagine his own psychological situation here, but—alas!—the private rule did not fit into the philosophical text. In the next sentence, Wittgenstein fitted carefully the philosophical pages "normally" with the mathematical formulas of logic. He must have realized at this moment that the one entry in code was a departure from the norm, an unhappy exit from his own rule. Since the personal message was unrelated to the philosophical text, the conclusion was that Wittgenstein abandoned making private remarks altogether. The 1944 notebooks of MS 179 and MS 180a were totally composed in plaintext, without secret script. After ending *Mathematik und Logik*, Wittgenstein had begun to get ahead with the reworked version of the final arrangement of his main work, the *Philosophical Investigations*.

The political situation of the period 1944–1945 changed the face of the Western world. After the Allied invasion of Normandy, American troops in April 1945 entered the Dachau concentration camp to free the Jewish and other prisoners. Berlin had to be reached by Russian troops to force the surrender of German armies. Occupied Europe was liberated by the Allied forces from the Nazi regime. The newspaper headlines of the outside world meant that the war was ending with cheerful and sad news. Wittgenstein, the Jewish *emigré*, felt at first optimistic about the military impact to remake Western mankind into a new continent, but his mood was even attracted by the fervor of Russia to overthrow the tsarist regime in the communist revolution. Soon, however, he saw that the revolutionary reforms of communism merely supported the illusion of free will, but the human catastrophe contributed nothing to improve the Russian population. The material progress after the war including the invention of the atomic bomb (1945) and other explosive and radioactive weapons by the military government activated uncertainty. Wittgenstein voiced his apocalyptic view of the dangers of technological weapons as a warning for future generations. As an essentially religious man, the technological progress of new offensive weapons was for Wittgenstein the unspeakable action of finding a military solution to the political problems.

As he wrote down in his private notebooks, Wittgenstein wanted to escape from the tragic future of mankind to make a new world (Monk 1990: 489–519). His fright and despair are mirrored in MS 130 and his notebooks written in the period 1946–1947. In these years, Wittgenstein's spiritual love for God also found the physical "temperature" of being a human individual (MS 127: 120, 1944) showing how his thermometer could "measure" the passionate love he felt for his young friend Ben Richards. The good and evil barometers of despair and love indicated Wittgenstein's high blood pressure changing his personality in ways of new behavior. In those years, the biographer Monk affirmed that, "the fly had at last found its way out of the fly-bottle" (1990: 492).

The texture of MSS 130, 131, 132, 133, and 134 consists of overlapping pocket notebooks made up of public text and private remarks. Wittgenstein discussed the new branch of psychological philosophy, including a number of inner reflections to measure his own "temperature." Regarding the character and motives of communicating in text or subtext, he mentioned the division between the inauthenticity (uncertainty, untruth) of half-automatic images in what he called the "pneumatic," that is, artificial, speech and the authenticity (certainty, truth) of automatic language with meaningful gestures, proposed for "behavioral" speech (MS 130: 1–4, 1946; repeated from MS 113: 42r, 1931–1942 and MS 114: 125, 1932–1933). The self-reflections about the use of language were not self-addressed, since Wittgenstein himself was symptomatic of the intellectual class, but there to instruct people's general habit of speech.

The social background of the general speakers integrated the logical language-game, adopting a narrower view without the description of verbal language. Wittgenstein focused on the non-verbal paralanguage in simple "gestures" (iconic pre-signs) to communicate to other speakers in emotional "speech" (Nöth 1990: 247–250, 392–401). Gesture language demonstrated the "artificial" modes of human communication accompanied with the "natural" modes of conversation. The multimessage (iconic and indexical signs) was incompatible with the "grammatical" thoughts of language but means a choice of interpretation. The following pages were Wittgenstein's background notes for giving rhetorical gestures to language. Following Rilke's minimalistic art of writing, Wittgenstein used vague gestures to give emphasis to single words via punctuation, quotation marks, lines, schemes, and colors as well as adding English words within the German apostrophes. He even used the notation of visual images and mathematical graphs to provide the sense of a stylistic gesture. Surprisingly, the secret code (*Geheimschrift*) was more than an airy gesture coded in a strange cryptogram; the positive knowledge was to enable the reader to assert the mental plan to learn the code system and understand the whole language.

In Wittgenstein's examples, the double coding of the same "objects" in positive (decorative) and negative (political) sign games would depend on his state of mind. Sometimes, he wrote in secret code to highlight the strangeness to others, but at other times he wrote in ordinary plaintext (Gorlée 2015c: 10, 43, 63–64, 83, 205, 221). The gestures formed visual ideas with "natural" and "necessary" elements to decorate Wittgenstein's style (MS 130: 73–78, 1946). The readers were immediately aware of the real and metaphorical tones of the expressive gestures that accompany or replace language. In his philosophy of language, Wittgenstein frequently depicted the art of color, flavor, sound, touch, etc. to oppose the "artificial" garden flowers (*Gartenblumen*) with "natural" wild flowers (*wilde Blumen*) (MS 130: 60, 1946, my translation; see MS 132: 26, 1946) (Sebeok [1994] 2001: 19–20). The artistic and dynamic signs of Wittgenstein's rhetorical gesture-tones was described in simple iconic signs to create immediate meaning but decorated with indexical schemes, drawings, mathematical symbols, descriptions, and stories. Wittgenstein used simple sign games to construct the symbolic structure of formal logic in the language-games.

In MS 130, Wittgenstein made self-addressed inner reflections written in common text. The paragraphs described how he observed the variety of "objects" surrounding him. He argued that the perception of visual signs (*visuelle Auffassung*) enabled the inner state of seeing these outer "objects," but not how he could be acquainted immediately with the meaning of the objects. He followed what happened to the beetles after their escape: Wittgenstein had several mental images of the beetles that came from different ideas or thoughts, signifying several meanings (MS 130: 111, 1946). The different meanings come from different actions of looking and seeing the future fate of the beetles, but he also created problems to define, nuance, or strengthen the meaning of animal life. Wittgenstein requires a solution to the observations of human observation and proposed fictional games to decipher animal gestures.

For example, Wittgenstein proposed the famous cryptogram of the duck-rabbit (*Hase-Ente*). Wittgenstein's own drawing is an ambiguous picture in MS 130 (133, 1946; Monk 1990: 507–508). The readers can learn to visualize the duck-rabbit image (*Bildhase* together with the *Bildente,* MS 130: 134, 1946). After seeing the mental mechanism of the head of the duck or the rabbit, Wittgenstein changed the visual perspective to "jump from one situation to the other" (*ein Überspringen von einem Zustand in die Anderen*) (MS 130: 131, 1946, my translation). The "faults" of viewing the rabbit or the duck would come from the movements of the human eyes observing the drawing. The viewer sees more than the vision of an animal organism; his mental vision also views the human *Umwelt* of the instrument of language—what Peirce called the perception of acquiring information and misinformation from visual, auditive, and other sense-semiotic signs of animals when seen artificially from the human mind's eye (see Sebeok [1994] 2001; Gorlée 2015c: 22, 79).

During Wittgenstein's analysis of the duck-rabbit image, he discussed the polysemous sketch of the duck-rabbit by reviewing the "grammatical" possibilities of the etymology, equivalences, and lexical parallels of using language. By "seeing" the problem of the sameness of the words "duck" and "rabbit," Wittgenstein tried to express the logical method to "think" the visual image of the duck and rabbit. This was a troublesome experiment, since there was no priority between the two meanings; one of the interpretations can be substituted for the other without effecting the general meaning. The double link signified that the exchange between both visions altered the effect on readers/observers. Wittgenstein's exclamatory cry, "M! Tmgg ori Afirvwvnsvrg org ovrnvo Hxsrxqhzsp tvyvn!" (Oh! May God give that I resign to my fate peacefully) was followed in normal text by "Life is like philosophy" (MS 130: 153–154, 1946, my translation).[14]

After writing more than 150 pages of notebook MS 130, Wittgenstein confessed on August 8, 1946, that he wanted to change his style of writing. Since his temperament had changed from high to low blood pressure, Wittgenstein continued MS 130 in secret code, including words translated into English. The emotional sentence was "secretly" enclosed in the bracketed parenthesis: "[Znw ozb Tmw szev ovixb mn ob hmfp]" ([And may God have mercy on my soul]) (MS 130: 188, 1946, my translation).

It seemed that the duck-rabbit image had turned Wittgenstein's daring experiment of thought into a disappointment. The strategy of "seeing" and "thinking" must produce the practical sense of a certain rule to guide the double method of the image. Wittgenstein was unable to give a logical or final definition, instead he presented something like a go-between arrangement to show the transit (*Durchgang*) (MS 130: 280–281, 1946, my translation) of the observer to judge the animals. Wittgenstein wandered or floated in a passageway between duck and rabbit to land in one "landscape" of one or two images. He deduced either the head of the duck or that of the rabbit, but finally mediated his doubts of passing from one to the other to rethink and reorder the doubts of his impulses and skills into feeling one sensibility of the complex figure.

As Wittgenstein settled into the last lectures of the summer term of 1947 and Part II of the *Philosophical Investigations* (PI/PPF: 118 and following), the duck-rabbit figure reflected the prominent aspects of what can be patterned as the psychological *Gestalt* figure, but without giving real evidence for the patient of the complexities of the first stimulus to the second stimulus. According to semiotician Charles Morris, the stimulus is any physical energy that acts upon a reaction in an organism, but causes not necessarily a response (a reaction of a muscle or gland) (1946: 8–9). Morris quotes the famous example of the "series of responses of a hungry dog which sees a rabbit, runs after it, kills it, and so obtains food is a response-sequence" (8–9). There was for Wittgenstein (and the readers) no real proof to exercise control or auto-control (like the dog's food) to respond to the fugitive objects of duck and rabbit.

In the *Denkbewegungen*, the coded script interconnected the philosophical texture with the subtext of the diary. Although Wittgenstein, now in his late fifties, felt himself relatively well, he at the same time felt himself as a false friend. He tried to win or lose the battle with friends and colleagues. Also he attempted to be a good partner to Ben Richards, but on the academic side, he could not be an authentic philosopher in the old English traditions of the University of Cambridge. He was extremely popular with the students, but his popularity among colleagues was at a low ebb. After the death of Frank Ramsey in January 1930, Cambridge became a philosophical desert for

Wittgenstein. The friendship with Bertrand Russell had broken up, the philosophical quarrel with Moore was unhealed, and Hardy's late essay *A Mathematician's Apology* (1940) about the painting and poetry of mathematics was in Wittgenstein's code a miserable publication (MS 131: 32, 1946). These controversies frightened him and he even feared that his own "talents"—his newly found habits of inquiry and interpretation of language—were enough to be suspended from his professorate.

In 1947, as he left Swansea for Cambridge, Wittgenstein wrote the following series of private paragraphs:

> Emppvi Znthg. "Wzh Tvufsp wvi Zysznträtqvrg."
>
> (Full of fear. "My feelings of dependence.")
>
> It does not depend just on me, whether I will receive what I am asking for. This is the kind of deliberation that makes all religious parables useless. Because if seen in the usual sense, the request, reward, punishment, and other things do not entirely depend from the image, but rather from the particular situation presented to us. That is why a fixed game is no game. (The mirror, on the face of which the "mirror image" is painted.)
>
> Hrnw zppv Pvfgv timhhv Ovnhxsvn? Nvrn.—Nfi, drv qznnhg wf wznnsmuuvn, vrn timhhvi Ovnhxs af hvrn! Dzifo hmpp ori vgdzh afgrp dviwvn, dzd wvrnvn Nzxsyzin nrxsg af gvrp driw? Dmufi?!—Dvnn vh nrxsg wvi Dfnhxs rhg, ivrxs af hvrn, wvi wrxs tpzfyvn ozxsg wf hvrhg ivrxs, hm ofhh vh wmxs vrnv Yvmyzxsgfny vrnv Viuzsifnt hvrn wrv wri wzh avrtg! Fnw dvpxsv Viuzsint szhg wf (zfhhvi wvi wvi Vrgvpqvrg)? Nfi wrv vrnv Gzpvngh. Fnw ovrnv Vrnyrpwfnt, rxs hvr vrn zfhhvimiwvngprxsvi Ovnxs, rhg rz ervp zpgvi, zph ovrnv Viuzsifnt,——ovrnvh yvhmnwvivn Gzpvngh.
>
> (Are all people great human beings? No.—what hope can you have then of being a great human being? Why should something be given to you that is not given to your fellow men? To what purpose?!—If it is not your wish to be rich that makes you think you are rich, then it must be some observation some experience that shows you! And what experience do you have (except that of vanity)? Simply that you have a talent. And my imagination that I am an extraordinary human being is of course much older than my experience of my particular talent.)
>
> The feeling of being dependent. How can one feel, that one is dependent? How can one feel: "It does not depend on me." But what an odd expression of feeling that is anyway. When one, for example, had every morning problems moving, lifting one's arm, for instance, & had to wait until the paralysis would subside & this would sometimes be a long and sometimes a short time, & one could not foresee & take medication to speed it up,—would that not make us conscious of being dependent? (MS 130: 292–294, 1946, my translation; one paragraph from CV 1998: 53–54 [punctuation modified])[15]

Wittgenstein was a man in trouble. He argued, both in code and uncoded, that his talent had denied him his self-identity and led him astray; and when he was "promoted" to university professor he felt paralyzed with administrative chores. He openly declared that he was reduced to functioning in the machinery of school teachers, having to officially submit his leave of absence to the bureaucratic system. In the battle against authoritarianism, Wittgenstein was controlled by all kinds of regulations. All dons, including professors, had to take their vacations outside the semester periods to have time to write their scientific work. Wittgenstein thought that this was an unreasonable complication to function well in an academic position.

Wittgenstein shared his intellectual thought experiment to train the brain and find a solution to his problem. As a paradigm, he used the physical example of the gymnastic exercise to control the mechanical skills of elevating the arm (MS 130: 292–294, 1946). The mechanical structure of the shoulder muscles facilitates the wide excursions of the arm across the front of the body, but flattens out to the rear. But the rotatory movement of the shoulder must be stimulated through nervous stimulation. If the nervous impulse is not carried further to move the arm, the arm becomes an immobile and non-functioning part of the body. Wittgenstein's body felt helpless and enervated, especially when dealing with impersonal bureaucracies. His text and subtext in secret code speak the same prayer for spiritual help.

Wittgenstein's response was a dramatic story: on the surface, his remarks commented about the anatomy of the biological motion of the arm (Scott [1942] 1963; Kelley 1971), but on a deeper level he wanted to change his spiritual and social life to create a new style of life, in which the study of the cultural or evolutionary forces seemed to control the moving body movements in time and space (Schutz 1976; Fürlinger 2004). Wittgenstein moved away from medical kinesiology into the psychological or ecological code of human thought (Maran 2012). He explained that the "logically necessary" picture of "conceptual" truth opposed the "motivational background in the intentional life of man" turning the illogical configuration into untruth (Von Wright 1984: 148).

Consequently, we see in Wittgenstein's game of writings during that period how the reality of the logical picture as a trademark of the *Tractatus* can be regenerated into the mirror image (*Spiegelbild*) of irreality focusing on the essential uncertainty of life (Hintikka and Hintikka 1986: 120–121). In the *Denkbewegungen*, text and inter- and subtext are structurally and thematically connected to Wittgenstein's "family resemblances" (Glock 1996: 120–124). Language is no essence but is a total process of human thought controlled by the medical, biological, and cultural elements of "movements." But when the inter- or subtext is taken away from the primary text—as unfortunately happened with the edition of Wittgenstein's published works—the philosophical text becomes a useless set of "muscles," losing a major part of the whole meaning and internally disconnecting it from Wittgenstein's real identity.

MS 130 continued in MS 131 (August 11–September 9, 1946). The notebook of MS 131 was not a monologue of private remarks like MS 130, but became a conversation—almost a "dialogue"—that functioned as the bases for Wittgenstein's last lectures in Cambridge (October 11, 1946–May 16, 1947). The lectures were addressed to the students and annotated during the lectures by Peter Geach, Kanti Shah, and A. C. Jackson, who edited and published their private notes (*Wittgenstein's Lectures on*

Philosophical Psychology, 1946-1947 [PGL; Wittgenstein 1988]). The editors recall that the difficulty in following Wittgenstein's lectures:

> Arose from the fact that it was hard to see where all this rather repetitive concrete detailed talk was leading to—how the examples were inter-connected and how all this bore on the problems which one was accustomed to put oneself in abstract terms. (quoted in Monk 1990: 502)

The informal lectures included descriptions and details of fictional games to bustle the text and subtext as generating the new "landscape" action. Wittgenstein looked with detachment at the conventions of formal lectures, but the constructed practice of stories exemplified (or better, illustrated) his philosophy.

The philosophical and psychological story of MS 131 returned to religious aphorisms about God's morality (CV: 54–57; Kerr 2008). His parables give rise to the model that Wittgenstein's human nature of philosophical psychology was grounded on moral virtues and mystical vices (Sebeok [1994] 2001: 140). It was true that Wittgenstein often wrote about religion, because he needed the biblical rules to keep him straight. He wrote that:

> Ivprtrmnm dfiwv ori vrnv tvdrhhv Yvhxsvrwvrg tvyvn, wrv ori uvspg. Wvnn rxs yrpwv ori zfu zppvh szpydvth Ovnhxsprxsv rn ori vgdzh vrn, drv zfu vrnv Vrtvnhxszug wrv orxs zfharxsnvg.
>
> (Religion would give me a certain modesty that I lack. Because I imagine I have something halfway human in me, like a quality that distinguishes me.)
>
> (MS 131: 15, 1946, my translation)[16]

Regarded by himself as a proud sinner, Wittgenstein did not submit openly to God, but he was conscious that his human "temperature" answered in the negative form of pride and other religious vices. The feelings of "Wrv Znthg, wrv Advruvp, wrv Hvsnhfxsg, wrv Yvqpvoofnt" (fear, doubt, nostalgia, oppression) (MS 131: 22, 1946, my translation)[17] led him to a desperate struggle between his weak human nature and the strong rules of the theological virtues. But those virtues turned out to be the vices, and Wittgenstein saw himself as the greedy and lustful demon, recalling the Faustian pact (Goethe 1958), in which he had been sold to Mephistopheles to be the ultimate sinner. In the struggle for devilish emancipation, Wittgenstein described himself as both sinner and saint. The contextual acts of piety were included among the philosophical text-pages of MS 131 to work further on both his inner way of life and the outward effort of humanizing the world's moral situations.

Wittgenstein's text of notebook MS 131 pursued the duck-rabbit image. The "grammaticalized" version about the double (*zweideutigen, dobbelsinnigen*) meanings were embodied in the single linguistic sign of the drawing. Wittgenstein gave as an example "Go to the bank" (*Geh zur Bank*) (MS 131: 10, 1946). The double reference of the word "bank" as either the establishment for custody of money or the side of a river left him as a linguist with two words of identical spelling, lexical synonyms, but unlike in sense. Synonyms are not perfect words but quasi-words, as near synonyms or quasi-synonyms of both words can have homonyms and homophones to distinguish them as separate words. The meaning depends on the etymology, style, and choice of the language speaker, but the cultural context stays unknown in the final meaning. For the reader, the double meaning remains a jigsaw game, embracing ambiguities, conflicts, and contradictions.

Jumping from code to non-code, on August 12, 1946, and subsequent days Wittgenstein created a textual and subtextual mixture of his writing. The feelings, reactions, and thoughts express criticism from others as well as his own self-criticism. He wrote that:

> Rvwvi Qirggrqvi qirggrhrvig org hvrnvo vrtvnvn avrtg hrxs rn hvrnvi Qirggrg. Vi uzhhg nfi hm ervp, zph hvrn Rnszpg vipzfyg
>
> (Each critic criticizes self and the measure [of his knowledge] rings through in his criticism. He comprehends only so far as his content allows.)
>
> (MS 131: 26–27, 1946, my translation)[18]

The question is: what is a critical scientist? Was he an investigator of the truth, or a benefactor of humanity? Wittgenstein's question-and-answer move from coded to non-coded experiences, confronting seeing and "blindness":

> What is a scientist? Is he an investigator of the truth, or a benefactor of humanity, or an artist, or is he an artisan? Had he religion, then his difficulties would be removed.
>
> <u>Pvinv</u> zfh wvn Hxsivxqvn wvh Pvynh.
>
> (<u>Learn</u> from the horrors of life.)
>
> The man who is blind to meaning must "register" his way of life: he will not be inclined to say that the meaning already lies in the atmosphere surrounding the word heard—or similar? Can one speak of subjective & objective distinctions between experiences?—Subjective experiences are those for which I have to take the subject's word—which I must accept from the subject on trust & faith … The meaning-blind then will not say: "I have now heard the word as a verb" or "heard it as verb in me." … It is no longer the same word—if one recognizes the conjunction as if it were a verb. It is as if two meanings meet in the same word, in the same order of letters.
>
> Flhvg. Smiv nrxsg emn I.. Rxs wvnqv qztprxs wzifyvi nzxs, & wzhh rxs wrv irxsgrtv Hgvppfnf af wrvhvo Veipfhg tvdrnnvn hmppgv. Nrxsgh hxsvrng ori dzsihxsvrnprxsvi, zph wzhh vi orxs evipzhhvn szg, mwvi ro Yvtiruuv hgvsh vh af gfn, & nrxsgh, rn vrnvo Hrnnv nzgfiprxsvi. Rz rxs ufspv zfxs wzhh rxs wrvhvo Tvhxsvsvn uivrvn Pzfu pzhhvn ofhh, wzhh rxs tvgzn szyv dzhh rxs qmnngv & vh rvgag zfh ovrnvi Sznw rhg. Fnw wmxs rhg ori zn rvwvo Omitvn, dvnn rxs drvwvi qvrnvn Yirvu—urnwv <u>fnsvroprxs</u> afofgv. Rxs ufspv, zph szggv rxs vgdzh nmxs nrxsg <u>vrntvhvsvn</u>; zph ofhhv rxs vrnvn Hgznwlfnqg urnwvn emn wvo zfh ovsi Dzsisvrg af hvsvn rhg.

(Upset. Hear nothing from R.. I think about this every day and how I should gain from this loss if I just take the right attitude. Nothing seems more likely to me than that he has left me, or is at the point of doing so, and it seems the natural thing to do. Indeed, I also feel, that I must let things run their course, that I have done what I could and that it is out of my hands now. And still, every morning, when again I find no letter—I feel uneasy; I feel as I have not yet had an insight; as if I had to find a position from where I could see more truth.)

(MS 131: 33–38, 1946, my translation)[19]

Trusting in God's mercy on us all, Wittgenstein seemed to discover his real self. He repeated the parable of the blind man, who had a similar "mechanism" as the street loafer (*Strassenköter*) of the previous story. Both of them discovered their "bad" habits and interpreted their evil behavior with the troublesome "facts of life" (Gorlée 2016b: 16–17, 22–24, 27–28). Wittgenstein narrated the next language-game of his (auto)biographical story of the blind man (now in an abbreviated version). The blind man is not seen as really blind but near- or short-sighted (*kurzsichtig*). He can "see" the objects around him (the figure of the duck-rabbit), but the visual image is not "interpreted" objectively in the usual "grammatical" or "behavioral" rules, but subjectively arranged in the special "pneumatic" rules of the blind man. In the "correct" version of the *Philosophical Investigations*, Wittgenstein did not dispute the "correctness" of the blind vision, but the "picture of blindness [came] as a darkness in the mind or in the head of the blind person" (PI: 134). The moral parable of Wittgenstein as a quasi-blind man was followed by his uncertainty about the truth of his romance with Ben Richards. It was obvious that the signs of utter doubt and despair crept into the emotional side of his diary.

As the pervasive endgame of MS 131, Wittgenstein communicated in code the strong paragraphs about the political signs provoked by the atom bomb. He emphasized that the atom bomb was not an iconic story of the good progress of humanity but signified the indexical catastrophe envisioning the fate of humanity. In Wittgenstein's emotional words:

Wrv sbhgvirhxsv Znthg, wrv wrv Muuvngpprxsqvrg wvi rvgag emi wvii Zgmo-Ymoyv szg, mwvi wmxs zfhwiifxqq, rhg yvnzsv vrn Avrxsvn, wzhh srvi vrnozp driqpriqprxs vrnv svrphzov Viurnwfnt tvozxsg dmiwvn rhg. Dvnnrthgvnh ozxsg wrv Ufixsg wvn vrnwifxq, wvi, emi vrnvi driqprxs driuqhzovn, yrggvin Ovwrarn. Rxs qznn orxs wvh Tvwznqvn nrxsg vidvsivn: dvnn srvi nrxsg vgdzh Tfgvh emipztv, dfiwvn wrv Lsprhgvi qvrn Tvhxsivr znsvyvn. Zyvi ervppvrxsg rhg zfxs vrnqrnwrhxsvi Tvwznqv. Wvnn zppvh, dzh rxs ovrnvn qznnm rhg wmxs nfi, wzhh wrv Ymoyv wzh Vnwv, wrv Avihgmifnt vrrnvh tizhhpxsvn Fyvph, wvi vqvpszugvn, hvruvndzhhirtvn Drhhvnhxdzug, rn Zfhhrxsg hgvppg. Fnw wzh rhg uiuvrprxs qvrn fnzntvnvsovi Tvwznqn; zyvi dvi hztg, dzh zuf vrnv Avihgmifnt umptvn dfiwv? Wrv Pvfgv, wrv svfgv tvtvn wrv Viavftfnt wvi Ymoyv ivwvn, hrnw uivrprxs wvi Zfhdfiu wvi Rngvpprtvna, zyvi zfxs wzh yvvdvrhg nrxsg fnyvwrntg, wzhh wzh af kivrhvn rhg, dzh hrv evizyhxsvfvn.

(The hysterical fear of the atom bomb the public now has, or at least expresses, is almost a sign that here for once a salutary discovery has been made. At least

> the fear gives the impression of being fear in the face of a really effective bitter medicine. I cannot rid myself of the thought: if there were not something good here, the philistenes would not be making an outcry. But perhaps this too is a childish idea. For all I can mean really is that the bomb offers the prospect of the end, the destruction of a ghastly evil, of disgusting soapy water science and certainly that is not an unpleasant thought; but who is to say what would come after such a destruction? The people now making speeches against the production of the bomb are undoubtedly the dregs of the intelligentsia, but even that does not prove beyond question that what they abominate is to be welcomed.)
>
> (MS 131: 66–67, 1946; CV 1998: 55–56; Gorlée 2012: 210–214)[20]

The contextualism of the paragraphs of MS 131 guided Wittgenstein's emotional clues of being a "dependent" or "independent" person guiding the future of the world. Inspired by the religious fate of humanity, his verbal clues were translated into the cryptic style of his discourse, in which the linguistic experiment of code with varieties of non-code has been applied by applying a game of "chance" (Peirce's iconic firstness) situated in primary text and secondary subtext. Wittgenstein's writings vaguely blended philosophy and diary in his collage of statements, quotes, and notes gathered in the lexical imagination of the *Denkbewegungen*. He wanted to expose that the fuzzy logic with a religious feeling must be pieced together from the fragments of the anecdote, religious legend, and dramatic chronicles to grow into the language-game to make sense at all. In the secret code, he did not discuss his own identity but stimulated the readers (Peirce's interpreters) to construct the educational steps of the fictional games to build up the critical rigor of the philosophical speech-act and to draw their own conclusions.

Concretely, Wittgenstein exposed in the diary of manuscripts 130 to 134 the cryptographical code not only as a medium of self-reflection but also as a stimulus for his readers to introduce the language-games. He wanted his readers to stumble at the regular details and irregular alphabetic order to feel in themselves the disorder of the textual and subtextual scripts. His goal was to construct out of the magical stories of fictional games the collective enterprise of language-games. The experience of reading existed in order to learn the linguistic-cultural enigma of the secret code. Wittgenstein's form of reading aims to thrill the students into the excitement of learning the (de)constructive code of the subtextual codes. Not all unschooled readers were "instinctively" inclined to be energetic cryptanalysts, most of them were superficial and or sensational listeners to his lectures. The energetic interpreters gave plausible reasons to Wittgenstein's philosophical method; they tried not to appreciate his inner reflections but instead his outward remarks to other readers when discussing the good or evil situation of the world. It seems that the emotional behavior of accepting the formal word-by-word literalism was not enough for Wittgenstein's plan to introduce the subtext of playful games to solve the whole problem of communication. The teaching of psychosemiotic philosophy had to generate the radical family of meanings moving away from the mainstream to follow Peirce's and Wittgenstein's pragmatism (Smith 2007: 5, 141, 221–223, 246–257; White [1955] 1983: 135–236, esp. 236–243).

Text and contexts

The narrative information of Wittgenstein's *Denkbewegungen* gave a highly personal stamp and strength to the literary structure of his fictional games. Wittgenstein's desire was that the fictional games were not reduced to merely tell their own story; when upgraded, they would represent the final causes of language-games. The psychological symptoms of fictional games were Wittgenstein's form of gesture language, shadowing the philosophy in the first sensation of emotion. The connection between text and subtext of MS 131 was continued in the following notebook (MS 132). But in the linguistic text of MS 132, text and subtext remain separate in the languages of text and subject of the diary. Wittgenstein stated that the *loose connection* of MS 132 and MS 133 was to organize the public use of fictional games as they did not learn automatic knowledge by practical experiment but by the expertise of the collective language-games (Gorlée 2016b: 20–31).

The text of MS 132 concerned the human sensation for the exercise of physical movements to set the physical muscles into motion (MS 131). Since images and words do not have a static sensation, but need to work properly to function in bodily and spiritual movement, Wittgenstein stressed the analogy between word-symbol and man-symbol. In Peirce's man/sign metaphor (CP: 5.313–5.317) each symbol embodies a history of bodily experiences to work in the machinery of life. The semiotic story used the physical machinery of the body for ordinary practice, but had a higher degree of power to grow steadily to the level of language-games.

In MS 132, Wittgenstein repeated his worries about the happiness of love, possibly disturbed by disease or accidents to lead to what he feared most. He was frozen with terror awaiting personal crisis. His examples took a dramatic turn for the worse:

> In a bullfight, the bull is the hero of the tragedy. First he is driven crazy by pain, then he dies a long & horrible death.
>
> (MS 132: 12, 1946)[21]

> Vrn Svpw hrvsg wvo Gmw rnh Zntvhrxsg, wvo driqprxsvn Gmw, nrxsg ypmh wvo Yrpw wvh Gmwvh. Hrxs rn vrnvi Qirhv znhgznwrt af yvnvsovn, svrhhg nrxsg vrnvn Svpwvn, tpvrxshzo drv zfu wvo Gsvzgvi, tfg wzihgvppvn qmnnvn, hmnwvin vh svrhhg wvo Gmw hvpyhg rnh Zftv hxszfvn qmnnvn. Wvnn wvi Hxszzfhlrvpvi qznn vrnv vrnv Ovntv Imppvn hlrvpvn, zyvi zo Vnwv ofhh vi wmxs hvpyhg zph Ovnhs hgviyvn.
>
> (The hero stares death in the face, real death, not just the image of death. To behave decently in a crisis, does not mean playing the hero, as in the theater, it means staring death itself in the eye. Because no matter how many roles an actor can take on, in the end he himself must die as a man.)
>
> (MS 132: 46–47, 1946, my translation).[22]

Wittgenstein's text and subtext are about the self-identity of heroism and courage. For him, as a former soldier, selfhood is protagonized in the process of the full semiosis of thirdness. Courage is seen in the semiosis of the language-games. In the art of thirdness, the emotional firstness and bodily secondness are interrelated into correct communication in the ideological form of language. In concrete terms, the nervous system and the movements of the body are *directly connected* to the biological and mental organism to work correctly with language-games.

Wittgenstein considered himself an imaginative person with a creative brain. In the text of MS 132, he described the intelligent sign-action of the symbol (thirdness). But while he generated logical texts in philosophy, his brain was crisscrossed by the private subtext in fragments of his non-logical diary. The subtext follows the text about the fabric of his emotions working in his organic body (firstness and secondness) to find the semiosis of his thirdness (Colapietro 1989: 84–86). The existence of the three-way identity of Wittgenstein's text, context, and subtext could change into the dramatic performance of different selves (Wilshire 1982: 143–234). In Wittgenstein's diary, the real facts of reality can be transfigured from reality into mythical signs of irreality, when the diarist feels morally disconnected from his self. The separateness of texts and subtexts leaves the reader with the danger of broadening the divergence of Wittgenstein's brain into separate cross-sections of real and theatrical stories, in which facts are gone, leading to fiction or misrepresentation.

Wittgenstein returned to Cambridge to teach his classes—indeed, his last classes (PGL). Life together with Ben Richards was happy with no unhappy incidents and no crisis. Wittgenstein wrote in the subtext of his diary that "Zpp ahg Tpfxg!!" (All is happiness!) (MS 132: 147, 1946, translated by Monk [1990: 503]), but commenting that "Rxs yrn rn wvi Prvyv af dvnrt tpzfyrt fnw af dvnrt ofgrt" (In love I have too little faith and too little courage) (MS 132: 147, 205, 1946, translated by Monk [1990: 503]).[23] The "theatrical" play about the virtue of heroism and courage in Wittgenstein's philosophical text is also *directly* and *indirectly connected* with his worries about finding real love. The language of MS 132 was written partly in plaintext to describe his "heroic" role, and partly in code to describe his lack of courage.

From October 1946, Wittgenstein focused on writing the common text. But the final question of MS 132—"Why then does one say, one knows ... one's thoughts" (MS 132: 133, 1946, my translation)[24]—was asked to his own text and context. Wittgenstein seemed to echo at that moment the last remark of *Tractatus*: "Whereof one cannot speak, thereof one must be silent" (TLP: 7).[25] He presented a pause for thought, a moment to think and reflect about what reality and irreality would *stand for* in his life. The reply of silence and secrecy came up in the text of the philosophical thoughts in the following notebook (MS 133, written in the longer period of October 22, 1946–February 28, 1947), which he indirectly used in the context of his lectures for the students in Cambridge (October 11, 1946–May 16, 1947).

Wittgenstein returned to the double explanation of the meaning of uncertainty. The meaning must not be negatively formulated in his own anxiety when he foresaw his own "madness" (*Wahnsinn*) formulated in non-coded text. Instead of madness, he wanted to regenerate his habit of life in the positive "change of character" (*Charakterveränderung*) (MS 133: 2r, 2v, 1946). The desire and decision (*Wollen und Können*) converted the inner input into outer speech. In non-coded text, Wittgenstein proposed that:

> "Man has given man the gift of thinking in secret." Imagine one would say "Although nature has given to speak out loud, man can also speak low in his mind." So there are two ways for doing the same thing ... But with internal speech, speech is concealed better than an internal process can be ... Nobody sees, nobody hears, nobody perceives, what I think. (MS 133: 3r, 4r, 1946)[26]

In the psychological interaction of Peirce's semiosis, humans communicate via many channels, among which are the "*heard-spoken*" and "*seen-written*" varieties of inner and outer speech (Shands 1970: 259–260). Language can be reformulated into inner and outer, vocal and nonvocal, verbal and non-verbal speeches (Sebeok 1985b: 301–310). Wittgenstein's silent and sounded, vocal and voiceless forms of language in his diary and philosophy expressed how the characters of verbal messages were used differently in social and personal forms of communication. To avoid the personal limitations of the isolated single individual, language to the group is transformed from intimate gossip and idle chat into the opening the mind to serious conversation. Wittgenstein as an "open" author always remained the "silent" interpreter of unknown, even anonymous, forms of message, but his self was the response of inner with outer signs.

In the seminars Wittgenstein held during the weeks of October 11–21, 1946, he concretized the textual explanations of outer and inner speech in the context (lectures) and text (philosophy) talking about the modalities of "thinking" and "talking" (PGL: 119–127; see 3–10, 235–239). Wittgenstein mentioned that thinking is a rare and extraordinary phenomenon in the classroom. Although thinking would be for students a frequent occurrence, he said that thinking was "different from what happens in the adding machine: for example, thinking shows inventiveness" (PGL: 120). Thinking is not the straightforward and simple "adding machine" of students, but is the puzzle of learning the technique of using linguistic forms to communicate with one another through pictures with the details of gestures of shades, colors, and numbers. The simple sign games must be retranslated into more complex picture words to communicate (PGL: 121–124). Language does not express in itself a rule but is a heterogeneous game playing with rules and unrules.

The simple activity of "talking" in conversation lacks serious and creative "thinking" to define the rules of the linguistic sign. To reconvert language's misunderstanding into full understanding, the language speaker uses the practical rule of Wittgenstein's term of "signpost" (*Wegweiser*) (PGL: 127). Wittgenstein's indexical signpost paves the way from non-communication to half-communication and further to real communication (see PI: 85, 87, 198). The signpost is represented by Wittgenstein in the German term for "road sign" (*Wegweiser*) to show the road leading through the individual sign to the rule of the actual (or even physical) connection to give full meaning. The index gives speech but does not occur alone in genuine "thinking," which happens in a technical sign to experience the real world. The signpost mobilizes the practical energy of the index, but it points further to a cause-effect that relates the original sign to the correlated meaning of sign and object(s). In terms of language, the index is clear in the deictic expressions of language, such as "*this* or *that* and *here* or *there*" (Danesi 2009: 156). The pointer-words give the individual replica of the concrete sign but stay in themselves passive demonstratives in weak words. They point indexically to the active forms in full words and sentences. For Wittgenstein, language must be a signpost of "thinking."

The diary entry of October 25, 1946, and subsequent days changed the tone-color of Wittgenstein's long and virulent monologue about his love affair (MS 133: 7r-9r, 1946). He narrated in secret code about his happiness with Ben Richard, but the fragile luck with him could, as Wittgenstein expected, never last. He feared that the pain of love would continue forever (Monk 1990: 503–506). As he wrote:

> Rxs szyv nrxsg wvn Ofg fnw nrxsg Qizug & Qpzisvrg wvn Gzghzxsvn ovrnvh Pvyvnh tvizwv rn'h Tvhrxsg af hxszfvn.—Y. szg af ori vrnv Emi-Prvyv. Vgdzh, dzh nrxsg szpgvn qznn.
>
> (I do not have the courage or the strength & clarity to look the facts of my life straight in the face.—B. [Ben Richards] has for me a pre-love, something that cannot last.)
>
> Wzomnvn szyvn wrvhvh Yznw tvdmyvn … fnw szpgvn vh rn wvi Sznw (wnv Sznwnv). Hrv qmnnvn'h aviivrhhen, mwvi wzfvin (pvyvn) pzhhvn.
>
> (Demons have woven this bond … and hold it in their hands. They can destroy it or let it live.)
>
> (MS 133: 7r-8r, 1946, translated by Monk [1990: 504] and my translation)[27]

The day after, the evil spirits have vanished and Wittgenstein wrote happily in the diary that:

> Wrv Prvyv rhg vrn Tpfxq. Ervppvrxsg vrn Tpfxg org Hxsoviavn, zyvi vrn Tpfxg. Uvspg wzh Tpfxq, mwvi hxsifolug vh zfu vrn qfiavh Zfuupzxxqvin afhzoovn, hm uvspg wrv Prvyv.—Rn wvi Prvyv ofhh rxs hrxsvi ifsvn qmnnvn.—Zyvi qznnhg wf vrn dziovh Svia afifzqvrhvn? Rhg vh vrn Svia, wzh dzio ufi orxs hxspztg? … Wvi Ovnxs qznn zfh hvrnvi Szfg nrxsg svizfh. Rxsqznn nrxsg vrnv Umiwvifnr, wrv grvu rn ori, org ovrnvo tznavn Pvyvn eviznqvig, prvtg, zfutvyvn. Wvnn wrv Prvyv rhg org wvi Nzgfi eviyfnwvn; fnw dfiwv rxs fnnzgfiprxs, hm ofhhgv (dfiwv) wrv Prvyv zfusmivn.—Qznn rxs hztvn: "Rxs dviwv evinfnugrt hvrn, &wzh nrxsg ovsi evipzntvn"?
>
> (Love is joy. Perhaps joy mixed with pain, but joy nevertheless. Without joy or just a flickering, there is no love.—In love I should be able to rest secure.—Is there a heart that beats warmly for me? … A person cannot come out of his skin. I cannot give up a demand that is anchored deep inside me, in my whole life. For love is bound up with nature; and if I became unnatural, the love would have to end.—Can I say: "I will be reasonable and no longer demand it"?
>
> (MS 133: 8r-9r, 1946, translated by Monk [1990: 505] and my translation)[28]

Wittgenstein tormented himself into the closeness and strangeness of what love can bring. He wrote that love must overcome disorder through sacrificial efforts, but importantly love will also give a sentiment of order to his life. He found Ben's pseudo-love (*Vorliebe*) a form of selfless devotion of brotherly kindness with sexual love rooted in forms of self-love (Fromm [1986] 1965: 38–61). But he feared that the sense of a pre-sign of love for oneself and friendship to others had the possible meaning of "madness" (*Wahnsinn*) by losing his balance and falling on stony ground. To reach the destination, Wittgenstein desired genuine love to relieve him of the "fundamental insecurity of life" (MS 133: 35r, 1946).

For Wittgenstein, the practical and theoretical questions of love must have the lasting quality of homecoming, resolving the nostalgia of life into unselfish harmony. He tried to do two things: in one story, real love is God's spiritual harmony, lacking the trickery of vanity, greediness, estrangement, egotism, and other vices. But in the second story, love combines the dreamy firstness with brute secondness. Wittgenstein was aware that "Love, as a mediation of real, separable individuals through a bond of affectionate concerns, is preeminently the activity of Thirdness in its more advanced stages" (Esposito 1980: 177). Love was for Wittgenstein his critical point of view, but with the surrogates of love, such as self-love, sexual love, brotherly love, and other sentiments, love remained an impossible dream. Possessed by this anguish, he remained caught in the single habits of iconicity (firstness) and indexicality (secondness). Love's symbolicity (thirdness) confounds a fully agreed-on description of real life, for which, as he wrote, he was ironically disabled (*Fesseln*) (MS 133: 9r, 1946). Continuing in plaintext, Wittgenstein claimed his mental handicap in the philosophical inquiry of language philosophy in plaintext, for everyone to see. He added that the reader sees the "fun of research into the philosophy of language yet fail[s] to see that [they] are entangled in utter confusion about the concept [of love]" (MS 133: 9r, 1946).[29]

At this point, the diary became ordinary plaintext. Wittgenstein seemed to discuss in the pages of MS 133 the psychological aspects of the language-game. On October 31, 1946, he implied what good order requires from the language speakers:

> Think about the proper name which can only be proposed and understood when the carrier is present. Freud has been through his fantastic pseudo-explanations (just as for the spiritual nature) of little help. (All asses have such images near at hand for "explaining" the pathological symptoms). Instead, the philosopher wants to reshape (reinfluence) the methods [into something new]. (MS 133: 11v, 1946, my translation; for Wittgenstein's term "name," see Glock 1996: 254–257)[30]

In plaintext, Wittgenstein was not "making an ass of himself" in his illustrations of the speaking, that is unthinking, thoughts of the biblical characters of Philistines (Gorlée 2012: 211–212). Since Wittgenstein excluded the directives to follow Freud's psychoanalysis as a helpless error, he discussed healing the breach between friends in the rational-emotive therapy of his goal, the language-games. In Wittgenstein's evangelizing tone of a believer, the language-game "only signifies with the presence of the carrier [patient], [so that it] must be as when the carrier's word plays for us the unusual role" (MS 133: 12r-12v, 1946, my translation).[31] The language-game is not the game played by Wittgenstein, but speaks for all the collective speakers.

In the semiotic experience proposed by Peirce's doctrine of semiotic signs, Wittgenstein's "carrier" of linguistic signs refers to the miracles of the sign-maker, whose vivid presence knows the real existence of the sign referring to the object. The sign-maker transforms the real sign into the linguistic sign for all sign-users (that is, the readers or observers, called semiotic interpreters). The sign-user receives the sign from the sign-maker. The sign-user is geographically "absent" from the sign-maker. The task of the sign-user is to play—to speak and think about the sign and object—to give the interpretant-signs talking about the information of the sign in the new form (Sebeok [1994] 2001: 3–6).

Wittgenstein's philosophy of language understands the fictional games of the sign-maker to eventually close down the subtext into marginalizing the meaning of the language-game. The linguistic and cultural *differences* of the language-games are contextual associations, not surfaced in textual references of subtext (Derrida 1973: 141). The cry of Wittgenstein's heart was written in code: "M, dzifo rhg ori afofgv, zph hxsirvy rxs vrn Tvwrxxg, dvnn rxs Lsrpmhmlsrv hxsivryv?" (Oh, why do I feel, as if I write a poem, when I write philosophy?), but with the appendix in plaintext: "The search for explanation [prevents me from writing] prevents the description of the full construction of facts [meaning] of the description]"; and he continued "The preconceived hypothesis works as a strainer that allows just a very small part of the facts into our minds [our observation]." (MS 133: 13r, 1946).[32] Wittgenstein must have condensed or reduced the information into the sense of misinformation.

With hypotheses such as this, Wittgenstein's prophetic process of thought-intermingled the habit of diary and philosophy with his real emotions, creating what looks like a poem or metapoem of his life. The literary form involves more than the depiction of the biographical facts, but for Wittgenstein there is a radical distinction between different levels of language: the language of science and the language of poetry. In the *Denkbewegungen*, Wittgenstein twisted together philosophy and diary. The effect was emotional and mental contortions in a mixed language. Philosophy (text) and diary (subtext or intertext) can hardly untwist the binding interactions of Wittgenstein's ethical intuition, because identifying the emotions is the anti-language belonging to the literary genre of poetry (Gray 1975: 523). In Wittgenstein's lectures (context), information turned again into the literary-visual machine for writing the final "poem" of seeing the duck-rabbit. This double image of duck or rabbit gave a physical *Gestalt* for the context of human pain, pleasure, fear, desire, and other emotional visions of human psychology (Monk 1990: 507–516) but provided no logical conclusion.

The coded diary about Wittgenstein's double images of duck and rabbit showed his "fundamental insecurity of life" (MS 133: 35r, 1946). The coded remarks of the diary seem to be *vaguely connected* to the philosophy written in plaintext. Wittgenstein's preparatory work of the fictional games was his clear and unequivocal story, but his mind was elsewhere: the possible (or impossible) *entrée* of the collective language-games. Until the end of MS 133 (October 28, 1946), Wittgenstein was unhappy and seemed to live in two worlds, diary and philosophy (or philosophy and diary). The coded remarks were about himself as the degenerate, or even disabled, person and he imagined himself as the "blind" man. See, for example:

Rxs yrn vrnv nvrwrhv, vruvihfxsgrtv Nazgfi.

(I have the envious, jealous nature.)

Wvi Hgmxg, wvi sfynnxs zfhhrvsg, hm pzntv ozn rsn giztg, zyvi hrxs yrvtg, hmyzpw [dvnn] wfwrxs zfu ran hgfgag, rhg nrxsgh dvig.

(The walking-stick that looks pretty so long as one carries it, but bends as soon as you rest your weight upon it, is worth nothing.)

Yrn hvsi vrnhzo.
(I am very lonely.)

Rxs hvsv vrn ymhvh Vnwv ufi ovrn Pvyvn emizfh. Vrnhzoqvrg, ervppvrxsg Dzsnhrnn. Ovrnv Emipvhfntvn tvsvn tfg, hrv dviwvn nrv yvhhvi tvsvn. Zivi dvpxsv Driqfnt pzhhvn hrv afifxg? Svpuv rxs ritvnw rvoznw? Rvdrhh nrxsg ovsi, zph dvnn rxs vrn timhhvi Hxszfhlrvpvi dziv, wvi rsnvn Giztmwrvn emihlrvpgv. Dzh hrv pvinvn, rhg nrg nrxsg dvig tvpving af dviwvn; & wvi lvihmnprxsv Vrnwifxq nfgag rsnvn nrxsgh. Wzh trppg ufi Zppv, org ervppvrxsg vrnvi, mwvi advr Zfhnzsoovn.

(I foresee a chilling end to my life. Loneliness, perhaps madness. My lectures go well, will never go better. But what effect will they leave? Do I help someone? Certainly not more, as if I were a big actor playing tragedies for them. What they learn, is perhaps not worth learning, & their personal impression does not help them. This goes for all [students], with perhaps one or two exceptions.)

Rn fypvo Afhgznw.

(Feeling unwell.)
(MS 133: 35v- 41v, 1946, translated by Monk [1990: 506] and my translation)[33]

Wittgenstein's imperfection of accepting Ben's self-love radiated for him to the falling short in his duties. To feel his way out of the maze of certainty and uncertainty, Wittgenstein used the physical and metaphorical help of the "walking-stick" to stand independently on two feet. See:

I cannot bow down in prayer because of my stiff knees. I fear the release (before my disintegration) when I turn weak. ... The question is: can I go upright, without leaning on this support. Or is it rather that I cannot decide to let it go? Or is it both?

(MS 133: 42r, 43v, 1946)[34]

During the last lectures in the spring semester of 1947, Wittgenstein's attention was distracted from his personal worries about losing the love of his friend and trying to forget his academic function to concentrate fully upon his own work and writings. He encouraged himself to live in one world, writing in code that "Nfi nrxsgh Gsvzgihxsvh! Wzemi ofhhg wf wrxs afgvn" (Please no theatrics! You have to avoid those) (MS 133: 78r, 1947).[35]

Wittgenstein moved away from the gestures of melodramatic poses. He abandoned the subtext of the diary and returned to writing the philosophical text. He reduced the experimental reasoning of philosophy to short paragraphs, as was usual in his diary. Not once but even twice, he argued that "The problem with philosophy is that the movements of thought are too long. The problem of philosophy is the length of the movements of thought" (MS 133: 41r, 1946).[36] The short epigrams of Wittgenstein's diary strictly associate with the strict accuracy of the readable epigrams in all texts. In the preface of the *Philosophical Investigations* (PI: 3), Wittgenstein wrote that he wanted to compose not a real book but something like what he called the "album" of the "landscape" of his philosophy. To guide the students from the incoherencies of the "landscape" to the whole research did not work. Wittgenstein changed the philosophy into readable paragraphs standing as fragments on their own strength.

Good and evil

Notebook MS 133 was followed by MS 134 (February 28–June 27, 1947). Most of MS 134 was written during Wittgenstein's last lectures "secretly" annotated by students (PGL). As discussed earlier, MS 134 changed the philosophical program but in a different sense from that expected in MS 133. Wittgenstein's content is described as the mathematical "grammar" of the language-game, but seen from the psychological use of language (now called psychosemiotics). The contexts of Wittgenstein's lectures (PGL: 209–232) were connected to his philosophical text—that is, the subjects were not the same but the lectures were *loosely connected* to the philosophical text.

Wittgenstein prepared the first manuscript of Part II of the *Philosophical Investigations* (PI/PPF: 1–372) about the newest field of the philosophy of psychology. The discussion was about the emotions affecting the physical sensation of "pain," one of Wittgenstein's favorite subjects (PGL: 209–210). The image of "pain" was followed by the "after-image" of the image (*Bild*), named the "Nachbild" of the sign of pain, signifying the false imagery of the copy or imitation of the sign (or any other image or symptom). The after-image was not the real thing (PGL: 210–212) but split the discussion of the "sense-impressions" of psychological motives, reasons, and causes of Wittgenstein's complex images into three steps: looking at the view of the sign-object is the first step, feeling the sensation of the sense-experience of the material or fabric of the sign is the second step, and finding the explanation (almost a judgment) was the final step (PGL: 216–232). The lectures bring to mind something like fragments of the outward sign in Wittgenstein's text of MS 134, in which the fragment is suggestive of the image of the inward sign. Since the after-image is dressed in a different form, one has to learn the method to understand and give the explanation. Wittgenstein's lectures ended on May 16, 1947, but he continued writing Part II during his summer vacation, spent in Swansea.

Wittgenstein's last writings turned over a new leaf. Surprisingly, he wrote in the first one hundred pages of MS 134 the philosophical text without any diary entries. The pages defend the psychological position of the mathematical language-games. Wittgenstein described the evolution of the motivated (sign a) and unmotivated signs—that is, sign a numerated with the series of signs a^2, a^4, a^8 (MS 134: 2, 1947)—to create the elastic series of solved and unsolved mathematical signs. Then, the reader of the sign is asked to "close the eyes to describe the after-image" (*Schliess die Augen, beschreib dein Nachbild)* (MS 134: 9, 1947) of the sign. In Wittgenstein's explanation, the after-image of the sign (say, the table) can be seen as red (*rot*) or having a specific smell (*Geruch)* (MS 134: 5–9, 1947). These "codes" motivate the reader (interpreter) to imitate the sign in inward and outward signs of belief and conviction (*Glaube*) (MS 134: 15, 1947). In Wittgenstein's domain of language, the linguistic signs have an unresolved meaning of individual scenes and detailed moments of practice—that is, Peirce's indexical experience, zooming out to give the global view of the symbolical language-games (Sebeok [1994] 2001: 84–88).

Language-games prophesy Wittgenstein's idea of "oracle" (*Orakel*) (MS 134: 19, 1947). The willingness to trade in the souls of the language-games was that he used the fictional games to upgrade the oracle into language-games. As ascertained from the *Oxford English Dictionary*, the oracle was etymologically adopted from the Latin *oraculum,* meaning "the place or site where one watches the sky for omens to conduct private and state business" (OED 1989: 10:884). The ancient oracle is given as the divine response or prophesy of a question. The voice of the "oracle"—like the temple of Apollo at Delphi, with the priestess called the Pythoness, sitting on a tripod to reply to questions—referred to the "response, decision, or message, given usually by a priest or priestess of a god, and, as was supposed by his inspiration at the shrine or seat where the deity was supposed to be thus accessible to inquirers" (OED 1989: 10:884). Since these responses were for the most part obscure or ambiguous messages, many of the divinations were misleading and the receivers had to form their own judgment in or against the omens. The Greek oracle played the game of examining the liver of a sacrificial goat, the movements of birds, or the rustle of leaves. Wittgenstein's "oracle" was situated outside the divine response in the linguistic message placed in metaphorical quotation marks. His combat was with the rhetoric of other philosophers with the weapon of his private argument (MS 134: 20, 1947; see also in other notebooks MS 109: 252, 1930–1931; MS 124: 42, 1941–1944; MS 127: 87, 1944; MS 156b: 47r, 1940; MS 176: 73v, 1951; see OC: 609).

The ancient priest or priestess and the modern philosopher "differ in their methods, one working by magic, the other by logic," but both of them "speak to us in some metalanguage about itself, a feeling that nature is written in a kind of role" (Sebeok 1988). The oracle in the secret code needs to be deciphered by the human questioner to reveal the underlying plaintext of the entranced priests or priestesses. Sebeok stressed the semiotic nature of the oracle, when he wrote that "Understandings of this kind are reached by a reverse application of semiotic procedures, pursuant to certain key transcription rules, laid back by privileged cogniscent of the craft of decryption" (Sebeok 1988). The oracle is a divination of love or war in the god's mysterious code, which was for Wittgenstein, the special language of the secret *Geheimschrift*.

In formal logic, the oracle generates inferences and/or hypotheses from Wittgenstein's long inventory of symptoms taken by a rational way of reasoning, by mentally reconstructing the similarities of the effects to the cause. If the hypothesis is true, there is reason by analogy to accept that the words of the oracle can be true. But if the hypothesis is not true, the oracle becomes useless. In semiotic terms, the oracle is regarded as the strong message of symbolic thirdness, but it can also be explained as the weak (or Peirce's degenerate) message in coded text speaking of icons (firstness) or indices (secondness). The cryptography works on the human instinct of the attendants to break the code and guess from the cause the effect. Peirce's conclusion would be that the hypothesis of the "abductive" style of reasoning means "abduction," that is, reasoning backwards by the example of the oracle, to bring from the indexical-iconic game of reasoning good or evil news to the listeners (Gorlée 2015c: 408).

Turning to his grammatical to rhetorical constructions, Wittgenstein discussed in MS 134 the truth and untruth of the fictional game to work as a message for real communication. He used the verb "to believe" (MS 134: 19, 1947) written in the first-person "I believe" (*Ich glaube*) to describe the life of a private person, opposed to the language-game of "It rains" (*Es regnet*) (MS 134: 16–24, 1947) written as a public event in the third person. In between the "pseudo-automatic" and "automatic" sentences lies "I believe it rains" (*Ich glaube es regnet*), "It appears to rain" (*Es scheint zu regnen*), and "It might rain" (*Es dürfte regnen*), which reasoned the psychological event in the intermediate formulas of "It rains, but I don't want it to be true" (*Es regnet, aber ich will es nicht wahr haben*) (MS 143: 23, 1947). Wittgenstein criticized his own argument, noticing that:

> "I believe it will rain," "I believe, that my friend is true to me." The words "it has been written into my soul ..." do not apply to no. 1, but to no. 2. One could say that the second example concerns a thought process, while the first one does not. One will be inclined to say: to rely on something is a condition of man (his soul); to believe it will rain, is not. (MS 134: 24, 1947)[37]

During the "automatic" belief and "non-automatic" unbelief of the grammatical verb "to believe" (or "to disbelieve") the conditions of the weather, Wittgenstein broke out in the impromptu remark, "I believe, that my friend is true to me." This sentence is loaded with Wittgenstein's emotion, precisely calibrated to opening his heart and posing an emotional alternative crisscrossing of the philosophical facts of his philosophy as usual in the non-existent diary. Evidently, Wittgenstein was still in despair over his lover's intention to leave him and makes no secret of his immediate feeling.

Finally, after the last lecture of May 16, 1947, to end the 100-pages without a diary entry, Wittgenstein's structure of writing the uncoded philosophy as well as the coded diary continued his old habit in the *Denkbewegungen*. It was clear that Wittgenstein's habit was in low spirits, despairing of finding meaning and purpose in life. Bitterly writing that his life was "Emn Vegvpqvrg tvylzsg!z!" (Over-inflated with vanity!) (MS 134: 168, 1947),[38] he tried to work out his failure to define the empty fame, glory, and power as false images of himself as a lover and scholar (Schimmel 1992: 55–82). Wittgenstein's opinion, that he was superior to others, led him to strongly feel the anxiety of the possible breakage with Ben Richards, and to feel the damage to his professorial life, which culminated in a love crisis. Wittgenstein then abandoned the professorate in October 1947 to feel free.

Since Wittgenstein wrote the last pages of MS 134 alone in Swansea, he had no audience for his writings (no intertextuality) and the coded diary pages shrunk to nothing (no subtext). He continued the preliminary sketches of interpreting the elastic term of the puzzle pictures—later rewritten and edited in the *Last Writings on the Philosophy of Language* (LW1, LW2). In Wittgenstein's final work, the observation of the puzzle pictures no longer worked with the visual eyes (like the rabbit-duck picture) but with the mental brain. He learned from the puzzle picture that "I see things in different contexts" (MS 134: 163, 1947).[39] These moral lessons of the human brain agree to the uncertainty of life in truth and untruth. In MS 134, the text, the context of the lectures, as well as the subtext of the diary could be brought together as one single, but disconnected, argumentation. Text, context, and subtext corresponded to Wittgenstein's goal: the universal categories of thirdness, secondness, and firstness in semiosis.

Without the coded subtext, the form of the text of the philosophy of psychology is based on Wittgenstein's first-draft raw material of MS 134, not later revised or repolished in typescripts. The drafts of MS 134 with many variants and repetitions of words and sentences create the impression of Wittgenstein's provisional and improvised fragments. As promised in MS 133 (41r, 1946), Wittgenstein now attempted to shrink from the lengthy argument of philosophy into brief epigrams. Starting the next manuscript (MS 135), Wittgenstein wrote on July 12, 1947, that "This volume will contain just <u>one</u> halfway decent section every 10 or 20 pages" (MS 135 front cover, 1947).[40] The little shards of philosophical commentary had a minimum of coded diary. Wittgenstein's new strategy is visible in his last book, *On Certainty*, written in the last years up to his death on April 29, 1951. *On Certainty* was posthumously published in 1969 by the Wittgenstein trustees, Elizabeth Anscombe and Georg Henrik von Wright, and presented the attractive and intelligible text to read (Moyal-Sharrock 2007; Gorlée 2012: 273–317).

After closely studying the *Denkbewegungen* of 1946–1947, we can conclude that in those years the structural and thematic connectedness of text, context, and subtext (MSS 130–132) was drawn away to acknowledge the disconnectedness of a unit of text with secondary texts (MSS 133–134). The first reason was Wittgenstein's own plan to reorganize the argument of his philosophical writings, making shorter paragraphs to communicate widely to his readership (including students). The second reason was the improvement of Wittgenstein's temperament. After the agonizing worries on his mind and heart, he now seemed to count his blessings as perhaps a sign of good luck. In Wittgenstein's sixties, there grew a sense of happiness in which his private remarks in the diary lost the great urgency to share the alienation and nostalgia of the exile he previously suffered. Wittgenstein's task was writing in relative isolation, steeped in religion, but not speaking out in seminars or lectures to others. The communion with the generative force at the heart of things inspired the final decision of striving toward old age, moving Wittgenstein from his evil to good behavior.

Since the secret code of the diary was a means of instruction to the readers to learn the code and understand the variety of paths through Wittgenstein's "landscape" to understand his philosophy. Wittgenstein's stimulus to the readers was to face the secrecy of the code to promote the cryptanalysis. Yet the eternal enigma ceased when he gave up his professorate in 1947. Giving up his academic position, Wittgenstein cleared his mind and was liberated to write. He equally gave up the habit of the emotional interpretant in writing his diary, focusing instead on the energetic interpretant in the examples and explanations, to tell the stories of the fictional games. The impasse which resulted from accepting the hypothetic premises of the fictional games was basically the denial of the final or definitive interpretant. Most importantly, he had lost the certainty of the familiar sense of language-games. His aims and the achievements of certainty had been the social interaction of all speakers of the collective language-games, but now with more free time, he left the readers the wide margin for the symptomatology of confusion and misunderstanding. From 1947, Wittgenstein's identity had to develop the art of personal compromise to communicate with his readers. In his escapism from "pursuers," he limited the debate of the crypto-autobiography but upgraded the primacy of the language-games in his last writing. Wittgenstein himself had no reservations about the vagueness of uncertainty to speculate on the logic of language.

6

Cryptosemiotician

> *"What happens when a man suddenly understands?"—The question is badly framed. If it is a question about the meaning of the expression "sudden understanding," the answer is not to point to a problem to which we give this name.—The question might mean: what are the symptoms of sudden understanding; what are its characteristic mental accompaniments?*
>
> (PI: 321)[1]

Forked tongue

The entries of Wittgenstein's diary are closely modeled on the symptoms of the diarist himself. The activity of writing the diary was motivated by his energy to record the day-to-day events of his life, but instead he wrote the quasi-secret "album" to describe the history and story of his own anxiety and loneliness. In Wittgenstein's day, there were no cures for psychiatric illnesses. The lack of medical knowledge reached the critical point that Wittgenstein's diary was not merely a self-portrait (pure icon) of his self asking for help. The diary was his crypto-autobiography (icon with index) to direct attention to the language-games (symbolic signs) used by all language speakers. The language-games were presented by Wittgenstein as final confessions, to consider his actions on particular occasions and to instruct the class of students and other readers to become ready to start their own philosophical inquiry.

Wittgenstein's experimental method was writing in diary form the self-description of "painful behavior." The diary was transformed into the therapeutic grammar of language needed to heal the diarist's alien soul. Miraculously, Wittgenstein's notes about his sensations of "painful behavior" seemed in themselves to self-heal through the intimate process of the diary messenger. When the diarist writes about his own life, the auto-communication responds to the autofiction of his life corresponding to his emotional firstness (CP: 6.585; see Lotman 1990: 20–35; Sebeok 1979: 263–267). But when the message is transmitted to other readers, the autofiction becomes a biography containing the encoded life story, but shifting from the artistic communication of firstness to secondness (Gorlée 2015c: 114). Taking the lack of knowledge further into the performance of his lectures, in which Wittgenstein had to translate his German into English, secondness corresponds to thirdness. The readership (students) communicated with Wittgenstein's sense of "collective personality of the common memory and collective consciousness" (Lotman 1990: 35). The motion from secondness to thirdness also happened in the cultural stories of Wittgenstein's language-games, which seemed to be the ideal model to judge his behavior throughout his entire life. Wittgenstein's lectures were not a public performance but private occasions in his rooms of Trinity College, changing the thirdness into secondness, even firstness.

Wittgenstein's inner life as a diarist made him come to terms with the history and story of his anxiety in relation to the symptoms of his own state of affairs of aggression, fictionalized from the medical definition of writing the diary to the practical activity of keeping the diary going without hardly any interruptions. Yet the readers (not the sign-maker but the sign-receivers of the diary) observe the diary differently as a disguise of the code into Wittgenstein's "semiotic self" with strange words and unknown sentences. The feelings of melancholia and nostalgia were substituted by the action of using (or even misusing) quasi-language with his codes. Wittgenstein injected the crypto-arithmetic of his style of writing into the literary genre of the diary. In the therapeutic setting of the diary, he measured out a dose of medicine to experience in the fragmentary narrative his own emotions and sensations. Wittgenstein's speech was a paradox.

The private role of the secret code mediated Wittgenstein's habit of "how to talk" into "how to talk to himself" (Shands 1971: 19). For communication with other readers, Wittgenstein's habituality of coded messages communicated to the sign-receivers the scientific struggle of his violent "war with words" (Shands 1971: 19–21). As a psychiatric semiotician, Harley Shands knew the problems of split personality disorder, which he metaphorized as the "forked tongue" fighting against the confusions of common language. The activities of talk and metatalk kept conversation going, but Shands stressed that:

> Man is conscious, and he communicates with others and with the self, and the two are the same. The early part of a mans life is spent learning how to talk, and how to talk to himself. But to talk to himself he has to split himself and oppose self to self, questioning, commanding, urging and persuading himself. The latter part of life for some is spent in putting the self back together again, attempting—with rare and partial success—to heal the rift necessarily induced by learning to be human. Little wonder that those who truly learn the way to regain a unity at first of the ignorance of bliss fear the unity of non-being little or not at all. Miraculously evoked from the not-self by the genetic instruction with which we command one-alien material, we learn then how to control the self from a one-alien standpoint we ultimately value as the very center of the self. Then we learn that no matter what we try or hope, we are ourselves constrained by instructions which we must in time obey, and these instructions prescribe what we reckon the alien in re-attaining ignorance. In my beginning is my end; in my end is my beginning. (19)

To keep the diary as Wittgenstein's psychobiography going, he reasoned from the premise with definite figures of evidence to render the conclusion as an explanatory hypothesis to demonstrate the secret language. By writing the diary messages for other readers, he created the ambiguous conclusion in the symptomatic habituality, which was not strictly painful reasoning on its own but drifted with the logical-linguistical stream of Wittgenstein's certainty into accepting the artistic uncertainty of judging for him what was true and what was not true.

Regarding the primary remarks about experiencing his own symptoms of pain, Wittgenstein wrote in ordinary plaintext the following fictional game (published in the *Philosophical Investigations*). The "diary-keeper argument" (Smerud 1970: 8, 23–28) justified Wittgenstein's use of private language as his own cliché of making the diary (*Tagebuchführer*). Smerud stipulated that the basis for the anti-private-language thesis was that the private language must point to public habits of language-games. Wittgenstein wrote that:

> I want to keep a diary about a returning sensation. For that purpose I associate this sensation with the sign "S," and mark this sign in my journal when I have this sensation.—Let me begin by saying that a definition of the sign cannot be pronounced.—But I can use it for myself as some sort of indicative definition!—How? Can I point to the sensation?—Not in the ordinary sense. But I say, or write the sign down, and in doing so I focus my attention on the sensation—point to it inwardly, as it were.—But why this ceremony? Then that is what it appears to be! The point of a definition is to record the meaning of a sign.—Well, the same happens by focusing my attention; for that is how I imprint on my memory, for that is how I imprint the connection of the sign to the sensation on my memory.—But "I imprint on my memory" can only mean one thing: because of the process, I will <u>correctly</u> remember the connection in the future. In our case, I have no yardstick for what is correct. One would say: correct is whatever appears correct to me. And that only means that the term "correct" does not apply here. (PI: 258 = MS 129: 43–44, 1944, my translation)[2]

In this scene, Wittgenstein, the maker of the diary, must have a forked tongue to speak in this double manner. Wittgenstein's uses language from his own "color-blindness" in the "unity and simplicity" of his own "solitary and celibate" speech as a simple "dweller in the desert" (see Peirce's CP: 6.230–6.234, 1898). Wittgenstein's quasi-language of the diary was no paradox but the uncommon logic of his "Babel of strange tongues" to "make a chaos of fortuitously wandering atoms" (CP: 6.237). Wittgenstein's simple logic in the quasi-language transformed "through simplicity, freedom, necessarily results in endless multiplicity and variety" (CP: 6.237).

The biblical metaphor of the forked tongue (Ps. 140:11; Acts 2:4; see Gorlée 2012: 314) was about the story of the "evil man" with his tongue split into two speeches. The effect of Wittgenstein's own pain is omnipresent in his writings. He blanketed his fraud and falsehood to heal the confusions of the tongue experienced by himself and other speakers of his messages. In the dream imagery, he inspired each word with his own sensation (*Empfindung*) of pain and grief, then the pain-data was shaken up with the logical grammar to serve as a remedy for other speakers. As a "good man," Wittgenstein lost the tongue of the private sensation to speak with public language-games. He did not restrict himself to personal problems and torments in the straightforward portrayal of his life in his "facts of life," but he spoke to the public in the "family resemblances" of good and bad language-games (Shands 1970: 307; see Glock 1996: 120–124, 199). Wittgenstein's words reflected the double division in the early *Tractatus*: "Laws, like the law of causation, etc., treat of the network and not of what the network describes" (TLP: 6.35; see Bunn 1981: 98). Wittgenstein served as the "carpenter" (Isa. 41.7, 44.13) crafting the sensations of his life into the "hypothetical idea, a fiction, a fantasy" (Bunn 1981: 1). He metaphorized the pain sensation into the hallucinations of spoken language (Gorlée 2016a: 50–53).

In the role of spontaneous as well as intelligent "tinkerer" of language (Fr. *bricoleur*, derived from Claude Lévi-Strauss [1962] 1966: 16–36; see Gorlée 2007: 224–233), Wittgenstein's textual signs were transformed into coded symbols. Against the usual habit of encrypting the remarks, he wrote the pain sensations in ordinary plaintext, fully understandable for other cryptanalysts. Gregory Bateson, who also injected autobiographical scenes into his own research, called the rule of transformation the art of decoding on a different plane to create his mythological message ([1972] 1985: 130). His habitual narrative was more than an intimate personal record as a private diarist, as he did try to speak to others. Wittgenstein started with special initials when communicating messages that were part of conversations with friends, students, and colleagues. The code of the abbreviated shorthand—initial "S" (short for "sensation")—coded the habituality of public language addressed to all speakers.

Wittgenstein's natural initials and inscriptions of pain and grief were monologues to himself, which he converted into logical symbols to achieve the "ceremonial" threeness of cultural dialogue (Sebeok [1994] 2001: 104). But the "soft" iconic-indexical signs, ruled by non-logical sense, did not reach the "hardness" of logical symbols, exclusively ruled in logical grammar for all participants. The hidden symbols of his diary referred as icons to his own self-medication, but as indexes they conditioned the readers to learn the didactic tool. Wittgenstein also missed the final goal: to follow the symbols of the language-games. The classification for the therapeutic setting of the forked tongue was the remedy in Bateson's "metalogue" as an intermediate party between monologue and dialogue. The causal classification of monologue, quasi-dialogue, and dialogue seem to follow Peirce's three categories in the subtext of Wittgenstein's diary, the context of his minor writings, and the major text of his language philosophy. The final meaning was to introduce Peirce's semiosis in the togetherness of the three categories.

Bateson wrote that the meaning of the initial is the "approximate synonym of pattern, redundancy, information, and 'restraint'" as in the telegraphic code ([1994] 2001: 130–131). The telegraphic code gives visible information coded in the vulnerable "guess with random success" (131). But the coded language is a quasi-language and the solution involves the unraveling of the keynumbers to find the underlying code. If we have the initial "T," which in the English alphabet can be the cliché that is followed by a "H" or an "R" or a vowel, Bateson cautioned about the risk of wrong conclusions (131). Wittgenstein stated that the initial "S" represented his graphic thought (firstness and secondness). This abstraction is a basic sign on its own (short for Wittgenstein's physical or mental "sensation"), but can also be regarded as Peirce's degenerate sign of firstness and secondness with respect to fully triadic signs implying thirdness. It seemed that the letter "S" is the first sketch of the full sign of semiosis, but for Wittgenstein, "S" is the impression of iconic pain. "S" suggested the open stimulus of the bodily and mental index, but also was the symbol that associated the subjective pain sensation with the objective mark of the grammatical syntax. The initial "S" broadened the remedy of his diary into a mathematical or statistical formula, working as a special code or quasi-code to reformulate (or retranslate) the direct sensation of emotions building the indirect dynamic forms of scientific (mathematical, statistical, or chemical) symbols.

Wittgenstein's art of oratory in public speaking was called the "signposts" of speech. He conjectured or hypothetized the pain sensation into private or public language to force the interpretation and signify new messages to the interpreters. Peirce wrote to Lady Welby in 1905 that he wanted to write a book on the process of thinking. Thinking was a rhetoric of non-technical and technical signs. For Peirce, the non-technical narratives involved a pure guess to upgrade the monologue of his own symptoms in the quasi-language of parables and metaphors. Yet Peirce misconstrued the non-technical talk of public speaking according to his logical structure of existential graphs "which expresses everything with a precision that no human tongues can approach, so that exercize in it strengthens the mental power of apprehension" (MS 280: 35). In his letter to Lady Welby, Peirce continued to explain the logical diagrams of existential graphs. He wrote that:

> Existential graphs are to be conceived as scribed upon the different leaves of a whole book. The whole book represents the thought (upon a given subject) of one mind. Each leaf represents a single stage of that thought. In the beginning, the successive leaves must represent strictly successive stages of thought—I speak of *logical* succession. But afterward when the minute anatomy of the thinking process has been mastered by the reader one can successively enlarge the intervals of development between the states of thought that successive leaves represent. (*Semiotic and Significs* [SS]: 195)

Peirce concluded that thinking moves from monologue to dialogue, meaning that logical thinking can have loose ends and partially determine the causal series of elements. He wrote that "A thought is a special variety of sign. All thinking is necessarily a sort of dialogue. An appeal from the momentary self to the better considered self of the immediate and of the general future" (SS: 195). Following Peirce, Wittgenstein's albums contained allusive, uncharacterized, or even self-contradictory signposts written in improvisational notebooks. The lack of a conventional rule signified that the reader (inquirer) needed to ascertain and explain what "actually is" (CP: 5:171) programmed in the "facts of life" of his diary. Wittgenstein shows the "diary" as the signposts of the crime scene. As in the detective novel, he tracks the isolated acts of clues and catchwords. These are at first impression meaningless until they can be regulated into the form of a "real" story. The detective story remains a horrible shadow of feeling and action of the crime scene, until the conclusion brings the existential specification of Peirce's three habits to discover the hidden signs to organize the criminal investigation and then dismiss the case.

The coded initial "S" is the "existential" sign used in logical investigation. As a double replica, "S" refers forward to the symbolic signs of habit to give general rule and law, but can also return backwards to mean the illogical vagueness of indexical habituality and iconic habit. Wittgenstein expected that the system of language would end the narrative of "facts of life" and focus upwards on the symbolic point of language-games, but the final output of habituescence was not working for Wittgenstein's language-games. Although the formula "S" already worked quasi-imperfectly as a symbolic sign, the single initial lacked the precise definition to identify with the other signs—the habitual signs of index and icon. The symbol is not the way to the real signpost, the replica is not a logical sign and does not connect with illogical and degenerate signs.

The signpost has lost its definitive meaning and again becomes the imperfect sign. The degenerate imperfect symbol tries to handle Wittgenstein's symptoms of medical disorder without the help of the logical rule of symbols. The quasi-semiosis is the defective transaction without interactive semiosis, but the initial "S" was no habitual sign nor the arbitrary degenerate sign, but a replica (that is, a copy or reproduction of a sign). In Peirce's system of existential graphs, the graph is reduced to the weak sense of a "pseudograph" (Roberts 1973: 67). The fundamental question of Wittgenstein's regenerative idea of reaching the law of the community turned the replica "S" progressively into the solitary sign that forced him to live with himself and forget the common language. The sensation of nothingness (Rotman 1987) meant that the use of "S" was recognized as meaning nothing. The daydream of senseless signs would darken into Wittgenstein's nightmares of keeping the imperfect message silent (TLP: 7), but he needed to let go of the "correct" grammar of the language-games. Obeying the "weak" quasi-semiosis of nonsymbolic signs, Wittgenstein had to explore the interdisciplinary forms of quasi-dialogue.

The dual opposition of private and public languages produces the major rule of human grammar, which German speakers such as Wittgenstein mainly saw in the example of the causal place of adverbials. Placed in the initial position, the series of adverbials give the human nuance of mood to the logical sentence, but they equally flavor the whole paragraph for sentimental reasons. Wittgenstein's use of "dazu" (for that purpose) started with the "zuerst" to launch Wittgenstein's private remarks at the public. Without mentioning "zweitens" or following numbers, Wittgenstein repeated the habituality of the demonstrative adverb "but" (*aber*) four times, but returned with an adversative nuance, see "Aber ich kan sie doch mir selbst als eine Art hinweisende Definition geben!" (But I can use it for myself as some sort of indicative definition!), "Aber ich spreche oder schreibe das Zeichen" (But I say, or write the sign down), "Aber wozu diese Zeremonie?" (But wherefore this ritual [of the collective noun]), and ending with "Aber in unserem Falle habe ich ja kein Kriterium für die Richtigkeit" (In our case, I have no criterion for what is correct). Wittgenstein's initial adverb "aber" is the challenge of the man/sign struggle with oneself (CP: 5.313–5.317). The formal solution is the compromise of the positive adverb "nun"; see "Nun, das geschieht ebendurch ds Konzentrieren die Aufmerksamkeit" (Well, the same happens by focusing my attention).

Although the attention of the target language is different from that of the source language, the English undertranslation of the German adverbs turned into the verbal modes to generate in English form the slight sense of overtranslation of the German style. But the crucial element of the diary anchored Wittgenstein's style in providing attention (*Aufmerksamkeit*) to oneself (the diarist) to communicate with others. In

Wittgenstein's quasi-dialogue, the diarist serves as his own iconic subject to himself to produce as quasi-interpreter the object (the diary), but at the same place or time he interacts indexically with other interpreters and readers to guarantee a "correct" answer to the public dialogue. For Wittgenstein, the collective argument does not mean that subjective questions and objective answers are alike. In the thought process of quasi-semiosis, they can interact to retain the memory of the double process. In actual practice, Wittgenstein recalled that both methods can "richtig an die Verbindung erinnere[n]" (correctly remember the connection) for the future. He had learned by heart to commit the illogical "sensation" to rewrite in the logical "S," but in public discourse he might not even remember or call it back.

The insecurity of storing the sensation solidly in your memory is different from rewriting the sensation into the written report to describe the very same sensation to others. This is what Wittgenstein argued in the "manometer argument" (Smerud 1970: 9, 57–66). He wrote, again in plaintext to the readers, that:

> Let's think of a use for the entry of the sign "S" into my diary. This is my experience. Whenever I feel a particular sensation, a manometer tells me that my blood pressure is raised. This enables me to report that my blood pressure is rising without the aid of the apparatus. This is a useful result. And it appears entirely unimportant whether or not I have *correctly* identified the sensation. Let's assume, I am constantly wrong about the identification, it wouldn't make a difference. And that in itself is a sign that the assumption of this mistake was an illusion. (We flip a switch, as it were, that looked as if it would serve to adjust something on the machine, but it was simply there for decoration and not at all connected to the mechanism.) And what reason do we have here, to call "S" the symbol of a sensation? Perhaps the way in which this symbol is used in this language-game.—And why a "particular sensation," the one every time? Well, we assume this, we write "S" every time. (PI: 270, my translation, MS 129: 46, 1944)[3]

The symbolic value of "S" is a struggle again in Wittgenstein's next thought experiment, including the error messages of the manometer to medical personnel. The "correct" point of the sign "S" can easily be twisted up or down the scale to correct what an "incorrect" signal could possibly signify. Concretely, the storage of the memory in the manometer must be different from short-term to long-term phrases and will remain an open question. The manometer has now turned into the puzzles of Wittgenstein's misreasoning of instructions.

The rule of thumb of the manometer is the mechanical scale consisting in the device of the elastic U-tube filled with a liquid. The apparatus reads the index of the pressure read from the scale. This machinery can give "rough" (that is, indexical and iconic) measurements of the patient's pulse, but the physical machine remains scientifically a meaning-blind mechanism (recalling Wittgenstein's image of the blind man). The manometer seems to measure "correctly" but with variable abstract numbers, without giving final and real constants. For the general solution, the manometer does not mirror the real point of the patient, but the additional guesswork approximates the measurements of the mathematical standards to the blood circulation from the pumping of the heart through the arteries and veins back again to the heart. The numbers of the heart rate per minute is the point of the "domestic" pressure in the cyclic nature of data-structures, but the genuine "sense-data" remain the guesswork of the "ideas in our minds" (Dilman 1998: 41). The inquirer's ideas do not represent the thought of the reliable scientific measurements but are only speculative hypotheses.

One can conclude that, in Wittgenstein's example, the diary was the iconic-indexical habit of spontaneous or even mechanical attitudes of his "play-act" (PI: 23; see Gorlée 2012: 159, 242) of quasi-semiosis. The theatrical scenes returned to the stories of Edgar Allan Poe's unsolved mysteries (Rotman 1987: 51–53) and relate the conjectural elements with the meaning of the crime puzzle. The "stage" voice caused patient Wittgenstein to sketch in the scenes of the diary the eternal premises of his own pain-expressions. At the same time, he trusted the secret figures and numbers believing in the logical play-act. The patient took the true conclusion of the pain game for granted. In the diary scenes, Wittgenstein created a theatrical make-believe. In the artistic illusion, he did not narrate his negative self-portrait, nor did he enact the performance of a certain role of detective playing "on the crime scene." Instead, he tried to create from the role-playing attitude the artificial mode of stage setting the introduction of the symbolic language-games. Since the function of the language-games mediate between ideology and literary form, they create the inner monologue to make possible the outer correspondence to others (Waugh 1984: 136, 148). But in Wittgenstein's radical point of view, the symptomatic habits of signs were translated from his physical and mental "sensations" into mathematical symbols (called "S") and other "strange" words and numbers to generate strange code numbers or code words.

The initials in phrases, letters, and syllables served as codes for other readers. They encouraged them to learn the "landscape" of the language philosophy, but turned into Wittgenstein's success as well as his failure. The quasi-language of the diary also introduced readers to the world of philosophical skepticism. What is true and what is not true? Wittgenstein's diary narratives were not a mirror image of his life (icon, firstness), nor did they reflect the narrative episodes of confession about his conduct or behavior (index, secondness). Instead, the quasi-language of words and sentences contained the crypto-biographical sketches addressed to be learned by readers to attain full knowledge (symbol, thirdness). The ordinary and coded quasi-language gave new directions to Wittgenstein's words and sentences, mixing freely the artistic genre of the diary with the alternative fragments of language philosophy. The conclusion of Wittgenstein's logical reasoning became the unsystematic and even arbitrary argumentation of uncertainty to "surprise" the readers. The readers did not receive the logical or "correct" argument, but Wittgenstein still proposed them to accept the hypothesis of language-games.

Wittgenstein's cries of exclamations, movements, or gestures in the diary tend to produce an atmosphere of uncertainty or disbelief in the mental processes of language-games (Glock 1996: 58–63; Gorlée 2015a: 76, 77). Wittgenstein suffered the hesitation of his personal anxiety and anger. To support his doubts, he stuck at least indirectly to the judgmental construction of Peirce's steps and phases of the fixed reasoning of semiotic arguments. Although they were anticipated by the logical system of Peirce's reasoning, the works of Wittgenstein were not sharply divided by their logical-linguistic conclusions. Reflecting on the vague principle of experimental reasoning between both logical philosophers, they generated philosophical propositions of certainty to understand the various descriptions of life experiences turned from the senseless "things" of nothingness (quasi-propositions) into the meaningful scale of full propositions. Thus one can apply the final evidence or proof of Peirce's three-way reasoning (for example, CP: 6.32–6.33) into Wittgenstein's own strategy of deduction, induction, and (Peirce's discovery) abduction, corresponding to thirdness, secondness, and firstness.

Peirce suggested that the human mind carried out three sorts of reasoning to consider what goes right and wrong in the activity of human reasoning (CP: 5.108). The first phase is the hypothetical model of abduction; the second phase moves to the more traditional models of induction and deduction (CP: 2.755). The three modes of reasoning served as Wittgenstein's "ideas [received in] a nominalistic, individualistic, sensualistic way" (CP: 6.150). The modes of thought served to formulate the facts and experiments surrounding any observation of real things. The observer was the self-inquirer who looked and saw to write about the practical habits of philosophy. Since philosopher Wittgenstein wrote about his personal symptoms in ordinary language, his "poetizing" anxiety remained uncertain reasoning for philosophy of science and the psychiatry of his time (Shands 1970, 1971; Shands and Meltzer 1973). His crypto-arithmetic description of his mystical habilts of thought were, to use Deely's formulation, the style of "cryptosemiotician." Wittgenstein was a modern thinker, secretly "involved with but not thematically aware of the doctrine of signs, still a prisoner theoretically of the solipsist epistemology of modern philosophy" (Deely 2015: 98 quoted in Sebeok 1979: 259).

Habits of reasoning

Wittgenstein seemed to insert the story of his own "painful" behavior into his philosophy to transform the pain into language-games and to move the qualities of his feelings from private remarks into public possessions (see CP: 5.112–5.113). These passages were the remedy for Wittgenstein's severe symptoms of pain, but in semiotic terms they were generalized into Peirce's different habits of reasoning. In the talking self-therapy of patient Wittgenstein, he practiced the technique of logical reasoning to grasp the causal rules of thought in his *Denkbewegungen,* written in ordinary language. The philosophy was in plaintext, the diary was mostly coded. Due to his style of writing, Wittgenstein was an "informal" scholar, but in his theatrical pose he pursued the "formal" ways of logician and active scientist Peirce to take the whole apparatus of logical methodology back to the old habits of reasoning. Peirce's "laboratory" evolved a series of things and ideas in three-way reasoning, while Wittgenstein was drawn into Peirce's logical models.

Originally, the scientific modes of reasoning were orthodox models, linked to the classical rules of logic to reach the true sense of pain, but seemingly under Peirce's more radical doctrine of semiotics, the causal reasoning served other working forms of semio-reasoning induction and deduction (Dilman 1973: 29–96, 99–194). Peirce added induction (indices) to deduction (based on symbols) to "discover" the iconicity of abduction. The three-way categories of reasoning were generally the experiment of revolutionary thinking and writing. But these three divisions could help one grasp and describe the flux and flow of Wittgenstein's thoughts in the movement of ideas (*Denkbewegungen*). After using deduction and induction for his philosophy, Wittgenstein imagined abductive reasoning as the sensational method to create his diary (Gorlée 2016a; see 2012, 2017).

The modes of reasoning were the continuation of the Roman *trivium* of grammar, logic, and rhetoric. Peirce's speculative rhetoric (also called aesthetics) was divided into images, diagrams, and metaphors to mark the grades of the sign-maker (writer, artist) in the effort of firstness (icon). Speculative grammar relates to the thirdness (symbol) and secondness (index) of the linguistic signs (*The Essential Peirce* [EP]: 2:327) to guarantee the "validity and degree of force of each kind" (Peirce 1955: 62) of the produced sign (in writing or art work). Peirce stated that the identity of "speculative rhetoric has been comparatively neglected" (EP: 2:327). To explain the beautiful "rhetoric of fine arts," he needed the "practical persuasion" of the intuitive dreams of the narrator (sign-maker). The writer engages in the story the "interest, curiosity, fear, tensions, expectation, and sense of order" of the readers (interpreters) to "remember, anticipate, hope, despair, believe, doubt, plan, revise, criticize, construct, gossip, learn, hate, and love" the story (Hardy 1969: 5). The stable self of the rhetoric includes the individual feeling of the writer to question the collective action of writing in practical forms and shapes to characterize her/his aesthetic activity. The specific answer creates the "certainly" true arguments to write the story. The methodology of speculative rhetoric makes the different levels of writing come "true."

Speculative rhetorics, or Methodeutic, emerges from the formalistic treatment to suggest that the three sciences grow from intuitive impressions to the unity of the perfect sign. Speculative rhetoric gives reliable information to the cohesive structure of writing. Peirce wrote that "Each division [of the argument] depends on that which precedes it" (1955: 62), but Peirce's semiotic method signifies that each sign must bring the new judgment as a symbolic sign to be regarded as the rhetoric of the writer's logical truth. But, according to Peirce's three interpretants, the argument of speculative rhetoric can also correspond to the lack of truth in pure speculation. In the "formal" volume of the *Tractatus*, Wittgenstein's strategy of writing contained a good deal of fragmented versions, in which he narrated about the "informal" experiences of sense-data as his "family resemblance" of pleasure and pain. Yet he never displayed in his subsequent works and writings the final version to qualify for the cohesive structures of the language-games. Wittgenstein's rhetoric remains a rhetorical question.

Instead of reaching Peirce's semiosis, which gains some information and "truth" from the sense-data of pain, Wittgenstein's game was halfway to semiosis but had fallen into the trap of quasi-semiosis (see Gorlée 2012). Wittgenstein's speculative conclusions were attempts to construct semiosis, but due to the errors of human workmanship his noble efforts were reduced to quasi-semiosis. The human concept of fallibilism is the maladaptive, and sometimes distressing, habit of reasoning in the ordinary or usual facts of writing. There, the logical system of interpretation accepted cases of false signs based on misreading or misunderstanding the ideas or facts in one or two categories: quasi-semiosis works with icons and indices, but without symbols (Gorlée 2004a: 145–239).

In his defense, Wittgenstein argued that the "weak" choice of quasi-semiosis is found in unusual words, sentences, or fragments found in ordinary language. These words are illogical and uncomfortable signs, which need to defend, in his own words, the "dry-cleaning" process of formal logic to recover them from the strangeness of their unusual interpretation and restore them to their usual working order (CV: 39, 44, 1998; see Gorlée 2012: 61). Wittgenstein's grammatical puzzle explained the rules of thirdness weakened into usual language, as follows:

> Every proposition has a content and a form. We get the picture of the pure form if we abstract from the meaning of the single words, or symbols (so far as they have independent meanings). That is to say, if we substitute variables for the consonants of the proposition. The rules of syntax which applied to the consonants must apply to the variables also. By syntax in this general sense of the word I mean the rules which tell us in which connections only a word gives sense, thus excluding nonsensical structures. The syntax of ordinary language, as is well known, is not quite adequate for this purpose. It does not in all cases prevent the construction of nonsensical pseudopropositions. (RLF 1929: 162)

Peirce's informative content of different forms and shapes of language expressed the same process as Wittgenstein's struggle. In philosophy Wittgenstein saw strong evidence for the belief in "grammatical" rules to guide away from "confusions," but in practice he degenerated from genuine semiosis into human quasi-semiosis. As a writer, he suggested a more positive tone of sympathy for human art:

> But it seems to me too that there is a way of capturing the world *sub specie aeterni* other than through the work of the artist. Thought has such a way—so I believe—it is as though it flies above the world and leaves it the way it is—observing it from above, in flight. (CV 1998: 7)

Later, Wittgenstein fought against the certainty of the *Tractatus*. Now everything can be said clearly. The creative argument of his later period showed the possible interaction of possibility and impossibility in the three-way categories. The sign-action of quasi-semiosis depended on Peirce's three modes of reasoning to communicate not merely to himself but for interaction with others. Wittgenstein's total communication rested upon the formal norms and standards of semiosis, but his argument did not reach formal semiosis, but rather the less formal approach of Peirce's quasi-semiosis. This reduction of the real certainty into the irreal uncertainty occurred, for example, in Wittgenstein's oral talks produced in his usual style of writing (Gorlée 2017). In semiotic terms, Wittgenstein's final occurrence to give the definitive conclusion was weakened from full semiosis to the reactor-interpretants to describe the thinking, speaking, and judging process of language. The weaker interpretants gain their proposed unity from the psychological events and ideas of the "facts of life" of the writer or language speaker, written in dynamic interpretants (index) and emotional interpretants (icon). But for other readers the surprise of secondness and firstness did not create the real conclusion of final interpretants but hypothetical guesswork (as previously demonstrated in Wittgenstein's manometer argument).

Although Wittgenstein's style of reasoning minimized the risk of the subjectivity of words to provide maximum objectivity in his rhetoric, he hoped to achieve the ideal of seeking the rational truth. He hated "confusions" in language, but he himself degenerated into a variety of inferential meanings, puzzling the readers with the "untruth" of hypothesis, mainly in his secret writings. Logical reasoning was traditionally either deductive or inductive reasoning, but Peirce revolutionized the dichotomy with abductive reasoning to generate three categories to model reasoning. Deduction was the strong method of explicatory (or analytic) reasoning, going from ideas to ideas and giving one truth as the final conclusion. Induction was ampliative (or synthetic) reasoning, going from ideas to things giving truth, but also certain untruths. Abductive reasoning went from ideas to things giving more than one meaning in Peirce's notion of "guesswork." Peirce's steps of logic are clearly present in the steps and stages of Wittgenstein's notebooks and manuscripts, for example the sensuous movements of his *Denkbewegungen* written as habits and habituality during the course of his life.

Explicatory or analytic reasoning corresponds to deductive logic, based on the formal power of symbols. Peirce explained this using the example of a beanbag:

Rule	All the beans from this bag are white.
Case	These beans are from this bag.
Result	These beans are white. (CP: 2.623)

All deductive reasoning simply substitutes from the possible premises what is implicit (present) in them. Deduction goes from one symbol to another related symbol, explaining directly or automaticaly the logical conclusion. Deduction corresponds to the idea of Peirce's symbol in the terms of law and habit. Deduction is necessary reasoning, since the logical conclusion is regarded as truth. In Peirce's exemplification, all of the beans in Peirce's sample are white, but the sample from the known whole is in deduction also true for the parts of the bag. Deductive argument moves from ideas to ideas, meaning that the state of affairs stays as it is (the whiteness of the beans) without drawing upon the possibility of new ideas. Unknown (or partially unknown) beans of other colors or different shapes could be secretly mixed between the white beans, but the deductive reasoning forecloses critical examination or evaluation of its premises and does not engage in the introduction of "creative" insights. Instead of renewing the interpreter's rhetoric of ideas, deduction blindly follows the adopted rule and case without further question to give the logical truth. Deduction is the final interpretant of Peirce's semiosis, but it is secretly struggling against the degenerate hypothesis of quasi-semiosis. Wittgenstein's early rhetoric sought to provide the readers with rational certainty. Accordingly, he justified himself in the truth claim of this hard law of reasoning deductively.

Wittgenstein centered the argument of his early book *Tractatus Logico-Philosophicus* (1922) on the formal principle of deductive thinking. With the causal chain of philosophical stages, he opposed making daily "confusions" of language speakers. The crucial questions for early Wittgenstein were:

> [What] logical propositions say or mean, what logical constants symbolize, what sanctions or justifies the logical inferences we make, what logical or necessary truths are based on, how we know or recognize them, in what way they differ from and how they are related to each other. (Dilman 1973: 100)

In the *Tractatus Logico-Philosophicus*, Wittgenstein answered these questions through deductive logic, in which "the symbol alone [works] that they are true; and this fact contains in itself the whole philosophy of logic" (TLP: 6.113). The "symbolic" nature of deduction brought Wittgenstein to his goal: the philosophical truth.

Wittgenstein's scholarship started with the formal speech of the *Tractatus*, in which he measured the effectiveness of this early volume against the total work of the philosophy of language. He wanted to judge the "confusions" of words, sentences, and paragraphs made by language speakers and to correct them. Wittgenstein's pattern of numbered and subnumbered items in the *Tractatus* reflects the symbolic nature of mathematical or statistical rules. The basic thoughts about the formal content harmonized the doubtful points in language through the rules of grammar and logic. This procedure determined the "good" and "false" meaning of linguistic problems, not through finding sporadic experiments to search for human errors but by strictly imposing the rules of the general symbolism (*Zeichensprache*) of language. He wanted to calculate, reason and plan the logical properties of mathematical symbols (TLP: 6.233, 6.234). Wittgenstein's general model of premises and cases followed in the *Tractatus* give valid and formal conclusions of deduction to attain the material form of logic and truth (Monk 1990: 67–72).

In the *Tractatus*, the sign and symbol are not uniform (Monk 1996: 345–347). Language, when spoken or written, for Wittgenstein, stands as the depository of signs (*Zeichensprache*), meaning that the sign (*Zeichen*) must have the *same* form and content (TLP: 3.31). Wittgenstein's notion of signs refers to "simple" or "complex" signs (*einfache Zeichen* and *komplexe Zeichen*). The "simple" signs, called "names" (*Namen*), are easily explained items without any real definition (TLP: 3.26). These "simple" signs attempt to "gather points" to belong to a quasi-proposition to have a fixed object with a real sense (TLP: 3.201–3.23, 3.26; Gorlée 2015a). Singular "names," such as exclamations, interjections, and other separate signs, are regarded as very "simple" signs, staying forever undetermined and basically without real sense (Gorlée 2015a). "Complex" signs approximate real signs in actual facts with a real meaning to discover. They belong to the propositional sentence relating to the sign to give them symbolical sense (TLP: 3.1432, 3.26).

Wittgenstein's symbol is different from the sign. The sign is seen as an element of the symbol, so that the symbol is larger than the sign, even *including* the sign (or various signs). Since the symbol merely implies the significant "complex" sign, it requires thought to function well. The symbol follows the logical grammar but can complexify the interpersonal communication because the *variable* form and content can "confuse" the argument. For example, to imagine how the linguistic symbols can serve to distinguish the class of word-signs, Wittgenstein noticed that:

> In the proposition "Green is green"—where the first word is a proper name and the last an adjective—these words have not merely different meanings but they are *different symbols.* (TLP: 3.323)

The logical environment (syntax) of symbols serves as the "functional sign" (TLP: 3.34), but Wittgenstein's symbols (not Peirce's symbols) are the sign with different meanings (TLP: 3.326–3.327). This makes deduction an easy but troublesome symbolism of Wittgenstein's reasoning in the *Tractatus.* He mentioned the mixture of symbols in the use of mathematical or statistical formulas, in which they still have the same "prototype" as the ordinary symbol but have independent meanings (TLP: 3.333). The *Tractatus* had the symbols of numbered and subnumbered paragraphs and sections to reflect Wittgenstein's formal symbols. Symbolicity is not a mixture of words, but in the *Tractatus* is the conventional system used to rule the formal framework of language.

The meaning of "sign" was for Wittgenstein and Peirce more or less the same "thing," but different in the "symbol." Peirce included a variety of:

> The term "sign" [in] every picture, diagram, natural cry, pointing finger, wink, knot in one's handkerchief, memory, dream, fancy, concept, indication, token, symptom, letter, numeral, word, sentence, chapter, book, library. (MS 74: 3)

These "things" show *seriatim*—the categorical object of icon, index, and symbol, which hardly has any meaning in itself but sees the sign as the semiotic variable of the "thing" against the non-semiotic "non-thing" without distinct meaning (exemplified in Gorlée 2014). Peirce's sign was generalized into the semiotic interaction of object and interpretant, expanded into the symbolic habit of law or rule. Wittgenstein's *Tractatus* transformed the "thing" of the formal symbol into the practical and less formal agreement of the causal "ideas" to rule the relatively simple and idiomatic system of language. He organized the commonsense analysis of words and sentences into the logical system, but beyond the logical atomism of the structure of the *Tractatus* (*Sachverhalt*) (TLP: 4.0311 and further) he applied the rhetorical use of language in the didactic interaction between himself (scholar) and his readers (students). In common speech, he hardly used any logical symbols but simplified himself in illogical icons and indices.

Peirce's "representations" and Wittgenstein's "expressions" treat the "symbol" as a logical sign with a meaning. The representation includes the expression of a less formal sign (icon, index) being transformed into a formal sign (symbol). In Wittgenstein's sense, the symbol is the conventional sign ascribing formal qualities to the sign to determine the logical place of truth or perhaps indicating a lack of truth (TLP: 3.12–3.14, 4.44–4.46). Wittgenstein's German rhetoric emphasized the foreign word "Kontradiktion" (TLP: 4.46) not something like "Wortstreitigkeit" to speak about the dispute of signs within symbols. By avoiding the term "untruth," Wittgenstein used the clear or unclear rules of the sign to color the symbols without losing the formal theory of the *Tractatus*. In the *Tractatus*, the term of language-games did not exist yet, so the signification of language was not symbolic signs but, rather, iconic or indexical forms of gestures.

Wittgenstein's "expressions" of the symbol was essentially different from Peirce's "representations" with attention and observation to upgrade feeling into action and thought (CP: 6.585). Yet both Peirce and Wittgenstein shared the interaction of the strong symbol with the weaker signs to build the rational and semiotic rule of communicating with language. For both thinkers, the symbol was essentially deductive reasoning. The semiotic rule was expanded by Peirce into the law and habit to reflect the *invariant* thought, but Wittgenstein completed the articulate form and content of signs by introducing the *variable* symbols. Instead of the "mixture of words" to express the weak and unsteady argument of language, both Peirce and Wittgenstein wanted to integrate the system of language with formal rules. But for Wittgenstein the social, moral, psychological, and other consequences of sign games or gestures would extend beyond their symbolic significance to communicate the thoughts through the weaker rules of contemporary language speakers.

Wittgenstein's lecture to the joint session of the Aristotelian Society and the Mind Organisation of 1929 reflected his change in direction:

> Such rules, however, cannot be laid down until we have actually reached the ultimate analysis of the phenomena in question. This, as we all know, has not been achieved. (1993: 35)

In the *Tractatus*, Wittgenstein described speech and language in deductive policy, which he compared with the musical idea of a "mixture of tones" (TLP: 3.141). The indexical "contradiction" of various tones would make room for the iconic quasi-code of Wittgenstein's diary and the symbolic code of the language-games.

At the end of the *Tractatus*, Wittgenstein abandoned the mental logic containing formal rules of deduction. He acknowledged the relevant state of affairs by building the internal model of "practical" induction. At this point, he confirmed the basic fact that "The process of induction is the process of assuming the *simplest* law that can be made to harmonize with our experience" (TLP: 6.363). The inductive method "has no logical foundations but only a psychological one," so it must be "clear that there are no grounds for believing that the simplest course of events will really happen" (TLP: 6.3631). Instead of the absolute truth of the logical conclusion, there is now the "probable" hypothesis of making individual choices. See Peirce's definition of induction:

Rule	These beans are from this bag.
Case	These beans are white.
Result	All the beans from this bag are white. (CP: 2.623)

The inductivist form of reasoning puts forward the typical form of reasoning of what "actually is" (CP: 5.171) in the concrete reality of the speaker. Induction checks the practical "course of experimental investigation" (CP: 5.168), but assuming that "what is true for a whole collection is true of a number of instances taken from it at random" (CP: 5.275). The conclusion of the fair sample taken from the bag takes for granted that we can judge that all the beans of the beanbag are, both now and in the future, white beans. Induction is the statistical proposition of the indexical sign, pointing outside itself to the object to which it refers to make sense. The index gives the "fragment torn away from the object, the two in their Existence being one whole or a part of such whole" (CP: 2.230).

Induction establishes a clear opposition between premise and conclusion (semiotically, between the original sign and the corresponding reactionary habit of the interpretant). The conclusion (interpretant-sign) requires the inquirer (interpreter, reader) to follow the judgment of the unknown almost blindly, but importantly for the conclusion there can be no absolute certainty in inductive truth. The active inquirers are spurred by their intellectual sense of curiosity (CP: 5.584), but are in fact making some predictions about the future, thereby judging the unknown by what the interpreter would see now: the extensive or even partial knowledge of the sign situation merely gives the "practical truth" (CP: 6.527). New knowledge is inferred by simply extrapolating from actual fact toward the unknown universe of the future; but the truth of induction brings the inquirers (readers) halfway on the path of logic, leading them closely from interrogation and doubt to their own belief in "certainty," which could indeed be turned into "uncertainty."

Induction serves as a "signpost" signaling the practical principle of the readers' sensations and thoughts as verbal clues. The signpost would help Wittgenstein's students understand the separate paragraphs his lectures, in the hope that they would turn into cryptanalysts. *The Blue and Brown Books* and the mainwork of the *Philosophical Investigations* are full of personal life experiences, other images in language-games as well as the stories of other language-games, to transform the basic procedure of narratives into the purely logical induction. Thus Wittgenstein trained his readers (students) to belief in induction to solve the reasoning problems of quasi-language. His belief led them to write not in the "natural" rule of the real world but in the "unnatural" diaries of the diary. The probable reasoning must go from the known real world through the inductive syllogism to grasp the arguments with real meaning.

Language has the "reagent" signpost of demonstrative and other deictic signs pointing to the objects of facts to describe the practical phenomena of certainty. In the detective story, we mainly observe the history of the indexical sign as verbal and non-verbal clues—a letter, a bloodstain, a footprint, or other forensic signs (Gorlée 2015d)—to point directly to another sign to explain the inexplicable story of the crime (Sebeok [1994] 2001: 84–86; Danesi 2014). In the mode of deduction, the human brain of the interpreter (here, the detective's brain) must be "under the dominion of a habit or association by virtue of which a general idea suggests in each case a corresponding reaction" (CP: 6.144). The detective's habit is the "intelligent" sign, degenerated into the habit of reaction to solve the sign-clues. The habit works backwards from the case to the causes, trying desperately to develop against the law of certainty without indulging deeply in the psychological aspects of belief and doubt. The habit senses the moral choice of "blind compulsion" (CP: 1.558) to solve the "criminal" case in ordinary language philosophy (Gorlée 2016b).

Von Wright described induction as "the best mode of reasoning about the unknown" (Von Wright [1941] 1965: 159). In the inductive policy, the "unknown" method of reasoning is "our way out from a complicated labyrinth" (159). He proposed the migration of *Tractatus*' mental signs of deduction into Peirce's "self-correcting operation" of induction (CP: 2.727–2.7230; see Lenz 1964; Von Wright [1941] 1965: 159–175, fns. 223–224). In *The Logical Problem of Induction* ([1941] 1965), Von Wright did not mention the use of the *Philosophical Investigations*. In later publications, he justified the imperfection of inductive reasoning but allowed that this led to mathematical calculation and statistical error.

Von Wright's "natural" example of induction was exemplified by the black plumage of ravens. Looking at the black birds, he wrote that in the uniformity of nature, one would assume that the color of all ravens was black. But he realized that:

> Why would we say we know that ravens are black? How many ravens have we seen? Most of us very few, if any. We have seen pictures of ravens; we have read about ravens in zoology books; we are familiar with what may be called the "proverbial" blackness of ravens. This is "second-hand" knowledge. (1984: 86)

The ravens are for most individuals basically unknown birds. Hardly seen in reality, in common knowledge they do exist as black birds. The case of white ravens would possibly be the exception from the inductive obligation, generating a new species.

In folktales, the raven was not a "natural" but an "unnatural" thing, surrounded by myth (Leach and Fried [1972] 1984: 927–929), as happened to Wittgenstein's beetles put into the box. It looks like we know the characteristics of the raven, but our knowledge is partial and random talk, at times merely the metatalk of secrets of witchcraft rather than commonsense analysis. Von Wright concluded that:

> At most a philosopher, who wishes to maintain that the reason why we *know* that ravens are black is that blackness is conceptually tied to ravenness. He would be wrong, however. An ornithologist, I think, would not insist on a conceptual tie there.
>
> For some purpose, however, blackness could be *made* a defining characteristic of ravens. This could be some practical, transient purpose—such as counting the number of live ravens in a district. Or it could be some scientific purpose—such as creating a taxonomy. (But even given such purposes as those mentioned one would, presumably, be willing to admit "exceptions.") (Von Wright 1984: 86–87; my emphasis)

In his words, Von Wright shows that the inductive policy of the logical experiments was regarded as a "primitive" habit, which can correct itself in the "frozen" standards of repeated habits but could equally "grow" into the political dangers of the scientific routine of Peirce's habituescence (Von Wright 1984: 147–148).

In *The Blue and Brown Books* and the *Philosophical Investigations*, the logical movements of thoughts depend on the indexical signs belonging to Wittgenstein's symbolic philosophy. But since the indexical signs were mixed with the personal events of the mathematical images, drawings, and stories, this must be the way to introduce the pictography of symbolic language-games. The procedure of the *Denkbewegungen* was not purely logical arguments but had psychological, anthropological, and indeed daily ingredients suggesting Peirce's concept of different habits. The scientific conclusions of induction can only become true when the underlying elements are also logical connections, but in the metaphorical discourse Wittgenstein used the excessively weak sense of inductive inference to offer good reason. In the opinion of orthodox rationalists, Wittgenstein reflected true or false understanding of the dependence on induction. The reason was that the induction hardly justifies the version of logical evidence without falling into the risks of "exceptions" with his narrative examples.

Wittgenstein's philosophical entries were now written in plaintext, first in deduction, then induction. Yet the diary was focused differently: mostly written in secret code, it focused the attention of the readers on Wittgenstein's sensation of alien Otherness. The readers (interpreters) of the cryptography were stimulated to analyze the strange "landscapes" to learn Wittgenstein's philosophy. Since the argument in the *Philosophical Investigations* is not the direct understanding of Wittgenstein's philosophy of language, the focus is the indirect (that is, unwritten and uninterpreted) thoughts of the diary entries to see the "secret" logic of Wittgenstein's abductive imagination.

Guessing

While deduction as thirdness is straightforward reasoning without making any error, non-deductive reasoning does not lead to necessary conclusions but to probable or plausible habits as a fair solution to the problem. Abduction works on the playful and rational guesses of Peirce's "experiences" (CP: 6.454) to confirm the hypothesis to solve the puzzling problem. While deductive policy "proves that something *must be*" in theory, induction generalizes the experience in secondness, showing that "something *actually is* operative" to solve the problem (CP: 5.171). Peirce suggested, however, that the alternative method of abduction goes further than deduction and induction. Abduction represents the "law of liberty" (CP: 6.450) to enlighten the truth through the hypothetical abstraction from work. The "Humble Argument" (CP: 6.483, 6.487–6.488) of abduction draws from the personal work of firstness. The conclusion causes open-ended guessing of one meaning or more than one meaning, merely suggesting that "something *may be*" the truth (CP: 5.171). Abduction fulfills Peirce's three stages in the non-logical and logical arguments of individual firstness. The play of imagination applied to Wittgenstein's evolutionary stages moves from public to personal writing, that is from philosophy to diary.

The source of insight into the original meaning of Peirce's "experiences" offered the "facts of life" split into two things. Firstly, the three "universes" were argued in deduction as "brute actuality of things and facts" to accept with moral blindness the established premises of the object studied. Secondly, the experience gives way to the "active power to establish connections between different objects" of the object seen as the indexical imperatives of induction (CP: 6.455). The center of reasoning lies, however, elsewhere in the iconic argument, which:

> Comprises mere Ideas, those airy nothings to which the mind of the poet, pure mathematician, or another *might* give local habitation and a name within that mind. Their very airy-nothingness, the fact that their Being consists in mere capability of getting thought, not in anybody's Actually thinking them, saves their Reality. (CP: 6.455)

Those "airy-nothings" are realized in the vague signs to find the "mystic experience" from the "visual physiology" to find the facts of life. The observation ascends from these ideas into the real vision of the puzzling problem (Shands 1971: 102–104 and throughout). The dream-work of the "reminiscences of sights, sounds, feelings, tastes, smells, and other sensations" (CP: 4.433) deeply influences the human brain to develop the first "thought-sign" (CP: 4.549, 5.283–5.309) to turn from these ideas into the creative reason of abduction. Abduction starts as personal firstness in Wittgenstein's cry for help. The cries cause chaos in body and psyche, but are anthropologically re-visioned by Bateson ([1994] 2001: 177–193) into the quasi-communication to strengthen the psychosomatic anxieties and get the health of the patient back (Staiano 1986: 14). The therapy (or self-therapy) of the spontaneous but brute experiments of Wittgenstein's cries was the basic ingredient of abductive speculation. The "Humble Argument" was Wittgenstein's intuitive knowledge to rewrite his *vie privée* for his diary.

The playful argument of abduction starts with implying the firstness in the "pure play" of "musement" (CP: 6.458, see 6.452–6.473). The reasoner lets herself/himself go and indulges freely in the delights of leisure. The idle speculation in abduction is not a bad habit but a good habit. Peirce's "meditation," "reverie," or "recreation" (CP: 6.452–6.465) unifies the "Sign's Soul" as a basic sign for mental tranquility (CP: 6.455; see Shands 1971: 94–123). The strictness of the intellectual discipline of reasoning is the active work of the reasoner's mind to be restive before doing the job. Indulging this relaxation, the active brains are left behind and the meditation takes over. The reasoner has transformed into a dreamer or play-actor showing in the musement the compliance with the creative intuition breathing originality and new ideas into what would otherwise be a "reasonable" (CP: 5.174), but utterly rationalistic and lifeless, procedure of strict reasoning.

In the recreative spirit of fancies and fantasies, the reasoner stays in the passive, but receptive, state of mind to let their "experience" happen in life to give itself form and meaning. The active consciousness has increased the level of the unconscious to find beyond the surface of the situation the spiritual and instinctive symptoms that let the ideas do their dream-work (CP: 7.45). The generation of personal ideas helps to bring the logical solution closer. The surrender to the instinctive intimation of musement makes the mystery of human guessing the real possibility of finding the logical truth. When applied to the medical case of Wittgenstein's symptomatic signs, the playful atonement of musement heightens the full understanding of his own problematic situation to heal his fears and anxieties.

Peirce encouraged the "playful" idea of Peirce's musement in metaphor: "Enter your skiff of Musement, push off into the lake of thought, and leave the breath of heaven to swell your sail. With your eyes open, awake to what is about or within you, and open conversation with yourself; for such is all meditation" (CP: 6.461). Wittgenstein let go of the intelligence of the brain to jump with simple words into musement:

> The feeling of an unbridgable gulf between consciousness and brain process: how come this plays no role in reflections of ordinary life? This idea of a difference in kind is accompanied by slight giddiness—which occurs when we are doing logical tricks ... When does this feeling occur in the present case? It is when I, for example, turn my attention in a particular way on my own consciousness and, astonished, say to myself: "THIS is supposed to be produced by a process in the brain!"—as it were clutching my forehead.—But what can it mean to speak of "turning my attention on to my own consciousness"? ... What I described with these words (which are not used in this way in ordinary life) was an act of gazing. I gazed fixedly in front of me—but *not* at any particular point or object. My eyes were wide open, brows not contracted (as they mostly are when I am interested in a particular object). No such interest preceded this gazing. My glance was vacant; or again, *like* that of someone admiring the sky and drinking in the light. (PI: 412;[4] see Shands 1971: 103)

Musing on the introspection between various meanings was inseparable from guessing the meaning of the private code in Wittgenstein's diary pages. The wild guesses of the coded script formalized human thought with informal emotions and actions into written discourse—the meaning was a puzzling wordplay (Gorlée 2005, rev. 2014a).

Abduction is playing over the hidden and uninterpreted details to see the decisive data of the problem. Thanks to the selection of data, the inquirer can guess the logical conclusion to solve the question. By giving way to spiritual impulses, the inquirer must be in the dreamlike situation of musement to catch the intuitive sense of the known parts of the brain to solve the unknown parts and explain the whole case. The abductive idea is to "feel" the data of the case to come up with the hypothetical conclusion (final interpretant). Indeed, abduction was Peirce's absolute talent of mankind to guarantee and justify the human labor of guesswork to reach a satisfactory and correct conclusion. Instead of induction serving the "statistical inference" for logic, the secret transpires in human chance: "Out of a bag of black and white beans I take a few handfuls, and from this sample I can judge approximately the proportions of black and white in the whole" (CP: 5.349). While induction and deduction are similar viewpoints of dealing with open systems about details, the human mystery senses the meaning through abductive reasoning.

Every scientific inquiry and pseudo-scientific story formulates a logical case to adopt certain beliefs leading from rough hypotheses to build further argumentation. Wittgenstein's diary used the raw and undefined version of human play to come to an abductive ideograph to strike the happy medium of the problem. Peirce noted that we catch the new "*case* from a *rule* and *result*" (CP: 2.623) to make the conclusion. Peirce's novelty of abduction explains the case of Wittgenstein's mode of thought (*Denkbewegungen*) as seen in the light of Peirce's technical example of the beanbag:

Rule	All the beans from this bag are white.
Case	These beans are white.
Result	These beans are from this bag. (CP: 2.623)

Or rephrased in the practical situation, "On the table there is a handful of white beans; and, after some searching, I find one of the bags contains white beans only. I at once infer as probability, or as a fair guess, that this handful was taken out of that bag" (CP: 2.623).

Abductive behavior takes on the chance of some clues as a medium to break the puzzle of the mysterious (or even criminal) case and to redefine the whole case in the new light. The radical leap in the dark moves away from the reasonable formulation of deduction and induction, not to trust the reasoned rules but to confide in the secret of the inquirer's instinct to generate personal ideas and to render disorder into order. The relaxation of the brain enables one to come up with the quasi-mathematical guesses to treat the word games. Abductive reasoning is what Peirce called "*il lume naturale*, which lit the footsteps of Galileo" which is "really an appeal to instinct" (CP: 1.630). Human instinct prevents man's (and woman's) vital crises of illness, life, and times of difficulty, danger, or anxiety to promote physical or mental health.

In Peirce's semiotic logic, the abductive experiment starts with the observation of the real signs of the insoluble puzzle (the rule of the case). After dreaming and studying the situation in the "Play of Musement" (CP: 6.460), the interpreter introduces their own image ideas to grasp instinctively the metaphorical signs to serve as abductive stages to check the "fingerprints and footsteps" (Gorlée 2015d) of the case. The inquirer interrogates the problem (the result of the case) to decipher the case as the unruled activity catching the proper ideas of their free mind. The catchwords can be compared to the cultural prejudices of the ordinary "grammar" of life, but in abduction they are removed from the rules of "grammar" to play psychologically in the interpreter's intuitive mind. Escaping from the emotional or affective attitudes, the interpreter creates enough free space to solve the problems to reach a logical conclusion.

Peirce's abduction could possibly include the intellectual strategies of deduction and induction, but instead is basically concentrated on the interpreter's creative brain deciphering the enigma of the case. The intuitive opportunities stay away from traditional possibilities of prejudices and judgments, but make a mental shortcut. Instead of trusting the standard of "sentimentalism [implying] conservatism," abductive guesses take the more direct route of "advocat[ing] radical reforms" changing the "code of morals at the dictate of a philosophy of ethics" (CP: 1.633). For Peirce, the interplay of musing abduction exposed the free creativity of firstness to solve the intertwined variety of emotional and sensational matters of the case to end in a logical conclusion.

The inquirer's readaptation, retranslation, and rebuilding of the details of the puzzling case establishes a sense of the new base for reasonable doubt to change the troublesome case as part of the world of logic. The inquirer tested, confirmed, and self-corrected the attention to Peirce's capitalized "Observation" in three categories, demonstrating how the human sensation and feelings guess correctly the abductive methods of unruled reasoning. Staying away from the internal "observation made from the parts of the diagram" and the "external observation of the objects," abduction presents no less than the signpost of trusting ourselves to this "*force majeure*" (CP: 5.581) of free reasoning.

The experimental power of abductive observation requires the unconditional "surrender to the Insistence of this Idea" in the abduction to oneself, since the "hypothesis is, as the Frenchman says, *c'est plus fort que moi*" (CP: 5.581). The hypothesis through speculation breaks through the heuristic programming in the "Humble Argument" to trust the observation of the facts, to rearrange the image ideas, and see the explanatory solution of the troubles (CP: 6.488). For Peirce, abduction is more than gratuitous guesswork providing neither trial nor error, but rather it allows a wider range and character of good and evil moods to think instinctively beyond consciousness to arrive at logical intellect. This is also Wittgenstein's work in his diary.

For example, Wittgenstein's secret dialect (or quasi-language) can be compared with David Savan's article "Abduction and Semiotics" (1980). Savan discussed the past history of Old Czech, called the Teták dialect. As an example, he introduced the scientific strategy of the religious reformer Jan Hus, who in the early fifteenth century made linguistic changes to Old Czech to give new directions for new forms of language. As a linguist, Hus investigated the structure of facts and features to find fresh linguistic forms, taking into consideration the geographical decline of older habits to speak with the political and social division of the regions of Bohemia and Moravia (the western and eastern parts of Czechoslovakia, with similar languages). As a preacher, Hus's changes were ruled by the old tone of political speech to adapt to the new theological speech. He was ready to announce to the Czech-language speakers the replacement of old "grammar" by new habits of speech.

Hus's clerical task was preaching in the Czech language. His outlook on the Old Czech language was approached as a collection of linguistic units unable to relate to the creation of the renewed national language. Imposed by Hus as a priest and linguist, this task led to hostility against his plan for the disappearance of their native language. Hus was popularly considered a bad prophet foreseeing the radical change to the old stream of dialect with it disappearing in the future. To be sure, the novelty of Hus's method of changes removed the old forms of language in the hands of a single inquirer. His labor was critical and relative, because normally this process takes place in evolutionary adaptive steps, meant to break through the external facts of Old Czech and compose contemporary ideas of the Czech language. Contrary to Hus's conversion of script to speech, the language speaker tends to slowly develop a certain style of reasoning to serve how language is conveyed for the native community of speakers.

Savan stated that the modes of reasoning generated logical forms of language, starting with deduction to find through analytic reasoning the peculiar changes. Then, he treated words in statistical pattern to see how often they were used in formal induction (CP: 5.349). However, Hus's scientific idea of Peirce's black and white induction existed to prove that personal ideas of abduction might replace non-logical signs with logical signs, primitive signs with contemporary signs, and emotional signs with intellectual signs. The readaptation of the pronouncements introduced new sensuous habits to change the native language. This change was of course different from Wittgenstein's secret arrangement of the native German language turning into the crypto-habit, imposing the sense of an artificial "grammar" to decipher the code system. In both cases, abduction was regarded as more of a revolutionary experiment. The bold experiment of abduction breathed originality into what would otherwise be the "best explanation" against the "procedure of testing and confirming hypotheses" (Hintikka 1998: 506–511). The inquirer of the world-tool of language must bring different knowledge to solve the "psychological" problem of language speakers.

Hus's abductive experiment provoked something like a troublesome revolution in speech. As the single "inventor," he needed to build freely on his earlier observations to open up new ground. Surprisingly, he introduced new ideas to scientific inquiry to generate a whole "grammar" for native speech. The "ordinary" language speakers were prevented from speaking out publicly. The Czechoslovakian speakers had no explicit notion to convert the new courses of action into their own vocabulary. Is Hus's rational argument the logical operation handling new "ideas" to serve as clerical and ordinary language? Remember that in Hus's era he had to work exclusively with people using spoken language, for example replacing the dental "alico-alveolar consonants /t d n/" for the corresponding "bilabial consonants /*p *b *m/" (in present-day notation) (Savan 1980: 252). At that time written work was reserved solely for biblical priests and legal documents for nobles. Hus's work of sound emission and sound reception of language was indeed an ambiguous and confusing revolution that would change, literally, the voice of all speakers and even change the learned history of the Slavish population (Sebeok 1985: 304–310).

Wittgenstein's diary tried to find in the quasi-language a written standard form with technical control over the survival of the oral dialect. He used the "restricted code" to redefine the redundant orthography with minimal syntactic diversity (Bernstein 1974: 1550–1557; see Bateson 1975: 60; Fiske [1982] 1987: 74–79). Wittgenstein's idea of quasi-language introduced the coded dialect of non-technical variants. He applied the less formal statements written in the familiar "secret" code to communicate with others. His revolutionary change was indexically using the unfamiliar idiom as his familiar code. When Wittgenstein's emotional idiom was decoded into the linguistically implicit alphabet structure, the code dialect was treated as a formally framed dialect. Its usage was confined to the discrete similarities between the speakers to serve their linguistic speech. Wittgenstein's secret dialect oriented the readers to establish new social relations with their psychology of language. The content was naturally bound to the single items of the intimate and autonomous diary text, but the restricted code meant that the dialectical differences of Wittgenstein's speech pattern manufactured a sense of iconic likeness to the original, shaped in the evidence-based system of Hus's indexical code. As in Hus's work, deduction and induction were shared in the informal echo of abduction, meaning that in the case of Wittgenstein's diary the grammatical rule promoted the mere chance to muse, almost naïvely, the use of language and to take this one step further. The descriptive activity inverted the riddles of his own life into the anecdotal evidence of the iconic and indexical differences. Wittgenstein's readers were forced to disentangle the truth of his quasi-episodes.

The stereotyped communication of the "restricted code" demonstrated the dual signs of icons and indexes to self-generate the triadic signs of icons, indexes, and symbols. Wittgenstein's quasi-language formed the area of surrogate signs to share the territory of communication. The discreteness of the numbers and word-features revealed the common ground to share the passageway of codes (Gorlée 2015c: 114–123, following the important articles included in Sebeok, Hayes, and Bateson [1964] 1972). To conclude Wittgenstein's verbal and clinical puzzle, his diary identified his individual sensations as an emotive writer, but at the same time he tried to educate the metasemiotic interaction by his interpretants to bring together the companions, friends, students, and readers to mediate the function of his thoughts with others (Parmentier 1985: 25–31, 45). The outcome of Wittgenstein's quasi-communication was his way of real communication.

The conjectural aspects of abduction liberate the inquirer from the rules of deduction and induction to relabel and christen the surprising mode of thinking from human instinct. This thinking was, for all the tentative rhetoric of the diary, more than gratuitous guesswork. Peirce wrote the fragmentary draft in the article about "Guessing" ([1929] 1966; reduced version in CP: 7.36–7.48; see Sebeok 1981: 20ff.). There Peirce explained how the human nature of pragmatic reasonableness can lead from surprising facts to exact truth. Through the entrée of abduction, human intelligence is a chemical reaction manifesting heat as proof that the condition of practical matters is definable in the scientific conclusion. In the article, Peirce explained that the process of the mental dimensions of abduction was articulated by the instinctive strategy to make final (or logical) interpretants. He wrote that:

> Knowledge of any subject never goes beyond collecting observations and forming some half-conscious expectations, until we find ourselves confronted with some experience contrary to those expectations. That at once rouses us to consciousness: we turn over our recollections of observed facts; we endeavour so to rearrange them, to view them in such new perspective that the unexpected experience shall no longer appear surprising. This is what we call explaining it, which always consists in supposing that the surprising facts that we have observed are only one part of a larger system of facts, of which the other part has not come within the field of our experience, which larger system, taken in its entirety, would present a certain character of reasonableness, that inclines us to accept the surmise as true, or likely. (Peirce [1929] 1966: 267)

Peirce's first example is the investigation of the observation of Rafael's painting to extract the instinctive ideas to illustrate the possible hypothesis of the whole:

> For example, let a person entering a large room for the first time, see upon a wall projecting from behind a large map that has been pinned up there, three-quarters of an admirably executed copy in fresco of one of Rafael's most familiar cartoons. In this instance the explanation flashes so naturally upon the mind and is so fully accepted, that the spectator quite forgets how surprising those facts are which alone are presented to his view; namely, that so exquisite a reproduction of one of Rafael's grandest compositions should omit one-quarter of it. He guesses that that quarter is there, though hidden by the map; and six months later he will, maybe, be ready to swear that he saw the whole. This will be a case under a logico-psychical

> law of great importance ... that a fully accepted, simple, and interesting inference tends to obliterate all recognition of the uninteresting and complex premisses from which it was derived. The brighter the observer's intelligence ... the more confident he will soon be that he saw the entire composition. Yet, in fact, the idea of the whole's being on that wall will be merely evolved from his *Ichheit*: it will be a surmise, conjecture, or guess. (267–268)

To harden the belief in human guessing, Peirce jumped to the work for scientific language brought together by the semiosis of abduction. Instead of the physiological method of induction, he chose the psychological approach to treat the case. In other words, instead of the "habitual element," he indicated the "sensuous element" (CP: 2.643). The abductive procedure passes to "attentive observation, observation into musing, musing into a lively give and take of communion between self and self" (CP: 6.450). Peirce's playfulness of musement relies on the intuitive and instinctive power of the mind, which is almost impossible to formulate but resort from emotional interpretant (firstness) to dynamical interpretant (secondness). If the rules of good processes of reasoned thinking, "one's observations and reflections are allowed to specialize themselves too much, the Play will be converted into scientific study"—however, Peirce as a scientist himself added that the jump to play in science "cannot be pursued in odd half hours" (CP: 6.459).

Peirce's second example of abductive argument in formal terms was the story of his own detective story, written in 1879 ([1929] 1966: 270–275). This anecdote took up the historical narrative of the theft of Peirce's watch from his cabin. Peirce was a passenger on the Fall River boat from Boston to New York and he was transformed into a detective, persecuting the symptoms of the suspect in New York. Peirce's narrative was fully discussed in Sebeok's "'You know my method'; A Juxtaposition of Charles S. Peirce and Sherlock Holmes" (Sebeok 1981: 21–23 and throughout, Sebeok in Eco and Sebeok [1983] 1988: 11–19).

Peirce's story as a detective starts with traditional reasoning. After the theft, Peirce related that he ordered that all the waiters of the boat "come and stand up in a row" ([1929] 1966: 271). Peirce's plan to apprehend the watch and detain the criminal was no great success and he changed the routine from deduction to induction. He persuaded Pinkerton's Pawnbrokers in New York to check for the indications of the theft of the personal property. The Pinkerton's agent followed his own plan to check the "fingerprints and footsteps" on the boat (Gorlée 2015d). Again, no success. Opposing the traditional reasoning of deduction and induction, Peirce reverted against the old attitude to embrace the detailed manner of secret drop-off points, illegal border crossings, and personal inquiries to play the abductive kind of thriller–but without involving the police. Peirce's anecdote illustrates an abductive experiment *in action*. The action is a real history, but in writing the story he initiated the conflicts of figures and episodes in the "Play of Musement" (CP 6.458) to require cultural participation from the readers. Peirce's playful mind treated the concrete habits of speech and human conduct to respond to the solution of the criminal case. In the psychological brain of a detective, the story interpreted the unresolved case not through deduction or induction, but through the psychoanalytical strategy of the abductive experiment *in action* (Sebeok 1981: 16; Eco and Sebeok [1983] 1988; Danesi 2014: 136–137).

Peirce's anecdote is a didactive thriller to prove that the literary saga of Sherlock Holmes and other "historical" detectives played the musement of their working brain to work on abductive ideas. Musement gave the preparatory material to solve the mysterious stories for the detective. The detective's role embodied the scientific brain of the inquirer (or interpreter) to bring new ideas to the creative mind to solve criminal cases. In the abductive investigation, the detective explored all kind of signs, signals, and signposts to detect the open and hidden paradoxes to interpret the case and find the criminals. The detective was inspired by the moral and mental details of the actual scene of the crime to find the special indeterminacies–in contrast to the determinacies of the deductive search. The dogmatic rationalism of deduction disagrees profoundly with the quasi-theoretical musement of abduction working on a probabilistic basis.

The conjectural element of guessing correctly is precisely the sense of haunting experience lodged deeply in the human brain. Abductive reasoning led Wittgenstein to write the diary to provide a remedy for his anxieties. In the later philosophy, he avoided the "movements of thought" of deduction and induction to amplify in the diaries his own "transition of thought" (CP 6.461). Wittgenstein trusted his psychological intuition. The radical changes of writing was similar to the procedure of Rilke's frozen visions of life or death, Kafka's half-human and half-animal stories, and even Pepys's secret adventures reformulated in code. The hieroglyphic puzzle of abduction will start as open conversation with yourself to store the detective's arsenal of thought in the unthought and uninterpreted habit of the psychological brain to instruct the class of advanced students. Thanks to the passive but receptive dream of Peirce's musement, Wittgenstein's diary pages served "not [as] playthings but edge-tools" (CP: 6.461) to know more. It formed the brain to go from likely speculations with several meanings to reach the proximity of the amazing faculty of "logical analysis … to its full efficiency" (CP 6.465). Wittgenstein's diary was not meant as an idle amusement to narrate the story of intimate events but as an encouragement to possible readers to learn the pertinent case of the code system (Gorlée 2015c: 130–139).

Diary as self-therapy

Wittgenstein as a foreigner tried to solve his own medical (or psychiatric) condition through the sign processes of communicating his different interpretants with friends, companions, and students. His identity involved the clear and vague inscriptions of the "visiting card" (see Chapter 1). Wittgenstein felt like the deviant figure of the "hanged man" (Highwater 1994: 191–211). In the Tarot game of divination, the metaphorical image of the "hanged man":

> Usually hangs upside down, usually tied by his ankle to a horizontal beam supported by two leafless tree trunks. The man's unbridled leg is bent at the knee, forming a triangle. The hands of the figure are tied behind his back, so his arms form another triangle. Despite his precarious situation, the young man is relaxed

> and smiling, appearing somewhat playful, as if he sees himself as being free while the rest of the world is fettered; seeing himself as upright while the rest of the world is upside down. (193)

Wittgenstein's urgent cries yearned for a better, or more just, life. In the physical and mental position of the "hanged man," the reversed meanings of symptoms identified him as the *other* man. He felt strange from the manners of English civilization, and even estranged from his professorate in Cambridge. He struggled with mental illness and contended with the psychotic state of a foreigner or outlaw. Throughout his life he was fraught with the danger of losing his real person. He entrapped his thoughts as the entanglement of a trickster working through philosophizing to be free.

Wittgenstein's sexual partners figure prominently in the self-addressed monologues of his diary. The emotional and sensational trajectory with David Pinsent, Marguérite Respinger, Francis Skinner, and Ben Richards is often initialized to the first letters of their names, but they are present persons in Wittgenstein's autobiographical piece as parts of Wittgenstein's oneness (firstness). But written mainly in codification, he estranged himself as the "hanged" sign in the alien Otherness. The quasi-language was the pre-verbal thoughts of his sensory experience and impressionistic language in the abductive description of his coded diary. In the diary, he mused about the emotional pleasure and pain he deeply felt in his heart—and sometimes an indication of his general physical health.

In his monologues, Wittgenstein spoke of things he would never say out loud in the dialogue of promoting the collective language-games. Keeping the diary was Wittgenstein's private affair of firstness, which with the indexical code made the details visible to outsiders. It seems that Wittgenstein needed to struggle with his emotions to settle the friendship with Marguérite Respinger. Their friendship flourished but brought burning questions. Did he and she desire a sexless marriage or did he transfer his affection to being homosexual? Choosing the radical love of male homosexuality, Wittgenstein's first love after the shell shock of the First World War was Francis Skinner. The inner speech of his symptoms actualized his intelligent thought-forms alone in his philosophical "mission," but the habit of the diary also left him in a social vacuum. Most of the time he lived alone.

The coded pseudo-confession of Wittgenstein's *libido* offered the paradox of erotic love in homosexuality offered with or without religious sins. Wittgenstein was in his time a modern thinker: he rejected the old sexual mores which did not reflect the new liberal standpoints of moral and ethical considerations of being "different." He accepted the controversial issues of transient thought-forms of sexual romance—that is, autosexuality and heterosexuality, which can be altered rapidly or turned off entirely. At the same time, by keeping the diary he used the musement to vacate his brain and inflect his wounded brain away from intelligent thought to enter the dream of abductive reverie and meditation. Wittgenstein nursed the relaxing climate of sentimentality to give him some rest. The playful idea of musement sprung up to color the surface of language in his coded pseudo-language, and Wittgenstein hoped that writing the diary could heal the symptoms of his future environment (*Umwelt*).

Wittgenstein struggled to save his soul from his own evil spirit troubled by pain and grief in the regime of Nazified Europe. His wounded person was the disease ofted caused by the usual course of events, such as the plague of buzzing insects surrounding his head when he worked in the summer season. He realized that his soul was far from God's mercy, while he had drifted into a life of vices. He even thought that he would eventually become blind or deaf, and even considered the idea of suicide. His liver operation placed him as a patient under the care of bad nurses, as he wrote in code. To free himself from his duties, he read Kafka's animal-human stories to inject some humor in the text of his works. He even considered his public confession as a would-be catharsis of tears and blood to his friends. The story of the beetles lifted his mind from the limits of the box to observe the dimensions of the world. Wittgenstein spent time on the fjords of Norway, attempting to compose in absolute tranquility the final version of the *Philosophical Investigations*. Later, the metamorphosis of his mind went further: by abandoning the professorate in Cambridge, he liberated his troubled soul from all kinds of psychological pressures. Wittgenstein's sense of reality was infected by the false notes of irreality. The effect on himself was the disease of his own symptoms (Staiano 1986: 13 and throughout). To recuperate from the personal shocks, he needed first and foremost the therapeutic care of family members, especially the intimacy of his older sister Hermine Wittgenstein and the comfort of his sisters Margarethe, Helene, Hermine, and their families (McGuinness 2018), but their correspondence was impossible in the war.

The sweeping theory of philosophy made Wittgenstein popular as a scientific philosopher (Gray 1969: 32). Yet the psychoneurotic condition of the "sentimental" diaries remained the unknown and unanalyzed subject. The scientific style moved from safe deduction (must be) and operative induction but avoided the surprising information of his talent for abduction (maybe). Abduction was used in the secret idiom of quasi-language playing in the code. The "playful" nature of musement gave shades of meaning in new and unexpected ideas to intelligent analysis. Wittgenstein followed Peirce's educational method of abductive reasoning with his students. His lectures were "not a conversation in words alone, but [were] illustrated, like a lecture, with diagrams and with experiments" (CP: 6.461). The affection to his students was the new learning method of Peirce's abduction through musement (argued here), which has been called the "mystical" vision (Glock 1996: 251–253) but is a form of meditation. Wittgenstein's real problem was the disorder of the symptoms, he felt the reversed "hanged man." His soul was constantly under fire, crushing him with neurotic despair. More memoir than autobiography, his diary was the coded pressure of his disease. He wanted to manifest his mental confession to other readers, but how? The readers of his diary came to learn the code of the language-games with the promise to go from cryptanalysts to real philosophers.

Wittgenstein's educational role asked for a therapeutic response from intellectual friends to help heal the emptiness of his monologue. Since the dialogue with others was troublesome due to the presence of Wittgenstein's symptoms, he liked to speak to a friend, companion, or colleague, such as Paul Engelmann, Bertrand Russell, Frank Ramsey, Rudolf Koder, Piero Scraffa, George Edward Moore, Nicholas Bachtin, and others. In the "investigative togetherness" (Shands 1970: 15) of these intellectual conversations, Wittgenstein fully explained the rough drafts of his language philosophy. He also created a wider and more abstract circle of "intimate" but "frozen" co-workers. The same sense of "album" of philosophical togetherness is the collection of lectures he gave as a professor to students at the University of Cambridge to find a diagnosis of objective knowledge in their subjective learning (Wiesenthal 1997: 188). The students gave him a social togetherness.

Teaching the new philosophy to Elizabeth Anscombe, Rush Rhees, Maurice Drury, Yorick Smythies, Norman Malcolm, and other "selected" students was not only Wittgenstein's daunting task to be given in the English language, but for himself and the students it stood as a synonym for "learning to learn" (Bateson in Ruesch and Bateson [1951] 1987: 215). The students memorized the lectures, took notes, and participated in discussions with him. The interchange of opinions made possible their publication at a later date. The "album" of Wittgenstein's lectures was in itself a process of learning, in which he clarified issues, while the students tested the strength of revision to edit his lectures (see Wittgenstein's LA; *Wittgenstein's Lectures Cambridge, 1930–1932* [LWL]; McGuinness, Ascher, and Pfersmann 1996). For the later, more professional, edition of Wittgenstein's lectures, see Klagge and Nordmann's volume *Ludwig Wittgenstein: Public and Private Occasions* (2003).[5]

Beyond learning and teaching students, Wittgenstein conveyed the intense debate concerning the new philosophy during various talks to the Cambridge Moral Science Club and other societies, he left numerous letters and postcards of both a private or professional nature, and wrote a number of articles and reviews. These "minor publications" or "shorter writings" were published from "a mass of papers [of] notes, typescripts, dictations" in Wittgenstein's *Philosophical Occasions 1912–1951* (1993: vii). The editors of this volume, Klagge and Nordmann, added humbly that the "activity of two modest collectors may have produced an avenue in its own right into Wittgenstein's thought," but they stressed that "From this picture of short writings emerges a picture of Wittgenstein that is obviously far less detailed, but no less faithful, than the picture that emerges from the series of book-length publications" (vii). The letters to Wittgenstein's family members were published in German in McGuinness, Ascher, and Pfersmann (1996) and as an English translation in McGuinness (2018).

Wittgenstein undertook to heal his pain by communicating the therapeutic experience—now called Gregory Bateson's "metalogue." Bateson preannounced metalogue in "Metalogue: What is an instinct?" (1969), but the idea of metalogue was understood in cooperation with his daughter Mary Catherine Bateson in the book *Steps to an Ecology of Mind* ([1972] 1985). Teaching the synonym of Bateson's "learning to learn" (Ruesch and Bateson [1951] 1987: 215), his remedy as an anthropological teacher seemed to cure the pathology between reality and false beliefs. Bateson made clear that the revolutionary discipline of metalogues could change the future of the human ecosystem into something of a better life. He briefly defined the notion of metalogue, saying that:

> A metalogue is a conversation about some problematic subject. This conversation should be such that not only do the participants discuss the problem but the

structure of the conversation as a whole is also relevant to the same subject. Only some of the conversations here presented achieve this double format.

Notably, the history of the evolutionary theory is inevitably a metalogue between man and nature, in which the creation and interaction of ideas must necessarily exemplify evolutionary process. (Bateson [1972] 1985: 1)

Concretely, in the metalogue, Bateson played a "fictional" game with his young daughter Mary Catherine Bateson. As Wittgenstein's student, Bateson's daughter was a young girl, full of curiosity and eager to learn the scientific approach to eventually become a scholar. Father and daughter talked about various subjects bothering mainly the younger brain of the daughter. The costs and benefits of their metalogues were exposed in autobiographical conversations to solve the internal and external puzzle between family members, as used in Bateson's experiment. The series of questions and answers revealed the critical ways of play and fantasy happening between the use of speaking to survive the mental uncertainties of the political involvement of the United States in the Second World War and the eventual atomic bombing of Hiroshima and Nagasaki. The contrasts and contradictions stressed the individual differences of the metalogue of father and daughter. The narrative conflicts between father and daughter responded to the anxieties leading to survival in an evolutionary stable state of mind. The mistakes and misunderstandings of the uncertainties of life were similarly suggested in the special manner in which Wittgenstein gave his lectures. He went beyond the didactic action of him and his students discussing military conflicts to handling how to create a peace settlement in their lessons.

For example, Bateson wrote a number of narratives (3–58) to inspire the motoring behavior of metalogues. In the first metalogue, Bateson's young daughter showed that she was not a tidy person, but her question, "Daddy, why do things get into a muddle" (3) garnered the reply that "tidy" and "untidy" have several meanings, while the word "muddle" implies confusion and entanglement, all jumbled together in the critical situation of making lots of mistakes. Father Bateson tried to exemplify the misunderstanding of language with the cinematic story of the movies, in which:

You will see a lot of letters of the alphabet all scattered over the screen, all higgledy-piggledly and some are even upside down. And then something shakes the table so that the letters start to move, and then as the shaking goes on, the letters all come together to spell the title of the film. (5)

The daughter agreed that ordinary language must make sense, but the fate of other languages had a different, and unknown, background. Father Bateson ended the bedtime story with his daughter saying that in the real world that underlies our lives, things do not get stirred up but always stir up troubles between us.

In the following metalogue, "How Much Do We Know?" (21–26), Mary Catherine wanted to know how knowledge works to "help" the human brain to act properly in life. Her father replied with a metaphor, saying that knowledge is "knitted together, or woven, like cloth, and each piece of knowledge is only meaningful or useful because of the other pieces," but it works "in three dimensions—perhaps four dimensions" (21–

22). The illusion of unity and disunity shows that the game of talk and metatalk can be reconciled as the play-act of assembling different pieces of knowledge in the inventory of the brain. Bateson told his daughter that to calculate error she must figure out the dynamical system of other speakers. Immediately, she exclaimed that "I don't like arithmetics" (23). Father Bateson gave practical examples to observe how "Arithmetics is a set of tricks for thinking clearly and the only fun of it is just its clarity" (25). The human brain seems to work in an orderly and disorderly ways through the paradox of arithmetic and amusement.

The same fluctuation between logic and drama played in young Wittgenstein's syndromes about virtues and vices. Living in his religious reality, Wittgenstein felt in pain of death. He cried for help, communicating in metaphor, that he had to live with "wild beasts" to get near to the divine "other" kingdom of "angels" (Mk 1:9–15; see Gen. 9:8–15). To construct the business of conversation with other living beings, Wittgenstein's cry for peace was his prayer exclaiming the voice of complaints to ask for justice for all. The prayers were not the same as Bateson's personal metalogues, since the collection of biblical instances were made universal among different languages and cultures. They were incorporated into the general prayers of one of God's creatures to ask a personal favor (James ([1902] 1982): 116–130). Wittgenstein's prayers moved away from Bateson's intimate conversations with patients to communicate the more abstract intercourse of the experience of sickness, weakness, and depression expressed to the divine healer.

In another metalogue, Mary Catherine asked her father "Why do things have outlines?" (Bateson [1972] 1985: 27–32). Bateson referred this abstract question to the methodology of behavioral science. Bateson got angry about the lack of theory, missing the structures, the weak production of data, and the lack of definitive theory in the experiences he had of bad research. The father's strong insistence on the practice of pseudo-theoretical and pseudo-conceptual scholarship was enough to make the innocent daughter cry with grief. After apologies—"I suppose I muddled you by starting to let off steam" (28)—the metalogue started again with the theme of tolerance (including intolerance). Father Bateson criticized bad research made by superficial researchers, who worked on the chief facts of the internal task but neglected all outlines as external playthings (Lotman 1990: 51, see 136–137). These researchers always "muddle" through to finish the task, but to what end? The same thing engaged father and daughter in their discussions. Father Bateson stressed that, "The point is that our conservations do have an outline, somehow—if only one could see it clearly" (Bateson [1972] 1985: 29). Father Bateson gave again the literary example of Lewis Carroll's *Alice in Wonderland* ([1865] 1982), in which the author:

> Amused himself with little Alice by imagining a game of croquet that would be all muddle, just absolute muddle. So he said they should use flamingos as mallets because the flamingos would bend their necks so the player wouldn't know even whether his mallet would hit the ball or how it would hit the ball … So that is so muddled that nobody can tell at all what's going to happen. (Bateson [1972]1985: 30)

The daughter asked "Did everything have to be *alive* so as to make a complete muddle?" and the father agreed with her:

> It's curious but you are right. Because if he's muddled things any other way, the players could have learned how to deal with the muddling details. I mean, suppose the croquet lawn was bumpy, or the balls were a funny shape, or the heads of the mallets just wobbly instead of being alive, then the people could still learn and the game would only be more difficult—it wouldn't be impossible. (30–31)

The sense of metalogue, including the metaphor of the game of croquet, is not an unpredictable game but a real, but unfinished, game played with a detailed outline to draw together the whole problem in some conclusion.

The same process transpired in Wittgenstein's sketch of his unfinished "album" (discussed in Gorlée 2012: 68–70). The "album" is the metalogue of his borderline cases of doubtful conversations with himself, friends, and other readers. The "album" provides the writing pages with external "things"—numbers, points, lines, spaces, functions—prior to the internal mind with "its own objects" of words, sentences, paragraphs, interpunction, and so on. To structure the "album" with borders, margins, and boundaries as the main features of his "landscape" was troublesome. The "landscape" proposes the scenic meanderings between major and minor works generating a series of connecting meanings to signify the qualities of the "album" according to Bateson's metalogues. Wittgenstein introduced the concept of "album" in the preface (*Vorwort*) of the *Philosophical Investigations.* The text of the "album" was crisscrossed with diary entries to puzzle his readers. Wittgenstein's goal was to analyze the "landscape" of his major works of philosophy. The metalogues also included other "minor publications" such as lectures, debates, correspondence, notes, typescripts, and narrative fragments, as discussed earlier.

The morality of Bateson's metalogues was articulated in his half monologue–half dialogue personal conversation. Acting on the unconscious level of the brain by the exclamations and wishes of the diary, Peirce's musement kept the stream of consciousness mixed in actual movement. The metalogue attempted to communicate between the borders of private firstness (pure iconicity) of the diary to reach the public thirdness (symbolicity) of the analysis of the language-games. The metalogue was the rational sign of secondness (indexicality) in half-paraphrased messages to stimulate the flow of ideas (that is, codes). The metalogue codifies the rough information with that of some other living person, who is hoping for a better life for himself and others. Wittgenstein's metalogue tried to communicate his messages to other speakers to let them know the first "information" of scientific messages. He shared with his readers or listeners the moral counsel of his style of language. But Wittgenstein's version of metalogue remained a one-sided sermon: he talked more of his own experiences than of those of other informants. The pulpit oratory was more indirect speech to believers than direct speech in a public setting. In semiotic terms, Wittgenstein's metalogue was the recodification of his native language to encodify the world. He wanted to codebreak the remarks, comments, and opinions of other people, but his code was the mechanical tool to index the higher order of learning, in Bateson's efforts "to learn to learn."

The morality of Bateson's metalogues was engaged to work for anthropological fieldwork, but the same professional view could be applied to linguistics through the emotional and energetic habits of private metatalk, without final habits. The human events and interactions represent in Bateson's metalogues the notions of "memory, voice and narration to explore methodologies from active inquiries and commonplace means of documentation, to more passive conditions of 'being there' coupled with serendipitous, context-bound documentation" (Chawla and Anderson 2015: 133). Bateson's theatrical play-act of metalogues did not exactly follow the semiotic hierarchy of Peirce's three categories, but in *Steps to an Ecology of Mind* ([1972] 1985: xvi–xxiv, 308, 402) he pursued his cultural-anthropological research by using the "hard" methods of deduction and induction to hope to instruct his students to work with the "soft" reasoning of abduction. Bateson touched on the use of instinct in human and animal metalogues (as in the metalogue of Bateson [1972] 1985: 38–58) but without mentioning the semiotic term of abduction. Yet it seems that Peirce's three categories were Bateson's hidden game to play the conversational activity in metalogues and achieve the goal of coherent communication with patients.

After Bateson's death in 1980, the notion of metalogue was concluded with the daughter-and-father essays of *Angels Fear: Towards an Epistemology of the Sacred* (1987). This book was not religious in the ordinary sense but included the notion of play to generate the sorcery of knowledge, transmitted from father to daughter—now the daughter was the eminent anthropologist (Bateson and Bateson 1987: 50–64). The evolution of the ecobiological world was healed in the aesthetic value of the semiotically unspecified metalogue, but the base of the creative narratives lies in the togetherness of the abductive play-act of father and daughter (Bateson and Bateson 1987: 36–49, 174–175). Abduction is regarded as the central "meeting-place" or human "niche" to shift off the burden of the outlines of conversations from Bateson's shoulders to heal the patient's physical and spiritual symptoms.

Old reasoning became an encounter with abductive reasoning. The anthropological vision transformed into the medical insight of the treatment of the psychiatric, and even drug addicted, habits of patients (Schutz 1975; Cannizzaro and Anderson 2016). Bateson's method of disorder remained the same: "Where does order come from?" (Bateson 1972: 343). He remembered how he recalled during his youth the Old Testament mythology of Genesis (Bateson 1972: xxv, 343). The first book of the Bible is the story of creation, recording how the Jewish people created order from disorder in the wilderness. The historical outlines of Genesis started the abductive destiny of the Jewish people. The Jewish people tried to fufil God's strange promise to reach Canaan, the Promised Land. The stories of Genesis re-created the mythical desert, inspired and influenced by the faith of nature.

The Jewish people were guided by God's call to Abraham to fulfill the promise to help Abraham's family and the Jewish people to traverse from Mesopotamia to the Promised Land. In their diaspora, they moved away from the moral "nothingness" of slavery to obey the covenant with God and become healthy individuals. The patriarch Abraham was the leader in reinstating the sense of justice within God's people. As the moral basis of Bateson's metalogues, the narrative of Genesis was retold in the conversations of father to son or father to daughter. One generation needed to talk to the next to create the laws and duties of the family to arrange marriages and funerals. In Genesis, Abraham spoke to Rebecca and her family to select her as a wife for his son Isaac (Gen. 24:1–51) and, in his last days, Abraham made Isaac his heir and talked to his sons Isaac and Ismael about the estate and his burial (Gen. 25:1–11). Then and now, the continuance of metalogues re-creates tokens of God's care and ratio toward the faithful men and women.

Translated from the mythical world of the sacred writings to the twentieth-century science of medicine, the mélange of anthropology and psychiatry provided patients with a method that could heal human wounds. Some drugs can be effective against the idea of the symptom but are in general insufficient for genuine healing. The physicians gave Bateson's patients "no information, no humor, no logical types, no abstractions, no beauty or ugliness, no grief or joy," but for Bateson the effects of inert sugar pills, tranquilizers, stimulants, alcohol, analgesics, or other pain-relieving drugs can sometimes work as a stimulus for the patient. Even more bluntly, he exclaimed that "Even placebos would not work on such a creature" (Bateson and Bateson 1987: 51).

Is the placebo effect more than folkloric superstition, but is the scientific term for a personal service? According to the *Oxford English Dictionary*, the word "placebo" has two senses. The first and original is the biblical phrase "I will please," that is to appeal to others as a "plea" for understanding or sympathy. The placebo is adopted from the Latin *Vulgata* in the psalm "Placebo Domino in regione vivorum" (I will please the Lord in the land of the living). The Christian hymn encourages the dead to sing to appeal to God's grace (OED 1989: 11:942). The second, and later, sense is replaced by the neurophysiological ideal to explain and predict human behavior. There, the placebo means "a substance or procedure which a patient accepts as a medicine or therapy but which actually has no specific therapeutic activity for his condition or is prescribed in the belief that it has no such activity," meaning that the "beneficial (or adverse) effect produced by a placebo that cannot be attributed to the nature of the placebo" (OED 1989: 11:942).

The old pejorative definitions expected, ideally, that the cause of the placebo was the patient's faith in the explicit promise of better health. Instead, contemporary medical science has a more skeptical view of the possible workings of the placebo as a fundamental role of persuasion and suggestion to influence human psychology (Gorlée 2016a). See the old and new definitions from *Black's Medical Dictionary*:

> Traditionally, placebos were used to pacify without actually benefitting the patient. They are inactive substances formerly given to please or gratify the patient but now only used in controlled studies to determine the efficacy of drugs. We now realize that pharmacologically inert compounds can relieve symptoms and we call this the placebo effect. The reassurance that is associated with placebo administration is accompanied by measurable changes in body function which are affected through autonomic pathways and humoral mechanisms. Alterations in blood pressure and pulse frequency are especially common. (1987: 543–544)

Healing is more than the therapeutic intervention of simply giving the materialistic (that is, deductive and inductive) drugs, it is the more complex transaction of prescribing nonspecific placebos with reasonable doubts of any effects of their work. The medical transaction of giving placebo pills is still judged "unethical since it involves deception" (Benson and McCallie 1979: 1424).[6] But, despite this skepticism, the placebo pills do actually work for some patients. Indeed, the effectiveness of placebos is a highly problematic and inconsistent substance for therapy. In Bateson's psychosomatic medicine, the operation of healing must *stand for* the natural, as well as supernatural, unification of personal forms of reasoning and unreasoning. This unification is the central part of Bateson's conversations with "sick" patients, when he tried to solve the puzzle of their health. Looking closely at the patient's way of observing the world around them, Bateson's antimaterialistic therapy could mythically change the narcotic world into the natural picture of the patient's physical world.

Bateson's sacred grounds of psychotherapy went through the new ritual of metalogues, which is not the same as Freud's essentially scientific interrogations with patients–a method which Wittgenstein abhorred. Freud received clinical patients plagued with psychological inhibitions, symptoms, and anxieties. In the treatments, Freud diagnosed their mental disease by analyzing their symptoms as they presented themselves, but Freud's real goal was writing scientific publications addressed to fellow-psychotherapists (Freud 1977; see Shands and Meltzer 1973: 7–8, 34; Stanley Cavell quoted in Appignanesi 2017: 38). Bateson's metalogues are "organized" into personal talks (and metatalks about previous talks) with people ("patients") about their human environment. Paradoxically, Bateson changed the unreal worlds of anxiety and loneliness during the intimate setting of metalogues into the sense of real life without pain. In semiotics, Freud's dogmas of logical interpretants are the opium of the symbolic routine, as seen in Peirce's habituescence. Freud's semiosis is radically different from Bateson's remedy in the emotional and dynamical habits of quasi-semiosis. Bateson concentrated his metalogues on the unreality of the "sick" habits and habituality of the "sick" patients to upgrade their interpretation of their body and mind to let them feel better.

In *Angels Fear: Towards an Epistemology of the Sacred* (1987), the anthropologist Mary Catherine Bateson played the "fictional" game-act in secret cooperation with her father. In the essay "Metalogue: Why Placebos?" (Bateson and Bateson 1987: 65–68), they reflected on the use of psychosomatic medicines in the real story of father Bateson's death-bed. The medical care programmed the placebos to help the affected patient, but Bateson himself wanted to get better without taking care of any accompanying symptoms. He pursued another way to self-heal the natural and supernatural habits into his own thoughts and ideas to guide him to the "good" life. A vexing question, because chemical placebos are psychedelic drugs that, indeed, promise miracles. Mary Catherine baptized placebos as pure "nonsense" (68), trying to heal the soft differences of the human mind in the patient's "ideas, information, even absences" to paralyze the escapism of the patient from clinical anxieties. Instead, Bateson's self-therapy was a fight for the perfection of the soul. He was helped by the play-act of abductive musement to take other, psychoactive drugs. The musement could treat the patient not through but with the individual will of the patient's mind. The mystical experience of musement lies in the patient's "floating devotion" to liberate the mind and "*fit together*" the medication with the diversity and differences of the patient's own beliefs and disbeliefs (65, 68).

Mary Catherine wrote in *Angel Fears* that the ethnographer can distinguish between tuberculosis as "real" and sorcery as "not real" illness, while the physician must transact with a diversity of mental and bodily variables "isolated from the laboratory" (185). For her, the therapy in human events and interactions "may be sorcery that is 'real' and not tuberculosis," coming to the conclusion that the alternative "idea of medication represented by placebo may be effective against the idea of the symptom—and pain as we experience it is itself an idea, a kind of mental image" (185). The physical reality of the human organism could heal itself merely through the belief of the patient in the truth of the medication. Importantly, the medication must be understood not in the medical sense of escape, but ethnographically in the belief in abductive musement. Bateson's religion-with-play emphasized the truth of the patient. This truth, not real but personal truth, assembled the pieces of thought into the pragmatic "hypothesis" to fit the spiritual soul of the patient.

Wittgenstein thought intensely about which drug he needed to remedy himself. As a quasi-model, the self-therapy consisted of iconic and indexical experiments to play-act the experiment of abduction. The "method" was a Bateson-inspired metalogue, stepping back from controversial dreams and sensations by communicating his life experiences with intimate colleagues and confidants. Wittgenstein's self-therapy equally attended to the musement of the sensory and affective words of close friends to find comfort in evaluative words (Schonauer 1994: 51–52). The words of these intellectual conversations helped him to compose the series of ideas and thoughts in what Wittgenstein called his personal "album," intending to help his neurotic attitude and strengthen his mind to rise to the occasion of composing language philosophy in meandering paths of his own *Denkbewegungen*.

The conversations with intimate friends helped Wittgenstein's desperate cries to cease shouting and to bury some of his neurotic habits. I have discussed in the chapters of this book that Wittgenstein's neurophysiological symptoms included the crisis and conflict of being a Jewish citizen politically and idelogically separated from his home in Vienna, due to the Nazi occupation. He was equally displaced from his native Austrian-German language. His homosexuality was judged as criminal and poisonous behavior "against nature." Wittgenstein thought that he could remove the frightening fantasies of the hospital and break up the antagonistic attacks of university administration to start afresh. The intuitive method of conversational metalogues helped him to find rest in his brain, to paralyze the puzzle of his aggression, to solve as a religious man the good or bad forms of behavior, and finally to compose his life without the intensities of "pain." This journey undertook the experimental "hypothesis" of abduction as a hard road through desolate terrain. By being abjected into darkness, he regained the freedom of a new self.

In his self-treatment, Wittgenstein shared the intellectual pertinence with the persons he could confide in. With his own physical resistance, his privacy searched the medical drug to relieve himself of the anxiety of grief and anger and move forward without pain. Wittgenstein responded to the secrecy of his heart (Peirce-inspired musement) consisting of spiritual prayer in Bateson's metalogues. To shortcut the uncertainties of writing the objective philosophy for logical certainty, he nursed his private play-act by keeping the comfort of writing his diary. Indeed, the intimate diary disguised the desire, depression, and melancholia coming from his environment, but he found the withdrawal and idleness of his life by taking the placebo drugs. The secrecy to change his life was implicit in the indexical sign of the code. Wittgenstein's diary in itself was the iconic image of his identity. But the crypto-biography integrated the code as a surplus sign bringing its own meaning and signification to self-heal. The code served as a double index of therapeutic diary and instructional learning, transforming the diary entries into the raw material of iconical indexes (or indexical icons). The total effect of the "secret" code supplied Wittgenstein with the usual therapy, but for outsiders the script suggested a strange code pointing to current teaching and practice to be decoded.

As a chronic patient, he wrote in his diary about the facts of life bothering him, but he added the narcotic "opium" of the placebo pills he had to take to heal the "bad" pains he suffered. With the musement of the body and mind without pain, Wittgenstein's ideas were refreshed by the placebo, making him see the horizon of the "good" future (Shands 1970: 148), yet the pain-relieving use of the placebo had, as usual, serious provisos. The placebo was not a "natural" sign. The "artificial" quasi-sign did relieve pain but had no specific value to heal patients. For Wittgenstein the placebo had a double identity: healing the psycho-biological effect of his almost "natural" pain, and escaping from the private neuroscience of suffering "unnatural" causes of pain. The first therapy was the iconic diary, while the second was the indexical code serving as an appendix in the diary. The coded diary could in some contexts heal the patient's complaints, but on other occasions it was totally unhealing but only driven by the patient's stimulus to work. Sometimes the setting of the "secret" code was helpful to believe that the placebo could achieve the serious effort of healing the symptoms, but often nothing happened. In the nothingness of the placebo, disbelief could take over to drive the patient into despair. Fortunately, Wittgenstein reacted positively to the qualities of the placebo.

The double identity of Wittgenstein's abductive therapy of treating himself was essentially expressed in the vagueness of his metaphorical meaning. In the *Philosophical Investigations*, Wittgenstein recalled the double identity of visualizing the neuroanatomical image of the duck-rabbit drawing (PI/PPF: 118–140, see Gorlée 2012: 22–23). The human eye sees in the black and white drawing the "seeing" and "thinking" in different moods (PI/PPF: 138). Firstly, one observes the rabbit and secondly the duck, but can it be switched back to the rabbit. What is really there? For Wittgenstein, the switch to the placebo is his "cry to pain" (PI/PPF: 138), but the alternative medicines do not heal any symptoms. Without changing the form or shape of the placebo, the response from one code to different codes in other forms is not a sharply delineated border to make a conclusion with one meaning (PI/PPF: 136). The image prompts the stimulus of the human eye with two retinal responses–either the duck or the rabbit. The human eye creates ambiguous figure-ground reversals, "that's why the lighting up of an aspect seems half visual experience, half thought" (PI/PPF: 140). With this, Wittgenstein created a double enigma.

In his later years, Wittgenstein replaced the certainty of the text and diary with one code by the uncertainty of the sign with various codes. For example, the images of the duck-rabbit and the blind man were unanalyzable paradigms, because to analyze them the code did not express the mere iconic quality (firstness) of the image, nor stressed the representations of the indexical character (secondness). He created a variety of human visions. The symbolic uncertainty of the language-games in the duck-rabbit and the blindness was communicated by his image but not further explained. Wittgenstein's *Remarks on Colour* ([1977] 1988b, written 1950–1951 close to Wittgenstein's death; Glock 1996: 81–84) were communicated by his image but without any conclusion. Since Wittgenstein was weakened by cancer, the unfinished collection of undated pages about color were written as the spontaneous pieces discussing the certainty and uncertainty of the coded (that is, cultural and linguistic) impressions of color. Wittgenstein's first-draft writing was published as pages of his pre-"album" selected, edited, revised, and translated as "minor publication" of quasi-communication edited in three rough sections.

Returning to the symbolism of the language-games, Wittgenstein discussed the empirical (that is, indexical and iconic) habits of "color-blind people" throughout the *Remarks on Colour*.[7] The ideas of color-blind people tinkered "defectively" with manipulating adequately the normal logic of deduction and induction, but seeing colors was the uncertain and indeed impossible activity. The color was observed as a pre-reflective code as the abductive signal to forget the uncertainty by seeing the variety of "possibilities" of the world (ROC: 3:301–316). Wittgenstein's code recalled the story of the beetles. The jar was opened and the half-dead beetles could escape from the darkened room to see the light dimensions of the world. Wittgenstein's diary explored the wordplay with a different geometry of mathematical (that is, "grammatical" and "non-grammatical") codes trying to communicate the coded message to others. Seeing and thinking was one of Wittgenstein's main matters of language philosophy. The possibility of seeing the "thing" surrounded by colored codes was the fundamental role to act and think the final language-games (Glock 1996: 330–336).

Firstly, the color/code confronted the symbolic language-games with indexical and iconic codes. The strange color problem was framed by Wittgenstein as the *mimesis* of the "transparent" substance to describe the "intermediary" and "saturated" marks of one of various colors as described by the logical or non-logical codes (A, B, X, Y).[8] Secondly, the color/code can simply work as a vague impression of experimental feeling in Wittgenstein's lectures and other "minor" publications, at that moment lacking the final logical conclusion of philosophy (ROC: 3:19). Finally, the meaning of the color impression can turn into the complex meanings of analytical, ambiguous, and metaphorical codes leading to an unusual coloration of coded language or psychological color-blindness (Riley 1995: 25–34, 35–45, 65–69, 103–104, 298 and throughout; Portmann et al. [1977] 1994).

The coloration with codes to the notion of language-game can substitute Wittgenstein's native speech for the "dark" secrets of his coded quasi-language. Speech and language do have a certain stability to speak about the sameness of the etymology of common meaning, but they do not build universal or stable systems. Speech and language consist of flexible or elastic variables, making the meaningful variables constantly shift to change their color/code through time and space. The iconic meanings of color can accurately reflect the same ideas as the code but are they actively making room for the indexical notion of cultural and linguistic communication to provide "destructive" information (Goffman 1959: 141–166). They transplant the old social conventions of Wittgenstein's codes and colors to fit the contemporary structure of neurological psychology. The habits of the wordplay of language and quasi-language will be that code and color can share the multiple senses of the superficial and deep meanings of Wittgenstein's psychology and parapsychology. The "knowing" is not a scientific habit but his own psychological habit (or better, pre-habit). Wittgenstein stated at the end of the *Remarks on Colour* that this psychological knowledge "will be of no help" (ROC: 3:350).

The cultural principles of code/color can have emphatic, ornamental, humorous, or other iconical aspects that "color" the public restricted code in Wittgenstein's indexical code of the "idiolectal and quasi-professional" quasi-language (Eco 1985: 168–169). The code turned the varieties of meaning into three stages—emotional, allegorical, and metaphorical—of interpretants depending on Wittgenstein's mood. For the readers, the experimental notions and technological conceptions worked as an instructive tool to work with. But for teacher, writer, diarist, and patient Wittgenstein, the code turned the evil he suffered for many years into the magical remedy to find his true sign. To alleviate his symptoms, the persuasion to take the placebo was taken by a sick man dulled with pain-killing drugs. The illusion of the placebo was to relieve the loss of his psychological self. The placebo taken as antidote, could cure Wittgenstein's pain but could equally have no effect at all. The diary with the code could color the double shadow into iconic-indexical expressions, but the "three-dimensional form" of the semiosis of the language-games was never exhibited (ROC: 3:53, 272–277). The zigzag line of possible interpretants of the diary reflected the ups and downs of the placebo effect. The quasi-language can possess hierographic codes to confuse the sign games almost with the gestures of language-games, but Wittgenstein took the chance to communicate the proviso of both remedies as his "luminous points" (ROC: 3:58) to cure his neurotic code.

The placebo of the code worked for Wittgenstein as an improvised sign of medical science and the pre-sign worked as the correct sign of incorrect degeneracy. Wittgenstein desperately needed the placebo to self-heal himself through the abductive experiment to treat himself: he wanted to make major life decisions to save his spiritual soul from his nervous breakdown. The diary was a preliminary sketch without good or false outlines, but the placebo effect transformed his iconic diary with the coded material into a good message for him as a mental patient. The double effect of the placebo was not full semiosis but the weak mediation of human quasi-semiosis, bringing for the interpreters of the diary opportunities with simple and straightforward interpretants. The indexical code functioned reasonably well as Wittgenstein's escapism to "re-organize" his therapeutic metalogues and to help him to make hard decisions on his future life. He wanted to change his life, abandon the professorate, survive without fixed abode to stay as a house-guest with friends. He wanted to gain free time to think and write the secret remedy of the linguistic code with creative language-games. Through the magical effect of the tranquilizing placebo, he was able to understand intuitively and practically, but not rationally, the two-way (not three-way) art of detaching his physical body and spiritual soul from the evil symptoms of anxiety and loneliness. Wittgenstein turned himself back into the real individual he was. The secrecy of Wittgenstein's effort of encoding and decoding for many outside readers remained a puzzle, but the truth was that he turned the emotion of the codes to strengthen the healing work of the placebo.

7

Tentative conclusion

Nothing is hidden here; and if I were to assume that there is something hidden the knowledge of this hidden thing would be of interest. But I can hide my thoughts from someone by hiding my diary. And in this case I'm hiding something that might interest him.

(LW1: 974)[1]

As this study of Wittgenstein's secret code comes to an end, the question of the secrecy of cryptography interspersed among his philosophical work naturally demands our attention. Wittgenstein recapitulated the events of the war diaries of 1914–1916. From 1929, the vital habit turned into the symptomatic habituality of his quasi-autobiography. He wrote that:

> Vh rhg pvoqdfiwrt wzhh rxs hvrg hm ervpvn Rzsivn uzhg nrv ovs wzh pvrhvhgv Yvwfuynrh volufnwvn hzyv Gztvyfxszfuavrxsnfntvn af ozxsvn. Rn wvi zppvrvihgvn Arg rn Yviprn zph rxs wzorg znurnt zfu Avggvp Tvwznqn fyvi orxs zfuafhxsivryvn, wz dzi vh vrn Yvwfiunrh. Vh dzi ven ufi orxs drxsgrtvi Hxsirgg. Hlzgvi vnghliznt vh afo Gvrp wvo Nzxszofnthgirvy (rxs szggv Qvppvih Gztvh Gztvyfxsvi tvpuhun) Gvrp wvo Yvwfiunrh wmxs vgdzh emn ori nrvwviafpvtvn. Vh dzi zphm afo timhzvn Gvrp Vrgvpqvrg. Afo Gvrp uivrprxs zfxs drvwvi wvi Vilzga ufi vrnvn Ovnhxsvn wvo rxs orxs znevigizfvn qmnngv. Hlzgvi orhxsgv hrxs wzaf zfxs Nzxszofnt wvi Lvlbhhxsvn Gztvyfxsvi. Uivrprxs rhg vh, drv roovim hxsdvi, srvi tvivxsg af hvrn, wvnn vh dzi nzgfiprxsvh & vrgpv Yvhgivyfntvn hgziq eviorhxsh.
>
> (It is remarkable that for so many years I have not had even the slightest inclination to write entries in my diary. When I was first in Berlin and started jotting down thoughts about myself, it was a need. An important step for me. Later I was inspired in part by the instinct to imitate (having read Keller's diaries), and in part by the need to make a record of my life. Vanity, mostly. Although partly also a substitute for someone in whom I could confide. To this came later the imitation of the Pepysian diaries. But, as always it is difficult to be fair, as natural & vain aspirations are strongly intertwined.)
>
> (MS 107: 74, 1929)[2]

Wittgenstein desperately needed to write the diary as a medication to tranquilize himself. In the entries, he pursued the diary of his life events to get better. The coded diary burned the cryptanalysis of his students and friends, but first of all the diary healed him of his symptoms and anxiety. Wittgenstein was a troubled man. His life-events left a wide margin between biofiction and confession. The interpretation is never safe and can easily stray from the proper course to suggest an iconic misreading of the codes.

Codification started out as the hidden script of Wittgenstein's diary, making the literal reading of Wittgenstein impossible. The discussion was that the diary was not readable in the "secret" language, but the fact that in the indexical art of quasi-language it was treated "normally" with Wittgenstein's logical codes. The diary was not simple talk, and the text was articulated with the "surrogate speech" in coded form (Sebeok and Umiker-Sebeok 1976). Translation was the linguistic habit of the symbolic interpretants, in which the language was changed into a new language. Wittgenstein's secret script was the "hidden" habit of indexical interpretants to compose the quasi-language of his diary. But translation and quasi-language were influenced by the iconic habit of the "sign-maker." Wittgenstein acted as the primary interpreter and secondary translator to give meaning to his works (Gorlée 2012: 17–23), but he considered that the readers would interpret his coded message and the underlying code. The code effect turned the readers into Jakobson's cryptanalysts (Jakobson and Halle [1956] 1971: 28–30) to decode the quasi-language and language and make with the new surface, environment, and social manners their own interpretants; if the suggestion was not taken up, the xenograms of Wittgenstein's "grammar" remained obscure script. Wittgenstein wanted to educate the "outside" readers to become fit for their own self-identity or self-development without any self-alienation and self-denial.

Like the inscriptions on the visiting card presented as an anecdote in the opening paragraphs of this book, the codification of the diary was Wittgenstein's word game by showing the mythical quasi-language in half-secrecy. As an artful and strange subtext, the diary text in code was interspersed throughout Wittgenstein's philosophy, but the double word game stood there to recover the personal identity of living in the social and historical awareness of Wittgenstein's real world. The good and bad instances renewed his cultural awareness—no more self-love but self-esteem to others—to blend the tone of the diary with his inward voice in the "prophesy" for the education of students (and other readers). Wittgenstein wrote the outward mode of scientific discourse and the emotional phrases of the unscientific paragraphs of the diary as his example. The double identity of the formal philosophy, discreetly modulated with humor and imagings, with the less formal phrases of the events in the diary, was Wittgenstein's strange formula of writing.

Wittgenstein tried to find access to, and control over, the orientation of language by using the quasi-language called the "restricted code" (Bernstein 1974: 1550–1557). His private diary was composed of the "grammatical" invariants of the code system to comprehend the personal invariants of ordinary speech (Kahn ([1968] 1974, 1986). Wittgenstein's form of dialect opposed firstly the more formal idiom of philosophical language, but secondly he never attempted to decode the autonomous and informal subtext of the diary. The visual display of the coded dialect appeared at first sight a senseless activity, but Wittgenstein demonstrated that the formal proof of rational reasoning (deduction, induction) of the philosophy was not identical to the truth. The emotional guesses and personal clues involved the special atmosphere of play, sharing with others, and learning information. Abductive reasoning was not the law of Wittgenstein's reasoning, but it reflected the chance of his heart to survive the "danger in the wilderness, danger in the sea, danger among false brethren" (2 Cor. 11:26). He felt surrounded by the isolated, terrified, and enraged unreality of the foreign environment, politically and ideologically removed from his native background of Austria. In the monologue of the diary, he reflected, almost naïvely, on the episodes of his "journeys," saying that he described the intimate quasi-confessions to himself. At the same time, he transmitted the coded revelation to educate the fellowship of his close friends, companions, students, and possibly other readers.

Wittgenstein mixed philosophy with diary to render his works simultaneously into theoretical and practical pieces of writing. The whole independence and autonomy of text and subtext made the key point that the genuine information of Wittgenstein's pages was not identical but was carried from the action of "family resemblance" to the reaction of "family meanings." It seemed that Wittgenstein himself struggled with the difficulties of giving meaning to language, but he appeared to be en route to understand implicitly Peirce's logical semiotics. This helped him to base the human communication on the semiotic categorization of language and quasi-language. Peirce's universal categories and their reification in the strategies of human reasoning makes private and public genres of writing possible, clearly distinguishing between the much sharper and unambiguous identity of the philosophy and the private insight of the diary. The "secret" code was not some sad story sketched in sincere entries to provoke shivers of pain that ran through Wittgenstein's body and soul, but was at many moments the practical tool to instruct with clear messages to communicate Wittgenstein's messages to outside readers.

The history of personal messages was manifest in Wittgenstein's double bind—firstly, the sincerity of his personal, even intimate, experiences of life for himself and secondly, the authenticity arranged in public rhetoric for others. The double bind of communication and quasi-communication was Wittgenstein's reaction to the educational way of being a teacher. He was fully aware that the social messages of strangeness could alienate his students (and other readers) away from the coded fragments. How would the readers get acquainted with the diary's real content? In Wittgenstein's outlook, the troubled ambiguity of the unfamiliar code can be challenged and learned, but can also obstruct insight and put it aside–as in Wittgenstein's early term of "silence" (TLP: 7). But as happened to the oral Torah transcribed into the written Talmud, the wholly or partially understandable text can also trigger the reader's verbal imagination to formulate the new *pilpul* (Bateson 1975: 64). The religious code could rewire the reader's brain to generate different ideas of thought to solve the puzzle picture. The Torah scholar uses this sense of mental gymnastics to decipher the code system and analyze the hypothesis of the "puzzle." This must be the way of reading the sacred writings to come to the truth and find a way to work hard to understand Wittgenstein's comprehensible text together with the subtext. The latter option was in the psychological reasoning of semiotic abduction—which was Wittgenstein's alternative code.

The half-tones or shades of Wittgenstein's pain-symptoms are the subject of his diary. But the auto-messages equally have a double bind reflecting public and private forms of being self and other. He moved from "I" to the "Other" (Lotman 1990: 20–35) and back again. The ambiguous feelings that crisscross Wittgenstein's mental settings were played out in the fictional games to inform through philosophical arguments—as in the story of the beetles and the image of the duck-rabbit. The fictional games were written in plaintext to present the philosophical "landscape" to others without code problems. The coded fragments obstructed the direct understanding, but Wittgenstein did not redirect his readers away from the "mechanical process" of transforming the "form of shape" of the literary wordplays into new ideas. The creative ideas of Wittgenstein's wordplays solved the abductive novelty characteristic of his style of writing (Shands 1971: 29, 43).

As a writer, Wittgenstein started writing raw and rough drafts—not real "information" but improvised news formulated with the strange code. The medical sense-information of Wittgenstein's symptoms of pain and toothache was reduced pragmatically to his instructives to others to learn the code system. The coded subtext was simple enough to practice the right way of understanding the unfamiliar quasi-linguistic speech. When transformed from the code into the German language (Wittgenstein's native language) and the translation into the English language (for the students at Cambridge, a foreign language), the diary moved from merely ideas to a competence with a meaning. The importance of hard work to learn the code and the German language was the exercise of language-games with the effect of learning by experience (Hardwick 1971: 60). Yet Wittgenstein's private effort was elsewhere: to survive, he was in urgent need of medical supplies to cure his pain sensations. Simply formulated in the dual bind of iconic-indexical signs, Wittgenstein's story of pain seemed to feel the painful behavior for himself, but the code assisted him to ask others for help—indeed, the "primitive" version of a language-game. Communication in writing was, for Wittgenstein, an inspirational and emotional remedy to correct his mental ills.

Guided by the "magical" nature of the coded diary, Wittgenstein taught that there was no obstacle that will assist the cryptanalysts in mastering the difficulties. With the help of the code, he explained the "landscape" of how he combined language with quasi-language, but there is something unseemly about how he did not formulate the final speech-act theory to set up the general rule of coded messages. Wittgenstein's step-by-step methodology was the original habit represented by the "secret" codes of himself, the diarist. By expanding, in a manner of speaking, the simple habit of writing into the narrative sequence of re-habits (Peirce's habituality), Wittgenstein turned the ordinary performance of language into the educational treatment of quasi-language. By pushing the code as a prerequisite for quasi-language, Wittgenstein's atomistic processing was quasi-semiosis. But in serious art, the dramatic code effect was not absolute but relative. The code did not push his tolerance to its limits to allow entrance to the language-games. In his writings, Wittgenstein could not reach the strength of Peirce's semiosis to lead all speakers of language (Peirce's habituescence).

But Wittgenstein's theatrical styles of the mixture of *Denkbewegungen* gave some vague theorizing to upgrade non-communication and half-communication, but without reaching the real dialogue of the language-games.

To tell the confidentialities of the small things and intimate events, Wittgenstein used the requisite of the "secret" code, not as a secretive idiom but as a speculative dialect serving him to diagnose the private facts of each day (Peirce's firstness). The iconical phrases of the diary show what he ironically literacized as the "copy, portraiture, figure, diagram, icon, picture, mimicry, echo" (SS: 194; see Gorlée 2014a). The marginal code amplified the thought with quasi-language. The coded diary half-pointed to the quasi-secondness in the "gnomon, clue, trail, vestige, indice, evidence, symptom, trace" (SS: 194). The mixture of "weak" or degenerate signs communicated that Wittgenstein's "forms of life" were alive in his emotional cries for help (firstness) but implied that the coded diary was more than a private affair. The interpretative version reached further than the temporary adventures of sexual desires and intimate yearnings for sympathy. The diary was composed as an ambivalent, one might even say the biofictional, crypto-autobiography. It seemed that Wittgenstein escaped from his painful life with the help of the emotional and mental crypto-signs of the diary. The diary was the clandestine conceit to symbolize the "key, hint, omen, oracle, prognostic" (SS: 194) of the written life with code. Wittgenstein felt he lacked in the analysis of language the theoretical limits of language-games, but he still hoped to cure the sensations of pain and to be sometimes heard by a public audience.

Wittgenstein's analytic development of language derived from his early days in the Saussure-like *Tractatus Logico-Philosophicus*. Written in the early years of modern linguistics, the *Tractatus* marked the possibility and impossibility of logical truth (thirdness, symbol) in the epistemological (or *logisch-philosophisch*) science of language. But at the end of the *Tractatus*, his unspeakable message was the secrecy of silence. The certainty of thirdness (symbol) edged away in the silence of degenerate signs of secondness (index) and firstness (icon). The same process is followed in young Wittgenstein's diary entries during the First World War, written half normally and half in code. The war diary commented on his real life as a volunteer soldier serving on the Eastern front. He tried to write the first version of the *Tractatus*. But Wittgenstein's diary centered on the military etiquette (secondness), but without the emotional effects of nostalgia (firstness) that he later suffered. After the war, Wittgenstein experienced a mental turmoil of anxiety, thrown from his physical freedom into the academic decorum of lectures and conversations at the University of Cambridge. He moved from the orderliness of scientific books toward exposing the ineffective and playful notebooks of the uncertainty of the meaning of his "album."

In *The Blue and Brown Books* and the *Philosophical Investigations*, the formal symbolism of Wittgenstein's *Tractatus* was abandoned to focus on lectures and fragmentary works. The diary was oriented to reflect the uncertainty of his emotionalism (firstness) topped by the unknown code (secondness). The quasi-semiosis took care to give his works the shadow of total uncertainty, but this signified that Wittgenstein's lectures and works gave not a formal and definitive theory but reflected the temperament of his emotional and imaginative experiences. The new psychological habits of feelings and actions came from Peirce's idea of musement. The vagueness of the brain had formless or unformed habits, which could be clarified and organized by Wittgenstein himself. Since he was a religious man, his bad form of habit gave sadness, guilt, and even hopelessness to his spirit or soul (Schimmel 1992: 191–216). When he was courageous, he would accept responsibility for new habits (205–206). The habit of bodily and intellectual movements was strengthened in Wittgenstein's habituality for self-healing his mental symptoms.

From Wittgenstein's perspective of psychology, the bonus of his work of "devoted teacher [was] to learn that after many years his students use and appreciate what he taught them and remember him with affection and gratitude" (207). The "opaque and blurred" thoughts (TLP: 4.112) of uncertainty found a place in learning the quasi-language (iconic-indexical signs) of Wittgenstein's diary. The diary surrounded the whole language-game in the strangeness of the code. To give themselves the certainty of pleasure and goodness, the students had to traverse the uncertainty of displeasure to learn the unknown signification. The edge of chaos implied the paradox of language in Wittgenstein's formalization of the "soft" art of the diary with the "hard" grammar of the philosophy. In the post-*Investigations* writings, the last monograph published as *On Certainty* focused on dealing with the problems of living with uncertainties.

The play of quasi-dialect was Wittgenstein's psychological mood. Peirce's musement punctuated the readers with inspired hypotheses to play with different ideas and express his ideas to make his symptoms of pain disappear. The cries for help were visualized as straight lines (iconic-indexical signs) showing directly his anxieties as an outsider and émigré trying to live in a hospitable but foreign country. But the direct lines break into geometrical pieces to communicate with various subsigns. The readers learn Wittgenstein's playful details to break from common language into quasi-language. The mixed mechanism of language and quasi-language pursued Peirce's "lot of things jumbled higgledy-piggledy" (CP: 3.454), but Wittgenstein went further: he repaired the jumpy roads of a "deviant" life to invent the perspectives of quasi-language. He recalled quasi-language as a memory from his childhood, when he used to play word games with the "secret" key to his sisters and brothers. The cryptograms recalled the old feelings of his home. The strange focal points, the exotic combinations of letters, and other emphatic features were the usual marks of quasi-language. With the indexical signs of the code attached to the iconic diary, he composed the final summary of his mixed argument intertwining the calligraphical art object to make intricate puzzles (Gorlée 2009).

Wittgenstein worked artistically with the geometrical letters of the reversed alphabet to write his visual cryptanalysis (Kahn [1968] 1974): 81–82). To compose the shorthand, he decoded the alphabetical letters of his thoughts in German language into the method of Caesar's script to form the logograms. The varieties of indexical signs was clear to discover the literal decipherment, but the truth of the technical initials and artistic inscriptions was unclear. The cryptanalysts translated the actual codes, but the meaning was more than straightforward interpretation. Following the novels of Rilke, Kafka, and perhaps Keller, Wittgenstein depicted the diary as a graphic representation of himself as a human (and even psychiatric) patient. The vagueness of the symptoms was probably the lesson to explore in the work of these novelists, the reality of their word games, written in plaintext without code. Wittgenstein provided plenty of these lessons to explore the differences with the coded script.

Wittgenstein applied the special (not secret) code dialect as a practically amorphous type of private speech. He applied the strategic principle of abduction, nuanced into the personal mood of firstness, as it seems today, when he wrote the diary entries. The quasi-language was a fixed system, but it freed Wittgenstein to new forms of liberty. Wittgenstein built the reality of logical constructs from fugitive ideas or even erroneous thoughts, as he pleased. Logical conclusions came from "Pure Play" (CP: 6.458) turning the non-logical category of firstness into the concrete, even playful, activity of violating the original code to change the meaning (Riley 1995: 56–63). The artistic code can also be depicted by the visual and auditive references in other shapes and forms—such as, a color, a musical note, a drawing, or the technical note of a diagram, chart, or chemical symbol. The codes construct signs of pure imagination but demonstrate that the coded signs have many meanings. The code can affect the psychological flavor of the other sign, but the code gives no logical assurance to stay the same thing. The code can change into something else to build a new puzzle.

As Wittgenstein wrote, the logical code can "play me a trick. If we lay down rules for the use of color words in ordinary language, then we can admit that memory plays tricks regarding these rules" (Wittgenstein 1993: 296). Wittgenstein was a *homo ludens*, playing with logical rules to transform his diary into the visual display of psychological "color words" (Glock 1996: 47–48, see 81–84). Reading the diary with the code in color there is no easy way to tell whether the readers are held aloof by the diary's "facts of life." The color—say, red color—gives the immediate stimulus of pure firstness. The red color causes a sensory reaction to the reader, but not necessarily a psychological response. If the code of the diary is printed in red color, the reader has doubts about what it could mean. The red codes are not fixed characters in a single formula with mechanical and arithmetical understanding, but are vibrating designs in colored objects playing with initials, numbers, ciphers, shapes, or figures. The reader can adopt a different specter of the red code, but the reason is never complete. The coded diary stays the hypothesis of having more than one meaning. The color/code of Wittgenstein's diary could remove the readers out of healthy knowledge into an unknown stigma. The power of the stimulus of the code implies the intellectual curiosity of learning the code system. But in psychology the color/code was waves of colors in uninterrupted flows of points, lines, and fragments.

The code can involve the musements of Wittgenstein's psychological state. The stimulus of the coded diary triggered off the gestures of words and sentences into meaningful propositions. The coded formulas appealed to Wittgenstein's students to exchange the logical style of deduction and induction to enter the personal interplay of abductive dreams. In Peirce's concept of firstness, the reader is away on "holiday," resting from work to explore the new environment codified with insights. In spiritual meditation, the inquirer imagines herself/himself as a "free spirit" creating new ideas on the case. Imagine the "secret" exchanges of monochromic color to a color with stripes or two or three colors as the fleeting opportunities of the code can be. The code effect of the artistic exercise of abductive musement can mentally stimulate the readers. Wittgenstein's codification represented the color/code as the emotional art and thrill of his diary—but the technical jargon of the diary was not explained in *Remarks on Colour*. By learning what the coded signs could be decoded for, Wittgenstein's "facts of life" would go from abstract hypotheses to concrete evidence. The visible interplay of colors and punctuation, and the mental codes implied a certain ridicule of playing ambiguous games with and without rules (Glock 1996: 274–278).

The exchange from logical semiotics into visual semiotics simplifies the status of Wittgenstein's idea of code. The diary-and-code marks the purely visual pattern of Wittgenstein's scientific (mathematical, chemical, logical) formulas in Peirce's system of existential graphs (see Chapter 3). The visual graph is a network of "words" connected by lines, dots, hyphens, and curves to construct sentences in "natural" speech. The dramatic script of the coded diary remains the puzzle of "unnatural" speech, because the private drawing gives geometrical ideas of words to disentangle the disorder of Wittgenstein's life. The mental formula of the color/code was not the story of reading Pepys's diary and not even the play with his sisters and brothers, but instead his personal word game. Wittgenstein was bemused with the relaxed attentiveness of encoding the diary by hand. In between, as a yogi, Wittgenstein daydreamed about the thought-forms as a means of increasing physical stamina to expersonate his pathology to a meditative quasi-language.

The quasi-language was not a paranormal faculty but a seemingly normal activity. Wittgenstein gave no explanation nor any critical evaluation to explain the blind combination of language and quasi-language. The existential questions of code and non-code require radical answers from each diary entry to reflect Wittgenstein's forms of reality or unreality. To remove the diary away as intimate observations from the published works has certainly been a misinterpretation of the specialized tone and flavor of Wittgenstein's manual labor, as he regarded the code not as a conventional system but as the creative art of his entire work. The visual likeness between the invisible original and the visible transcription tends to confuse the reader's mind with her/his misreadings and misunderstandings (Catford [1965] 1974: 70, following Pike 1947: 46).

Returning to Wittgenstein's passion in his cries for help, they voiced both the private hope as well as the despair of learning to save his voice. Wittgenstein turned the codification of the private diary as the official regimentation, like his prayer to God for help. Wishful thinking was the personal expression of firstness to help his sorrow and anguish, but Wittgenstein's urgency changed the invocation into a religious sermon to others. The sermon would express the didactic or teaching functions of "arousing, persuading, and stimulating" (Hutchison 1963: 235) the activity of the readers. The original cries for help were transformed into the collective prayers as a sign of secondness. The prayer is "no vain exercise of words, no repetition of certain sacred formulæ, but the very movement itself of the soul" (James [1902] 1982: 486). Indeed, this kind of prayer can be called the "propagating, stimulating, and sustaining" (Hutchison 1963: 235) code, color, or other replica reflecting the togetherness of metalogues (Bateson [1972] 1985). The prayer converses with God for the recovery of sick people, but for Wittgenstein his own prayer means his own moral fight to remain non-critical and self-critical without pain and sadness.

Wittgenstein's monologue kept his symptoms to himself, but as a lone player the monologue made him live in darkness. The firstness offered no remedy to clear and brighten the unclear mind. Then, the alternative role of Bateson's metalogue ([1972] 1985) attempted to stimulate him to engage in the practice of teaching for the students. The lectures raised questions for the group of fellow-students. They derived further questions, answered by Wittgenstein, who reasoned further into a self-therapy for the students but also secretly for Wittgenstein himself. The lectures were pronounced in English and Wittgenstein struggled to translate them on the spot from German into English, Wittgenstein's "foreign" language. As a professor of philosophy, he took the lectures deadly serious, but the fatigue and nervousness they caused were no cure for his symptoms of pain. Wittgenstein's self-remedy was Peirce's abductive reasoning self-medicated as his private inquirer. In moments of Peirce's musement, he enjoyed during the working sojourns on the Norwegian fjords and in the seaside city Swansea. In this mental silence, he emptied his brain away from the pressures of the lectures in Trinity Hall and concentrate on writing the provisional pre-"album" to prepare the never final nor definitive "album."

Wittgenstein found in the controversial "placebo effect" (Schonauer 1994) the self-medication he needed as a tranquilizing drug to be able to work without troubles. Wittgenstein's idea of autosuggestion in the placebo was that his health would improve. The analgesics of his pain allowed him to continue to write the emotional remarks in Peirce's firstness that trigger a clinical routine of quasi-secondness to reach real secondness. The diary entries were the rough drafts (firstness) to help the habit in emergencies (quasi-secondness). The endorsement of the code to the diary also generated the mixture of firstness and secondness (icon-indexical signs) to become, as amply discussed in this book, the elliptical language-game of Wittgenstein's style of writing. Wittgenstein found the first antidote in writing the diary with the code. The firstness of his monologue about his medical problems taught him the lesson to play the games of dialogue (Carlson 1983: 107–110). To cross the pain-threshold (Gorlée 2004a: 228) from monologue to dialogue he used the intellectual conversations he had with friends and colleagues. Wittgenstein's metalogue was different from the formalized "art" of public speaking in dialogue. The metalogue of Wittgenstein's fragmentary "conversations" lacked the sociocultural boundaries established between "artificial" quasi-speech and the "natural" mode of speaking. The social remedy of Wittgenstein's self-medication tried to actualize the mental symptoms into the informal rhetoric of Bateson's metalogue. Real dialogue was not the ruled "grammar" of his philosophy, because Wittgenstein played the quasi-communication alone (Hintikka and Hintikka 1986: 242–243).

Finally, this book points out that Wittgenstein's wandering mind was troubled by psychological hardships and trials of the environment. His life was in fact seen as the emotional signs of the "fallen angel." His philosophical genius brought him bittersweet victory and fame, but he abhorred pride and arrogance. Beyond the superhuman genius of his mental brain, he suffered the half-human and half-animal symptoms of psychological disorders. He fell victim to all kinds of political, social, and religious "noises" of news and information to disturb and activate the messages of his religious soul. Wittgenstein even served as his own physician to lessen the pain himself. In his self-medication, he was the therapeutic agent to take the placebo as artificial proviso conveyed by different shapes, colors, names, and smells, all of them to rid himself of the madness of the psychic alienation he deeply suffered.

The proviso of Wittgenstein's drug therapy was the abductive self-effect of the placebos. The art of human persuasion took support from the medicosemiotic suggestion to bring him the truth of self-healing. This psychotherapy was a strong antidote to neutralize his pain. Wittgenstein's sense of placebos were no longer a theatrical pose of playful behavior; the placebos were the private play-act of sketching his own semiosis. Following the sensory words of his inner monologue (diary), he gave affective and critical comments during the metalogue (conversations, addresses, lectures), and he ended with the speculative hypothesis of dialogue (philosophy). The qualities and intensities of treating his painful behavior worked for patient Wittgenstein as his abductive sensationalism suggesting the self-medication of his human condition. But the long-term clinical success of the placebo was for him a questionable hypothesis (Gorlée 2005, rev. in 2014a).

Beyond the serious effort of self-therapy, Wittgenstein made a deliberate effort to co-educate his philosophy students and other readers. His goal was to unfold a lifestyle different from conventional and scientific philosophy into an artful, even colorful, style of teaching the narrative of philosophy. This was how Wittgenstein foresaw the work of the future generations of philosophers. The design of technological systems operate in synthetic patterns of rearrangement with symbolic scripts, which vary from the interplay of one strategy to the next, from one culture to the next, from one inhuman "thing" to the next idea. The science of philosophy went the same way. To illustrate the chronic incompleteness of old philosophy, Wittgenstein obscured the ordinary plaintext into the inflexibility of shape, form, and color to reconstruct the intuitive knowledge into fragmentary images. By exemplifying with philosophical images, he seemed to explore the emerging field of artificial intelligence. The didactic tool of Wittgenstein's coded quasi-dialect was about learning the new paradigm to program a built-in style of associatively learning the restricted speech of philosophical reasoning. In this search and research, I have approached Wittgenstein's game experiments to follow the hard path from the theory of meaning to the theory of truth and falsehood.

Appendix: List of coded passages from Wittgenstein's *Nachlass*

The following is the alphanumeric list of all secret code passages in Wittgenstein's *Nachlass*. The list was kindly provided by the Wittgenstein Archives at the University of Bergen (Norway) according to the formalization and codification of the *Nachlass* texts. Each single passage can be inspected in facsimile version on the website Wittgenstein Source at http://www.wittgensteinsource.org/ and as a transcription at http://wittgensteinonline.no/.

As illustration, "MS 101: 11r[2]" refers to the passage consisting of the second text block on page 11r of MS 101; "MS 101:11r[3]" refers to the passage consisting of the third text block on page 11r of MS 101; "MS 101:11r[4]et12r[1]" refers to the passage consisting of the fourth text block on page 11r and the first text block on page 12r of MS 101.

The uncoded paragraphs of two years of the First World War are published in Wittgenstein's *Geheime Tagebücher 1914–1916* (GT, Wittgenstein [1991] 1992). The plaintext in ordinary language describe military life at the frontier and do not reckon as real diary. Wittgenstein's coded diary in cryptography are the following:

MS-101,11r[2]
MS-101,1r[3]
MS-101,11r[4]et12r[1]
MS-101,3r[3]et14r[1]
MS-101,16v[2]
MS-101,17v[2]
MS-101,18v[2]
MS-101,20v[2]
MS-101,20v[3]
MS-101,20v[4]
MS-101,21v[2]
MS-101,22r[1]
MS-101,22v[2]
MS-101,23v[2]
MS-101,24v[2]
MS-101,24v[3]
MS-101,26v[2]
MS-101,26v[3]
MS-101,27r[4]
MS-101,27v[2]

MS-101,28v[2]
MS-101,28v[3]
MS-101,29v[2]
MS-101,29v[3]
MS-101,29v[4]
MS-101,29v[5]
MS-101,30v[2]
MS-101,31v[2]
MS-101,31v[3]
MS-101,31v[4]
MS-101,31v[5]
MS-101,32v[2]
MS-101,33v[2]
MS-101,34v[2]
MS-101,34v[3]
MS-101,35v[2]
MS-101,36v[2]
MS-101,37v[2]
MS-101,37v[3]
MS-101,38v[2]
MS-101,3r[2]et4r[1]et5r[1]
MS-101,40v[2]
MS-101,41v[2]
MS-101,41v[3]
MS-101,42v[2]
MS-101,42v[3]
MS-101,42v[4]
MS-101,43v[2]
MS-101,44v[2]
MS-101,45v[2]
MS-101,45v[3]
MS-101,45v[4]
MS-101,46v[2]
MS-101,46v[3]
MS-101,46v[4]
MS-101,48v[2]
MS-101,48v[3]
MS-101,48v[4]
MS-101,50v[2]
MS-101,51v[2]
MS-101,5r[2]
MS-101,5r[4]et6r[1]
MS-101,62r[4]
MS-101,6r[2]et7r[1]

MS-101,7r[2]
MS-101,8r[2]
MS-101,8r[3]
MS-101,9r[2]et10r[1]et11r[1]

MS-102,10v[2]et11v[1]
MS-102,11v[2]et12v[1]
MS-102,12v[2]et13v[1]
MS-102,13v[2]et14v[1]et15v[1]
MS-102,15v[2]et16v[1]
MS-102,16v[2]
MS-102,16v[3]et17v[1]et18v[1]
MS-102,18v[2]et19v[1]et20v[1]
MS-102,1v[1]
MS-102,1v[2]et2v[1]
MS-102,20v[2]et21v[1]
MS-102,22v[1]
MS-102,22v[2]et23v[1]
MS-102,23v[2]
MS-102,23v[3]et24v[1]
MS-102,24v[2]et25v[1]et26v[1]
MS-102,26v[2]et27v[1]
MS-102,27v[2]et28v[1]
MS-102,28v[2]et29v[1]et30v[1]
MS-102,2v[2]et3v[1]
MS-102,30v[2]
MS-102,30v[3]et31v[1]
MS-102,31v[2]
MS-102,31v[3]et32v[1]et33v[1]
MS-102,33v[2]et34v[1]et35v[1]
MS-102,35v[2]
MS-102,35v[3]
MS-102,36v[1]et37v[1]
MS-102,37v[2]
MS-102,38v[1]
MS-102,38v[2]et39v[1]
MS-102,39v[2]et40v[1]et41v[1]
MS-102,3v[2]
MS-102,3v[3]et4v[1]
MS-102,41v[2]
MS-102,41v[3]et42v[1]et43v[1]
MS-102,43v[2]
MS-102,43v[3]et44v[1]
MS-102,44v[2]

MS-102,44v[3]et45v[1]
MS-102,45v[2]
MS-102,45v[3]
MS-102,45v[4]
MS-102,46v[1]
MS-102,46v[2]
MS-102,46v[3]
MS-102,46v[4]
MS-102,46v[5]et47v[1]
MS-102,47v[2]
MS-102,47v[3]
MS-102,47v[4]
MS-102,47v[5]
MS-102,48v[1]
MS-102,48v[2]
MS-102,48v[3]
MS-102,48v[4]et49v[1]
MS-102,49v[2]
MS-102,49v[3]
MS-102,4v[2]et5v[1]
MS-102,50v[1]
MS-102,50v[2]
MS-102,50v[3]
MS-102,50v[4]et51v[1]
MS-102,51v[2]
MS-102,51v[3]
MS-102,51v[4]
MS-102,52v[1]
MS-102,52v[2]
MS-102,52v[3]
MS-102,52v[4]
MS-102,52v[5]et53v[1]
MS-102,53v[2]
MS-102,53v[3]
MS-102,53v[4]
MS-102,53v[5]et54v[1]
MS-102,54v[2]
MS-102,54v[3]et55v[1]
MS-102,55v[2]
MS-102,55v[3]
MS-102,55v[4]
MS-102,55v[5]
MS-102,56v[1]
MS-102,56v[2]

MS-102,56v[3]
MS-102,56v[4]
MS-102,57v[1]
MS-102,57v[2]
MS-102,57v[3]
MS-102,57v[4]
MS-102,57v[5]et58v[1]
MS-102,58v[2]
MS-102,58v[3]et59v[1]
MS-102,59v[2]
MS-102,59v[3]et60v[1]
MS-102,5v[2]et6v[1]
MS-102,60v[2]
MS-102,60v[3]
MS-102,60v[4]et61v[1]
MS-102,61v[2]
MS-102,61v[3]
MS-102,61v[4]et62v[1]
MS-102,62v[2]
MS-102,62v[3]et63v[1]
MS-102,63v[2]
MS-102,63v[3]
MS-102,63v[4]et64v[1]
MS-102,64r[7]et65r[1]
MS-102,64v[2]
MS-102,64v[3]
MS-102,64v[4]et65v[1]
MS-102,65v[2]et66v[1]
MS-102,66v[2]
MS-102,66v[3]
MS-102,66v[4]
MS-102,66v[5]
MS-102,67v[1]
MS-102,67v[2]
MS-102,67v[3]
MS-102,68v[1]
MS-102,68v[2]
MS-102,68v[3]
MS-102,68v[4]
MS-102,68v[5]
MS-102,69v[1]
MS-102,69v[2]
MS-102,69v[3]
MS-102,69v[4]

MS-102,69v[5]
MS-102,69v[6]
MS-102,69v[7]et70v[1]
MS-102,6v[2]
MS-102,6v[3]et7v[1]
MS-102,70v[2]
MS-102,70v[3]
MS-102,70v[4]
MS-102,70v[5]
MS-102,70v[6]
MS-102,71v[1]
MS-102,71v[2]
MS-102,71v[3]
MS-102,71v[4]
MS-102,71v[5]
MS-102,71v[6]
MS-102,72v[1]
MS-102,72v[2]
MS-102,72v[3]
MS-102,72v[4]
MS-102,72v[5]et73v[1]
MS-102,73v[2]
MS-102,73v[3]
MS-102,8v[1]
MS-102,8v[2]et9v[1]et10v[1]

MS-103,10v[2]
MS-103,10v[3]et12v[1]
MS-103,12v[2]
MS-103,12v[3]et13v[1]
MS-103,13v[2]
MS-103,13v[3]et14v[1]
MS-103,14v[2]
MS-103,14v[3]
MS-103,14v[4]
MS-103,14v[5]et15v[1]
MS-103,15v[2]
MS-103,15v[3]et16r[1]
MS-103,16r[2]
MS-103,16r[3]
MS-103,16r[4]et16v[1]
MS-103,16v[2]
MS-103,16v[3]
MS-103,17v[1]
MS-103,17v[2]

MS-103,17v[3]
MS-103,17v[4]et18v[1]
MS-103,18v[2]et19v[1]
MS-103,19v[2]et20v[1]
MS-103,1v[1]
MS-103,1v[2]
MS-103,20v[2]et21v[1]
MS-103,21v[2]
MS-103,21v[3]et22v[1]
MS-103,22v[2]
MS-103,22v[3]
MS-103,2v[1]
MS-103,2v[2]
MS-103,3v[1]
MS-103,3v[2]et4v[1]
MS-103,4v[2]
MS-103,4v[3]
MS-103,4v[4]
MS-103,4v[5]
MS-103,52v[1]
MS-103,5v[1]
MS-103,5v[2]
MS-103,6v[1]
MS-103,6v[2]et7v[1]
MS-103,7v[2]
MS-103,7v[3]
MS-103,7v[4]
MS-103,7v[5]et8v[1]
MS-103,8v[2]
MS-103,8v[3]et9v[1]
MS-103,9v[2]
MS-103,9v[3]et10v[1]

MS-105,105[3]
MS-105,46[2]
MS-105,67[7]
MS-105,73[6]
MS-105,85[2]

MS-106,233[4]
MS-106,239[2]
MS-106,247[4]
MS-106,253[2]et255[1]
MS-106,30[5]
MS-106,4[1]

MS-106,4[2]
MS-106,4[3]
MS-106,4[4]

MS-107,100[2]
MS-107,110[7]
MS-107,114[2]
MS-107,114[6]
MS-107,116[3]
MS-107,117[4]
MS-107,120[2]
MS-107,120[5]
MS-107,120[6]
MS-107,129[5]
MS-107,129[7]
MS-107,130[6]
MS-107,153[4]et154[1]
MS-107,154[2]et155[1]
MS-107,155[6]et156[1]
MS-107,156[4]
MS-107,156[5]
MS-107,156[6]
MS-107,156[7]
MS-107,156[8]
MS-107,156[9]et157[1]
MS-107,158[5]et159[1]
MS-107,159[4]et160[1]
MS-107,160[2]
MS-107,161[3]
MS-107,166[2]
MS-107,170[4]
MS-107,172[2]
MS-107,175[8]et176[1]
MS-107,176[5]
MS-107,178[1]
MS-107,179[1]
MS-107,179[3]
MS-107,179[4]
MS-107,184[4]et185[1]
MS-107,192[5]
MS-107,219[4]et220[1]et221[1]et222[1]
MS-107,247[5]
MS-107,295[2]
MS-107,70[4]
MS-107,72[2]

MS-107,74[2]
MS-107,74[3]
MS-107,74[4]et75[1]
MS-107,75[2]
MS-107,75[3]
MS-107,75[4]
MS-107,75[5]
MS-107,75[6]et76[1]
MS-107,76[2]
MS-107,77[2]
MS-107,78[10]et79[1]
MS-107,81[4]
MS-107,82[8]
MS-107,82[9]et83[1]
MS-107,87[5]
MS-107,88[3]
MS-107,97[8]
MS-107,98[8]

MS-108,102[2]
MS-108,133[6]
MS-108,24[2]
MS-108,24[4]et25[1]
MS-108,38[2]
MS-108,46[2]et47[1]

MS-110,208[2]
MS-110,226[4]
MS-110,231[6]
MS-110,240[3]
MS-110,242[5]
MS-110,246[5]et247[1]
MS-110,252[7]et253[1]
MS-110,260[3]
MS-110,261[6]
MS-110,268[4]
MS-110,290[5]

MS-111,2[2]
MS-111,81[3]et82[1]
MS-111,82[2]

MS-112,32v[4]

MS-114,IIv[1]

MS-117,151[4]
MS-117,152[2]
MS-117,153[3]
MS-117,159[3]
MS-117,160[4]
MS-117,164[2]
MS-117,168[4]
MS-117,171[3]
MS-117,193[2]
MS-117,201[3]
MS-117,257[2]
MS-117,268[3]
MS-117,269[1]
MS-117,270[3]et271[1]
MS-117,271[3]et272[1]
MS-117,272[2]
MS-117,272[3]
MS-117,272[4]et273[1]

MS-118,100r[2]et100v[1]
MS-118,104r[1]
MS-118,105v[2]
MS-118,10r[2]
MS-118,10r[3]et10v[1]et11r[1]
MS-118,12r[3]et12v[1]
MS-118,13r[2]
MS-118,15v[3]et16r[1]
MS-118,17r[2]et17v[1]
MS-118,1r[1]et1v[1]
MS-118,1v[2]et2r[1]et2v[1]
MS-118,23v[4]
MS-118,32r[3]
MS-118,34v[2]
MS-118,34v[4]
MS-118,35r[4]
MS-118,37r[1]
MS-118,45r[4]
MS-118,45v[4]
MS-118,56r[3]et56v[1]
MS-118,5r[2]et5v[1]et6r[1]et6v[1]
MS-118,62r[3]62v[1]
MS-118,62v[3]
MS-118,63r[2]et63v[1]
MS-118,65r[3]
MS-118,71v[2]

MS-118,87r[3]et87v[1]
MS-118,89v[2]
MS-118,8r[2]et8v[1]
MS-118,9v[2]
MS-118,9v[3]et10r[1]
MS-118,FCv[2]

MS-119,100r[2]
MS-119,101r[4]et101v[1]
MS-119,105[2]et106[1]
MS-119,108v[2]
MS-119,109v[2]et110r[1]
MS-119,111[2]
MS-119,117[3]et118[1]
MS-119,119r[2]et119v[1]et120r[1]et120v[1]et121r[1]
MS-119,123[3]et124[1]
MS-119,128r[1]
MS-119,130[2]et131[1]et132[1]
MS-119,131v[1]
MS-119,134r[4]et134v[1]et135r[1]et135v[1]et136r[1]et136v[1]et137r[1]et137v[1]
MS-119,137[2]
MS-119,139[4]et140[1]et141[1]et142[1]
MS-119,140r[2]et140v[1]
MS-119,140v[2]et141r[1]
MS-119,146[3]
MS-119,147[2]
MS-119,61[2]
MS-119,63[2]et64[1]
MS-119,6[3]
MS-119,70[3]et71[1]
MS-119,75v[2]et76r[1]
MS-119,79r[2]
MS-119,79v[3]et80r[1]
MS-119,80r[2]et80v[1]et81r[1]
MS-119,81r[2]
MS-119,81v[2]
MS-119,81v[3]
MS-119,84v[2]
MS-119,88v[2]
MS-119,91r[2]et91v[1]
MS-119,91v[2]
MS-119,92v[2]
MS-119,94v[1]et95r[1]
MS-119,95r[2]
MS-119,96r[2]et96v[1]

MS-119,98[2]et99[1]
MS-119,99[2]
MS-119,99[3]

MS-120,10v[3]
MS-120,10v[4]
MS-120,11r[1]
MS-120,121r[7]et121v[1]
MS-120,121v[3]
MS-120,127r[3]
MS-120,128v[2]et129r[1]
MS-120,130v[2]
MS-120,16r[2]et16v[1]
MS-120,17r[1]
MS-120,17r[2]et17v[1]et18r[1]
MS-120,1r[1]
MS-120,1r[2]et1v[1]
MS-120,20v[2]
MS-120,20v[3]
MS-120,21v[3]et22r[1]
MS-120,23r[4]
MS-120,25r[2]
MS-120,26v[2]
MS-120,26v[3]et27r[1]
MS-120,33v[1]
MS-120,34v[2]
MS-120,39r[3]
MS-120,41v[2]et42r[1]
MS-120,42r[2]et42v[1]et43r[1]
MS-120,48r[1]
MS-120,48r[2]
MS-120,4v[2]
MS-120,51v[2]
MS-120,54r[2]et54v[1]et55r[1]et55v[1]
MS-120,55v[2]et56r[1]
MS-120,56r[3]
MS-120,56r[4]et56v[1]
MS-120,56v[3]
MS-120,57r[1]
MS-120,57r[2]
MS-120,57v[1]
MS-120,57v[2]
MS-120,62v[3]et63r[1]
MS-120,65r[2]
MS-120,65v[3]

MS-120,68r[3]
MS-120,70r[2]
MS-120,70r[3]et70v[1]
MS-120,70v[2]
MS-120,71r[2]
MS-120,71r[3]
MS-120,72v[1]et73r[1]
MS-120,7v[2]et8r[1]
MS-120,85r[2]
MS-120,9v[2]et10r[1]

MS-122,111v[2]
MS-122,118v[2]
MS-122,28r[3]
MS-122,37r[3]et37v[1]et38r[1]
MS-122,43v[1]
MS-122,49v[4]
MS-122,88r[2]et88v[1]
MS-122,95r[3]
MS-122,95v[3]et96r[1]
MS-122,99v[3]

MS-123,10r[2]
MS-123,15v[4]
MS-123,16r[1]et16v[1]
MS-123,3r[2]
MS-123,3v[2]
MS-123,3v[3]et4r[1]
MS-123,8r[3]et8v[1]
MS-123,FCv[1]et1r[1]

MS-124,3[2]
MS-124,3[3]
MS-124,3[4]et4[1]
MS-124,4[2]
MS-124,4[3]

MS-125,13v[1]
MS-125,1r[1]et1v[1]et2r[1]
MS-125,26r[3]et26v[1]
MS-125,2v[1]
MS-125,31v[3]
MS-125,36v[3]et37r[1]
MS-125,50v[2]
MS-125,53v[4]

MS-125,56v[2]et57r[1]
MS-125,57v[1]
MS-125,58v[2]
MS-125,58v[3]et59r[1]
MS-125,59r[2]et59v[1]
MS-125,75v[1]et76r[1]

MS-126,105[4]et106[1]et107[1]et108[1]
MS-126,105[4]et106[1]et107[1]et108[1]
MS-126,132[4]et133[1]
MS-126,132[4]et133[1]
MS-126,21[2]et22[1]
MS-126,22[2]et23[1]et24[1]et25[1]et26[1]
MS-126,86[2]et87[1]
MS-126,86[2]et87[1]

MS-127,117[4]
MS-127,120[1]

MS-130,153[4]et154[1]
MS-130,185[2]
MS-130,188[3]
MS-130,286[2]
MS-130,291[2]
MS-130,291[3]et292[1]

MS-131,150[2]
MS-131,15[2]
MS-131,163[2]
MS-131,202[3]
MS-131,220[2]et221[1]
MS-131,222[2]
MS-131,22[2]
MS-131,26[2]
MS-131,26[3]
MS-131,32[2]et33[1]
MS-131,34[2]
MS-131,37[3]et38[1]
MS-131,41[3]
MS-131,41[4]et42[1]
MS-131,45[2]
MS-131,48[3]
MS-131,52[2]et53[1]
MS-131,56[2]
MS-131,57[3]et58[1]

MS-131,65[3]et66[1]
MS-131,66[2]et67[1]
MS-131,79[2]
MS-131,81[2]

MS-132,13[2]
MS-132,147[2]
MS-132,153[3]
MS-132,155[3]
MS-132,162[4]et163[1]
MS-132,190[2]
MS-132,191[2]
MS-132,205[1]
MS-132,46[2]et47[1]
MS-132,77[3]et78[1]
MS-132,85[3]
MS-132,85[4]

MS-133,13r[2]
MS-133,13r[5]et13v[1]
MS-133,32v[2]
MS-133,35r[2]
MS-133,35v[3]
MS-133,36r[3]et36v[1]
MS-133,39r[2]
MS-133,41r[3]et41v[1]
MS-133,41v[2]
MS-133,41v[3]
MS-133,41v[4]et42r[1]
MS-133,43r[4]et43v[1]
MS-133,46r[2]
MS-133,67v[2]
MS-133,78r[2]
MS-133,7r[3]et7v[1]et8r[1]
MS-133,8r[2]et8v[1]et9r[1]

MS-134,101[3]et102[1]
MS-134,105[5]et106[1]
MS-134,109[2]
MS-134,121[2]
MS-134,122[4]
MS-134,131[2]
MS-134,140[3]
MS-134,140[4]et141[1]
MS-134,143[2]

MS-134,152[1]
MS-134,152[2]
MS-134,156[4]
MS-134,163[2]
MS-134,168[4]
MS-134,1[2]

MS-135,39r[2]
MS-135,51v[3]
MS-135,52r[3]
MS-135,56r[4]
MS-135,58v[2]

MS-136,60a[2]

MS-137,106a[3]
MS-137,135a[4]
MS-137,135a[7]et135b[1]
MS-137,4b[3]
MS-137,50a[4]
MS-137,57a[3]et57b[1]
MS-137,71a[4]et71b[1]
MS-137,72b[7]et73a[1]
MS-137,73a[2]
MS-137,73a[3]
MS-137,73b[3]
MS-137,88a[4]

MS-138,11b[2]
MS-138,12b[3]
MS-138,14a[4]
MS-138,15b[1]
MS-138,18a[3]
MS-138,1a[1]
MS-138,27a[3]
MS-138,27a[4]
MS-138,29a[3]
MS-138,29b[1]
MS-138,30a[7]
MS-138,30b[2]
MS-138,8a[4]

MS-157a,59v[1]
MS-157a,59v[2]
MS-157a,61v[2]

MS-157a,61v[4]et62r[1]
MS-157a,65r[1]
MS-157a,66v[2]
MS-157a,67v[2]

MS-161,70r[2]
MS-161,70r[3]

MS-162b,21v[3]et22r[1]
MS-162b,22r[2]et22v[1]
MS-162b,25r[1]
MS-162b,36v[2]et37r[1]
MS-162b,37r[2]
MS-162b,37r[3]et37v[1]
MS-162b,42v[3]
MS-162b,48r[2]
MS-162b,62r[2]
MS-162b,62r[3]et63v[1]

MS-163,1r[1]
MS-163,37v[2]
MS-163,39r[2]
MS-163,40v[2]
MS-163,40v[3]
MS-163,42v[3]
MS-163,4v[2]et5r[2]
MS-163,58v[2]
MS-163,5r[1]
MS-163,63r[4]et63v[1]
MS-163,64v[2]et65r[1]
MS-163,68r[2]
MS-163,68v[2]et69r[1]

MS-165,200[2]

MS-166,12r[2]

MS-173,FCv[2]

MS-183,143[2]et144[1]
MS-183,145[3]
MS-183,145[4]
MS-183,146[1]
MS-183,146[2]et147[1]
MS-183,148[1]et149[1]et150[1]et151[1]et152[1]et153[1]

MS-183,153[2]et154[1]et155[1]et156[1]et157[1]
MS-183,157[2]et158[1]
MS-183,159[1]
MS-183,159[2]
MS-183,161[2]et162[1]
MS-183,162[2]
MS-183,164[3]et165[1]et166[1]
MS-183,166[2]et167[1]et168[1]
MS-183,168[2]et169[1]et170[1]et171[1]et172[1]et173[1]
MS-183,173[2]et174[1]et175[1]
MS-183,175[2]et176[1]
MS-183,176[2]et177[1]
MS-183,183[2]et184[1]et185[1]
MS-183,185[2]et186[1]et187[1]et188[1]et189[1]et190[1]et191[1]
MS-183,191[2]et192[1]et193[1]et194[1]et195[1]et196[1]
MS-183,196[2]et197[1]et198[1]et199[1]et200[1]et201[1]et202[1]
MS-183,202[2]et203[1]et204[1]
MS-183,204[2]et205[1]et206[1]et207[1]
MS-183,207[2]et208[1]
MS-183,208[3]et209[1]et210[1]
MS-183,210[2]
MS-183,210[3]
MS-183,210[4]et211[1]
MS-183,211[2]et212[1]
MS-183,213[3]et214[1]et215[1]et216[1]et217[1]
MS-183,217[2]
MS-183,217[3]et218[1]
MS-183,221[2]
MS-183,222[1]
MS-183,222[2]et223[1]
MS-183,223[2]et224[1]et225[1]et226[1]
MS-183,226[2]et227[1]
MS-183,232[2]et233[1]et234[1]
MS-183,234[3]et235[1]
MS-183,240[2]et241[1]
MS-183,241[2]
MS-183,241[3]

In the quotations of *Wittgenstein's Secret Diaries*, the labeling of the coded passages has been slightly modified, for example "MS 133: 41v-42r, 1946" with capitalization, extra spaces, and the year of writing.

Notes

Chapter 1

1 "Wovon man nicht sprechen kann, darüber muss man schweigen."
In terms of the quotations from Wittgenstein's work in the footnotes of this book, they are ordered as follows: (1) Wittgenstein's original code or cryptogram, (2) the English translation of (3) Wittgenstein's German translation.

The translations in this book are mine, except those of published works made by different translators. I have not followed the existing translations exactly. Often the translations have been modified to revise words, details, and punctuation. My principle has been to preserve the consistency of the synonymy and to make translations in Wittgenstein's style of writing (for my translation method of Wittgenstein's philosophical texts, see Gorlée 2012: 12–15, forthcoming a).

2 For a full English translation of McGuinness, Ascher, and Pfersmann 1996, see McGuinness 2018.

3 The prefix *quasi-* is a loan-word taken from Latin. The initial prefix of quasi-followed by the main noun involves the *as-if* comparison of the corresponding items of the main word or sentence to those of the similar words or sentence. Quasi- often serves to soften the main word in an unusual or strange expression. For example, the strong term of "language" is weakened in the forms of "quasi-language." Wittgenstein's quasi-language adopted a stranger code alphabet than normally applied in language. The readers are confounded by the dynamic of quasi-language, but Wittgenstein stressed the implication of a key to make itself understood. The code system operates on the process of transforming the verbal material of the strange quasi-language backwards into usual language.

4 Brown's *Wittgensteinian Linguistics* (1974) compared Chomsky's theory with general linguistics. Against the sharp rise of Chomsky's transformative-generative aspects of grammar, Brown was interested in the linguistic interactions of Wittgenstein's lexical and grammatical forms of language. Chomsky mainly concentrates on describing the "competence" of the speaker's knowledge of language, while Wittgenstein considered first and foremost the speaker's fragmented "performance." In the 1970s Chomsky was a poststructuralist linguist, while the role of generative grammar was only implicitly shared in semiotics. Brown's *Wittgensteinian Linguistics* shows the anti-Chomskian perspective, but semiotics was hardly noticed and only added in the Introduction (1974: 13–19). Brown's book was an early analysis of Wittgenstein's speech acts, in which semiotic relations are represented from different points of view.

5 Wittgenstein's *Denkbewegungen* is the German neologism of combining the verb *denken* (to think, to reflect, to conceive) with *Bewegung* (movement, motion, commotion, agitation) used in plural. In Wittgenstein's ambiguous style of writing, the German *Denkbewegungen* refers to the revolutionary "thought-movements" for the violent "transport of thoughts" to write in various forms and genres of literature. An accurate English translation is impossible. The German noun *Denkwegungen*

is the *abstract* noun to refer to Wittgenstein's many-branched quality of the brain, which corresponds to the *concrete* mood for the physical and emotional inspiration of the works. Thus, the plurality of Wittgenstein's works can be approached from the reality of his mental life and also experimentally from the psychological irreality of Wittgenstein's hidden emotions.

6 Peirce's semiotic doctrine—including the three categories in sign-object interpretant, icon-index-symbol, deduction-induction-abduction, semiosis, and other subjects—has, beyond the primary works of Peirce, an extensive bibliography. For interested students, Thomas A. Sebeok's book *Signs: An Introduction to Semiotics* ([1994] 2001) considers Peirce's semiotic doctrine as applicable manual to general academic disciplines and different fields of practice. Peirce's semiotics is also briefly explained in "Fundamentals of the Semiotics of Charles S. Peirce" (Gorlée 1994: 31–66). Peirce's notion of "habit" (for example, CP: 7.468–7.423) is studied by the articles of *Consensus on Peirce's Concept of Habit: Before and Beyond Consciousness*, edited by West and Anderson (2016). For the criminal code, see Marcel Danesi's *The Puzzle Instinct: The Meaning of Puzzles in Human Life* (2002).

Chapter 2

1 "Manches Mensch ist im ganzen Leben krank und kennt nur das Glück, das der fühlt, der nach langen geftigen Schmerzen ein paar scherzlose Stunden hat. (Es ist ein seliges Aufatmen)." Today, the totality of the coded diaries are made available in electronic format in the Wittgenstein Archives at the University of Bergen (Norway). Written by Wittgenstein from 1929 onwards, the text references are: MS number followed by page(s) and year.

2 "Es geschieht so viel, dass mir ein Tag so lange vorkommt wie eine Woche. Bin gestern zur Bedienung eines Scheinwerfers auf einem von uns gekaperten Schiffe auf der Weichsel befordert worden. Die Bemannung ist eine Saubande! Keine Begeisterung, unglaubliche Rohheit, Dummheit und Bosheit! Es ist also doch nicht wahr, dass die gemeinsame grosse Sache die Menschen adeln muss. Dadurch wird auch die lästigste Arbeit zum Frondienst. Es ist merkwürdig, wie sich die Menschen ihre Arbeit selbst zu einer hässlichen Mühsal machen.—Unter allen unseren äusseren Umständen könnte die Arbeit auf unserem Schiffe eine herrliche glückliche Zeit geben und stattdessen!—Es wird wohl unmöglich sein, sich hier mit den Leuten zu verstehen (ausser etwa mit dem Leutnant, der ein ganz netter Mensch zu sein scheint). Also in Demut die Arbeit verrichten und sich selbst um Gottes willen nicht (sich selbst) verlieren!!!! Nämlich am leichtesten verliert man sich selbst, wenn man sich anderen Leuten schenken will."
In this book, the emphasis of words and phrases in *italics* will be underlined.

3 "Von mir kann ich nichts sagen. Ich lebe noch immer."

4 Wittgenstein's hieroglyphic signs of the *Notebooks 1914–1916* can be regarded as the ideograms of the archaic visual writings of Wittgenstein's *Tractatus*. The paragraph about the origins of the alphabet illustrated the visual analogy with the "hieroglyphic writing, which pictures what it describes" (*Hieroglyphenschrift, welche die Tatsachen die sie beschreibt abbildet*) (*Tractatus Logico-Philosophicus* [TLP]: 4.016; see Saussure [1959] 1966: 25–27; Gorlée 2012: 150, 287, 288; 2015b). Wittgenstein was interested in hieroglyphics, but they have no connection with the secret code and cryptographic

imagination. In *Tractatus*, Wittgenstein mirrored the logical "grammar" of the linguistic sign referring to the object, which he perhaps derived from Saussure's formal relation of sign and referent, but looks forward to Peirce's formal and informal relation of sign, object, and interpretant to interpret the use of secret script in the diary. However, Royce, a disciple of Peirce, described the interpreting process of hieroglyphical translation as a semiotic movement from Saussure to Peirce: "Suppose that an Egyptologist translates an inscription. So far two beings are indeed in question: the translator and his text. But a genuine translation cannot be merely a translation in the abstract. There must be some language into which the inscription is translated. Let this translation be, in a given instance, an English translation. Then the translator interprets something; but he interprets it only to one who can read English. And if a reader knows no English, the translation is for such a reader no interpretation at all. That is, a triad of beings—the Egyptian text, the Egyptologist who translates, and the possible English reader—are equally necessary in order that such an English interpretation of an Egyptian writing should exist. Whenever anybody translates a text, the situation remains, however you vary texts or language or translators, essentially the same" (1918: 286). For Royce, "The triadic relation in question is, in its essence, non-symmetrical,—that is, unevenly arranged with respect to all three terms" (286). But if "you transpose the order of the terms," Royce wrote, "an account of the happening which constitutes an interpretation must be altered, or otherwise may become either false or meaningless" (286–287).

5 See Sebeok [1994] 2001: 46–50, 65–82; 1984b: 211–230; 1986a: 45–58; see Staiano 1986: 3–9 and throughout. Barthes (1972) made a double division of the form and substance of symptom and sign. Barthes views the general sign as the purely linguistic sign, merely expressed by the physician's clinical discourse. The physician attempts to define the linguistic and non-linguistic variety of the symptoms, about which the patient complains, into the medical anamnesis, diagnosis, and prognosis of the patient's illness or disease (Barthes 1972: 40; see Sebeok [1994] 2001: 47, 48).

6 See further, Peirce's remarks in CP: 2.304, 3.361, 5.138, 5.186, 5.473, 5.552, 7.356, 7.354, 7.628, 8.119, 8.335, 8.313.

7 Peirce spoke of genuine signs and degenerate signs. This contrast was used in two senses by Peirce. On the one hand, both iconic and indexical signs are considered degenerate with respect to symbolic, fully triadic signs, so that the only sign to be genuine or pure is the symbol where all of the terms equal a third. On the other hand, both thirds and seconds have degenerate forms. In a degenerate second the secondness partakes of firstness. A third can be degenerate in two degrees. The first degree of degeneracy is found in a third involving secondness, or in a second involving firstness, whereas the second of degeneracy is found in a third partaking of firstness.

8 "Das erlösende Wort" has also been translated by Klagge and Nordmann as "the liberating word" (Wittgenstein 1993: 164–165). The undertranslation, coming from Wittgenstein's *Big Typescript* (BT: 276), expresses how by his death Christ redeemed the moral debt of despair and forgiveness of humankind. Compare the further meaning to the "first" ordinary word, transformed by God into the proposition that "God redeems Christian from slavery to sin in order to adopt them as his children, thus perpetuating the idea that the redeemer assumes the role of familial protector over the redeemed" (Willis 2001: 434). Wittgenstein's task was to solve the philosophy of discourse by "healing" the old language of knowledge into the "second" revelation for future generations. The word "salvation" (*Erlösung*) is Wittgenstein's

"redemptive word" derived from the words of Christ the Redeemer to guarantee the legitimacy of the right interpretation of God's truth (Hick [1963] 1973: 59–60, 62–63; Klagge 2011: 125–142; Gorlée 2012: 77).

God's redemption is expressed in the Old Testament as the voices of the prophets: "Through me the spirit of the Lord has spoken: his words are on my tongue" (2 Kgs 23:2), "This covenant I will make with them, the Lord says: Spirit of mine that dwells in thee, words of mine entrusted to thy lips, on thy lips shall dwell, on the lips of thy children and thy children's children, henceforth and for ever" (Isa. 59:21; see Num. 23:5, 24:3; 1 Kgs 3:4–9).

In the New Testament, the (now capitalized) Word of God (Hebrew *dabar*, Greek *logos*) was intimately related to the force of the Holy Spirit. For example, "At the beginning of time the Word already was; and God had the Word abiding with him, and the Word was God" (Jn 1:1). Wittgenstein's mind articulated the new level of creative reality, taught by the "second" meaning to the "first" Word, rearticulated by the three visions of the Trinity (God and Christ, expanded in the world by the light of the Holy Spirit) (Gorlée 2012: 121–128).

9 "Meine Gedanken sind müde. Ich sehe die Sachen nicht frisch, sondern alltäglich ohne Leben. Es ist, als ob eine Flamme erlöschen wäre und ich muss warten und ich muss warten, bis sie von selbst wieder zu brennen anfängt. Mein Geist aber ist rege. Ich denke."

The flame of fire can be compared to the hope of bad or good habits in Wittgenstein's *Philosophical Grammar* (written in 1931–1934, before *The Blue Book*). He wrote about the commonsense use of two or more expressions: "Thought can only be something common-or-garden and *ordinary*. (We are accustomed to thinking of it as something ethereal and unexplored, as if we were dealing with something unknown like our brain)" (PG: 108, translated by Anthony Kenny). For Wittgenstein's sentence "Der Gedanke kann nur etwas ganz hausbackenes, gewöhnliches, sein," Kenny translated Wittgenstein's "hausbacken" as "common-or-garden" and "*ordinary*" (Somavilla in DB: 1:142). This meaning is rendered twice in my translation as "commonplace" and "lifeless."

10 I used the the King James Version of the Bible and the Torah edited by Rabbi W. Gunther Plaut (New York: Union of American Hebrew Congregations, 1981). The Jewish book of Jeremiah in English translation edited by Rabbi Dr. H. Freedman (London: The Soncino Press, [1949] 1966) and the Psalms edited by Rabbi Samson Raphael Hirsch (Jerusalem: Feldheim Publishers, [1960] 1997).

11 "Ich bin ganz im Dunkeln darüber, wie meine Arbeit weitergehen wird. Nur durch Wunder kann sie gelingen. Nur dadurch indem von ausserhalb mir die Schleier von meinen Augen weggenommen wird. Ich muss mich ganz in mein Schicksal ergeben."

12 "Von Gemeinheit umgeben! Soll in absehbarer Zeit zum Kader ins Hinterland abgehen. Bin froh darüber. Von Gemeinheit umgeben. Gott will helfen."

13 "Bin deprimiert. Allein allein! Gott sei dank."

14 "Unter Schmerzen: manches Gute im Grossen im einzelnen aber schlecht."

15 "Mein lieber Davy! Heute habe ich Deinen Brief von 27 Januar erhalten. Ich habe einen Wendepunkt erreicht. Ich fange an, wieder mehr zu arbeiten" (Noll 1998: 111, 1915).

16 Beyond the lectures and papers, mainly *Philosophische Bemerkungen* and *Philosophische Grammatik*, collected in *The Big Typescript*.

17 The fragmentariness in written signs, not in a real article or book but in short paragraphs (as discussed in Gorlée 2007), is now applied to Wittgenstein's style of fragments.

18 "Meine Art des Philosophierens."

19 "Mein Leben ist sehr seltsam! Ich weiss nicht wie hell oder wie finster es ist. Es ist gleichsam halb hell, halb dunkel. Respi erklärte mir vor ein paar Tagen dass sie micht mehr küssen werde weil ihr Gefühl für mich nicht desart sei dass es dieses Zeichen rechtfertigte. Ich bin nun davon schmerzlich getroffen and dabei doch fröhlich. Denn es kommt doch eigentlich darauf an, dass mich der Geist nicht verlässt. Denn wenn der Geist mich nicht verlässt, dann ist nichts was geschieht schmutzig und kleinlich. Ich aber muss viel auf den Zehenspitzen stehen, wenn ich nicht untergehen will."

20 "Ich bin in meine Art der Gedankenbewegungen beim Philosophieren etwas verliebt. Und vielleich sollte ich das Wort 'etwas' weglassen."

21 "Übrigens heisst das nicht, das ich in meinen Stil verliebt bin. Das bin ich nicht."

22 "beleidigte Leberwurst."

23 Wittgenstein's funny metaphor recalls Groucho Marx playing "Dr." Hugo Z. Hackenbusch in the film *A Day at the Races* (1937). A patient asks Dr. Groucho Marx "Are you a man or a mouse?" and he answered "Throw me a piece of cheese and you'll find out" (Abrams [1941] 1957: 64).

24 "Es ist beschämend sich als leerer Schlauch zeigen zu müssen der nur vom Geist aufgeblasen wird."

25 Wittgenstein's symptoms of "liverwurst" (and other examples) illustrate the semiotic terminology of Peirce's image, diagram, and metaphor. Peirce's three-way terms applied here to medical signs do *not* consider as literary figure of metaphor in the ordinary sense, but as calculated metaphor (Sontag 1978, 1988). The metaphor of the symptoms were elaborated into Wittgenstein's fictional games—such as the beetle story and the duck-rabbit image—materializing directly the physical and bodily proximity of danger.

26 "Es ist schwer einem Kurzsichtigen einen Weg zu beschreiben. Weil man ihm nicht sagen kann 'schau auf den Kirchturm dort 10 Meilen von uns und geh in dieser Richtung.'"

27 "Mein Gehirn wird wohl einmal gleichsam vor Alter erblinden. Aber nicht unbedingt erst wenn ich viel älter bin als jetzt."

28 "Ich erscheine mir selbst wie ein alter Mann … Man könnte sich einen Menschen vorstellen, der vor seiner Geburt bis zu seinem Tod immer entweder schliefe oder in einer Art Halfschlaf oder Dusel lebte. So verhält sich mein Leben zu dem wirklich lebendigen Menschen."

29 "Im Falle meines Todes vor der Fertigstellung oder Veröffentlichung dieses Buches sollen meine Aufzeichnungen fragmentarisch veröffentlicht werden unter dem Titel 'Philosophische Bemerkungen' und mit der Widmung 'Francis Skinner zugeeignet' — Er is, wenn diese Bemerkung nach dem Tode gelesen wird, von meiner Arbeit in Kenntnis zu setzen, an die Addresse: Trinity College, Cambridge."

30 "Dieses Buch kann allerdings gekürzt werden, aber es ist sehr schwer, es richtig zu kürzen. Diese Bemerkung bezieht sich nicht auf den "Versuch einer Umarbeitung."

31 "Einiges gearbeitet. Und doch ist mein Geist nicht 'wholeheartedly' bei der Arbeit. Dahinter steht doch ein vages Gefühl vom Problem dieses meines Lebens. Aus dem Schiff nach Skjolden."

32 "Schreibe mehr order weniger aus lange Weile. Ich fühle: ich treibe. Eitel, gedankenlos, ängstlich. Ich wünsche jetzt durchaus nicht, allen zu leben. Fürchte, ich werde bedrückt sein und nicht arbeiten können. Ich möchte jetzt bei jemandem wohnen. In der Früh ein menschliches Gesicht sehen.—Anderseits bin ich jetzt wider so verweichlicht, dass es viellecht gut wäre allein zu müssen. Bin jetzt

ausserordentlich verächtlich. Darin dass ich das schreibe liegt natürlich eine Unwahrheit.—Haltlos."

33 "In Skjolden. Fühle mich übel. Unglücklich, rastlos und gedankenlos. … Und da kam mir wieder zum Bewusstsein, wie einzig Francis ist und unersätzlich. Und wie wenig ich doch nach das weiss, wenn ich mit ihm bin.
Bin ganz in Kleinigheit verstrickt. Bin irritiert, denken nur an mich and fühle, dass mein Leben elend ist, und dabei ich auch gar keine Ahnung, wie elend es ist."

34 "Bin jetzt wirklich krank. Unterleibschmerzen und Temperatur."

35 "Arbeite weiter und sieh, was wird! … Werde ich damit zu Rande kommen? Arbeite weiter und überlass es der Schickung! … Auch Gedanken fallen manchmal unreif vom Baum."

36 "Die Lösung des Problems, das du im Leben siehst, ist eine Art zu leben, die das Problemhafte zum Verschwinden bringt. …
Das das Leben problematisch ist, heisst, dass Dein Leben nicht in die Form des Leben passt. Du musst dann dein Leben verändern, und passt es in die Form, dann verschwindet das Problematische.
Oder soll icht nicht sagen: dass wer richtig lebt, das Problem nicht als Traurigkeit, also docht nicht problematisch empfindet, sondern vielmehr als eine Freude, also gleichsam als einen lichten Aether un sein Leben, nicht als einen fraglichen Hintergrund."

37 "Genie ist nicht 'Talent und Character', sondern Character der sich in der Form eines speziellen Talents kundgibt. Wie ein Mensch aus Mut einem Wasser nachspringt, so schreibt ein anderer aus Mut eine Symphonie. (Dies ist ein schwaches Beispiel.)"

38 "Man könnte sagen: "Genie ist Mut im Talent."

39 "Der Mut, nicht die Geschicklichkeit; nicht einmal die Inspiration, ist das Senfkorn, was zum grossen Baum empor wächst."

40 "Auf seinen Lorberen auszuruhen ist so gefährlich, wie auf einer Schneewanderung auszuruhen. Du nicht Man schläft ein & stirbst im Schlaf."

41 "Man schläft."

42 "Im Krankensaal, warte ich auf die morgige Operation. Es scheint ein recht abscheulicher Ort. Ausser Männern sind hier auch ein Paar kranke Kinder da, eines wimmert unaufhörlich. Es ist zugig, unbequem und ungemütlich. Ungemütlich auch die Pflegerinnen."

43 "Ein Mensch ist in seinem Zimmer gefangen, wenn die Türe unversperrt ist, sich nach innen offnet; er aber nicht auf die Idee kommt zu ziehen, statt gegen sie zu drücken. / Bring den Menschen in die unrichtige Atmosphäre & nichts wird funktionieren wie es soll. Er wird an allen Teilen ungesund erscheinen. Bring ihn wieder in das richtige Element, & alles wird sich enfalten & gesund erscheinen. Bring ihn wieder in das Richtige Element, & alles wird sich enfalten & gesund erscheinen. Wenn er nun aber in unrechten Element ist? Dann muss er such also damit abfinden, als Krüppel su erscheinen."

44 "Mein Unglück ist so komplex, dass es schwer zu beschreiben ist. Aber wahrscheinlichist doch Vereinsamung die Hauptsache."

45 "ich war ein Fisch und ein Fisch geblieben."

46 "Die Liebe hat sozusagen zwei Temperaturen; einen Hitzegrad und einen Wärmegrad."

47 "Alles am Ort stösst mich ab. Das Steife, Künstliche, Selbstgefällige der Leute. Die Universitätsatmorphere ist mir ekelhaft."

48 "Das Gefühl der Abhängigkeit."

49 "eine Bitte, ein Lohn, eine Strafe, u.s.f.„ ist nicht nur von dem Bild anhängt, das uns eine gewisse Situation darbietet."
50 "von einem bösen Geist im Kreis herum geführt, und rings umher ist schöne, grüne Weide."
51 "Möge das Herzweh mich zur richtigen Handlung führen."
52 "Ich fühle mich nicht wohl, weiss aber nicht recht warum. Ich bin ermüdet, fühle mich fremd in der Welt. Wenn dich kein Band an Menschen und kein Band an Gott bindet, so bist du ein Fremdling. … Kann wegen schlechten Schlafe und Müdigkeit nicht arbeiten."
53 "Gott bewahre mich vom Wahnsinn!"
54 "Ob das meine letzte Krankheit ist?"
55 "War beim Arzt, der sagt, mir fehle nichts Ernstes, nur Gastritis. Ich glaube er hat recht, vertraue aber seine Therapie nicht."
56 "Gestern von Wien zurück. Danach kommt mir London furchtbar trübselig vor. Die Ordnung selbst ist hier ekelhaft. Die Menschen sind vor den Bedürfnissen selbst getotet. Jeder Schwung ist, wie durch eine ungeheure Reibung, ganzlich ausgezehrt."
57 "Wenn Einer glaubt, vor weniger Tagen von Amerika nach England geflogen zu sein, so glaube ich, dass er sich darin nicht irren kann.
Ebenso, wenn Einer sagt, er sitze jetzt am Tisch & schreibe.

"Aber wenn ich mich auch in solchen Fällen micht irren kann, ist es nicht möglich, dass ich in der Narkose bin? Wenn ich es bin & wenn die Narkose mir has Bewusstsein raubt, dann rede & denke ich jetzt nicht wirklich. Ich kann nicht im Ernst annehmen, ich träume jetzt. Wer träumend sagt 'Ich träume', auch wenn er dabei hörbar redet, hat sowenig recht, wie wenn er im Traum sagt 'Es regnet', während es tatsächlich regnet. Auch wenn sein Traum wirklich mit dem Geräusch des Regens zusammenhängt."

Chapter 3

1 "Ich drücke, was ich ausdrücken will doch immer nut "mit halben Gelingen" aus. Ja auch das nicht, sondern vielleicht nur mit einem Zehntel. Das will doch etwas sagen. Mein Schreiben ist oft nur ein "Stammeln."
2 The moral import of science is described in the word-tool of human language. To control (and self-control) the value of scientific thoughts, Scheffler expected, or demanded, the Jewish imperatives of teaching formal education to question dogmas and seek relevant reasons. Then, he wanted students to embark on new situations of creative thinking and critical dialogues (Scheffler [1973] 1989, 1985). It seems that, for Scheffler, rationality (objectivity) rests upon irrationality and non-rationality (subjectivity) (Scheffler ([1967] 1978).
3 The growth from outside to inside draws from Peirce's triadic idea of "evolutionary love" (CP: 6.287–6.317, 1983; see Potter 1997: 171–190), which gives the cumulative continuity of science (CP: 2.15). In the modes of evolution, Peirce's semiosis gives an endless and infinite series of interpretants. The interactive semiosis ends the negative process of seeing the mystery of the verbal signs in shaping the strange forms in positive interpretants. In Peirce's evolutionary philosophy, "Love, recognizing germs of loveliness on the hateful, gradually warms it to life, and makes it lovely" (CP: 6.289, 1893). For Peirce, love and hate must be understood as marginal sensations,

but the opposite "synonyms" work against those signs to make "equivalent" habits. Growth changes strange emotions and knowledge magically into genuine feelings and activity.

4 "ein Paar freundliche Worte (es könnten auch Kraftworte à la Luki sein)."

5 "Du alter Hxszhrn!"

6 Serres adorned the rhetorical style of French philosophy with the poetic speech and multilingual puns of the act of translation. The mixed pseudo-literary narration makes Serres's logic in *The Parasite* (1982) apply to the labyrinth of the verbal themes in translation (Nöth 2012: 124–128).

7 "fere plerisque accidit, ut praesidio litterarum diligentiam in perdiscendo ac memoriam remittant."

8 "Epistulae quoque eius ad senatum extant, quas primum videtur ad paginas et formam memorialis libelli convertisse, cum antea consules et duces non nisi transversa charta scriptas mitterent. Extant et ad Ciceronem, item ad familiares domesticis de rebus, in quibus, si qua occultius perferenda erant, per notas scripsit, id est sic structo litterarum ordine, ut nullum verbum effici posset; quae si qui investigare et persequi velit, quartam elementorum litteram, id est D pro A et perinde reliquas commutet."

9 Different from the rhetorical structure of the English language, German nouns have an initial capital letter. The nouns are often composed words of several nouns together, which have a longer average length than other languages. All nouns are of male, female, or neuter gender, and the adjective accompanying the noun must be accordingly declined with reference to the nominative, genitive, dative, and accusative cases. Moreover, the verb often comes at the end of the sentence, meaning that the initial objects are central to the sentence, while the verbal action is stated as the terminal item.

10 CP 2.303f., 322, 326f., 3.73, 4. 424, 455f., 471, 515.

11 See Jakobson's zero sign arguing the dysfunction of communication in language (Jakobson [1939] 1971).

12 Cryptography climbs down from the contrastive spectrograms in the final years of symbolic logician Charles S. Peirce, who believed that discourse was the monologue growing into the dialogue. Peirce's "existential graphs" was his pioneering system of logical diagrams to define the universe of discourse. In the imitation game of existential graphs, Peirce transferred alphabetical letters to a coding "machine" in order to decipher and decode the inferential meaning of the habits of language (Roberts 1973). Peirce was an early computer scientist who worked feverishly on composing a logical kind of cable code, to be used in mathematical reasoning machines. He wrote that "I could make a machine which would write a cipher dispatch, as secure as a combination lock, and as readily as an ordinary typewriter, and a companion machine would translate it as fast as a stock ticker,—every dispatch in a different cipher which the machine itself would discover" (MS L254: 12, 1898; see MS 831: 2–12, 1900). Peirce's logical calculations count as the mechanical language-games destined for a limited number of cryptoanalysts (Beaulieu 2008; 2014).

13 "Alles was überhaupt gedacht werden kann, kann klar gedacht werden. Alles was sich aussprechen lässt, lässt sich klar aussprechen."

14 "Wovon man nicht sprechen kann, darüber muss man schweigen."

15 "Es gibt allerdings Unaussprechliches. Dies z e i g t sich, es ist das Mystische."

16 "Diese [mystische] Methode wäre für den anderen unbefriedigend—er hätte nicht das Gefühl, dass wir ihn Philosophie lehrten—aber s i e wäre die einzig streng richtige."

17 Wittgenstein's philosophy of language anticipated the evolution of technical, statistical, and mathematical roots of meaningful information to mark the cryptographical codes of communication technology (Cherry [1957] 1966), prior to the introduction of political security to the computer-based cryptology (Kahn [1968] 1974).

18 The Kabbalistic provenance of Atbash has been investigated by Elias Lipiner in *The Metaphysics of the Hebrew Alphabet* (1989). Since Lipiner's book was written in Hebrew, a more detailed discussion lies beyond the scope of this chapter.

19 Poe's "The Gold Bug" might have inspired Wittgenstein's story of the beetle, as discussed here.

20 "Was ist die primitive Reaktion, mit der das Sprachspiel anfängt? Die dann in Worte umgesetzt werden kann?"

21 "Die Unsichterkeit das "Spannende" vieler Detektivgeschichten aufgebaut? darauf das Problem jeder Detektivgeschichte gegründet?"

22 "entsprang es zum Teil dem Nachahmungstrieb (ich hatte Kellers Tagebücher gelesen) zum Teil dem Bedürfnis doch etwas von mir niederzulegen. Es war also zum grossen Teil Eitelkeit. Zum Teil freilich auch wieder der Ersatz für einen Menschen dem ich mich anvertrauen konnte. Später mischte ich dazu die Nachahmung der Pepysschen Tagebücher. Freilich ist es, wie immer, schwer hier gerecht zu sein, denn es war natürliches und eitle Bestrebungen stark *vermischt*."

Chapter 4

1 "Eine Beichte muss ein Teil des neuen Lebens sein."

2 "Ich bin ein Schwein und dabei bin ich doch nicht unglücklich. Ich bin in der Gefahr noch seichter zu werden. Möge Gott es verhuten!"

3 "Ich fühlte dass ich ein Schwein bin weil ich auch echter mit unechtes mische. Möche mir Gott Reinheit und Wahrheit schicken."

4 "(Beichte, etc.) und ich muss froh sein, wenn ich schon ein Schwein bin, dass ich mich noch manches mal darüber beunruhigen kann. Wäre die Beunruhigung nicht so oberflächlich, so würde eine Besserung eintreten."

5 "Die Wahrheit über sich selbst kann man in dem verschiedensten Geist schreiben. Im anständigsten und unanständigsten. Und danach ist es sehr wünschenswert oder sehr unrichtig dass sie geschrieben werde. Ja, es gibt unter den wahrhaften Autobiographien die man schreiben könnten alle Stufen vom Höchsten zum Niedrigsten. Ich zum Beispiel kann meine Biographie nicht höher schreiben als ich bin. Und durch die blosse Tatsache dass ich sie schreibe hebe ich mich nicht notwendigerweise ich kann mich dagegen sogar schmutziger machen als ich schon war. Etwas in mir spricht dafür meine Biographie zu schreiben und zwar möchte ich mein Leben einmal klar ausbreiten um es klar vor mir zu haben und auch für andere. Nicht so sehr, um darüber Gericht zu halten als um jedenfalls Klarheit und Wahrheit zu schaffen."

6 "Ein gutes Gleichnis erfrischt den Verstand."

7 "Wenn ein 'Strassenköter' seine Biographie schreibe, so bestände die Gefahr a. dass er entweder seine Natur verleugnen, oder b. einen Grund ausfindig machen würde auf sie stolz zu sein, oder c. die Sache so darstellte als sei diese seine Natur eine nebensächliche Angelegenheit. Im ersten Falle lügt er, im zweiten ahmt er eine für den Natur dem Naturadel natürliche Eigenschaft, den Stolz nach ein vitium splendidum ist das er ebensowenig wirklich besitzen kann, wie ein krüppelhafter Körper natürliche Grazie. Im dritten Fall macht er gleichsam die socialdemokratische Geste, die die Bildung über die rohen Eigenschaften des Körpers stellt, aber auch das ist ein Betrug. Es ist was er ist und das ist zugleich wichtig und bedeutsam aber kein Grund zum Stolz aderseits immer Gegenstand der Selbstachtung. Ja ich kann den Adelsstolz des Andern und seine Verachtung meiner Natur anerkennen, denn ich erkenne ja dadurch nur meine Natur an und den andern des zur Umgebung meiner Natur, die Welt, deren Mittelpunkt dieser vielleicht hässliche Gegenstand, meine Person ist."

8 "Diese Methode ist in Wesentlichen der Übergang von der Frage nach der Wahrheit zur Frage nach dem Sinn."

9 "Ich habe 14 Tage lang nichts gearbeitet. Nun wollen wir sehen ob es wieder gehen wird. Ich bin noch nicht zur Ruhe gekommen. Und meine Gedanken flattern um den Gegenstand herum."

10 "Ich trödle gerne. Vielleicht jetzt nicht mehr so sehr wie in früherer Zeit."

11 "Es ist merkwürdig dass ich seit so vielen Jahren fast nie mehr das leiseste Bedürfnis empfunden habe Tagebuchaufzeichnungen zu machen. In der allerersten Zeit in Berlin als ich damit anfing auf Zettel Gedanken über mich aufzuschreiben, da war es ein Bedürfnis. Es war ein für mich wichtiger Schritt. Später entsprang es zum Teil dem Nachahmungstrieb (ich hatte Kellers Tagebücher gelesen) zum Teil dem Bedürfnis doch etwas von mir niederzulegen. Es war also zum grossen Teil Eitelkeit. Zum Teil freilich auch wieder der Ersatz für einen Menschen dem ich mich anvertrauen konnte. Später mischte ich dazu die Nachahmung der Pepysschen Tagebücher. Freilich ist es, wie immer, schwer hier gerecht zu sein, denn es war natürliches und eitle Bestrebungen stark vermischt."

12 "Aber dieses Vorkommen des Paradigmas und der Klasse im Symbolismus bedeutet nicht, dass ein bestimmter Satz des Symbolismus wahr sein muss. Rousseau hat etwas jüdisches in seiner Nature."

13 See Wittgenstein's word "primitive" in Gorlée 2012: 181 fn.

14 "Du musst erst auf die Wanderstaft gehen und dann kannst Du in die Heimat zurückkehren und dann wirst Du sie anders verstehen."

15 "Soweit das Tagebuchschreiben nicht selber leben ist, ist es in meinem Fall schlecht. Denn es wird für mich, wie alles, was ich mache beinah sicher zum Anlass der Eitelkeit und je weiniger Zeit ich habe mich auf eitle Weise selbst zu bespiegeln, desto besser. Das Leben zerstreut, verblässt am besten diesen Rauch und er ist auch wenn er vorübergehend gedacht wird harmloser."

16 "Ich muss aus meinem Tagebuch, wenn es in Ordnung sein soll quasi eben ins Freie—in das Leben—treten und weder wie aus einem Kellerloch ans Licht steigen, noch wie von einem höheren Ort wieder auf die Erde herunterspringen müssen."

17 "Wo Wärme ist da kann Eitelkeit nicht gut gedeihen. Was die anderen von mir halten beschäftigt mich immer mehr aussenordentlich."

18 "Wenn ich nicht recht weiss wie ein Buch anfangen so kommt das daher dass noch etwas unklar ist. Denn ich möchte mit dem der Philosophie gegebenen, den

geschriebenen & gesprochenen Sätzen, quasi den Büchern anfangen. Und hier begegnet man der Schwierigkeit des "Alles fliesst." Und mit ihr vielleicht überhaupt anzufangen."

19 "Maman wünscht, dass ich ein kleines Mädchen wäre und nicht dieser Junge, der ich nun einmal war … Und wenn ich dann eintrat (in dem kleinen, mädchenhaften Hauskleid, das ich ohnehin trug, mit ganz hinaufgerollten Ärmen), so war ich einfach Sophie, Maman's kleine Sophie, die sich häuslich beschäftigte und der Maman einen Zopf flechten musste, damit keine Verwechslung stattfinde mit dem bösen Malte, wenn er je wiederkäme."

20 "Silber Freude Rohheit Runde Loos Lieber / Ausguss Sand Weshalb Nimmer Achtung / Lauer Nieder Neid Vielfrass Seegen Sucht / Nager Weg Ast vertieft Zaun Sage Einfalt/Wespe Herz Kino (Kind) Trauer Taufall / … / Saumzwang Niefeln Hieber Beherzung / Ichthüs Nomenclatur Beinung Richter / Regulus Galgen Wehrkraft Karde Spule / Spielt langsam aber keine Musik reicht / An den Reigen Naumann."

21 "*Mendikant / Reblaus / Schönbern / Kleborn / Bornmouth / Valborn / Friborn / Kalbausen / Kleebon.*"

22 "Die Bedeutungen dieser Zeichen 'Wörter' wird im Sprachspiel sowie in … durch hinweisende Erklärung festgelegt."

23 The expressive images of Wittgenstein's multiple invocations of God—for example, "O God, thank God, for God's sake, may God forbid, it is God's will, God is with me, and many others, often with exclamation points (!)"—are the spontaneous cry of his heart to speak to God (Hutchinson 1963: 228–236). The utterances to God are personal prayers, in which Wittgenstein visualized and summarized his self-understanding. In emotional pain he asked for God's help to continue his duty—writing philosophy including his diary.

Chapter 5

1 Sebeok stated that the notion of *Umwelt* "has been employed differently by various investigators, but, broadly speaking, the term refers to the organism's cognizance of conditions and manner of appropriate and effective use of messages" (Sebeok 1991a: 29). Sebeok translated Von Uexküll's German term *Umwelt* into English as "*ecological niche*, *experienced world*, *psychological* or *subjective* or *significative environment*, *behavioral life space*, *ambient extension*, *ipsefact*, or, expressions that I prefer, *cognitive map* or *scheme*, or even *mind set*" (1979: 194).

2 "Beschreibungen … Instrumente für besonderen Verwendungen."

3 "Angenommen, es hätte Jeder eine Schachtel, darin wäre etwas, was wir 'Käfer' nennen. Niemand kann je in die Schachtel des Andern schaun; und Jeder sagt, er wisse nur vom Anblick seines Käfers, was ein Käfer ist.—Da könnte es ja sein, dass Jeder ein anderes Ding in seiner Schachtel hätte. Ja, man könnte sich vorstellen, dass sich ein solches Ding fortwärend veränderte.—Aber wenn nun das Wort 'Käfer' dieser Leute doch einen Gebrauch hätte?—So wäre er nicht der der Bezeichnung eines Dings. Das Ding in der Schachtel gehört überhaupt nicht zum Sprachspiel; auch nicht einmal als ein Etwas: denn die Schachtel könnte auch leer sein.—Nein, durch dieses Ding in der Schachtel kann 'gekürzt werden'; es hebt sich weg, was immer es ist."

4 "Das heisst: Wenn man die Grammatik des Ausdrucks der Empfindung nach dem Muster, von—'Gegenstand & Bezeichnung' konstruiert, dann fällt der Gegenstand als irrelevant aus der Betrachtung herausgenommen. Und was soll 'Ich weiss nur vom eigenen Fall …' überhaupt für ein Satz sein? Ein Erfahrungssatz?—Nein.—Ein grammatischer?"

5 "Ich denke mir also: Jeder sage von sich selbst er wisse nur vom—eigenen Schmerz, was Schmerz sei. Nicht, dass die Menschen das wirklich sagen, oder auch nur bereit sind, zu sagen. Aber wenn nun Jeder es sagte—nun, es könnte eine Art Ausruf sein."

6 "Man muss manchmal einen Ausdruck aus der Sprache herausnehmen, ihn zur Reinigung geben,—& kann ihn dann wieder in den Verkehr einführen."

7 "Wenn eine Kanone zum Schutz gegen Fliegerangriffe so bemahlt ist, dass sie von oben aussieht wie Bäume oder Steine, dass ihre wahren Konturen unerkenntlich & falsch an ihre Stelle getreten sind, wie schwer zu beurteilen ist dieses Ding. Man könnte sich Einen denken der sagt: 'das sind also alles falsche Konturen, also hat das Ding gar keine Gestalt.' Und doch hat es eine wirkliche Gestalt aber sie ist mir den gewöhnlichen Mitteln gar nicht so beurteilen?"

8 "Welches Naturspiel!—Welches Naturspiel, wenn ein Käfer ausschaut wie ein Blatt, aber dann ein wirlicher Käfer ist, & nicht ein Kunstblumenblatt."

9 "Es muss dazu, gleichsam durch die Decke, den Plafond, unter dem ich arbeite, über den ich nicht steigen will, ein Licht durchschimmern." "Wie das Insect das Licht umschwirrt so ich ums Neue Testament."

10 "Geometrie die zeigt Dir gleichsam eine neue Dimension des Raumes."

11 "Im richtige geschriebene Satz löst sich ein Partikel vom Herzen oder Gehirn ab & kommt als Satz aufs Papier. Ich glaube meine Sätze sind meistens Beschreibungen visueller Bilder die mir einfallen."

12 "Die Liebe hat sozusagen zwei Temperaturen; einen Hitzegrad und einen Wärmegrad."

13 "Ist es denn möglich eine Beobachtung zu machen."

14 "O! Möge Gott mir Zufriedenheit mit meinem Schicksahl geben! Es ist im Leben wie in der Philosophie."

15 "Voller Angst. 'Das Gefühl der Abhängigkeit.'

Es hängt micht nur von mir ab, ob ich erhalten werde, worum ich bitte, sondern auch, ob ich werde bitten können. Das ist die Art von Überlegung, die jedes religiöse Gleichnis als Erklärung wertlos macht. Weil eben ob etwas im gewöhnlichen Sinne, ein Bitte, ein Lohn, eine Strafe, u.s.f., ist nicht nur von dem Bild abhängt, das uns eine bewisse Situation darbietet. Darum nennen wir auch ein abgekartetes Spiel kein Spiel. (Der Spiegel, auf dessen Fläche das 'Spiegelbild' gemalt wird.)

Sind alle Leute grosse Menschen? Nein.—Nun, wie kannst du dann hoffen, ein grosser Mensch zu sein! Warum soll dir etwas zuteil werden, was deinen Nachbarn nicht zu teil wird? Wofür?!—Wenn es nicht der Wunsch ist, reich zu sein, der dich glauben macht du seist reich, so muss es doch eine Beobachtung seine Erfarung sein die dir das zeigt! Und welche Erfahrung (ausser der Eitelkeit)? Nur die eines Talents. Und meine Einbildung, ich sei ein ausserordentlicher Mensch, ist ja viel älter, als meine Erfahrung meines besonderen Talents.

Das Gefühl der Abhängigkeit. Wie kann man fühlen, man sei abhängig? Wie kann man fühlen: 'Es hängt nicht von mir ab.' Aber was ist das überhaupt für ein seltsamer Ausdruck eines Gefühls. Aber wenn man z.B. jeden moren zuerst Schwierigkeiten hätte, gewisse Bewegungen zu machen, den Arm zu heben u.

dergl., & warten müsste, bis die Lähmung vergeht & das brauchte manchmal lange, manchmal kurze Zeit, & man könnte es nicht vorhersehen & kein Mittel einnehmen, es zu beschleunigen,—würde uns das nicht eben ein Bewüsstsein der Abhängigkeit geben?"

16 "Religion würde mir eine gewisse Bescheidenheit geben die mir fehlt. Denn ich bilde mir auch alles halbwegs Menschliche in mir etwas ein, wie auf eine Eigenschaft die mich auszeichnet."

17 "Die Angst, der Zweifel, die Sehnsucht, die Beklemmung."

18 "Jeder Kritiker kritisiert mit seinem eigenen Ich und sein Mass zeigt sich in seiner Kritik. Er fasst nur so weit, als sein Inhalt erlaubt." For the translation of Wittgenstein's "*Mass*" into "measure," see Gorlée 2012: 2–3.

19 "Was ist ein Wissenschaftler? Ist er Wahrheitsforscher, oder Wohltäter der Menschheit, oder Künstler, oder ist er Handwerker? Hätte er Religion, so wäre seine Schwierigkeit behoben.
Lerne aus den Schrecken des Lebens.

Der Bedeutungsblinde wird also 'aufzeigen': & ist es nun so: er werde nicht geneigt sein, zu sagen, die Bedeutung sei schon in einer Atmosphäre gewesen, die das gehörte Wort umgeben haben—& ahnliches? Kann man von subjektiven & objektiven Unterschieden zwischen Erlebnissen reden?—Subjektive Unterschiede sind solche for which I have to take the subject's word — die ich vom Subjekt auf Treu & Glauben annehmen muss … Der Bedeutungsblinde wird also nicht sagen: 'Ich habe jetzt das Wort als Zeitwort gehört,' oder 'als Zeitwort in mir gehört.' … 'Es ist gar nicht mehr dasselbe Wort'—wenn man, was Bindewort war, als Zeitwort erkennt. Es ist als schnitten sich zwei Bedeutungen im selben Wort, in derselben Buchstabenreihe.

Upset. Höre nichts von R.. Ich denke täglich darüber nach, und dass ich in die richtige Stellung zu diesem Verlust gewinnen sollte. Nichts scheint mir wahrscheinlicher, als dass er mich verlassen hat, oder im Begriffe steht, es zu tun, und nichts in einem Sinne natürlicher. Ja, ich fühle auch, dass ich dieses Geschehen freien Lauf lassen muss, dass ich getan habe was ich konnte und es jetzt aus meiner Hand ist. Und doch ist mir an jedem Morgen, wenn ich wieder keinen Brief finde—unheimlich zumute. Ich fühle, als hätte ich etwas noch nicht eingesehen; als müsse ich einen Standpunkt finden von dem aus mehr Wahrheit zu sehen ist."

20 "Die hysterische Angst, die die Öffentlichkeit jetzt vor der Atom-Bombe hat, oder doch ausdrückt, ist beinahe ein Zeichen, daß hier einmal wirklich eine heilsame Erfindung gemacht worden ist. Wenigstens macht die Furcht den Eindruck der, vor einer wirklich heimsamen bittern Medizin. Ich kann mich den Gedanken nicht erwehren: wenn hier nicht etwas Gutes vorläge, würden die Philister kein Geschrei anheben. Aber vielleicht ist auch das einkindischer Gedanke. Denn alles, was ich meinen kann, ist doch nur, daß die Bombe das Ende, die Zerstörung eines grässlichen Übels, der ekelhaften, seifenwässrigen Wissenschaft, im Aussicht stellt. Und das ist freilich kein unangenehmer Gedanke; aber wer sagt, was auf eine solche Zerstörung folgen würde? Die Leute, die heute gegen die Erzeugung der Bombe reden, sind freilich der Auswurf der Intelligenz, aber auch das beweist nicht unbedingt, daß das zu preisen ist, was sie verabscheuen."

21 "Beim Stierkamp ist der Stier der Held einer Tragödie. Zuerst durch Schmerzen toll gemacht, stirbt er einen langen & furchtbaren Tod."

22 "Ein Held sieht dem Tod in's Angesicht, den wirklichen Tod, nicht bloss dem Bild des Todes. Sich inn einer Krise anständig zu benehmen, heisst nicht einen Helden, gleich

wie auf dem Theater, gut darstellen können, sondern es heisst dem Tod selbst in's Auge schauem können. Denn der Schauspieler kann eine Menge Rollen spielen, aber am Ende muss er doch selbst als Mensch sterben."

23 "Alles ist Glück!" "Ich bin in der Liebe zu weinig gläubig und zu weinig mutig."

24 "Wovon sagt man denn, man kenne … meine eigenen Gedanken."

25 "Wovon man nicht sprechen kann, darüber muss man schweigen."

26 "'Dem Menschen hat es die Natur gegeben, dass er im Geheimen denken kann.' Denk dir, man sagte: 'Die Natur hat es dem Menschen gegeben, dass er hörbar reden, aber auch dass er unhörbar in seinem Geiste reden kann.' Er kann also, heisst das, dasselbe auf zwei Arten tun … Nur ist beim Reden im Geiste das Reden besser verborgen als ein Vorgang im Innern des Körpers sein kann. … Niemand sieht, niemand hört, niemand nimmt wahr, was ich denke."

27 "Ich habe nicht den Mut and nicht die Kraft und Klarheit den Tatsachen meines Lebens gerade in's Gesicht zu schauen.—B. hat zu mir eine Vor-liebe. Etwas, was nicht halten kann … Dämonen haben dieses Band gewoben … und halten es in der Hand (den Händen). Sie können's zerreissen, oder dauern (leben] lassen."

28 "Die Liebe ist ein Glück. Vielleicht ein Glück mit Schmerzen, aber ein Glück. Fehlt das Glück, oder schrumpt es auf ein kurzes Aufflackern zusammen, so fehlt die Liebe.—In der Liebe muss ich sicher ruhen können. —Aber kannst du ein warmes Herz zurückweisen? Ist ein Herz das warm für mich schlägt? … Der Mensch kann aus seiner Haut nicht heraus. Ich kann nicht die Forderung, die tief in mir, mit meinem ganzen Leben verankert liegt, aufgeben. Denn die Liebe ist mir der Natur verbunden; und würde ich unnatürlich, so müsste (würde) die Liebe aufhören.—Kann ich sagen: 'Ich werde vernünftig sein, und das nicht mehr verlangen'?"

29 "die Sprachuntersuchungen in der Philosophie spotten & nicht sehen, dass sie selbst in tiefen Begriffsverwirrungen verstrickt sind."

30 "Denke dir, in welcher man einen Namen nur in Anwesenheit der Träger gebrauchen & verstehen kann. Freud hat durch seine phantastische pseudo-Erklärungen (gerade weil sie geistlich sind) einen schlimmen Dienst erwiesen. (Jeder Esel hat sie (diese Bilder) nun zur Hand, mit ihrer Hilfe Krankheitserscheinungen zu 'erklären'). Ja: der Philosoph will Methoden umgestalten (beeinflussen)."

31 "Das Sprachspiel, in welchen das Wort nur bei Existenz des Trägers Bedeutung hat, müsste eines sein worin der Träger des Worts eine andere als die uns gewohnte Rolle spielt."

32 "O, warum ist mir zumute, als schreibe ich ein Gedicht, wenn ich Philosophie schreibe? … Die Sucht nach Erklärung [ist dem Beschreiben hinderlich] ist der vollen Auffassung der Tatsachen, [d.h. also] der Beschreibung hinderlich]. Die vorgefasste Hypothese wirkt wie ein Sieb, das nur einen ganz kleinen Teil der Tatsachen zu unserm Blick gelangen lässt. [zu unserer Betrachtung gelangen lässt.]."

33 "Ich bin eine neidische, eifersüchtige Natur."
"Der Stock, der hübsch aussieht, so lange man ihn trägt, aber sich biegt, [sobald] wenn] du dich auf ihn stüzt, ist nichts wert."

"Bin sehr einsam."

"Ich sehe ein böses Ende för mein Leben voraus. Einsamkeit, vielleicht Wahnsinn. Meine Vorlesungen gehen gut, sie werden nie besser gehen. Aber welche Wirkung lassen sie zurück? Helfe ich jemand? Gewiss nicht mehr, als wenn ich ein grosser Schauspieler wäre, der ihnen Tragödien vorspielte. Was sie lernen, ist nichts wert

gelernt zu werden, und die persönliche Eindruck nützt ihnen nichts. Das gilt für Alle, mit vielleicht einer, oder zwei Ausnahmen."
"In üblem Zustand."

34 "Ich kann nicht niederknien, zu beten, weil gleichsam meine Knie steif sind. Ich fürchte mich vor der Auflösung (vor meiner Auflösung) wenn ich weich würde."
"Denn das ist die Frage: kannst du nicht aufrecht gehen, ohne dich auf diesen Stab zu lehnen? Oder kannst Du dich nicht entschliessen ihn aufzugeben? Oder ist es beides?"

35 "Nur nichts Theatralisches! Davor musst du dich hüten."

36 "Eine Schwierigkeit der Philosophie ist, dass die Gedankengange in ihr so lang sind. Eine Schwierigkeit der Philosophie ist die Länge ihrer Gedankengänge."

37 "'Ich glaube, es wird regnen,' 'Ich glaube, dass mein Freund mir treu ist.' Die Worte 'Es ist mir in die Seele geschrieben …' passen nicht auf No 1, aber auf No 2. Man könnte auch sagen das zweite Beispiel redet von einer Denkweise, das erste nicht. Man wird geneigt sein, zo sagen: auf etwas vertrauen ist sei ein Zustand (der Seele) des Menschen; glauben, es wird regnen, sei keiner."

38 "Von Eitelkeit gebläht!"

39 "Ich sehe etwas in verschiedenen Zosammenhängen."

40 "In diesem Band kommt auf 10 oder 20 Seiten nicht mehr als ein halbwegs guter Abschnitt."

Chapter 6

1 "'Was geschieht, wenn ein Mensch plötzlich versteht?'—Die Frage ist schlecht gestellt. Fragt sie nach der Bedeutung des Ausdrucks 'plötzlich verstehen', so ist die Antwort nicht das Hinweisen auf einen Vorgang, den wir so nennen.—Die Frage könnte bedeuten: Was sind Anzeichen dafür, dass Einer plötzlich versteht; welches sind die characteristischen psychischen Begleiterscheinungen des plötzlich verstehen?"

2 "Stellen wir uns diesen Fall vor. Ich will über das Wiederkehren einer gewissen Empfindung ein Tagebuch führen. Dazu assoziiere ich sie mit dem Zeichen 'E' und schreibe in einem Kalender zu jedem Tag, an dem ich die Empfindung habe, dieses Zeichen.—Ich will zuerst bemerken, dass sich eine Definition des Zeichens nicht aussprechen lässt.—Aber ich kann sie doch mir selbst als eine Art hinweisende Definition geben!—Wie? Kann ich auf die Empfindung zeigen?—Nich im gewöhnlichen Sinne. Aber ich spreche, oder schreibe das Zeichen, und dabei konzentriere ich meine Aufmerksamkeit auf die Empfindung—zeige also gleichsam im Innern auf sie.—Aber wozu diese Zeremonie? denn nur eine solche scheint es zu sein! Eine Definition dient doch dazu, die Bedeutung dieses Zeichen festzulegen.—Nun, das geschieht ebendurch das Konzentrieren die Aufmerksameit; denn dadurch präge ich mir die Verbindung des Zeichens mir der Empfindung ein.—'Ich präge sie mir ein' kann doch nur heisse: dieser Vorgang bewirkt, dass ich mich in Zukunft richtig an die Verbindung erinnere. Aber in unserem Falle habe ich ja kein Kriterium für die Richtigkeit. Mann möchte hier sagen: richtig ist, was immer mir als richtig erscheinen wird. Und das heisst nur, dass hier von 'richtig' nicht geredet wird. Und das heisst nur, dass hier von 'richtig' nicht geredet werden kann."

3 "Denken wir uns eine Verwendung des Eintragens des Zeichens 'E' in mein Tagebuch. Ich mache folgende Erfahrung: Wenn immer ich eine bestimmte

Empfindung habe, zeigt mir ein Manometer, dass mein Blutdruck steigt. So werde ich in den Stand gesetzt, ein Steigen meines Blutdrucks ohne Zuhilfenahme eines Apparats anzutragen. Dies ist ein nützlich es Ergebnis. Und nun scheint es hier ganz gleichgültig zu sein, ob ich die Empfindung richtig wiedererkannt habe, oder nicht. Nehmen wir an, ich irre mich beständig bei ihrer Identifizierung, so macht es gar nichts. Und das zeigt schon, dass die Annahme dieses Irrtums nur ein Schein war. (Wir drehen gleichsam, an einem Knopf, der aussah, als könnte man mit ihm etwas an der Maschine einstellen; aber er war ein blosses Zierrat, mit dem Mechanismus gar nicht verbunden.)
Und welches Grund haben wir hier, 'E' die Bezeichnung einer Empfindung zu nennen? Vielleicht die Art und Weise, wie dies Zeichen in diesem Sprachspiel verzendet wird.—Und warum eine 'bestimmte Empfindung,' also jedesmal die gleiche? Nun, wir nehmen ja an, wir schreiben jedesmal 'E.'"

4 "Das Gefühl der Unüberbrückbarkeit der Kluft zwischen Bewusstsein und Gehirnvorgang: Wie kommt es, dass das in der Betrachtung des gewöhnlichen Lebens nicht hineinspielt? Die Idee dieser Artverschiedenheit ist mit einem leisen Schwindel verbunden,—der auftritt, wenn wir logische Kunststücke ausführen. … Wann tritt, in unserm Fall, dieses Gefühl auf? Nun, wenn ich z. B. meine Aufmerksamkeit in bestimmter Weise auf mein Bewusstsein lenke und mir dabei staunend sage: DIES solle durch einen Gehirnvorgang erzeugt werden!—indem ich mir gleichsam an die Stirne greife.—Aber was kann das heissen: "meine Aufmerksamkeit auf mein Bewusstsein lenken? … Was ich so nennte (denn diese Worte werden ja im gewöhnlichen Leben nicht gebraucht) war ein Akt des Schauens. Ich schaute steif vor mich hin—aber nicht auf irgend einen bestimmten Punkt, oder Gegenstand. Meine Augen waren weit offen, meine Brauen nicht zusammengezogen (wie sie meistens sind, wenn ein bestimmtes Objekt mich interessiert). Kein solches Interesse war dem Schauen vorgegangen. Mein Blick war 'vacant'; oder ähnlich dem eines Menschen, der die Beleuchtung des Himmels bewundert und das Licht eintrinkt."

5 After Wittgenstein's death in 1951, the fellowship he had with his co-workers was made official in the history of his trustees—Elizabeth Anscombe, Georg Henrik von Wright, and Rush Rhees. This collegium stewarded the heritage (*Nachlass*) of the publications of his mainly unpublished work. In the trustees' perspective, Wittgenstein's diary after the First World War was considered private, not publishable with Wittgenstein's other publications (see Chapter 1).

6 The role of placebos is evaluated in inter- and transdisciplinary research, but in medical science the placebo remains the controversial discussion of serious doubts about using these methods as medical strategies (Staiano 1986: 14, 34; Hippius et al. 1986; Harrington [1997] 2000). The semiotic therapy of Klaus Schonauer's *Semiotic Foundations of Drug Therapy: The Placedo Problem in a New Persperctive* (1994) is important. This book threw a new light on the sad story of Wittgenstein's beetle-box (50–54). The human knowledge of the beetle was based on partial and random intuition by quick looks at the situation, while the real sensation of the life of the insect remained unknown and unanalyzed. This story is compared to relevant passages of Thomas Mann's diary and a letter from Franz Kafka (Schonauer 1994: 54). In Schonauer's view, the beetle needed individual medication by attributing aspirin or some other placebo as the effective instrument of medical control.

7 See ROC: 1:13, 16, 27, 32, 77, 81–88, 3:31, 112–120, 128, 165–170, 278–281, 284–294, 319–322, 342–347.

8 See ROC: 3:14–15, 34, 129, 131, 146–153, 172–183, 211, 239, 259.

Chapter 7

1 "Es ist hier nichts versteckt; und ich nähme ich an, es sei etwas versteckt, so hätte die Kenntnis dieses Versteckens kein Interesse. Ich kann aber meine Gedanken vor ihm verbergen, indem ich ein Tagebuch verstecke, Und hier verstecke ich etwas, dessen Kenntnis für ihn von Interesse sein könnten."

2 "Es ist merkwürdig dass ich seit so vielen Jahren fast nie mehr das leiseste Bedürfnis empfunden habe Tagebuchaufzeichnungen zu machen. In der allerersten Zeit in Berlin als ich damit anfing auf Zettel Gedanken über mich aufzuschreiben, da war es ein Bedürfnis. Es war ein für mich wichtiger Schritt. Später entsprang es zum Teil dem Nachahmungstrieb (ich hatte Kellers Tagebücher gelesen) zum Teil dem Bedürfnis doch etwas von mir niederzulegen. Es war also zum grossen Teil Eitelkeit. Zum Teil freilich auch wieder der Ersatz für einen Menschen dem ich mich anvertrauen konnte. Später mischte ich dazu die Nachahmung der Pepysschen Tagebücher. Freilich ist es, wie immer, schwer hier gerecht zu sein, denn es war natürliches und eitle Bestrebungen stark vermischt."

Bibliography

Abrams, M. H. ([1941] 1957). *A Glossary of Literary Terms*. New York: Holy, Rinehart and Winston.

Alston, William P. (1964). *Philosophy of Language*. Englewood Cliffs, NJ: Prentice Hall.

Alston, William P. ([1967] 1972). svv. "Emotive meaning," "Language," and "Philosophy of Language." In *The Encyclopedia of Philosophy*, edited by Paul Edwards. 9 vols. Reprint. New York: Macmillan Publishing and the Free Press; London: Collier Macmillan Publishers.

Anderson, Myrdene and Dinda L. Gorlée (2011). "Duologue in the Familiar and the Strange: Translatability, Translating, Translation." In *Semiotics 2010*, Proceedings of the Semiotic Society of America, edited by Karen Haworth, Jason Hogie, and Leonard G. Brocchi, 221–232. Toronto: Legas Publishing.

Appignanesi, Lisa (2017). "Freud's Clay Feet." *New York Review of Books* 64 (16): 36–38.

Arango, Ariel C. (1989). *Dirty Words: Psychoanalytic Insights*. Northvale, NJ: Jason Aronson.

Augustine, Saint ([1961] 1974). *Confessions*, translated by R. S. Pine-Coffin. Harmondsworth: Penguin.

Bamberger, Bernard J. (1981). "The Torah and the Jewish People." In *The Torah: A Modern Commentary*, edited by W. Gunther Plaut, xxix–xxxvi. New York: Union of American Hebrew Congregation.

Bär, Eugen (1979). "Things are Stories: A Manifesto for a Reflexive Semiotics." *Semiotica* 25 (3/4): 193–205.

Barr, Andrew (2002). *Songs of Praise: The Nation's Favourite Hymns*. Oxford: Lion Publishing.

Barthes, Roland (1957). *Mythologies*. Paris: Seuil.

Barthes, Roland (1972). "Sémiologie et médicine." In *Les sciences de la folie*, edited by Roger Bastide, 37–46. Paris: Mouton.

Barthes, Roland ([1977] 2010). *Roland Barthes by Roland Barthes*, translated by Richard Howard. New York: Hill and Wang.

Barthes, Roland ([1979] 1983). *Barthes: Selected Writings*, edited by Susan Sontag. Oxford: Fontana and Collins.

Barton, Christina (1990). "Entries." In *Now See Hear! Art, Language and Translation*, edited by Ian Wedde and Gregory Burke, 215–221. Wellington: Victoria University Press.

Bateson, Gregory (1969). "Metalogue: What is an Instinct?" In *Approaches to Animal Communication*, edited by Thomas A. Sebeok in cooperation with Alexandra Ramsay, 11–30. Approaches to Semiotics, 1. The Hague: Mouton.

Bateson, Gregory ([1972] 1985). *Steps to an Ecology of Mind*. 13th edn. New York: Ballantine Books.

Bateson, Gregory and Mary Catherine Bateson (1987). *Angels Fear: Towards an Epistemology of the Sacred*. Toronto: Bantam Books.

Bateson, Mary Catherine (1975). "Linguistic Models in the Study of Joint Performance." In *Linguistics and Anthropology in Honor of C.F. Voegelin*, edited by M. Dale Kinkade, Kenneth L. Hale, and Oswald Werner, 53–66. Lisse: The Peter de Ridder Press.

Bauman, Zygmunt (1996). "From Pilgrim to Tourist—Or a Short History of Identity." In *Questions of Cultural Identity*, edited by Stuart Hall and Paul Du Gay, 18–36. London: Sage Publications.

Beaugrande, Robert de (1991). *Linguistic Theory: The Discourse of Fundamental Works*. London: Longman.

Beaulieu, Yvan (2008). "Peirce's Contribution to American Cryptography." *Transactions of the Charles S. Peirce Society* 44 (2): 263–287.

Beaulieu, Yvan (2014). "Peircean Inquiry and Secret Communication." In *Charles Sanders Peirce in His Own Words: 100 Years of Semiotics, Communication and Cognition*, edited by Torkild Thellefsen and Bent Sørensen, 45–55. Semiotics, Communication and Cognition, 14. Berlin: De Gruyter Mouton.

Benjamin, Walter (1978). "Paris, Capital of the Nineteenth Century." In *Reflections: Essays, Aphorisms, Autobiographical Writings*, edited by Peter Demetz, translated by Edmund Jephcott, 146–162. New York: Schocken Books.

Benson, Herbert and David P. McCallie (1979). "Angina Pectoris and the Placebo Effect." *New England Journal of Medicine*, June 21: 1424–1429.

Bernstein, Basil B. (1974). "Social Class, Language and Socialisation." *Current Trends in Linguistics*, vol. 12: 3 *Linguistics and Adjacent Arts and Sciences*, edited by Thomas A. Sebeok, 1545–1562. The Hague: Mouton.

Black's Medical Dictionary (1987). Edited by C. W. H. Havard. 35th edn. London: A & C Publishers. [BMD 1987]

Blake, Barry J. (2010). *Secret Language: Codes, Tricks, Spies, Thieves, and Symbols*. Oxford: Oxford University Press.

Blanchard, Marc Eli(1980). "Montaigne's Preserve of the Self." In *Description: Sign, Self, Desire*, edited by Marc Eli Blanchard, 157–166. Approaches to Semiotics, 43. The Hague: Mouton.

Bloomsfield, Leonard ([1933] 1967). *Language*. Reprint. London: George Allen and Unwin.

Boklund-Lagopoulou, Karin and Alexandros-Ph. Lagopoulos (2017). "The Role of Methodology in Semiotic Theory Building." *Punctum: International Journal of Semiotics* 3 (2): 5–32. doi:10.18680/hss.2018.0002.

Bouwsma, Oets Kolk(1986). *Wittgenstein: Conversations, 1949–1951*. Indianapolis, IN: Hackett Publishing Company.

Brent, Joseph (1993). *Charles Sanders Peirce: A Life*. Bloomington: Indiana University Press.

Brooks, Peter (2000). *Troubling Confessions: Speaking Guilt in Law & Literature*. Chicago: University of Chicago Press.

Brown, Cecil H. (1974). *Wittgensteinian Linguistics*. The Hague: Mouton.

Bunn, James H. (1981). *The Dimensionality of Signs, Tools, and Models*. Bloomington: Indiana University Press.

Buruma, Ian (2018). "Art of a Degenerate World." *New York Review of Books* 65 (14): 78–79, 84.

Cannizzaro, Sara and Myrdene Anderson (2016). "Culture as Habit, Habit as Culture: Instinct, Habituescence, Addiction." In *Consensus on Peirce's Concept of Habit: Before and Beyond Consciousness*, edited by Donna E. West and Myrdene Anderson, 315–339.

Studies in Applied Philosophy, Epistemology and Rational Ethics SAPERE). New York: Springer.
Capra, Fritjof ([1976] 1985). *The Tao of Physics: An Exploration of the Parallels between Modern Physics and Eastern Mysticism*. London: Fontana.
Carlson, Lauri (1983). *Dialogue Games: An Approach to Discourse Analysis*. Dordrecht: Reidel Publishing Company.
Carroll, Lewis ([1865] 1982). "Alice's Adventures in Wonderland." In *The Complete Illustrated Works of Lewis Carroll*, 17–114. London: Chancellor Press.
Catford, J. C. ([1965] 1974). *A Linguistic Theory of Translation*. 4th edn. Oxford: Oxford University Press.
Cavell, Stanley (1979). *The Claim of Reason: Wittgenstein, Skepticism, Morality, and Tragedy*. Oxford: Oxford University Press.
Chambers, Robert (2010). *Parody: The Art that Plays with Art*. Studies in Literary Criticism & Theory, 21. New York: Peter Lang.
Chawla, Devika and Myrdene Anderson (2015). "Acknowledging Affect in Ethnography." *Semiotics 2015: Virtual Identities. Semiotic Society of Amerika* (2015): 133–141. doi:105840/cpsem2015201514.
Chatterjee, Ranjit (1991). "Rossi-Landi's Wittgenstein: 'A philosopher's meaning is his use in the culture.'" *Semiotica* 84 (3/4): 275–283. doi:10.1515/semi.1991.84.3-4.275.
Cherry, Colin ([1957] 1966). *On Human Communication: A Review, a Survey, and a Criticism*. Cambridge, MA: MIT Press.
Colapietro, Vincent M. (1989). *Peirce's Approach to the Self: A Semiotic Perspective on Human Subjectivity*. Albany: State University of New York Press.
Conan Doyle, Sir Arthur ([1887] 1953). *A Study in Scarlet: The Complete Sherlock Holmes*, introduced by Christopher Morley. 2 vols., 1: 3–47. New York: Doubleday & Company.
Conan Doyle, Sir Arthur ([1903] 1953). *The Adventure of the Dancing Men: The Complete Sherlock Holmes*, introduced by Christopher Morley. 2 vols., 2: 593–612. New York: Doubleday & Company.
Crystal, David (1987). *The Cambridge Encyclopedia of Language*. Cambridge: Cambridge University Press.
Danesi, Marcel (2002). *The Puzzle Instinct: The Meaning of Puzzles in Human Life*. Bloomington: Indiana University Press.
Danesi, Marcel (2009). *Dictionary of Media and Communications*. Armonk, NY: M. E. Sharpe.
Danesi, Marcel (2014). *Signs of Crime: Introducing Forensic Semiotics*. Berlin: De Gruyter Mouton.
Darwin, Charles ([1858] 1958). *On the Origin of Species*. London: Dent; New York: E. P. Dutton.
Davis, Norbert ([1943] 2001). *The Mouse in the Mountain*. Boulder, CO: Rue Morgue Press.
Deely, John (2015). "'Semiotics today'. The Twentieth-Century Founding and Twenty-First-Century Prospects." In *International Handbook of Semiotics*. 2 vols., 1: 71–113 (in "Appendix: Sebeok's Synthesis [The Tartu-Bloomington-Copenhagen School]," 1: 98–99). Dordrecht: Springer.
Demsky, Aaron (1977). "A Proto-Caanite Abecedary Dating from the Period of the Judges and its Implications for the History of the Alphabet." *Tel Aviv: Journal of the Tel Aviv University Institute of Archaeology* 4 (1–2): 14–27.
Derrida, Jacques (1973). *Speech and Phenomena and Other Essays on Husserl's Theory of Signs*, translated by David B. Allison. Evanston, IL: Northwestern University Press.

Derrida, Jacques (1985). "Des Tours de Babel." In *Difference in Translation*, edited and translated by Joseph F. Graham, 165–207. Ithaca, NY: Cornell University Press.

Derrida, Jacques (1987). *The Post Card: From Socrates to Freud and Beyond*, translated by Alan Bass. Chicago: University of Chicago Press.

Di Leo, Jeffrey (2014). "Don't Fear the Reaper." *American Book Review* 35 (2): 2, 25.

Dilman, Ilham (1973). *Induction and Deduction: A Study in Wittgenstein*. Oxford: Basil Blackwell.

Dilman, Ilham (1998). *Language and Reality: Modern Perspectives on Wittgenstein*. Leuven: Peeters.

Donnellan, Keith S. ([1967] 1972). "Paradigm-Case Argument." In *The Encyclopedia of Philosophy*, edited by Paul Edwards. 9 vols., 6: 39–44. Reprint. New York: Macmillan Publishing and the Free Press; London: Collier Macmillan Publishers.

Douglas, Mary ([1966] 1979). *Purity and Danger: An Analysis of the Concepts of Polluted and Taboo*. London: Routledge & Kegal Paul.

Eco, Umberto (1979). *A Theory of Semiotics*. Advances in Semiotics. Bloomington, IN: Indiana University Press.

Eco, Umberto (1984). *Semiotics and the Philosophy of Language*. London: Macmillan.

Eco, Umberto (1985). "How Culture Conditions the Colours We See." In *On Signs*, edited by Marshall Blonsky, 157–175. Oxford: Basil Blackwell.

Eco, Umberto ([1995] 1997). *The Search for the Perfect Language*, translated by James Fentress. London: Fontana Press.

Eco, Umberto and Thomas A. Sebeok (eds.) ([1983] 1988). *The Sign of Three: Dupin, Holmes, Peirce*. Advances in Semiotics. Bloomington: Indiana University Press.

Emerson, Ralph Waldo (1910). *Die Sonne segnet die Welt. Auswahl aus dem Werken Essays und Vorträge*, edited by Maria Kugn. Düsseldorf: Karl Robert Langewiesche.

Esposito, Joseph L. (1980). *Evolutionary Metaphysics: The Development of Peirce's Theory of Categories*. Athens: Ohio University Press.

Farb, Peter (1974). *Word Play: What Happens When People Talk*. New York: Knopf.

Farber, Assi and Claude Gandelman (1993). "Iconizing the Text/Textualizing the Body: Judaism as a Graphocentric Religion." *American Journal of Semiotics* 10 (1–2): 11–34.

Fiske, John ([1982] 1987). *Introduction tio Communication Studies*. Studies in Communication. London: Methuen.

Foucault, Michel (2014). *Wrong-Doing, Truth-Telling: The Function of Avowal in Justice*, edited by Fabienne Brion and Bernard E. Harcourt, translated by Stephen W. Sawyer. Chicago: University of Chicago Press.

Freedman, Rabbi Dr. H. (ed. and trans.) ([1949] 1966). *Jeremiah: Hebrew Text & English Translation*, vol. 14, *Soncino Books of the Bible*, edited by Rev. Dr. A. Cohen. London: Soncino Press.

Frege, Gottlob (1879). *Begiffsschrift eine der Aritmetischen nachgebildete Formelsprache des reinen Denkens*. Halle: Nebert.

Freud, Sigmund (1938). *The Basic Writings of Sigmund Freud*, edited and translated by A. A. Brill. New York: Random House.

Freud, Sigmund (1977). *Inhibitions, Symptoms and Anxiety*, edited by James Strachey, translated by Alix Strachey. New York: W. W. Norton & Company.

Freudenthal, Hans (1960). *Lincos: Design for a Language for a Cosmic Intercourse*, Part 1. Amsterdam: North-Holland.

Fromm, Erich ([1986] 1965). *The Art of Loving*. 4th edn. London: Unwin Books.

Fürlinger, Anton (2004). "Die Situation—Erleben, Beschreiben, Verstehen." In *Macht der Zeichen Zeichen der Macht: Signs of Power Power of Signs: Essays in Honor of Jeff*

Bernard, edited by Gloria Withalm and Josef Wallmannsberger, 216–225. Vienna: INST.

Gedo, John E. (2000). "Protolinguistic phenomena in psychoanalysis." In *Peirce, Semiotics, and Psychoanalysis*, edited by John Muller and Joseph Brent, 27–48. Psychiatry and the Humanities, 15. Baltimore: Johns Hopkins University Press.

Ginzburg, Carlo ([1986] 1989). *Clues, Myths, and the Historical Method*, translated by John and Anne C. Tedeschi. Baltimore: Johns Hopkins University Press.

Ginzburg, Carlo (1990). *Myths, Emblems, Clues*, translated by John and Anne C. Tedeschi. London: Hutchinson Radius.

Glock, Hans-Johann (1996). *A Wittgenstein Dictionary*. Malden, MA: Blackwell Publishers.

Goethe, Johann Wolfgang von (1958). *Faust: A Tragedy*, translated by Alice Raphael, illustrations by Eugene Delacroix. New York: Heritage Press.

Goffman, Erving (1959). *The Presentation of Self in Everyday Life*. Garden City, NY: Doubleday Anchor Books.

Goffman, Erving (1981). *Forms of Talk*. Philadelphia: University of Pennsylvania Press.

Gorlée, Dinda L. (1990). "Degeneracy: A Reading of Peirce's Writing." *Semiotica* 81 (1/2): 71–92.

Gorlée, Dinda L. (1994). *Semiotics and the Problem of Translation: With Special Reference to the Semiotics of Charles S. Peirce*. Approaches to Translation Studies, 12. Leiden: Brill [formerly Amsterdam: Rodopi].

Gorlée, Dinda L. (1998). "Der Fall Kenneth L. Pike: Neue Perspektiven für den sprachwissenschaftlichen Ansatz in der Übersetzungsforschung." In *Text, Sprache, Kultur*, edited by Peter Holzer and Cornelia Feyrer, 69–86. Frankfurt am Main: Peter Lang.

Gorlée, Dinda L. (2004a). *On Translating Signs: Exploring Text and Semio-Translation*. Approaches to Translation Studies, 24. Leiden: Brill [formerly Amsterdam: Rodopi].

Gorlée, Dinda L. (2004b). "Horticultural Roots of Translational Semiosis." In *Macht der Zeichen Zeichen der Macht: Signs of Power Power of Signs: Essays in Honor of Jeff Bernard*, edited by Gloria Withalm and Josef Wallmannsberger, 164–187. Vienna: INST.

Gorlée, Dinda L. (2005). "Hints and Guesses: Legal Modes of Semio-Logical Reasoning." *Sign Systems Studies* 33 (2): 239–272.

Gorlée, Dinda L. (2007). "Broken Signs: The Architectonic Translation of Peirce's Fragments." *Semiotica* 163 (1/4): 209–287.

Gorlée, Dinda L. (2008a). "Jakobson and Peirce: Translational Intersemiosis and Symbiosis in Opera." *Sign Systems Studies* 36 (2): 341–374.

Gorlée, Dinda L. (2008b). "Wittgenstein as Mastersinger." *Semiotica* 172 (1/4): 97–150.

Gorlée, Dinda L. (2009). "A Sketch of Peirce's Firstness and its Significance to Art." *Sign System Studies* 37 (1–2): 205–269.

Gorlée, Dinda L. (2011). "Traduttore traditore?" In *Semiotics Continues to Astonish: Thomas A.Sebeok and the Doctrine of Signs*, edited by Paul Cobley, John Deely, Kalevi Kull, and Susan Petrilli, 161–190. Semiotics, Communication and Cognition, 7. Berlin: De Gruyter Mouton.

Gorlée, Dinda L. (2012). *Wittgenstein in Translation: Exploring Semiotic Signatures*. Semiotics, Communication and Cognition, 9. Berlin: De Gruyter Mouton.

Gorlée, Dinda L. (2014a). "Peirce's Logotheca." In *Charles Sanders Peirce in His Own Words: 100 Years of Semiotics, Communication and Cognition*, edited by Torkild

Thellefsen and Bent Sørensen, 406–409. Semiotics, Communication and Cognition, 14. Berlin: De Gruyter Mouton.

Gorlée, Dinda L. (2014b). "Hints and Guesses: Legal Modes of Semio-Logical Reasoning." In *Zeichen und Zauber des Rechts: Festschrift für Friedrich Lachmayer*, edited by Erich Schweighofer, Meinrad Handstanger, Harald Hoffmann, Franz Kummer, Edmund Primosch, Günther Schefbeck, and Gloria Withalm, 1041–1070. Berne: Weblaw. [Rev. edn. Gorlée 2005]

Gorlée, Dinda L. (2015a). "From Words and Sentences to Interjections: The Anatomy of Exclamations in Peirce and Wittgenstein." *Semiotica* 205: 37–86.

Gorlée, Dinda L. (2015b). "Kenneth L. Pike and Science Fiction." *Semiotica* 207: 217–231.

Gorlée, Dinda L. (2015c). *From Translation to Transduction: The Glassy Essence of Intersemiosis*. Tartu Semiotics Library, 15. Tartu: University of Tartu Press.

Gorlée, Dinda L. (2015d). "Fingerprints and Footsteps." *American Book Review* 36 (1): 17. [Review of Danesi 2014]

Gorlée, Dinda L. (2016a). "Wittgenstein's Persuasive Rhetoric." *Semiotica* 208: 49–77.

Gorlée, Dinda L. (2016b). "On Habit: Peirce's Story and History." In *Consensus on Peirce's Concept of Habit: Before and Beyond Consciousness*, edited by Donna E. West and Myrdene Anderson, 13–33. Studies in Applied Philosophy, Epistemology and Rational Ethics (SAPERE). New York: Springer.

Gorlée, Dinda L. (2017). "From Peirce's Pragmatic Maxim to Wittgenstein's Language-Games." In *Semiotics and Its Masters Volume 1*, edited by Christian Bankov and Paul Cobley, 325–350. Semiotics, Communication and Cognition, 18. Berlin: De Gruyter Mouton.

Gorlée, Dinda L. (forthcoming a). "How to Wrestle with the Translation of Wittgenstein's Writings." Lecture, Wittgenstein Archives, University of Bergen, June 22, 2017. Published in Sâo Paulo (Brazil).

Gorlée, Dinda L. (forthcoming b). "The Semiotic Story of Translation: Paraphrase or Parasite." Plenary lecture 14th World Congress of International Association of Semiotics (IASS), Buenos Aires, Argentina, 2019.

Gorlée, Dinda L. and Myrdene Anderson (2011). "Kenneth L. Pike's Semiotic Work: Arousing, Disputing, and Persuading Language-and-Culture." *American Journal of Semiotics* 27 (1/4): 243–255.

Gray, Bennison (1969). *Style: The Problem and Its Solution*. The Hague: Mouton.

Gray, Bennison (1975). *The Phenomenon of Literature*. The Hague: Mouton.

Gray, Bennison (1977). *The Grammatical Foundations of Rhetoric: Discourse Analysis*. The Hague: Mouton.

Gregory, Richard L. (ed.) (1987). *The Oxford Companion to the Mind*. Oxford: Oxford University Press.

Hackett, Jo Ann (2001). "Shibboleth." In *The Oxford Guide to Ideas & Issues of the Bible*, edited by Bruce M. Metzger and Michael D. Coogan, 459–460. Oxford: Oxford University Press.

Hall, Calvin S. (1954). *A Primer of Freudian Psychology*. New York: New American Library.

Hardwick, Charles S. (1971). *Language Learning in Wittgenstein's Later Philosophy*. The Hague: Mouton.

Hardy, Barbara (1969). "Towards a Poetics of Fiction: An Approach through Narrative." *Novel: A Forum of Fiction* (Fall): 5–14.

Hardy, G. H. (1940). *A Mathematician's Apology*, introduced by C. P. Snow. Cambridge: Cambridge University Press.

Harrington, Anne (ed.) ([1997] 2000). *The Placebo Effect: An Interdisciplinary Exploration*. Cambridge, MA: Harvard University Press.
Harris, Roy (1988). *Language, Saussure and Wittgenstein: How to Play Games with Words*. London: Routledge.
Hastings, Max (2015). *The Secret War: Spies, Ciphers, and Guerrillas*. London: HarperCollins Publishers.
Heller-Roazen, Daniel (2013). *Dark Tongues: The Art of Rogues and Riddlers*. New York: Zone Books.
Henry, Paul (1960). *Saint Augustine on Personality*. The Saint Augustine Lecture 1959. New York: Macmillan.
Hick, John H. ([1963] 1973). *Philosophy of Religion*. 2nd edn. Englewood Cliffs, NJ: Prentice Hall.
Highwater, Jamake (1994). *The Language of Vision: Meditations on Myth and Metaphor*. New York: Grove Press.
Hintikka, Jaakko (1998). "What is Abduction? The Fundamental Problem of Contemporary Epistemology." *Transactions of the Charles S. Peirce Society* 34 (3): 503–533.
Hintikka, Merrill B. and Jaakko Hintikka (1986). *Investigating Wittgenstein*. Oxford: Basil Blackwell.
Hippius Hanns, Karl Űberla, Gregor Laakmann, and Joerg Hasford (1986). *Das Placebo-Problem*. Stuttgart: Gustav Fischer Verlag.
Hofmann, Michael (2015). "A Puzzling Heroine of German Literature." *New York Review of Books* 62 (16): 43–44.
Holy Bible: A Translation from the Latin Vulgate in the Light of the Hebrew and Greek Originals, The ([1945, 1955] 1956). The Knox Translation Authorized by the Hierarchy of England and Wales and the Hierarchy of Scotland. London: Burns & Oates.
Hoskisson, Paul Y. (2010). "Jeremiah's Game." *Insights* 30 (1): 3–4. Available online: http://publications.mi.byu.edu/fullscreen/?pub=1367&index=3 (accessed December 23, 2015).
Hutchinson, John A. (1963). *Language and Faith: Studies in Sign, Symbol, and Meaning*. Philadelphia, PA: Westminster Press.
Immler, Nicole L. (2011). *Das Familiengedächtnis der Wittgensteins. Von verführerischen Lesarten von (auto-)biographischen Texten*. Bielefeld: Transcript Verlag.
Jakobson, Roman ([1939] 1971). "Signe zéro / Das Nullzeichen." In *Selected Writings*, vol. 2, *Word and Language*, edited by Roman Jakobson, 211–220, 211–222. The Hague: Mouton.
Jakobson, Roman (1972). "Verbal Communication." *Scientific American* (September): 73–80.
Jakobson, Roman (1980). *Brain and Language: Cerebral Hemisphere and Linguistic Structure in Mutual Light*. New York University Slavic Papers, 4. Columbus, OH: Slavica Publishers.
Jakobson, Roman and Morris Halle ([1956] 1971). *Fundamentals of Language*. 2nd rev. edn. The Hague: Mouton.
James, William ([1890] 1950). *Principles of Psychology*. 2 vols. London: Dover.
James, William ([1902] 1982). *The Varieties of Religious Experience: A Study in Human Nature*. 11th edn. Glasgow: Collins.
James, William ([1907] 1981). *Pragmatics: A New Name for Some Old Ways of Thinking*. Indianapolis, IN: Hackett Publishing Company.
Janik, Allan and Stephen Toulmin (1973). *Wittgenstein's Vienna*. Touchstone Book. New York: Simon and Schuster.

Jensen, Hans (1970). *Sign, Symbol and Script: An Account of Man's Efforts to Write.* London: George Allen and Unwin.
Jeremias, Joachim (1963). *The Parables of Jesus*, translated S. H. Hooke. Rev. edn. New York: Charles Scribner's Sons.
Jung, Carl G. ([1956] 1976). *Symbols of Transformation*, vol. 5, *The Collected Works of C.G. Jung*. Princeton, NJ: Princeton University Press.
Jung, Carl G. ([1964] 1979). *Man and his Symbols*. London: Aldus Books.
Kafka, Franz ([1916] 1992). "Metamorphisis." In *Metamorphosis and Other Stories*, translated by Willa Muir and Edwin Muir, 7–63. Harmondsworth, Middlesex: Penguin Books.
Kahn, David ([1968] 1974). *The Codebreakers*. London: Weidenfeld and Nicolson.
Kahn, David (1986). "Cryptology." *Encyclopedic Dictionary of Semiotics*, edited by Thomas A. Sebeok. 3 vols., 1: 154–157. Approaches to Semiotics, 73. Berlin: Mouton de Gruyter.
Keller, Gottfried (1942). *Das Tagebuch und das Traumbuch*, edited by Walter Muschg. Klosterberg: Benno Schwabe.
Keller, Gottfried (2003). *Green Henry: A Novel*, translated by A. M. Holt. Woodstock, NJ: Overlook Press.
Keller, Werner ([1956] 1980). *The Bible as History Revised: Archaeology Confirms the Book of Books*, translated by William Neil. London: Hodder & Stoughton.
Kelley, David L. (1971). *Kinesiology: Fundamentals of Motion Description*. Englewood Cliffs, NJ: Prentice Hall.
Kerr, Fergus (2008). *"Work on Oneself" Wittgenstein's Philosophical Psychology*. Arlington, VA: Institute for the Psychological Sciences Press.
Kimball, Miles Spencer (1984). "Language, Linguistics and Philosophy: A Comparison of the Work of Roman Jakobson and the Later Wittgenstein, with Some Attention to the Philosophy of Charles Saunders Peirce." MA thesis, Brigham Young University, Provo, UT. Available online: http://www-personal.umich.edu/~mkimball/pdf/linguistics-thesis.pdf (accessed August 7, 2019).
Kishik, David (2008). *Wittgenstein's Form of Life*. London: Continuum.
Klagge, James C. (1999). "Wittgenstein on Non-Mediative Causality." *Journal of the History of Philosophy* (October): 653–667.
Klagge, James C. (2011). *Wittgenstein in Exile*. Cambridge, MA: MIT Press.
Klagge, James C. and Alfred Nordmann (eds.) (2003). *Ludwig Wittgenstein: Public and Private Occasions*. Lanham, MD: Rowman & Littlefield Publishers.
Krey, Angela (2016). "Geheimschrift bei Ludwig Wittgenstein: Computerlinguistische Untersuchungen." MA thesis, University of Munchen, Munich.
Kripke, Saul A. ([1982] 1985). *Wittgenstein on Rules and Private Language: An Elementary Exposition*. Oxford: Basil Blackwell.
Kull, Kalevi and Peeter Torop (2003). "Biotranslation: Translation between *Umwelten.*" In *Translation Translation*, edited by Susan Petrilli, 315–328. Approaches to Translation Studies, 21. Leiden: Brill [formerly Amsterdam: Rodopi].
Kydd, Ronald A. N. (1984). *Charismatic Gifts in the Early Church*. Peabody, MA: Hendrickson Publishers.
Lackey, Michael (2017). "Introduction to Focus: Biofiction—Its Origins, Natures, and Evolutions." *American Book Review* 39 (1): 3–4.
Langer, Susanne K. ([1942] 1948). *Philosophy in a New Key: A Study in the Symbolism of Reason, Rite, and Art*. New York: Penguin Books.
Lawless, Elaine J. (1994). "Peirce, Semiotics, and Strange Tongues: A Folk Religious Theory of Signs." *Semiotica* 99 (3/4): 273–295.

Leach, Maria and Jerome Fried (eds.) ([1972] 1984). *Funk & Wagnalls Standard Dictionary of Folklore, Mythology, and Legend*. San Francisco, CA: Harper & Row.
Lemberger, Dorit (2015). "Dialogical Grammar: Varieties of Dialogue in Wittgenstein's Methodology." *Dialogical Pedagogy: An International Oneline Journal* 3: 158–173.
Lemoine, Roy E. (1975). *The Anagogic Theory of Wittgenstein's "Tractatus."* Janua Linguarum, Series Minor, 214. The Hague: Mouton.
Lenz, John W. (1964). "Induction as Self-Corrective." *Studies in the Philosophy of Charles Sanders Peirce* (Second Series), edited by Edward C. Moore and Richard S. Robin, 151–162. Amherst: University of Massachusetts Press.
Lévi-Strauss, Claude ([1962] 1966). *The Savage Mind*. London: Weidenfeld & Nicolson.
Lipiner, Elias (1989). *The Metaphysics of the Hebrew Alphabet*. Jerusalem: Hebrew University Magnes Press.
Lotman, Yuri M. (1990). *Universe of the Mind: A Semiotic Theory of Culture*. London: I.B.Taurus & Co.
Lotman, Yuri M. (1991). *Universe of the Mind: A Semiotic Theory of Culture*. Bloomington: Indiana University Press.
Lubbe, Jan C. A. van der (1998). *Basic Methods of Cryptography*. Cambridge: Cambridge University Press.
Macintyre, Ben (2016). "Nostalgia isn't a Patch on What it Used to Be." *The Times*, December 17: 28.
Mallery, Garrick (1972). *Sign Language among North American Indians Compared with That among Other Peoples and Deaf-Mutes*. The Hague: Mouton.
Maran, Timo (2012). "Are Ecological Codes Archetypal Structures?." In *Semiotics in the Wild: Essays in Honor of Kalevi Kull on the Occasion of his 60th Birthday*, edited by Timo Maran, Kati Lindström, and Morten Tønnessen, 147–156. Tartu: University of Tartu Press.
Markoš, Anton (2012). "Are We Cryptos?." In *Semiotics in the Wild: Essays in Honor of Kalevi Kull on the Occasion of his 60th Birthday*, edited by Timo Maran, Kati Lindström, and Morten Tønnessen, 25–29. Tartu: University of Tartu Press.
Marks, Jonathan D. (2010). "Rousseau's Use of the Jewish Example." *Review of Politics* 72 (3): 463–481.
Masters, Roger D. (1986). "Jean-Jacques Rousseau (1712–1778)." In *Encyclopedic Dictionary of Semiotics*, edited by Thomas A. Sebeok, 2:837–839. Berlin: Mouton de Gruyter.
McCormick, Donald (1980). *Love in Code or How to Keep Your Secrets*. London: Eyre Methuen.
McGuinness, Brian (1988). *Wittgenstein A Life. Young Ludwig (1889–1921)*. London: Duckworth.
McGuinness, Brian F. (1996). *Wittgenstein: A Life Young Wittgenstein (1889–1921)*. Los Angeles: University of California Press.
McGuinness, Brian F. (2018). *Wittgenstein Family Letters: Correspondence with Ludwig*, translated by Peter Winslow. London: Bloomsbury.
McGuinness, Brian, Maria Concetta Ascher, and Otto Pfersmann (1996). *Wittgenstein Familienbriefe*. Schriftenreihe der Wittgenstein-Gesellschaft, 23. Vienna: Verlag Hölder-Pichler-Tempsky.
Monk, Ray (1990). *Ludwig Wittgenstein: The Duty of Genius*. New York: Free Press of Maxwell.
Monk, Ray (2001). "Philosophical Biography: The Very Idea." In *Wittgenstein: Biography and Philosophy*, edited by James C. Klagge, 3–15. Cambridge: Cambridge University Press.

Monk, Ray (2016). "'One of the Great Intellects of His Time.'" *New York Review of Books* 63 (20): 80, 86–88.
Montaigne, Michel E. de ([1580, 1588] 2005). *Essays. Selections*. The Collector's Library of Essential Thinkers. London: CRW Publishing.
Morris, Charles (1946). *Signs, Language, and Behavior*. New York: George Braziller.
Morris, Charles (1971). *Writings on the General Theory of Signs*. Approaches to Semiotics, 16. The Hague: Mouton.
Mounce, H. O. (1997). *The Two Pragmatisms from Peirce to Rorty*. London: Routledge.
Moyal-Sharrock, Danièle (2007). *Understanding Wittgenstein's On Certainty*. Basingstoke: Palgrave Macmillan.
Nedo, Michael (ed.) (2012). *Ludwig Wittgenstein: Ein biographisches Album*. Munich: C. H. Beck.
Nedo, Michael, Guy Moreton, and Alec Finlay (2005). *Ludwig Wittgenstein: There Where You Are Not*. London: Black Dog Publishing.
Net, Mariana (2009). "How We Read Postcards: Iconicities, Ideologies." *Transmodernity: Managing Global Communication*, edited by Doina Cmeciu and Traian D. Stănciulescu, 62–67. Bacău: Alma Mater.
Neville, Robert Cummings (1996). *The Truth of Broken Symbols*. Albany: State University of New York Press.
Newmark, Peter (1982). *Approaches to Translation*. Oxford: Pergamon Press.
Nida, Eugene A. (1964). *Toward a Science of Translating: With Special Reference to Principles and Procedures Involved in Bible Translating*. Leiden: Brill.
Noegel, Scott B. (1996). "Atbash in Jeremiah and its Significance: Part I." *Jewish Bible Quarterly* 24 (2): 82–89.
Noll, Justus (1998). *Ludwig Wittgenstein und David Pinsent: Die andere Liebe der Philosophen*. Berlin: Rowohlt.
Nordmann, Alfred (2001). "The Sleepy Philosopher: How to Read Wittgenstein's Diaries." In *Wittgenstein: Biography and Philosophy*, edited by James C. Klagge, 156–175. Cambridge: Cambridge University Press.
Nöth, Winfried (1990). *Handbook of Semiotics*. Advances in Semiotics. Bloomington: Indiana University Press.
Nöth, Winfried (2012). "Signs from the Life of Organisms, Species, Languages, and the Media." In *Semiotics in the Wild: Essays in Honour of Kalevi Kull on the Occasion of his 60th Birthday*, edited by Timo Maran, Kati Lindström, Riin Magnus, and Morten Tønnessen, 123–130. Tartu: University of Tartu Press.
Nuessel, Frank (1996). "The Symbolic Nature of Esperanto." *Semiotica* 109 (3/4): 369–385.
Ogden, Charles K. and I. A. Richards (eds.) ([1923] 1969). *The Meaning of Meaning; A Study of the Influence of Language upon Thought and of the Science of Symbolism*. Reprint of 8th edn. (1946). New York: Harcourt, Brace and Company.
Oxford English Dictionary, The (1989). Edited by J. A. Simpson and E. S. C. Weiner. 2nd edn. 20 vols. Oxford: Clarendon Press. [OED 1989: vol.#:page#]
Parmentier, Richard J. (1985). "Signs' place *in medias res*: Peirce's Concept of Semiotic Mediation." In *Semiotic Mediation: Sociocultural and Psychological Perspectives*, edited by Elizabeth Mertz and Richard J. Parmentier, 23–48. Orlando, FL: Academic Press.
Peirce, Charles S. (Unpublished manuscripts). Peirce Edition Project. Indianapolis: Indiana University-Purdue University. [MS#: page#]
Peirce, Charles S. ([1929] 1966). "Guessing." *The Hound and Horn: A Harvard Miscellany*, 2: 267–282.

Peirce, Charles S. (1931–1966). *Collected Papers of Charles Sanders Peirce*, edited by Charles Hartshorne, Paul Weiss and Arthur W. Burks. 8 vols. Cambridge, MA: Belknap Press of Harvard University Press. [CP: vol.#:paragraph#]

Peirce, Charles S. (1955). *Philosophical Writings of Peirce*, edited by Justus Bucher. New York: Dover.

Peirce, Charles S. (1977). *Semiotic and Significs: The Correspondence between Charles S. Peirce and Victoria Lady Welby*, edited by Charles S. Hardwick. Bloomington: Indiana University Press. [SS: page#]

Peirce, Charles S. (1991–1998). *The Essential Peirce: Selected Philosophical Writings*, edited by Nathan House and Christian Kloesel. 2 vols. Bloomington: Indiana University Press. [EP 1: and EP 2: page#]

Pepys, Samuel (1985). *The Shorter Pepys*, edited by Robert Latham. London: Bell & Hyman Limited. [This selection of Pepys's unpublished diaries of 1660–1669 is taken from Samuel Pepys (1970–1983). *The Diary of Samuel Pepys: A New and Complete Transcription*, edited by Robert Latham and William Matthews. 11 vols. London: Bell & Hyman Limited]

Perloff, Marjorie (2016). *Edge of Irony: Modernism in the Shadow of the Habsburg Empire*. Chicago: University of Chicago Press.

Perl, Jed (2016). "In the Sculptor's Studio." *New York Review of Books* 63 (1): 30–32.

Pichler, Alois (2004). *Wittgensteins Philosophical Untersuchungen: Vom Buch zum Album*. Studien zur Österreichischen Philosophie, 36. Leiden: Brill [formerly Amsterdam: Rodopi].

Pichler, Alois (2006). "'Ich habe 14 Tage lang nichts gearbeitet …' Ein Blick auf die Schreibarbeit Wittgensteins." In *Festschrift für Allan Janik. Mitteilungen aus dem Brenner-Archiv*, 24–25: 131–149. Innsbruck: University of Innsbruck.

Pike, Kenneth L. ([1943] 1961). *Phonetics: A Critical Analysis of Phonetic Theory and a Technic for the Practical Description of Sounds*. 7th printing. Ann Arbor: University of Michigan Press.

Pike, Kenneth L. (1947). *Phonemics: A Technique for Reducing Languages to Writing*. Ann Arbor: University of Michigan Press.

Pike, Kenneth L. ([1952] 1972). "Operational Pronemics in Reference to Linguistic Relativity." *Kenneth L. Pike Selected Writings to Commemorate the 60th Birthday of Kenneth Lee Pike*, edited by Ruth M. Brend, 85–99. The Hague: Mouton.

Pike, Kenneth L. (1957–1958). *Language and Life*. Glendale, CA: Summer Institute of Linguistics.

Pike, Kenneth L. (1967). *Language in Relation to a Unified Theory of the Structure of Human Behavior*. 2nd rev. edn. The Hague: Mouton.

Poe, Edgar Allan (1841). "A Few Words on Secret Writing." *Graham's Magazine* 19 (July): 33–38.

Poe, Edgar Allan ([1843] 1993). "The Gold Bug." *Tales of Mystery and Imagination*, edited by John S. Whitley, 1–30. Ware: Wordsworth Classics.

Pope, Maurice ([1975] 1999). *The Story of Decipherment From Egyptian Hieroglyphs to Maya Script*. Rev. edn. London: Thames & Hudson.

Popovič, Anton (1975). *Dictionary for the Analysis of Literary Translation*. Edmonton: Department of Comparative Literature, University of Alberta. [Typescript based on Popovič's *Teória umeleckého prekladu* (*Theory of Literary Translation*) (1975) and *Problémy literárne metakomikácie—Teória metatextu* (*Problems of Literary Metacommunication—Theory of Metatext*) (1975).]

Portmann, Adolf, Dominique Zahan, René Huyghe, Christopher Rowe, Ernst Benz, and Toshihiko Izutsu ([1977] 1994). *Color Symbolism*. Six Excerpts from the Eranos Yearbook 1972. Dallas, TX: Spring Publications.

Posner, Roland (1980). "Semantics and Pragmatics of Sentence Connectives in Natural Language." In *The Signifying Animal: The Grammar of Language and Experience*, edited by Irmengard Rauch and Gerald F. Carr, 87–122. Advances in Semiotics. Bloomington: Indiana University Press.

Potter, Vincent G. (1997). *Charles S. Peirce On Norms & Ideals*. New York: Fordham University Press.

Powell, James Newton (1982). *The Tao of Symbols*. New York: Quill.

Pratt, Fletcher (1939). *Secret and Urgent: The Story of Codes and Ciphers*. London: Robert Hale Limited.

Putnam, Hilary (2008). *Jewish Philosophy as a Guide to Life*. Bloomington: Indiana University Press.

Rhees, Rush (ed.) (1984). *Recollections of Wittgenstein*. Rev. edn. New York: Oxford University Press.

Riley, Charles A. (1995). *Color Codes: Modern Theories of Color in Philosophy, Painting and Architecture, Literature, Music, and Psychology*. Hanover, NH: University Press of New England.

Rilke, Rainer Maria ([1910] 1988). *Die Aufzeichnungen des Malte Laurids Brigges*. Berlin: Buchverlag der Morgen.

Rilke, Rainer Maria ([1921] 1974]). *Das Testament*. Frankfurt am Main: Suhrkamp Verlag.

Rilke, Rainer Maria (1955). *Sämtliche Werke*, edited by Ernst Zinn. Rilke Archiv, assisted by Ruth Sieber-Rilke. Vol. 1, *Gedichte*. Frankfurt am Main: Insel Verlag.

Rilke, Rainer Maria (2012). *Letters to a Young Poet*, edited by Franz Xaver Kappus. New York: Merchant Books. [English translation of *Briefe an einen jungen Dichter*, 1929]

Roch Lecours, André, Jean-Luc Nespoulous, and Alain Viau (1986). "Glossolalia." In *Encyclopedic Dictionary of Semiotics*, edited by Thomas A. Sebeok, 1:292–293. Approaches to Semiotics, 73. 3 vols. Berlin: Mouton de Gruyter.

Roberts, Don D. (1973). *The Existential Graphs of Charles S. Peirce*. Approaches to Semiotics, 27. The Hague: Mouton.

Rosen, Charles (2008). "The Genius of Montaigne." *New York Review of Books* 55 (2): 48–53.

Rosenheim, Shawn James (1997). *The Cryptographic Imagination: Secret Writing from Edgar Poe to the Internet*. Baltimore: Johns Hopkins University Press.

Rossi-Landi, Ferruccio (1992). "Wittgenstein, Old and New." In *Between Signs and Non-signs*, edited by Susan Petrilli, 87–108. Amsterdam: John Benjamins.

Rotman, Brian (1987). *Signifying Nothing: The Semiotics of Zero*. New York: St. Martin's Press.

Rousseau, Jean-Jacques ([1781] 1973). *The Confessions*, translated by J. M. Cohen. Reprint. Harmondsworth: Penguin.

Rousseau, Jean-Jacques ([1782] 1982). *Reveries of the Solitary Walker*, translated by Charles E. Butterworth. New York: Harper & Row.

Royce, Josiah (1918). *The Problem of Christianity*. Chicago: University of Chicago Press.

Ruesch, Jurgen and Gregory Bateson ([1951] 1987). *Communication: The Social Matrix of Psychiatry*. New York: W. W. Norton & Company.

Rundle, Bede (1993). *Facts*. London: Duckworth.

Samarin. William J. (1972). *Tongues of Men and Angels: The Religious Language of the Pentecostalism*. New York: Macmillan.

Samarin, William J. (1975). "Theory of Order with Disorderly Data." *Linguistics and Anthropology: In Honor of C.F. Voegelin*, edited by M. Dale Kinkade, Kenneth L. Hale, and Oswald Werner, 509–519. Lisse: Peter de Ridder Press.
Saussure, Ferdinand de (1916). *Cours de linguistique générale*. Paris: Payot.
Saussure, Ferdinand de ([1959] 1966). *Course in General Linguistics*, edited by Charles Bally and Albert Sechehaye, in collaboration with Albert Riedlinger, translated by Wade Baskin. New York: McGraw-Hill Book Company.
Savan, David (1980). "Abduction and Semiotics." *The Signifying Animal: The Grammar of Language and Experience*, edited by Irmengard Rauch and Gerald F. Carr, 252–262. Advances in Semiotics. Bloomington: Indiana University Press.
Scheffler, Israel ([1967] 1978). *Science and Subjectivity*. Indianapolis, IN: Bobbe-Merrill Educational Publishing.
Scheffler, Israel ([1973] 1989). *Reason and Teaching*. 2nd edn. Indianapolis, IN and Cambridge: Hackett Publishing Company.
Scheffler, Israel (1985). *Of Human Potential: An Essay in the Philosophy of Education*. Boston, MA: Routledge & Kegan Paul.
Schimmel, Solomon (1992). *The Seven Deadly Sins: Jewish, Christian, and Classical Reflections on Human Nature*. New York: Free Press; Toronto: Maxwell Macmillan.
Schonauer, Klaus (1994). *Semiotic Foundations of Drug Therapy: The Placebo Problem in a New Perspective*. Approaches to Semiotics, 112. Berlin: De Gruyter Mouton.
Schulte, Joachim (1990). "Kontext." In *Chor und Gesetz: Wittgenstein in Kontext*, edited by Joachim Schulte, 146–161. Frankfurt am Main: Suhrkamp.
Schulte, Joachim (2001). "Letters from a Philosopher." In *Wittgenstein: Biography and Philosophy*, edited by James C. Klagge, 176–194. Cambridge: Cambridge University Press.
Schutz, Alfred ([1962] 1967). *Collected Papers*, vol. 1, *The Problem of Social Reality*. Phaenomenologica, 11. The Hague: Martinus Nijhoff.
Schutz, Jr., Noel W. (1975). *On the Autonomy and Comparability of Linguistic and Ethnographic Description*. Lisse: Peter de Ridder Press.
Schutz, Jr., Noel W. (1976). *Kinesiology: The Articulation of Movement*. Lisse: Peter de Ridder Press.
Scott, M. Gladys ([1942] 1963). *Analysis of Human Motion: A Textbook in Kinesiology*. New York: Appleton-Century-Crofts.
Sebeok, Thomas A. (1976). *Contributions to the Doctrine of Signs*. Bloomington: Indiana University (Research Center for Language and Semiotic Studies); Lisse: Peter de Ridder Press.
Sebeok, Thomas A. (1979). *The Sign & Its Masters*. Austin: University of Texas Press.
Sebeok, Thomas A. (1981). *The Play of Musement*. Bloomington: Indiana University Press.
Sebeok, Thomas A. (1984a). *Communication Measures to Bridge Ten Millennia. Technical Report*. Columbus, OH: Office of Nuclear Waste Isolation, Battelle Memorial Institute.
Sebeok, Thomas A. (1984b). "Symptom." In *New Directions in Linguistics and Semiotics*, edited by James E. Copeland, 211–230. Current Issues in Linguistic Theory, 32. Amsterdam: John Benjamins Publishing Company.
Sebeok, Thomas A. (1985a). "Enter Textuality: Echoes from the Extra-Terrestrial." *Poetics Today* 6 (4): 657–663.
Sebeok, Thomas A. (1985b). "Zoosemiotics Components of Human Communication." In *Semiotics: An Introductory Anthology*, edited by Robert E. Innis, 294–324. Advances in Semiotics. Bloomington: Indiana University Press.

Sebeok, Thomas A. (ed.) (1986b). *Encyclopedic Dictionary of Semiotics*. 3 vols. Approaches to Semiotics, 73. Berlin: De Gruyter Mouton. [vol.#:page#]

Sebeok, Thomas A. (1986a). *I Think I Am a Verb: More Contributions to the Doctrine of Signs*. New York: Plenum Press.

Sebeok, Thomas A. (1988). "On Cue." *Times Literary Supplement* 4447, June 24–30: 714. [Review of Giovanni Manetti (1987). *Le teorie del segno nell' antichità classica*. Milan: Bompiani]

Sebeok, Thomas A. (1991b). *Semiotics in the United States*. Bloomington: Indiana University Press.

Sebeok, Thomas A. (1991a). *A Sign is Just a Sign*. Advances in Semiotics. Bloomington: Indiana University Press.

Sebeok, Thomas A. ([1994] 2001). *Signs: An Introduction to Semiotics*. 2nd edn. Toronto Studies in Semiotics and Communication. Toronto: University of Toronto Press.

Sebeok, Thomas A., Alfred S. Hayes, and Mary Catherine Bateson (eds.) ([1964] 1972). *Approaches to Semiotics: Cultural Anthropology—Education—Linguistics—Psychiatry—Psychology*. Transactions of the Indiana University Conference on Paralinguistics and Kinesics. Janua Linguarum, Series Maior, 15. The Hague: Mouton.

Sebeok, Thomas A. and Donna Jean Umiker-Sebeok (1976). *Speech Surrogates: Drum and Whistle Systems*. 2 vols. Approaches to Semiotics, 23. The Hague: Mouton.

Sebeok, Thomas A., Sydney M. Lamb, and John O. Regan (1988). *Semiotics in Education. A Dialogue*. Issues in Communication, 10. Claremont, CA: Claremont Graduate School.

Segre, Cesare (1986). "Co-text and Context." *Encyclopedic Dictionary of Semiotics*, edited by Thomas A. Sebeok. 3 vols., 1:151–152. Approaches to Semiotics, 73. Berlin: Mouton de Gruyter.

Serres, Michel (1982). *The Parasite*, translated by Lawrence R. Schehr. Baltimore: Johns Hopkins University Press.

Shands, Harley C. (1970). *Semiotic Approaches to Psychiatry*. Approaches to Semiotics, 2. The Hague: Mouton.

Shands, Harley C. (1971). *The War With Words: Structure and Transcendence*. Approaches to Semiotics, 12. The Hague: Mouton.

Shands, Harley C. and James D. Meltzer (1973). *Language and Psychiatry*. Janua Linguarum, Series Minor, 165. The Hague: Mouton.

Shelton, Thomas ([1642–1647] 1970). "A Tutor to Tachygraphy, or Short-Writing" and "Tachygraphy." *Augustan Reprint Society*, edited and introduced by William Matthews Clark Memorial Library, UCLA, 145–146.

Shipley, Joseph T. (ed.) (1972). *Dictionary of World Literature. Criticism—Forms—Technique*. Totowa, NJ: Littlefield, Adams & Co.

Siegel, Lee (1996). "'The Work is to Live Without Dying." *Atlantic Monthly* 277–4 (April): 112–118.

Singer, Milton (1984). *Man's Glassy Essence: Explorations in Semiotic Anthropology*. Advances in Semiotics. Bloomington: Indiana University Press.

Smerud, Warren B. (1970). *Can There Be A Private Language? An Examination of Some Principal Arguments*. The Hague: Mouton.

Smith, Howard A. (2007). *Teaching Adolescents: Educational Psychology as a Science of Signs*. Toronto: University of Toronto Press.

Snyder, Timothy (2015). "Hitler's World." *New York Review of Books* 62 (14): 6–10.

Sontag, Susan (1978). *Illness as Metaphor*. New York: Farrar, Strauss and Giroux.

Sontag, Susan (1988). *Aids and Its Metaphors*. New York: Farrar, Strauss and Giroux.

Staiano, Kathryn Vance (1986). *Interpreting Signs of Illness: A Case Study in Medical Semiotics*. Approaches to Semiotics, 72. Berlin: Mouton de Gruyter.

Staiano-Ross, Kathryn Vance (2012). "The Symptom." *Biosemiotics* 5 (April): 33–45.

Stankiewicz, Edward ([1964] 1972). "Problems of Emotive Language." *Approaches to Semiotics: Cultural Anthropology—Education—Linguistics—Psychiatry—Psychology*, edited by Thomas A. Sebeok, Alfred S. Hayes, and Mary Catherine Bateson, 239–264. Janua Linguarum, Series Maior, 15. The Hague: Mouton.

Steiner, George (1975). *After Babel: Aspects of Language and Translation*. Oxford: Oxford University Press.

Steiner, Richard C. (1996). "The Two Sons of Neriah and the Two Editions of Jeremiah in the Light of Two Atbash Code-Words for Babylon." *Vetus Testamentum* 46 (1): 74–84.

Stern, David G. (2004). "Weininger and Wittgenstein on 'Animal Psychology'." In *Wittgenstein Reads Weininger*, edited by David G. Stern and Béla Szabados, 169–197. Cambridge: Cambridge University Press.

Stygall, Gail (1994). *Trial Language: Differential Discourse Processing and Discursive Formation*. Pragmatics & Beyond 26. Amsterdam: John Benjamins.

Suetonius ([1914] 1920). *The Lives of the Caesars, Book I*, translated by John Caren Rolfe. Loeb Classical Library, 31. Reprint. London: William Heinemann; New York: G.P. Putnam Sons. [paragraph# page#]

Thoreau, Henry D. (1854). *Walden: Or, Life in the Woods*. New York: Thomas Y. Crowell.

Tilghman, B. R. (1984). *But is it Art? The Value of Art and the Temptation of Theory*. Oxford: Basil Blackwell.

Tolstoy, Count Leo N. (1896). *The Gospel in Brief*. New York: Thomas Y. Crowell. Available online: http://archive.org/stream/cu31924029339078#page/n5/mode/2up (accessed August 7, 2019).

Toporov, V. N. (1977). "The Semiotics of Prophesy in Suetonius." In *Soviet Semiotics: An Anthology*, edited and translated by Daniel P. Lucid, 157–167. Baltimore: Johns Hopkins University Press.

Umiker-Sebeok, D. Jean and Thomas A. Sebeok (1978). *Aboriginal Sign Languages of the Americas and Australia*. 2 vols. New York: Plenum Publishing Corporation.

Von Wright, Georg Henrik ([1941] 1965). *The Logical Problem of Induction*. 2nd rev. edn. Oxford: Basil Blackwell.

Von Wright, Georg Henrik (1984). *Truth, Knowledge, and Modality*. Philosophical Papers. Vol. 3. Oxford: Basil Blackwell.

Walker, Benjamin (1977). *Encyclopedia of Esoteric Man*. London and Henley-on-Thames: Routledge & Kegan Paul.

Waugh, Alexander (2008). *The House of Wittgenstein: A Family at War*. London: Bloomsbury.

Waugh, Patricia (1984). *Metafiction: The Theory and Practice of Self-conscious Fiction*. London: Methuen.

West, Donna E. and Myrdene Anderson (eds.) (2016). *Consensus on Peirce's Concept of Habit: Before and Beyond Consciousness*. Studies in Applied Philosophy, Epistemology and Rational Ethics (SAPERE). New York: Springer.

White, Morton (ed.) ([1955] 1983). *The Age of Analysis: 20th Century Philosophers*. New York: New American Library.

Wilde, Oscar (2007). *Complete Works*, edited by Josephine M. Guy, vol. 4. Oxford: Oxford University Press.

Williams, Raymond ([1976] 1988). *Keywords: A Vocabulary of Culture and Society*. London: Fontana Press.

Willis, Timothy M. (2001). "Redeem." In *The Oxford Guide to Ideas & Issues of the Bible*, edited by Bruce M. Metzger and Michael D. Coogan, 434. Oxford: Oxford University Press.

Wilshire, Bruce (1982). *Role Playing and Identity: The Limits of Theatre as Metaphor*. Bloomington: Indiana University Press.

Wimsatt, William K., Jr. (1943). "What Poe Knew about Cryptography." *Publications of the Modern Language Association of America (PMLA)* 58 (September): 754–779.

Wittgenstein, Hermine (1984). "My Brother Ludwig." *Recollections of Wittgenstein*, edited by Rush Rhees, 1–11. Oxford: Oxford University Press.

Wittgenstein, Ludwig ([1922] 1962). *Tractatus Logico-Philosophicus*, translated by C. K. Ogden and Frank P. Ramsey, introduced by Bertrand Russell. 9th edn. London: Routledge and Kegan Paul. [TLP: paragraph#]

Wittgenstein, Ludwig (1929). "Some Remarks on Logical Form." Proceedings of the Aristotelian Society. Supplementary vol. 9, 162–171. London. [RLF: page#]

Wittgenstein, Ludwig ([1953] 2009). *Philosophical Investigations*, edited by P. M. S. Hacker and Joachim Schulte, translated by G. E. M. Anscombe, rev. translation by P. M. S. Hacker and Joachim Schulte. German text with a rev. English trans. Rev. 4th edn. London: John Wiley-Blackwell. [PI and PI/PPF (former Part II): paragraph#]

Wittgenstein, Ludwig ([1958] 1978). *The Blue and Brown Books: Preliminary Studies for the "Philosophical Investigations,"* edited and introduced by Rush Rhees. Reprint. Oxford: Basil Blackwell. [BBB: page#]

Wittgenstein, Ludwig ([1961] 1979). *Notebooks 1914–1916*, edited by G. H. von Wright and G. E. M. Anscombe, translated by G. E. M. Anscombe. 2nd edn. Chicago: University of Chicago Press. [TB: page#]

Wittgenstein, Ludwig ([1964] 1981). *Philosophische Bemerkungen*, edited by Rush Rhees. Frankfurt am Main: Suhrkamp. [PB: page#]

Wittgenstein, Ludwig (1966). *Lectures & Conversations on Aesthetics, Psychology and Religious Belief*, edited by Cyril Barrett. Berkeley: University of California Press. [LA: page#]

Wittgenstein, Ludwig (1967). *Letters from Ludwig Wittgenstein, With a Memoir of Paul Engelmann*, edited by Paul McGuinness. New York: Horizon Press. [CPE: page#]

Wittgenstein, Ludwig (1969). *Über Gewissheit / On Certainty*, edited by G. E. M. Anscombe and G. H. von Wright, translated by Denis Paul and G. E. M. Anscombe. Oxford: Blackwell. [OC: paragraph#]

Wittgenstein, Ludwig (1973). *Letters to C.K. Ogden with Comments on the English Translation of the Tractatus Logico-Philosophicus*, edited by G. H. von Wright. Oxford: Basil Blackwell; London: Routledge & Kegal Paul.

Wittgenstein, Ludwig ([1974] 1980). *Philosophical Grammar (Part I The Proposition and its Sense, Part II On Logic and Mathematics)*, edited by Rush Rhees, translated by Anthony Kenny. Oxford: Blackwell. [PG: page#]

Wittgenstein, Ludwig (1975). *Philosophical Remarks*, edited by Rush Rhees, translated by Raymond Hargreaves and Roger White. Oxford: Blackwell. [PR: page#]

Wittgenstein, Ludwig ([1977] 1988a). *Culture and Value*, edited by Georg Henrik von Wright, rev. edn. edited by Alois Pichler, translated by Peter Winch. German text with a rev. English trans. Rev. 2nd edn. Malden, MA: Blackwell. [CV: page#]

Wittgenstein, Ludwig ([1977] 1988b). *Remarks on Colour*, edited by G. E. M. Anscombe, translated by Linda L. M. McAlister and Margarethe Schättle. Oxford: Basil Blackwell. [ROC: paragraph#]

Wittgenstein, Ludwig ([1977] 1994). *Vermischte Bemerkungen: Eine Auswahl aus dem Nachlass*, edited by Georg Henrik von Wright and Heikki Nyman, rev. edn. edited by Alois Pichler. Rev. 2nd edn. Frankfurt am Main: Suhrkamp. [VB: page#]

Wittgenstein, Ludwig (1979). *Wittgenstein's Lectures Cambridge, 1930–1932*, edited by Desmond Lee, notes by John King and Desmond Lee. Chicago: University of Chicago Press. [LWL: page#]

Wittgenstein, Ludwig ([1982] 1990). *Letzte Schriften über die Philosophie der Psychology / Last Writings on the Philosophy of Psychology*. vol. 1, *Vorstudien zum zweiten Teil der Philosophischen Untersuchungen / Preliminary Studies for Part 2 of* Philosophical Investigations, edited by Georg Henrik von Wright and Heikki Nyman, translated by C. G. Luckhardt and Maximilian A. E. Aue. Oxford: Basil Blackwell. [LW1: paragraph#]

Wittgenstein, Ludwig (1988). *Wittgenstein's Lectures on Philosophical Psychology, 1946–1947*, edited by P. T. Geach, notes by P. T. Geach, K. J. Shah, and A. C. Jackson. London: Harvester. [PGL: page#]

Wittgenstein, Ludwig ([1991] 1992). *Geheime Tagebücher 1914–1916*, edited by Wilhelm Baum. 3rd edn. Vienna: Turia und Kant. [GT: page#]

Wittgenstein, Ludwig (1992). *Letzte Schriften über die Philosophie der Psychology / The Last Writings on the Philosophy of Psychology*, vol. 2, *The Inner and the Outer*, edited by Georg Henrik von Wright and Heikki Nyman, translated by C. G. Luckhardt and Maximilian A. E. Aue. Oxford: Basil Blackwell. [LW2: page#]

Wittgenstein, Ludwig (1993). *Philosophical Occasions 1912–1951*, edited and translated by James C. Klagge and Alfred Nordmann. Indianapolis, IN: Hackett Publishing Company.

Wittgenstein, Ludwig (1997). *Denkbewegungen: Tagebücher 1930-1932 and 1936-1937*, edited by Ilse Somavilla. 2 vols. (vol. 1, *Normalisierte Fassung*, vol. 2, *Diplomatische Fassung*). Innsbruck: Haymon. [DB: vol.#:page#]

Wittgenstein, Ludwig (2000). *The Big Typescript*, edited by Michael Nedo Wiener Ausgabe, 11. Vienna: Springer Verlag and Frankfurt am Main: Zweitausendeins. [BT: page#]

Wittgenstein Online (2018). "Wittgenstein Archives at the University of Bergen (WAB): Open Access to Transcriptions of the Wittgenstein Nachlass (2016–)." Available online: http://wittgensteinonline.no/ (last accessed August 7, 2019).

Wittgenstein Source (n.d.). "Wittgenstein Source." Available online: http://www.wittgensteinsource.org/ (last accessed August 7, 2019).

Wickler, Wolfgang (1968). *Mimicry in Plants and Animals*, translated by R. D. Martin. New York: McGraw-Hill.

Wiesenthal, Chris (1997). *Figuring Madness in Nineteenth-Century Fiction*. Basingstoke: St. Martin's Press.

Wouters, Els (2000). "Detective Fiction and Indexicality." *Semiotica* 131 (1/2): 141–154.

Index

abduction, guessing 16, 86, 159, 171–172, 174, 180–190, 194–198, 200–201, 205–206, 209, 211–212, 232
album 64, 81, 84, 104, 115, 128, 157, 191, 194, 198, 200, 207, 211
Anscombe, Elizabeth 32, 46, 49, 50, 130, 191
Atbash vii, 81–82, 239
Augustine, Saint 27, 30, 58, 65, 69, 105–106, 108–110
autobiography, crypto-autobiography, pseudo-autography vii, 1–2, 4–5, 7–8, 96–97, 101, 130, 166, 189–190, 192, 110–115, 122, 125, 127, 207
auto-communication, self-communication 21, 64
auto-da-fé 101–102, 115, 124

Babel, Babylon, *Sheshach* vii, 60, 72, 80–82
Barthes, Roland vii, 15, 100, 233
Bateson, Gregory 191–198
Bauman, Zygmunt 96, 118–119, 121
beetle (insects), image of 86, 129–134, 142, 190, 200, 206, 242, 235, 239
Benjamin, Walter 118
Bible, Biblical scripture 3, 10, 27–30, 34, 36, 42, 47, 59, 73–74, 83, 98, 103, 113, 122, 146, 165, 185, 193–194, 195–196
Bible translation 72, 77, 194
Big Typescript 35
biography, cryptobiography vii, 1, 5, 17, 96, 98–100, 141, 148, 155, 199, 239
Blake, William 47
blind man, image of 36–37, 147–148, 155, 165, 169, 190, 199–200, 235, 243
Blue and Brown Books (BBB) 21, 31, 36, 38–39 77, 106, 129, 179
Buddha, Buddhism 64–75, 83

Caesar's shorthand 63–82, 94, 208
censorship 30–31
Christian faith 27–30, 39–40, 42–43, 73, 75, 78–79, 105–112, 114, 196, 233–234
Christ Jesus 29, 78, 92, 122, 233–234
code, coded text (*Geheimschrift*), *passim*
color, code of 20, 49, 75, 111–112, 123, 142, 153–161, 163–174, 176, 179, 189, 200–201, 209–210, 212
Conan Doyle, Sir Arthur 84, 86–87
confession 24, 29–30, 32, 34, 36, 39, 42, 57, 65, 87, 95, 97–98, 101, 108, 112–116, 122–123, 124, 135, 143, 163, 170, 190, 204–205
confusion (of languages) 2, 21, 27, 39, 48, 72–80, 92, 137, 154, 161, 165
cries for help 13, 45, 129, 130, 134–135, 155, 170, 181, 189, 193, 207, 210, 241
cryptanalyst, cryptographer, cryptosemiotician vii, ix, 6, 54, 70–72, 161, 163, 166, 171, 204–206, 208
cryptography, cryptogram, cryptology vi–vii, 1, 8, 16, 35, 38, 53–94, 71, 82, 161, 163–166, 204–206
crypotomnesia vii, 95, 105–106, 110, 124–125
Culture and Value (CV) 33, 35–36, 42–43, 59, 88, 99, 102, 146, 149, 173

Danesi, Marcel vi–viii, 72, 232
Darwin, Charles 130, 138–139
decoding, encoding vii–viii, 4, 53–55, 59–63, 68, 75, 84, 86, 120, 163, 185, 194, 199, 201, 210
deduction and induction (also see abduction) 16, 171–188, 190, 195, 196, 200, 232, 205

degeneracy, degenerate signs 3, 23, 26, 51, 62, 70, 120, 127, 155, 159, 166, 168, 173–174, 178, 201
Derrida, Jacques 2, 15, 77, 132, 155
detective story, crime story 72, 84–88, 118, 167, 170, 178, 187–188
diaries (*Tagebücher*), *passim*
Di Leo, Jeffrey 14
disiecta membra 16
dream 34, 50, 105, 136
duck-rabbit, image of 71, 142–148, 155, 160, 199–201, 206, 235

Eco, Umberto 14, 68, 70, 80, 85
ego, egotism 4, 25–26, 75, 107–108, 115, 117, 121, 154
Engelmann, Paul 29, 190
exile 72, 80–82, 96, 109, 113, 134, 160
existential graphs 167–168, 210, 238

family resemblances 128
fiction, biofiction, metafiction, nonfiction vi, viii, 1, 4, 8, 11, 14–16, 32, 41, 45, 68–69, 80, 83–88, 94, 96, 98, 100, 117, 119, 121, 127–131, 137–140, 142, 146, 149–151, 155, 158–159, 161, 163–166, 192, 200, 204, 206–207, 235
fictional games 4, 14, 137–151, 155, 158–159, 161, 164, 192, 206–207, 235
firstness, secondness and thirdness 10, 12–13, 15, 22–24, 27, 50, 70, 73, 110, 118, 130–131, 149, 151, 154, 159, 172, 180–181, 183, 189, 194, 211, 233
forked tongue 164–166
forms of life, facts of life (*Lebensformen*) vi, viii, 5–6, 10–12, 16–20, 23–24, 41–42, 57, 74–75, 88, 97, 101, 104, 127–128, 139–140, 148, 165, 167–168, 174, 181, 199, 207, 209–210
fragment(s), fragmentary story 4–6, 8, 13, 15–16, 22–23, 26, 28, 31, 38, 48, 54–55, 69, 72, 84, 96, 98, 104, 106, 111, 115, 118–119, 122–125, 136, 149, 151, 157, 160, 164, 170, 172–173, 178, 186, 194, 205–206, 209, 211–212, 231, 234–235
Freud, Sigmund 24–25, 30, 50, 151

game of reasoning, habit of reasoning, sign-game vi, 2, 5, 9, 11, 16, 24, 27, 37, 55, 157, 170–184, 187–188
game of writing, word games, jigsaw games 93–94, 124–125, 127, 130, 133–134, 152, 157, 159, 161, 165, 177, 183, 192–196, 206, 208–212
Geheime Tagebücher (GT) 4, 17, 18, 19, 20, 27–28, 30, 107
gesture, sign game (of language-game) 24–26, 57, 71, 79, 100, 142–143, 150, 152, 157, 159, 161, 165, 177
glossolalia, xenoglossia 72, 76, 79
God, Lord 18, 24, 26, 28–30, 34, 42–43, 47–48, 50, 74, 76–77, 79–82, 83, 97–98, 102, 105, 107, 109, 125, 132, 141–142, 146, 148, 154, 190, 193, 195–196, 210, 233–234, 241
Goethe, Johann Wolfgang von 49, 146
Gorlée, Dinda L., *passim*

habit, habituality, habituescence (see Interpretant) viii, 2–3, 7, 10–15, 20–21, 23, 24–27, 30, 31, 45, 47, 50–51, 53–54, 58, 66, 70, 71, 72–73, 77, 79, 83, 85, 96, 103, 107, 114–115, 118, 119, 123–124, 129, 133–136, 140–141, 144, 148, 151, 154–155, 159, 161, 164–167, 170–181, 184–185, 187–188, 189, 195–198, 200–201
headache, toothache 19, 21, 45, 75, 130, 206
hieroglyphics 20, 84–86, 232–233
Holmes, Sherlock (fictional character) 86–87, 187–188
homosexuality 30, 39, 50, 105–107, 120–121, 189
humour, joke vi, 3, 5, 35, 59–60, 75, 190, 196, 201
Hus, Jan 184–185

icon, index vii, 10–16, 21–25, 35, 37, 58, 61, 82–83, 94, 95, 99, 109–110, 116–119, 123–124, 129, 132, 136, 141–142, 148–149, 152–153, 154, 158–159, 163, 166–179, 181, 185, 194, 198, 199–201, 204, 206–208, 211, 232
interpretant, interpretant-sign (see reagent sign, habit) 8, 10–12, 20, 37, 50–51, 54, 58–59, 69–70, 79, 83, 85, 87, 108, 110, 121–122, 133–137, 140, 155, 161, 173–174, 176, 178, 182, 186–188, 201, 204, 232–233, 237

interpreter, quasi-interpreter, reader 10–11, 21–22, 39, 50–51, 61, 69, 70, 110, 140, 149, 152, 155, 158, 167, 169, 172, 174, 178, 180, 183, 188, 204

James, William 24, 41, 74–75, 193, 210
jargon, dialect, idiom (see Quasi-language) 32, 61, 68, 72, 75, 82, 95, 129, 176, 184–185, 190, 204, 207–210, 212
Jeremiah (Biblical prophet) 43, 72–82
Jewish ancestry 19, 33–34, 39, 50, 101
Jewish symbols vii, 35, 56, 72–84, 83, 97–98, 101–102, 109

Kabala-X (Pike) 68
Kabbalah 60, 71–84
Kafka, Franz 132, 136–139, 188, 190, 208, 246
Kahn, David 54, 56, 70, 80, 86–87, 208, 239
Keller, Gottfried 89, 110–115

landscape (of philosophy) 13, 64, 84, 86, 104, 146, 157, 161, 170, 180, 194, 206
language, *passim*
language-game (*Sprachspiel*), word game vi, 2, 13, 15–16, 23, 26, 37, 39–45, 54, 57, 59, 65, 123, 134, 150, 155, 168, 170, 183, 204, 208–210, 239, 241, 244, 246
Last Writings on the Philosophy of Psychology (LW) 26, 160
learning, education, *pilpul* 9, 43, 81–83, 205
lectures, Wittgenstein's 31, 36, 38, 46, 56, 74, 77, 81, 96, 101, 105, 128–129, 131–135, 139, 143, 145–146, 149, 151–152, 155–157, 159, 177, 190–192, 194, 200, 207, 211–212
libido, sexuality 30, 66, 102, 105, 107, 116, 121–122, 124–125, 154, 189, 207
liverwurst (swine, pig), image of 35, 97–98, 101
love, self-love 154, 156, 91–92, 107, 113, 117, 121–122, 124–125, 204

madness (*Wahnsinn*) viii, 37, 47–48, 86, 151, 154, 156, 212
manometer argument 169–174, 245
man/sign 16, 82, 150, 168
marked (unmarked) signs 26, 67, 69, 72, 84
meaning, signification, *passim*
mediation 6, 11, 23, 47, 59, 72, 79, 143, 154, 159, 166, 170, 186
metaphor, analogy 3, 6, 8, 11, 16, 23, 28, 34–35, 37, 45, 58–59, 61, 83, 93–94, 97, 110–111, 115, 119, 122,124, 128–130, 135, 139, 142, 150, 156, 159, 165–167, 172, 180, 182–183, 199, 193–194, 200–201, 232, 235
monologue, quasi-dialogue, dialogue and multilogue 4, 19, 131, 133, 140–141, 145, 153, 166–170, 189–191, 194, 207, 211–212, 237–238, 240
metalogue (Bateson) 166, 191–201, 212
Montaigne, Michel Eyquem de 106–110
movements of thought, thought-movements (*Denkbewegungen*) 4, 13, 16, 21, 32, 34, 63, 65, 69, 96–97, 102–104, 106, 115, 122, 124, 127–139, 143, 145, 149–150, 155, 159–160, 171–172, 174, 180, 182, 198, 207, 231–232
musement 181–183, 187–190, 194, 197–199, 207–208, 211
mysticism, mystical 73–76, 79–83, 146, 181, 190

narcissism 15, 41, 102, 124
Nazism, fascism 4, 30, 31, 34, 45, 98, 101, 135–136, 140, 190
neurosis, psychoneurosis 25, 31, 45, 114, 122, 190, 198–199, 201
nonsense (*Unsinn*), sense 3, 27
nostalgia 19, 46, 111–112, 116, 135, 146, 154, 160, 164, 207
Notebooks 1914–1916 (TB), notebooks 2, 4–6, 15, 17, 20, 27, 43, 48–49, 63, 95, 98, 103, 117–118, 124, 128, 141, 157, 174, 207, 232

On Certainty (OC) 48–49, 160
oracle 64, 158–159, 207
Otherness 69–69, 109, 119, 180, 189

pain, anxieties, fears, *passim*
parables 34, 43, 75, 82, 94, 99, 122, 146, 148, 167

paragraph, epigram 4–6, 8, 13, 18, 20, 23, 29, 30–33, 36, 38, 49, 57, 60, 72, 84, 89, 94, 103–104, 106, 115, 119, 128–129, 133, 140, 142, 144, 148–149, 157
parasite, parasitism 35, 62, 238
Peirce's three categories 10–16, 22–24 and *passim*
Pepys, Samuel 65, 88–94, 103, 110, 125, 188, 210, 239–240, 247
Philistines 113, 149, 154
Philosophical Grammar (PG) 27, 37
Philosophical Investigations (PI) 27, 31, 35, 37–38, 40–41, 43, 48, 50, 58, 64, 72, 104, 106, 128, 130–132, 136, 143, 157, 163, 165, 179–180, 190
Philosophische Bemerkungen (PB) 33–34, 88, 235
phonetic transcription 65–68
Pichler, Alois ix, 43, 60, 96, 102, 104
pictography, pictograms 1, 8, 65, 70–71, 80, 82–87, 92, 94, 180
Pinsent, David 19, 30, 107, 189
placebo 196–199, 201
plaintext, uncoded text, *passim*
play-act, play-actor, theatrical pose 15, 25, 27, 37–38, 51, 74, 88, 93, 97, 150–151, 170, 181, 190, 193–198, 207–208, 212
Poe, Edgar Allan vi, 84–86, 132, 138
postcard 2–3, 15, 113, 191
prayer 24, 29, 47, 75, 79, 82, 105, 107, 119, 125, 156, 193, 198, 210, 241
private and public notebooks 2, 4–6, 15, 18, 38, 43, 46, 48–49, 63, 95, 98, 104, 112, 123–124, 128, 134, 140–141, 143, 145–146, 150–151, 157–158, 167, 173, 207
proposition, pseudo-proposition vi, 18, 23, 27, 36, 39, 55, 59, 70, 73–74, 77, 109, 122, 134, 171, 173, 175–176, 178, 209, 233
psychoanalysis 24–26, 30–31, 66, 101, 136, 154, 188
psychology, psychosemiotics vi, 57, 68, 74, 76–77, 88, 96, 105, 108–109, 114, 120, 128, 130, 132, 136–137, 140–143, 145–146, 149–150, 152, 154–155, 157–160, 164, 174, 177–178, 180–181, 183, 185, 187–188, 190, 196–197, 200–201, 206–209, 211–212, 232, 241

quasi-experience, anecdotal evidence 18, 73
quasi-speech, quasi-language, quasi-code 4, 7–8, 11, 36, 53, 74, 77, 81–86, 93–94, 123–125, 127, 135, 139, 147, 164–165, 167, 170, 177, 184, 186, 189–190, 198, 200–201, 204–210, 231
quasi-mind, quasi-thought 8, 73

Ramsey, Frank 102, 137, 143
reactor sign, reaction (see Interpretant)
Respinger, Marguérite 32–34, 103, 121, 137, 189
restricted code (Bernstein) 185, 201, 204
Richards, Ben 46, 48, 50, 141, 143, 148, 151, 189
riddles, puzzles, jigsaw vii, 2–4, 9, 12, 26, 32, 55, 69–72, 75, 82, 84–86, 89, 95, 128, 134, 139, 147, 152, 160, 170, 173, 183, 185, 188, 192, 194, 197–198, 205, 209–210, 232
Rilke, Rainer Maria 115–125, 141, 188, 208
Rhees, Rush 32, 36, 105, 134, 191, 246
Rossi-Landi, Ferruccio 6–7
Rousseau, Jean-Jacques 29, 108–110, 240

satirical writing 3
Saussure, Ferdinand de vii, 8–9, 20–21, 134, 207
Scheffler, Israel 56, 88, 237
Schimmel, Solomon 3, 26, 34, 46, 59, 101–105, 112, 114, 130, 132, 208
Schulte, Joachim 3, 46, 59, 130, 132
Sebeok, Thomas A. 6, 9, 10, 20–21, 22–24, 53–55, 62–64, 70–71, 82, 85–86, 110, 129, 132, 138, 142, 146, 152, 155, 158, 166, 171, 186–188, 204, 232–233, 241
secrecy, nonsense, (un)certainty vii, ix, 1–2, 3, 13–15, 33, 37, 46, 48, 49, 54, 74–75, 98, 106, 109–110, 122, 128, 136, 137, 139, 140–141, 145, 148, 151–152, 156, 160–161, 165, 170–173, 174, 178, 192, 197–200, 207–208
self-analysis, self-reflection, self-identity, self-game viii, 4, 8, 15, 23, 24, 25, 27, 31, 35, 37, 42, 73, 98, 100, 101, 106–107, 114, 115, 121, 127, 137, 142, 144, 147, 149, 164

self-remedy, self-therapy, therapy 135, 166, 171, 181, 188, 197–199, 201
semiosis, quasi-semiosis 10, 15, 23, 51, 62, 69–71, 73–74, 82, 110, 122, 150, 160, 166, 168–170, 172–174, 187, 197, 201, 206–207, 212, 232, 237
semiotics of Charles S. Peirce 7–16 and *passim*
sermon 94, 107, 118, 119, 194, 210
shibboleth 54, 72–83, 104, 131
sign, object *passim*
signpost, signal 12, 152
silence 2, 56, 74, 79, 151
Skinner, Francis 38–39, 41, 43, 189, 235
soul (*Seele*) 2, 15–16, 28–30, 33–35, 39, 41–42, 47, 57, 98, 103, 107, 121, 138, 143, 158–159, 163, 182, 190, 197, 201, 205, 208, 210–211
speech-act 127, 131–132, 139, 149, 206
spirit (*Geist*) 16–17, 20, 24, 26, 28–30, 32–36, 41, 43, 47–48, 66, 61, 73, 75, 77–79, 81–82, 96–106, 109–110, 112–114, 117–119, 110, 121, 123–124, 130–131, 133, 137–138, 141, 145, 150, 154, 159, 181–182, 190, 195, 198, 201, 208–209, 234
Staiano (Ross), Kathryn Vance 12, 22, 23, 25, 181, 190, 233, 246
stream of thought, stream of consciousness, stream of dialect 3, 12, 23, 74, 184
street loafer (beggar), image of 99–100, 112, 114, 148
students (Cambridge) 35, 38, 39, 55–59, 75, 81, 104, 133, 140, 143, 145, 151, 152, 157, 163, 166, 176, 178, 186, 188, 190–192, 195, 204, 205, 206, 208, 209, 211, 212
subtext, context, intertext 5, 12, 15, 27, 30, 44, 55–56, 72, 97, 104, 119, 124, 128, 132–133, 139–141, 143, 145–147, 149–157, 160, 167, 195, 199, 204–206
suicide (*Selbstmord*) 30, 100, 102, 122, 190
symbol, symbolism vii, 2, 5, 7, 9, 10–16, 21, 23, 24, 25, 35, 36, 37, 61, 73, 74, 77, 82, 83, 84, 86, 91–92, 93, 99, 100, 107, 108, 109–110, 112, 115, 117, 123, 134, 142, 150, 151, 154, 158, 159, 163, 166, 167–168, 170, 172, 173, 174, 175, 176, 177, 179, 180, 194, 197, 200, 204, 207, 209, 212, 232, 233, 238
symptoms, symptomatic action 12, 19–27

tachygraphy, stenography 65, 91–94
theatrical pose, performance art 15
Torah, Talmud 56, 81, 109, 205
Tolstoy, Count Leo 29–30
Tower of Babel 72, 75–76, 79
Tractatus Logico-Philosophicus (TLP) 1–2, 15, 17–18, 20, 23, 27, 29, 30, 34, 54, 73–74, 77, 102, 109, 115, 137
translatability, untranslatability 53, 61, 68, 77, 80, 94, 123
translation, semiotranslation 11–51, 53–61, 68–69, 72–73, 75, 77–79, 80–83, 92, 94, 96, 102, 105, 123, 149, 152, 163, 167, 168, 170, 196, 200, 204, 206, 208, 211, 231, 233, 234, 238, 241, 243

Umwelt (environment) 128, 139, 189, 241

virtues and sins 12, 42, 50, 101–103, 108, 146, 154, 190, 193

Winch, Peter 32
Wittgenstein, Hermione, Helene, Margarethe and Helene 48, 49, 59, 138, 97, 113, 190
Wittgenstein, Ludwig, *passim*
wordplay 56, 131, 182, 200–201, 206
Wright, Georg H. von 32, 49, 145, 160, 179, 246

www.ingramcontent.com/pod-product-compliance
Lightning Source LLC
Chambersburg PA
CBHW070022010526
44117CB00011B/1677
9781350277557